CHINESE REPORTAGE

ASIA-PACIFIC

Culture, Politics, and Society

Editors: Rey Chow, H. D. Harootunian,

and Masao Miyoshi

CHARLES A. LAUGHLIN

CHINESE REPORTAGE

The Aesthetics of Historical Experience

Duke University Press   Durham and London 2002

© 2002 Duke University Press   All rights reserved

Printed in the United States of America on acid-free paper ∞

Designed by Rebecca Giménez   Typeset in Quadraat by Tseng

Information Systems, Inc.   Library of Congress Cataloging-in-

Publication Data appear on the last printed page of this book.

In memory of my father

CONTENTS

ACKNOWLEDGMENTS

A project over a period of years usually incurs more debts than can be briefly acknowledged, but those who helped shape this project are in fact few in number. C. T. Hsia and David Wang contributed a great deal to the formulation of the topic, which uncannily and somewhat unexpectedly addressed a wide variety of my intellectual interests. The lion's share of my dissertation research in Beijing was made possible by a grant from the Committee for Scholarly Communication with China. While in Beijing I was fortunate to work under the guidance of Professor Zhao Xiaqiu of Renmin University. Through her and the assistance of her students Qin Xinchun, Hou Jin, and Chen Fensen, I was able to meet and interview writers like Xiao Qian, Huang Gang, and Chen Huangmei as well as modern prose scholars Yuan Liangjun, Lin Fei, Zhang Manjun, and Yin Junsheng, all of whose creative visions and ideas saturate this study.

Several classmates also writing dissertations at Columbia University contributed materially to the writing process by exchanging commentary and chapter drafts, a practice I highly recommend, especially across disciplines. Among them I would particularly like to thank Kristina Torgeson, Kristine Harris, Andre Schmidt, Margherita Zanasi, and Kim Brandt for their insights, criticism, and encouragement.

This project's long journey into book form is almost entirely due to the support and guidance of Rey Chow, who has been a caring and proactive mentor since I took her modern Chinese literature class at the University of Minnesota as an undergraduate. I would like to thank also my colleagues at Yale University, particularly Kang-i Sun Chang and Edward Kamens, for going out of their way to facilitate the completion of this and other academic endeavors. A Morse Junior Faculty Fellowship at Yale in 1999–2000 allowed me to bring this manuscript to a conclusion as well as to begin research on my next project on the late imperial influence on the modern Chinese essay.

My wife Ma Lan has endured a great deal during every stage of this project, and to her I owe all the rest of my gratitude, for her patience, understanding, and support.

FREQUENTLY CITED WORKS

BWYZX

Wang Ronggang 王榮綱, ed. *Baogao wenxue yanjiu ziliao xuanbian* 報告文學研究資料選編 (Selected Research Materials on Reportage Literature). 2 vols. Jinan: Shandong renmin chubanshe, 1983.

SNZWZX

Ma Liangchun and Zhang Daming 馬良春、張大明, eds. *Sanshi niandai zuoyi wenyi ziliao xuanbian* 三十年代左翼文藝資料選編 (Selected Materials on Left-Wing Literature and Art in the 1930s). Chengdu: Sichuan renmin chubanshe, 1980.

ZBWC

Huang Gang 黃鋼, Hua Shan 華山, and Li You 理由, eds. *Zhongguo baogao wenxue congshu* 中國報告文學叢書 (Compendium of Chinese Reportage Literature). 19 vols. Wuhan: Changjiang wenyi chubanshe, 1981–83.

ZXWD, 1927–1937

Zhongguo xin wenxue daxi, 1927–1937. Vol. 13: *Baogao wenxue juan* 中國新文學大係報告文學卷 (Compendium of New Chinese Literature, 1927–1937, Reportage Volume). 20 vols. Shanghai: Shanghai wenyi chubanshe, 1985.

ZXWD, 1937–1949

Lin Ailian 林愛蓮 and Xu Shaojian 徐紹建, eds. *Zhongguo xin wenxue daxi, 1937–1949*, Vol. 13: *Baogao wenxue juan* 中國新文學大係報告文學卷 (Compendium of New Chinese Literature, 1937–1949, Reportage Volume). 20 vols. Shanghai: Shanghai wenyi chubanshe, 1990.

ZXWD, 1949–1966

Mu Qing 穆青, ed. *Zhongguo xin wenyi daxi, 1949–1966*. Vol. 13: *Baogao wenxue juan* 中國新文藝大係報告文學卷 (Compendium of New Chinese Arts and Literature, 1949–1966, Reportage Volume). 31 vols. Beijing: Zhongguo wenlian chuban gongsi, 1987.

INTRODUCTION

NONFICTION AND MODERN CHINESE CULTURE

What is reportage literature? *Is* reportage *literature?* Many China watchers will associate the term *reportage* with the highly conspicuous efforts of such writers as Liu Binyan and Su Xiaokang in the 1980s, who used the reportage form to circumvent the strictures of journalism in the post–Mao Zedong era of "reform and opening." So much attention was lavished on Liu Binyan's efforts, in fact, that one gets the impression in reading about him that he pioneered and even created the form, or was at least its first Chinese practitioner.[1] However, reportage literature has been a continuous strand of China's leftist cultural legacy since the early 1930s, and indeed its popularity can be traced to practices and predispositions that *preceded* the Chinese adoption of the genre's name (as *baogao wenxue* in 1930) by at least a generation. This book illustrates the development of Chinese reportage from its origins up to the eve of the Cultural Revolution, endeavoring to do justice to both its complex origins and its close relationship with cultural leftism. In so doing, I offer an alternative to prevalent ways of reading in modern Chinese literary studies that have led both to a prejudice toward fiction and to a general dissatisfaction with the artistic efforts of modern Chinese authors.

As a working definition, I understand *reportage* to mean any deliberately literary nonfiction text that narrates or describes a current event, person, or social phenomenon. On the other hand, my selection of texts has largely been governed by the classification of a corpus of works as reportage by Chinese cultural institutions for over fifty years, a process I will describe in more detail toward the end of this introduction. Viewed in historical perspective, the word *reportage*, originally a French noun meaning any kind of journalistic work, was adopted by German communist writers in the 1920s to refer specifically to agitational investigative reports on the labor movement. Reportage was soon elevated to the status of a literary genre by the Czech writer Egon Erwin Kisch, who boldly claimed that reportage would displace fiction as the dominant genre of the age. Aided by the popularity of his works, Kisch's exuberant promotion of the genre helped it spread throughout the major urban centers of the world as part of the international proletarian cultural movement.[2]

"Deliberately literary"—the idea that nonfiction writing can be a creative art form takes some getting used to. Especially in light of today's conventional understanding of art, perpetuated through our education and the media, creative art is supposed to rely principally on the imagination, specifically the imagination of an autonomous individual. The notion of the individual that lay behind this understanding is part of the legacy of Enlightenment humanism. The private individual is one of the Enlightenment's principal epistemological and social categories, and its apparent universality is often critiqued as deceptively concealing its own historicity. The ideology surrounding the individual promotes certain narrative configurations, creating a canon and a standard of narrative writing (fictional and otherwise) that features a dramatic plot, structural closure, psychological exploration, and the construction and development of characters in ways that fulfill these expectations.[3] The relative prominence of these narrative conventions derives from the individual character's self-realization, conflicts with other individuals, and especially conflicts with "society," which is conceived homogeneously in opposition to the individual. These conflicts must generally be resolved within the system of the text so that the narrative functions not as a part of the social continuum but as a reproduction or re-presentation of it. In this context, nonfiction works intended or believed to be artistic are at best treated as novelties, experiments, or historical documents valued principally for their content, no matter how much respect their authors' artistic creativity otherwise commands. Fidelity to the facts, which lay *out there*, outside the domain of the imagination's influence, prevents the individual from exerting the manipulative power over their arrangement and presentation necessary to create art. We are so accustomed to such assumptions that it is difficult to see how typical they are of the thinking of our own time or that other eras and cultures might not so readily take such views for granted.

Nonfiction narrative literature challenges these formal and ideological expectations. The genre's claim of veracity requires that the course of events not be "tampered with," and the interior states of multiple characters cannot be simultaneously represented (because they are not available to the author's observation). At most, only the psychology of the author-narrator can be explored. This does not mean, however, that works of literary nonfiction are or are meant to be purely "objective" records of facts. Rather, the different set of expectations created by the promise of a true story actually creates new possibilities for imaginative literary expression, not the least of which are the exploration of modes of consciousness and identity other than individuality and a shift of focus in the production of meaning from characters to places and events. These difficult and uncharted directions of literary expression are exciting in part because they function subtly as a practical critique of the ideology of individualism and its literary muses.

In traditional Chinese prose creative originality—the trademark of the individual—is not given the same importance as in literature and the arts in Europe since the Enlightenment. The presence of tradition in the form of recognizable models is felt deeply, and the writer provides, if anything, discernible sincerity of feeling and authenticity of experience. By contrast, modern Chinese narratives are burdened with the specter of fictional realism. The perceived importance of individual liberty brought with it a conviction that Western fiction of the industrial era, with all its intricate verisimilitude, encyclopedic plenitude, and formal and technical rigor, is a more solemn and socially responsible literary enterprise than the casual, sometimes "frivolous" sentiments and adventures one finds in traditional Chinese narrative prose and fiction, especially in the late imperial period. As a result, there has been a tendency among modern Chinese and Western observers alike to give modern Chinese literature less critical leeway than traditional forms that could not have benefited from the Western example. Because of the supposed universality of the Enlightenment, modern literature is supposed to be on an even playing field in China and "the West" (Europe and North America), and so its products must be judged by the same standards. Some scholars, accepting this, register their disappointment in China's literary achievements; others find extraliterary excuses for literary shortcomings. Few have thought to explore the possibility that there is a divergence in artistic standards, and even worldviews, between *modern* China and "the West" that is not explicable in terms of an essential *Chineseness*. This has inevitably led to general disappointment in and, I would say, a failure to understand the productions of modern Chinese writers, including novelists and poets.[4]

To begin with, the indigenous legacies of authenticity in art and of nonfictional self-expression are perhaps the most significant and overlooked constitutive elements of the modern Chinese literary tradition. They are obscured not only by our late-twentieth-century myopia but by the influential May Fourth humanists' prejudice toward European-style individualism. May Fourth intellectuals' adoption and promotion of Enlightenment ideology has been so influential over Chinese and Western scholarship on modern Chinese culture that it has deeply obscured other elements of that culture, particularly those difficult to assimilate into Enlightenment categories. Nowhere is the legacy of authenticity more in evidence than in modern Chinese reportage literature. There may never have been forms in traditional culture quite like reportage, which of course is modeled superficially on modern journalistic writing, but the principal concerns and expectations reportage addresses for moderns are strikingly congruent with the concerns of a certain tradition of late imperial literati culture.

One of the most unprecedented contributions of Qing dynasty intellectual history is *kaozheng xue* (evidential studies), or the pursuit of empirical knowledge as a practical critique of the idealism influential in Ming neo-Confucianism.[5] *Kaozheng xue* is often understood as a rigorous philological skepticism limited to the textual interpretation of the Confucian classics, but early advocates like Gu Yanwu also emphasized the investigation of the contemporary physical and social worlds and the questioning of traditional assumptions and conventional wisdom on these matters. The pathbreaking geographical investigations of Xu Xiake (a contemporary of Gu Yanwu), for example, can be understood as motivated by the spirit of empirical research.[6] The function and development of this methodology over the centuries of the Qing is complex, but as an intellectual trend it constitutes an important foundation of Chinese intellectual modernity that was obscured and trivialized by the introduction of Western ideas and practices. This indigenous empiricism has left a methodological and textual legacy—a way for the literati to conceive of the practice of writing and its cultural function. This methodology deeply influenced precisely the generation that allowed Western thought to supersede Chinese culture and polarized Western culture against everything Chinese, lumping all Chinese tradition together and erasing any progress that might have been achieved in the early modern period.

The familiar story of late imperial intellectual history, largely based on Liang Qichao's *Intellectual Trends in the Ch'ing Period*,[7] focuses on the ancient legacies left to the modern literati (intellectuals) by their traditional forebears. This is one of the principal reasons why both intellectual and literary histories of modern China have traditionally viewed the last twenty years of the Qing dynasty and the May Fourth movement, rather than earlier periods, as the birth of Chinese cultural modernity. It is significant, though, that social historians look earlier, even as early as the late Ming, for the traces of modernity in social life that we have recognized in our own culture: urbanization, the population explosion, significant improvements in domestic transportation systems, increasing reliance on international trade, regional division of markets and interregional trade, the professionalization of the publishing and entertainment industries, the more rapid spread of literacy, and the enhanced social mobility all these changes afforded, especially to the growing merchant class.[8] The literate elite was becoming less homogeneous: given a certain level of literacy it was possible for wealthy merchants and socially ambitious Buddhist monks and priests to buy positions in the civil service hierarchy or, short of that, to live like literati by enjoying elite modes of entertainment and cultivating elite tastes in design and casual reading.[9]

Certainly such changes had their effects, no matter how subtle, in reading and writing, which conditioned twentieth-century Chinese literary culture as much as the theory and practice of elites. Without going into detail here on the full range of effects these changes had on the late imperial cultural world, it is generally accepted among scholars of late imperial culture at least that the rise of vernacular fiction and regional opera could not have occurred were it not for these social and economic changes.[10] By the same token, later changes in the Qing dynasty—the emergence of the newspaper, experimentation with standardizing the written vernacular, and Western material culture with its electric lights, appliances, elevators, automobiles, public transportation, and the telegraph—some of which can be closely associated with European and American influences—were similarly assimilated years before the artificially dualist rhetoric of East-West cultural conflict polarized young intellectuals in the first two decades of this century.

LEFTIST JOURNALISM AND ITS "ARTISTIC" QUALITIES

The newspaper began to flourish in China, along with all this other Industrial Revolution paraphernalia, before more metaphysical aspects of Western cultural influence attracted the attention of elites. Intellectuals, politicians, and businessmen alike appreciated what the newspaper had to offer. It appealed to the Qing value of fact-finding, the outward-directed dimension of empirical research, and as such served as an important link between late imperial intellectual culture and the emergence of reportage in China, in addition to serving more immediately as a stylistic model.

While the scholar-official class was displaced by (or *became*) a new Westernized literati after the May Fourth movement, the perspective of the commercial, the mercantile, and the quotidian persistently counterbalanced the elite, May Fourth voice. This perspective manifests itself in the continued flourishing of "traditional-style" fiction in the modern publishing industry, in the emergence of the modern Chinese familiar essay, and in the newspaper. Apart from the newspaper, these are often seen as evidence of the continuity of traditional Chinese culture in modern times, but I think it is more accurate to think of them as manifestations of a persistent *indigenous modernity* that challenges the dominant, redemptive discourses of modern Chinese culture.

Reportage, on the other hand, emerges from a leftist worldview that develops in the wake of the May Fourth movement, a perspective that is in principle at odds with the commercial, bourgeois perspective described above. Moreover, there is a clear trace of literati concerns in reportage's emphasis on authenticity and the moral certainty of historical experience in contrast to the quotidian emphases of the commercial/urban perspective. But what makes reportage literature fascinating is precisely its ability to satisfy such different expectations, especially in that through its commitment to concrete experience it resists easy assimilation into the machines of propaganda. That is, although it is ironically a form of great importance to and treasured by the Chinese Communist Party, it possesses within it more than other forms, such as fiction and poetry, the potential to critique the shortcomings of the socialist order it helped bring into being.[11]

Reconstructing the Leftist Worldview
It is difficult to appreciate how reportage could be conceived as being artistic unless we try to reconstruct the worldview that appealed to the creators of reportage in the 1920s and 1930s. The history of the end of the nineteenth and the beginning of the twentieth century, particularly in Asia for those who lived through it, cast a most unfavorable light on capitalism, imperialism, and their interrelationship. For the young intellectuals of the time, anguished by the irony of China's utter humiliation in the wake of its erstwhile cultural supremacy, the notion of "revolution," no matter how vague or ill conceived, carried almost unambiguously positive connotations of national and individual self-affirmation, social justice, and above all a radical departure from a complex of ills conventionally attributed to China's traditional culture. The one vestige of that cultural legacy that in general they could live with—the responsibility of the literate class to be the moral guides of society—led them to conceive of revolution initially in terms of its literary implications: how writing itself could be revolutionized and in turn could revolutionize China.

To the initiators of the New Culture movement in 1917, it was "revolutionary" enough that writing and speech should be united in a modern, standard, written vernacular, as had been done in Japan in the previous century;[12] but the younger generation harbored more radical expectations for social change. The May Fourth demonstration of 1919 split the New Culture movement into moderate and radical camps. The former were generally committed to an overall transformation of culture (literature, media, the educational system), while the latter were determined that China needed a drastic transformation that could only be accomplished by decisive social action. The moderates dominated the literary scene in the early 1920s, and thus the first substantial corpus of modern vernacular literature modeled itself on the major literary forms and accomplishments of Europe in the previous century. Fiction was the most popular choice, and the world depicted, with a few exceptions, was that of petty bourgeois intellectuals, with an emphasis on themes of individual freedom and the uncovering of inhumanity in traditional Chinese family relations.

What did this cultural situation look like to the many younger would-be writers entering the scene in the 1920s? The heady enthusiasm of "literary revolution" from around 1920 had already waned for some years. Those whose temperament was more inclined toward action were frustrated by an increasingly conspicuous gap between the content of the new literature and the notion of revolution. This generation was also the first to take an interest in Marxist theory as well as its apparently successful application in the Russian Revolution of 1917. The analogy between the two national situations was elementary, at least in their minds. Moreover, the importance of the fact that Marxism, like almost no other European doctrine that became available to them at the time, provided a sophisticated and sympathetic explanation of China's domestic and international plights that included a *way out* cannot be overemphasized.

Not long after the literary arena was shaken up by the conversion of the Creation Society to Marxism and the emergence of yet another radical leftist literary society (the Sun Society), an important debate on revolutionary literature flared. Representing the frustration of the radical camp of the May Fourth generation, members of these two literary societies launched an attack on the mainstream literary scene, complaining that even the arguably "revolutionary" stories of the decade's most radical author, Lu Xun, were hopelessly out of date and irrelevant to the current historical situation.[13] This shrill voice, to be sure, was that of a minority and one particularly out of touch with the broad masses whose interests these radical writers claimed to represent. However, this debate signified a tip in the direction of mainstream Chinese letters to the left, so that by the beginning of the next decade, literary and historical events worked together to legitimize "revolutionary literature" at the expense of the "literary revolution."

What did a revolutionary worldview entail? It would be naive to assume that most of the readers (not to mention the writers) of left-wing literature in the 1920s had even a rudimentary understanding of Marxist theory. This book is concerned more with a practical answer to this question—reportage literature—than theoretical ones gleaned from manifestos and public debates. It had to have been something more than the persuasive rhetoric of a few radical promoters of leftist literature that shifted readers' interest and the publishing industry's resources in a leftward direction.

As a community, these readers and writers (many of whom had been active in the modern literary arena since its establishment) shared a set of attitudes regarding the relationships between the individual, literature, and society largely consistent with Marxism. They shared a distaste for what they perceived as the excessive individualism of the literature of the early 1920s and felt comfortable labeling it "bourgeois individualism." The kind of socially effective literature that Liang Qichao had envisioned twenty years before as the "political novel" had not yet appeared in China, and such a literature, as it began to appear in the late 1920s and early 1930s, would have to attend more to the broader, collective experience of contemporary social life than the "May Fourth literature" of the 1920s. In the repeated political violence of the mid- and late 1920s, students and younger writers watched their moderate May Fourth mentors plead with them to "shut the door and attend to their studies" rather than leading them in protest, leaving them with a feeling of betrayal. Insofar as this apparent shrinking in the face of danger could be attributed to "humanism," the leftward-leaning literary community began to feel that, like the "Age of Ah Q" and Lu Xun's fiction, "humanism" and other Enlightenment-inspired banners held aloft by May Fourth moderates ("science," "democracy," "freedom") had become outmoded concepts in a ruthless and violent world and indeed could even pass themselves off as a rationalization for imperialist aggression or for laying down before the enemy.[14] These interpretations took on more poignancy in the early 1930s when the Japanese unofficially began their piecemeal invasion of China and the Nationalist government, unable to mount an effective military resistance, adopted a passive policy until the outbreak of war in 1937.

Finally, an attitude shared by this community on the subject of journalism was particularly conducive to the rise of reportage literature. Reportage literature as such is actually at some remove from newspaper journalism. While reportage consciously imitates journalism, it is generally the product of professional authors publishing in literary magazines. Reportage in the early days of its development had a different purpose than journalism and, as I will show, is often a conscious critique of professional journalism when the latter is conceived as a mouthpiece for bourgeois, capitalist, or imperialist interests. Reportage authors attempt to make actual historical experience meaningful, to rescue the truth of actual events from the hollowing, reifying effects of journalistic objectivity.

It has been clearly shown how important the evolving role of the Chinese newspaper was to the advent of modern culture, both behind the scenes and at center stage.[15] In many ways, the newspaper provided an unprecedented forum and catalyst for the May Fourth mode of social intervention (becoming informed of world and domestic events as they happen, communicating with the literate public in the form of positional articles, and finally taking to the streets and *making news* in the form of political protest). The last stage, however, and indeed the one that immortalized the date of May 4, 1919, in modern Chinese culture, embodies a critique of the newspaper as a catalyst for just social change. Chinese intellectuals at the end of the Qing dynasty depended heavily on the newspaper as a tool, but they were also alive to its ideological complexity. They were aware of the religious, economic, and political connections that brought it into existence and the effects these (in addition to government censorship) had on their content. They were also aware of the agitational possibilities of mass-produced and distributed publications and of the emerging new discourse on journalistic objectivity. For the radical camp of the May Fourth generation, the newspaper was a medium of ambiguous value at best.

More importantly, the young intellectuals who experienced the violent struggles of 1925–27 had often experienced events reported in the newspapers, and they were aware of consistent gaps between the way they were reported in the major Chinese newspapers of the time and the way they had experienced them. As I will show in chapter 2, although reportage is heavily indebted in principle to the model of journalism, one of the principal motives for its appearance was to remedy the *distortions* of journalism. This is a subtle point and requires consideration of the Marxist-Leninist view of journalism to be fully understood.

The subject of journalism is emblematic of the pitfalls of projecting one's own conceptions on an earlier era in a different culture, even within our own century. To us late-twentieth-century inhabitants of the postindustrial, developed world, newspaper and television journalism may at times seem biased, but the principle that it should work against such biases, that it should be objective and impartial, seems to go without saying. We also believe that journalists themselves (if not the boards of directors of media companies) generally adhere to this principle. However, the newspaper and journalism existed for a long time before the issue of objectivity arose toward the end of the nineteenth century.[16] In the early stages of their development from the Renaissance through the seventeenth century, though, early protonewspapers, apart from providing commercial information and chronicling important events, functioned principally as a forum for their well-known publishers and editors to express their opinions. The newspaper evolved in the eighteenth century in large part as a medium of communication about wars and revolutions in Europe and North America, a condition that did not put a premium on objectivity.[17] In America it was not until the end of the Civil War that certain practices and attitudes in newspaper reporting emerged that would lead a generation later to a discourse of journalistic professionalism, a clear practical notion of the "fact," and the value of "objectivity" came to define ethical journalism.[18] Even then, as the newspaper became more popular in the Industrial Revolution as reading material, many exploited its influence as a weapon to influence public opinion for reasons of political strategy or commercial profit. The issue of journalistic objectivity arose in *resistance* to what was then the normal, comparatively biased state of journalism.

From the Marxist point of view (and here I am still speaking of a worldview with shared assumptions, not fine theoretical points) the notion of journalistic objectivity itself is suspect; it is part of the whole positivistic rhetoric or ideology of the bourgeoisie that served to cement that class at the pinnacle of capitalist society. To V. I. Lenin, for example, "objectivity" is a myth that is used to conceal a journalistic enterprise that actually staunchly defends the dictatorship of the bourgeoisie.[19] Karl Marx himself was a journalist, emerging into the public sphere as an advocate for freedom of the press (which for him meant tolerance for the leftist press) and ultimately with Friedrich Engels establishing the *Neue Rheinische Zeitung, Organ der Demokratie* in 1848, which lasted nearly a year before it was closed down. Throughout the following decade he was a contributing columnist in Horace Greeley's progressive *New York Tribune*.[20]

Whatever Soviet and other communist journalism would become, leftist journalism in the nineteenth and early twentieth century was in practice and principle suspicious of any pretense at "objectivity" in the established press. Marx as a journalist was not a very objective one, because for him history is truth; the truth is objective in the sense that it is not *relative*, but it is not impartial. The true meaning of historical events consisted in the constant unfolding of class struggle and the teleological progress toward a classless society. Thus, an event, no matter how apparently insignificant, had a true meaning, and for communists it was just as much the journalist's responsibility to highlight that meaning as it was to narrate that event; it may be for such reasons that the Soviet Communist Party's official newspaper was named *Pravda* (The Truth).

This point is crucial in understanding the origin of reportage literature, not only in China but as an important genre in the proletarian literary movements of many nations in the 1920s (including the United States, Germany, and Japan as well as the Soviet Union).[21] If there was to be a leftist counterpart to bourgeois journalism, it would have to be self-consciously tendentious and not dishonestly pass itself off as objective, as bourgeois journalism was perceived by leftists as doing; it would proudly affirm its bias for the perspective of workers and peasants and reveal the unfolding of historical truth in current events.

Thus, subjective judgment played an important role in the presentation of current events, making socialist journalism itself into an almost artistic endeavor. The reporter would seek not "information" but *truth* immanent in actual events, and the perception and transmission of that truth would be neither impartial nor dispassionate. It made the interpretation of everyday experience into an almost religious hermeneutic, only this truth was not transcendental but historical. The narration of events becomes an exploration of the aesthetics of historical experience. Aware of this, leftist writers of reportage, including one of the genre's initiators, Egon Erwin Kisch, understood the form to be an *artistic* genre, indeed an inherently leftist artistic genre.[22]

The League of Left-Wing Writers and the Discovery of Reportage
Reportage as such only came into existence in China in 1930 when a certain kind of writing called *baogao wenxue* was promoted by the Chinese League of Left-Wing Writers, following the example of their German, Soviet, and Japanese counterparts. However, the genre had a notable *prehistory* in China. Earlier writing practices that served as a foundation for the reportage form included travel literature since the Qing dynasty as well as impressionistic accounts of historical events in progressive late Qing and early Republican journals and newspapers. It may seem odd that I devote two of six chapters to such "protoreportage," but in so doing I hope to emphasize the integral relationship between reportage and larger trends of Chinese literary culture in its transition from the late imperial to the modern period. To put that prehistory in perspective, I should first sketch the "history" of the emergence of Chinese reportage as such around 1930 in some detail.

Viewed from the vantage point of the left-wing literary movement in China, reportage provided a means to resolve the gap between theory and practice that divided leftist writers, a gap manifested in the rift between the Sun Society (Taiyang she) and the Creation Society (Chuangzao she), especially in 1928–29.[23] The Sun Society, led by Jiang Guangci, claimed to represent the interests of active revolutionaries who had experience in organizing demonstrations as well as serving time in prison for their political activities. Their aim was to produce polemical literary works that reflected the experience of the proletariat and directly called for revolution in practical, immediate terms. Because they did not stress (and even disdained) theoretical orthodoxy, they welcomed work from writers of a diversity of backgrounds, regardless of their specific political credentials, as long as it had the effect of exposing the evils of capitalism and imperialism and furthering the cause of revolution.

The Creation Society, on the other hand, led by Guo Moruo, was after

1928 dominated by a group that was studying in Japan during the peak of the Japanese proletarian literary movement. Influenced by Japanese "Fukumotoism," they stressed theoretical orthodoxy above all and felt that literary figures should engage wholeheartedly in theoretical battles in which true communists would be separated from fellow travelers and clearly establish the former at the vanguard of the leftist literary movement.[24] They denounced works of literature that were in the least ambivalent about the future or from where revolutionary leadership would come, ostracizing their authors from the revolutionary ranks. As a consequence, the Creationists tended to downplay the importance of actual literary creation in favor of direct theoretical struggle.

The difficulty created by this rift is that neither side was perceived as productive of compelling literature. Many viewed the literary works of the Sun Society members as artistically crude and dogmatic, failing to excite the sympathy and interest of their readers, while the Creation Society produced few literary works at all and, despite its emphasis on theoretical purity, was rather irrational and unsystematic. The Creation Society's "theoretical debates" often consisted of vitriolic personal attacks on prominent May Fourth generation writers like Lu Xun, Ye Shaojun, and Mao Dun, stigmatizing them by arbitrarily associating them with reactionary forces and thus disqualifying their literary contributions from having any revolutionary value.

At the same time, the more productive novelists (some veterans of the Literary Association, others associated with Lu Xun) were struggling with the limitations of realism as a means of promoting social change, which was the common aim of writers of all camps who were actively experimenting with new forms and the adoption of modern Western literary models.[25] From Lu Xun's superficial decoration of bleak works like his "Yao" (Medicine, 1919) and "Mingtian" (Tomorrow, 1920) with symbols of hope,[26] to Mao Dun's vain struggles with aesthetic closure in his otherwise promising and ambitious novels Shi (Eclipse, 1927–28), Hong (Rainbow, 1930), and Ziye (Midnight, 1933),[27] the aesthetic demands of realistic fiction seemed too inextricably rooted in a European, capitalist worldview to meet what these writers perceived as the immediate tasks of modern Chinese cultural engagement. Marston Anderson sums up the problem eloquently in his introduction to The Limits of Realism.

The Chinese assumed that, once successfully transplanted, realism would encourage its readers to actively involve themselves in the important social and political issues confronting the nation. That Chinese reformers credited realism with this kind of social efficacy was understandable, since theorists in the West (including those from whom the Chinese first learned about realism) had themselves frequently credited the mode with this power. But in its actual operation, ... realism is more given to encouraging an aesthetic withdrawal than an activist engagement in social issues. . . . It is therefore not surprising that in its practice realism proved to be other than the socially transitive medium Chinese reformers first saw it to be. (25)

Thus, while novelists inclined toward formal realism as it had evolved in Europe were criticized for failing to truly engage social problems in their literature, leftist writers, though much more tendentious, were often faulted by the literary mainstream and even from within their own ranks for being inadequately realistic. Reportage had much potential in this context in that it accommodated both a radical political stance and the employment of the techniques of literary realism. In this sense it held the promise, much more than fiction, of staking out an entirely new artistic territory for the proletariat.[28] Moreover, in its dual insistence on factual accuracy and political positioning (i.e., a radical interpretation of the facts), reportage offered a powerful new cultural strategy that exploited the reader's acceptance of its claim to veracity for agitational ends. By providing detailed, concrete information about common persons and events that illustrate issues at the center of the contemporary historical and political stage, reportage attracted the attention of students and political activists at this time of confusion and change.

Perhaps the major contributing factor to the closing of ranks within the Left and the radicalization of many liberal-minded artists and writers at the time was the brutal suppression of communism by the Nationalist Party from 1927 to 1930, which excited the sympathy and indignation of a significant portion of the educated population. The Chinese Communist Party (CCP) and leftist literature had to struggle for mere survival; the futility of internal bickering was increasingly obvious. The Mukden Incident ("September 18th") of 1931 and the Battle of Shanghai

("January 28th") in 1932 pushed patriotic activism into the mainstream of literary production by superimposing the theme of resistance to Japan (upheld weakly in the cultural realm by the Guomindang [GMD], also referred to as the Nationalist Party) on the revolutionary agenda.

Beginning with the 1927 purge in Shanghai, repeated military operations on the part of the Nationalist Party aimed at thoroughly wiping out the Communist Party made it clear to the latter that it was no match for the Guomindang in military terms. This awareness coupled with Comintern policy led to the conscious expansion of the Communists' struggle into the cultural realm. Until then, the communist movement had been largely the work of highly educated intellectuals (some of whom were creative writers) attempting to reach the proletariat directly through political organization. As it gradually gained momentum throughout the 1920s, Marxism also began to attract the sympathy of some of the foremost young writers and artists of the time, who sought to carry on the tradition of iconoclasm they felt was the true legacy of the May Fourth movement. Thus, by the end of the 1920s when the very survival of the Chinese Communist Party was at stake, the mobilization of the "literary front" became an essential and effective weapon against the Nationalists, who by then had little claim over the sympathies and imaginations of cultural figures.[29]

The League of Left-Wing Writers was established in March of 1930 as an attempt to unify the divisive leftist literary scene; its members represented, in roughly equal numbers, all of the major cliques on the Left, including the Creationists, the Sun Society, and Lu Xun and his followers. While its establishment was endorsed by the Communist Party and was beneficial to its interests, the Left-Wing League was not a Party organization. The purpose of the league was to promote the proletarian literary movement in China through a repertoire of initiatives centered on the inclusion of the proletariat in cultural production. The league membership went about achieving these goals by establishing committees, holding regular meetings, publishing journals and newspapers, and to some extent sending members into factories to carry out both cultural and organizational policies. Reportage was promoted for the first time in the early 1930s by the league as part of a package of various proletarian artistic and cultural initiatives imported from abroad. Its practical ability to resolve conflicts in leftist cultural politics (not to mention the dilemmas of socially engaged writers in general) enabled reportage to play a more important role in the development of the leftist literary movement in China than other forms, as well as to play a more important role in the development of modern literature than it had elsewhere in the world.

A few months after the inception of the League of Left-Wing Writers a resolution of the league's Executive Committee (entitled "The New Status of Proletarian Literature and Our Duties") includes the first explicit promotion of reportage literature by a Chinese organization.[30] The resolution also makes clear how reportage practice was to integrate all aspects of the proletarian literary movement.

> We call upon the entire membership of the "Left-Wing League" to go to the factories, the villages, the front lines, to the lower levels of society. There accumulate explosive feelings; there unfold inhuman, painful lives that urgently need revolution, layered ranges of volcanoes, buried loads of explosives waiting to ignite. How we take these emotions, these convergences of different lives, and organize them into a progressive struggle for liberation, this is precisely the work of the worker-peasant-soldier correspondent movement, work that we should begin decisively. This is not any ordinary communications work but rather a broad-based educational movement to organize the lives of workers, peasants, and soldiers, to elevate their cultural level and political education. From the midst of intense class struggle, from militant strikes, the smoldering village struggles, through community night schools, through factory newsletters, wall newspapers, through all kinds of inflammatory propaganda work, let us create our *reportage!* Only thus can our literature be liberated from the hands of the privileged few and truly become the property of the masses. Only thus can we make the literary movement develop closely, together with revolutionary struggle, and only thus will the lives of our authors undergo a true transformation, and the content of our works will be filled with the proletarian consciousness of struggle. Therefore, the process of development of the correspondent movement is undeniably the process of development of the proletarian literary movement. (152)

The Committee for Creation and Criticism formed in a 1932 re-organization of the league took up many of these duties. Shen Qiyu and Wu Xiru, both writers of reportage, were members of this commit-tee. Wu Xiru also served as head of the Committee of Mass Literature and Art in 1933 and 1934. Among the duties of this committee cited in the league's organ *Mishuchu xiaoxi* (News from the Secretariat) were (1) the creation of revolutionary mass literature and art; (2) the study of the organization and methods of the reportage movement; (3) the study and criticism of reactionary mass literature and art; (4) the organiza-tion of reading classes for workers, peasants, and soldiers, newspaper-reading groups, and the training of peasant and worker reporters; and (5) the organization of storytelling and letter-writing teams. Hu Yepin had been in charge of the Committee for the Correspondents Movement (*tongxun yundong*) among Workers, Peasants, and Soldiers until his as-sassination on February 7, 1931.[31] There were also a few prominent re-portage writers on the standing and executive committees of the league at one time or another, including Lou Shiyi, Ding Ling, Xia Zhengnong, and Zhou Libo, with Zhou being one of the genre's most ardent support-ers.[32] To help quicken the growth and enrichment of this movement, the league's journal *Wenyi xinwen* continuously published reportage and articles about reportage theory and method.[33]

Qu Qiubai, who had been a consultant for the Sun Society,[34] was from 1931 to 1933 closely involved in the administration of the League of Left-Wing Writers.[35] In this capacity, one of Qu's greatest concerns was the popularization of literature. Reportage, then referred to variously as *tongxun* (correspondence) or *baogao* (reporting), was an integral part of the campaign to popularize literature, including initiatives to bring workers, peasants, and soldiers into the creation of literature as well as its reception, the keystone of the league's literary policy under Qu's administration. Tu Ru's "Laobosheng lu" (Robison Road), discussed in chapter 3, manifests this aspect of the Worker Correspondents Move-ment in the form of a *bibao*, or "wall newspaper," a worker-managed medium in which factory news and other items of interest were written on a blackboard or pasted to the wall in a common area.

Few of the texts that directly reflect the activities of the Worker Cor-respondents Movement in China make use of the figurative techniques characteristic of reportage. However, the movement had the effect of attracting a significant number of left-wing creative writers, such as Xia Yan, Wu Xiru, Peng Zigang, and Ding Ling, to experiment with tendentious literary nonfiction. What the movement offered these writers was not only a more practical form of involvement with the always elusive "masses," who were supposed to be the primary beneficiaries of leftist literature, but an opportunity to integrate research, investigation, and interviewing into the process of literary creation. The implications of such integration extend beyond reportage itself to influence realistic fiction.

The works of these writers, published in left-wing literary journals and occasionally major newspapers such as *Dagong bao* and *Shen bao*, manifest a distinctively literary figuration of industrial space as well as the vivid characterization of individual workers as vehicles for the indictment of industrial capitalism and imperialism. However, because of persistent divisiveness within left-wing literary circles as well as higher level turmoil within the leadership of the Communist Party, and especially because of the inexorable threat of war with Japan, worker-oriented initiatives of the Left-Wing League were short-lived, almost disappearing after the outbreak of war in 1937. Nevertheless, the literary accomplishments of the movement firmly established conventions for the event- and environment-oriented expression of collective consciousness that would characterize reportage throughout the war and afterward.

THE FORMATION OF A REPORTAGE CANON IN CHINA

The conspicuousness of reportage literature in the 1930s Chinese literary scene notwithstanding, the idea of reportage literature as an independent literary genre, as a modern Chinese tradition, is the creation of mainland Chinese scholarship in the 1980s. At that time, huge anthologies were compiled, conferences organized, and magazines established, all in the name of reportage.

Incomplete statistics show that from 1977 to 1980, 1409 reportage texts appeared in 63 different newspapers and 81 literary magazines, representing an average of one text per day over the span of four years. In 1981 alone, more than 400 works were published. The same year saw the establishment of a national reportage contest—the first of its kind in history. Two national academic institutes were set up to conduct research in the theory and criticism of the genre. Since then, reportage has been introduced into university and high school literature classes as a separate and distinct literary genre.[36]

The anthologies include *Zhongguo baogao wenxue congshu* (Compendium of Chinese Reportage Literature, ZBWC);[37] *Zhongguo youxiu baogao wenxue xuanbian* (Selection of Outstanding Works of Chinese Reportage Literature) (Shanghai: Fudan daxue chubanshe, 1982); reportage volumes of the *Zhongguo xin wenxue daxi* (Anthology of New Chinese Literature, ZXWD), 1927–37, 1937–49, and 1949–66;[38] and various topical compendiums, including ones for Communist base areas and occupied areas during the war against Japan and the civil war. And this list does not even begin to cover the various annual anthologies of "outstanding reportage" published from 1978 on. In short, one could fill a small bookcase with Chinese reportage anthologies alone, not to mention critical, theoretical, and historical works. There has been more than one nationwide conference on Chinese reportage and at least one on international reportage. Journals include *Shidai de baogao*, which later became *Baogao wenxue*, *Baogao wenxue xuankan* (Readings in Reportage Literature), and the later *Fazhi wenxue* (Law Literature, perhaps better translated as "detective stories").

This entrenchment of reportage is indicative of the political, literary, and academic culture of the early 1980s. The appearance in 1978 of Liu Binyan's "Ren yao zhi jian" (Between People and Monsters) sent shock waves throughout Chinese society and initiated a new wave of reportage literature that flourished for six years or so.[39] In the political atmosphere of the times, Deng Xiaoping's motto of "seeking truth through facts" set the tone for all kinds of social interaction, and reportage literature was an exemplary way of putting this kind of thinking into practice. It was also at this time that all of the above-mentioned forms of institutionalization of reportage (compendia, research projects, academic conferences, etc.) fell into place. In retrospect, seeing how almost all of the scholars who swarmed upon this "hot topic" at the time later moved on to study other, often unrelated subjects gives one a sense of how limited the options of a Chinese scholar in the field of modern Chinese literature were at the time. In my interaction with many of these scholars (with the exception of Yin Junsheng), I rarely got the impression that they pursued research in reportage literature because they thought it was an interesting topic. In fact, they had often forgotten what specifically they had written at the time and were strangely united in their opinions and conclusions about the nature and limits of the genre.

There was of course genuine interest among readers and writers, primarily because contemporary reportage in the 1980s provided a rare window to information and ideas that had been taboo throughout the Cultural Revolution (1966–76). That is, its value derived from its supply of information that had previously been lacking, but once it had served its purpose of confirming the disillusionment of the Chinese reading public reportage became expendable: it declined sharply in quality and popularity after 1989. From another point of view, though, the value to readers and writers of reportage in the 1980s was that it provided a means of social critique that was able to circumvent the official news media and also provide a deeper analysis of the social and cultural roots of certain problems facing Chinese society.[40] The decline of reportage after 1989 cannot be interpreted as a sign that this function has become irrelevant, only that reportage is no longer a reliable medium for the performance of this function.

Be that as it may, the Chinese scholarship on reportage provides us with a wealth of bibliographic information, if not a much greater understanding of the nature and history of reportage literature in China. It also provides us with a clear idea of the significance of reportage for those who promoted its institutionalization. It was seen by official commentators and scholars as a repository of revolutionary history from an explicitly revolutionary perspective. It ties adherence to the facts to the revolutionary project, even going so far as to grant the Chinese Communist Party a nominal monopoly on factual accuracy.[41] Finally, it gives the Party a means to filter out texts that are not ideal for achieving these objectives by forming a canon of "outstanding" pieces of Chinese reportage and thereby making the other pieces even more inaccessible than before.

Having sketched out the place of reportage in leftist literary organizations, it is now possible to reconstruct how the emergent genre was transformed into a literary canon in the space of thirty-three years (from 1930 to 1963). The process began with the discovery of reportage in the form of translations of foreign articles on the genre as well as excerpts from prominent foreign works. Yuan Shu's "Baogao wenxue lun" (On Reportage Literature)[42] was possibly the first published article after the Left-Wing League's August 1930 resolution promoting reportage along with other genres to define reportage and link it with recent worldwide literary trends. Interestingly, the language Yuan uses and the specific points he makes about the genre's origins in the milieu of modern industrial production are remarkably similar to that of Kawaguchi Hiroshi's more extensive treatment of the genre (translated by Xia Yan), which was published the following year.[43] It seems quite likely that Yuan Shu was familiar with Kawaguchi's article in 1931 and based his comments on it. Ah Ying's (Qian Xingcun's) preface to the 1932 Shanghai shibian yu baogao wenxue (The Shanghai Incident and Its Reportage) includes a short section defining reportage based largely on Kawaguchi's account, with many passages almost identical to Xia Yan's translation.[44] From this it is apparent how seminal Kawaguchi's article was in the early 1930s to contemporary Chinese writers' understanding of reportage.

In all of these articles except the Shanghai Incident piece, reportage is conceived narrowly as agitational literary treatments of factory and mine conditions and the labor movement. There is no indication that it had occurred to anyone before 1932 to include other kinds of subject matter in this category until the appearance of The Shanghai Incident and Its Reportage, which is primarily concerned with war reporting. In this sense, The Shanghai Incident was a major breakthrough in reportage's development in China: it paved the way for war reportage in the following decade as well as opening the door for the inclusion of other kinds of subject matter, including political demonstrations in the city streets, the lives of beggars and homeless people, and the narration of the achievements of Communist social and political reform in Soviet base areas in the countryside. In short, reportage was quickly becoming a favored vehicle for the expression or construction of all aspects of the experience of modern Chinese history.

These introductions to the genre were also strident calls to promote reportage in China; there was a perception among contemporary commentators that China was in need of such a form. Ah Ying's introduction to The Shanghai Incident states as one of the collection's major goals "to cause young readers to grasp the importance of the 'reportage' form in these times and to exert efforts to study it . . . reportage is the newest form of literature, a form with unlimited agitational powers; our young readers must not forget that this form must be studied and actively put into practice."[45] Other promotional articles gave specific suggestions as to how to organize and develop reportage production among workers, peasants, and soldiers,[46] and the promotional efforts paid off to a certain extent as Chinese works of reportage began to appear in the 1930s. In part due to these works and the introductory articles, many professional writers began to experiment with the form.

The second step or aspect of institutionalization was the support of the publishing industry. Special columns for reportage or similar forms were established in several influential journals,[47] at least two journals were specifically devoted to reportage,[48] and, most significantly, by 1936 three widely read anthologies of reportage had appeared.[49] While columns and journals offer a place to publish and affirm a certain confidence in a new form, anthologies reflect the development of critical standards and an awareness that certain works are worth preserving.

As a result of the tremendous outpouring and variety of reportage in 1936 and 1937, commentators had a significant corpus of Chinese reportage to form the basis of the next stage of institutionalization: critical history. Two of the most important contributions to this were Mao Dun's 1937 "Guanyu 'baogao wenxue'" (About "Reportage Literature"),[50] and Zhou Gangming's introduction to his manual *Zenyang xie baogao wenxue* (How to Write Reportage Literature).[51] At this point, issues such as the definition of the genre, its essential characteristics, and its artistic techniques become crucial means of distinguishing reportage from other genres. In addition to defending reportage against certain critics who were calling for "great works," Mao Dun encourages formal diversity, including the use of diary, epistolary, and *yinxiangji* (impressions), rather than looking to a single model (such as Xia Yan's "Bao shen gong" [Indentured Laborers]) (Mao Dun, "Guanyu 'Baogao wenxue,'" 52). Both writers assess Chinese works such as *The Shanghai Incident and Its Reportage*, "Indentured Laborers," and the travelogues of Zou Taofen and Fan Changjiang in light of the Western reportage tradition, and Zhou Gangming clearly suggests that reportage was independently developing its own tradition in China. Finally, both writers strongly distinguish reportage from journalism, Mao by emphasizing its literary nature and Zhou by stressing that reportage is a critique of journalism.

Though not historical summaries, Hu Feng's 1935 "Lun suxie" (On the Sketch),[52] and 1937 "Lun zhanzheng shiqi de yige zhandou de wenyi xingshi" (On a Battling Form of Art in a Period of War),[53] are very much concerned with accounting for the genre's popularity in China and with improving its literary quality. However, his high literary standards and commitment to an independent, critical artistic vision led him to often find fault with existing reportage, particularly during the war. Hu must not be viewed as a detractor of reportage, however, for his wartime journal *Qiyue* (July) was a vehicle for some of China's finest reportage.[54]

Such early assessments of Chinese reportage were rounded out several years later by Yi Qun's (Ye Yiqun's) "Kangzhan yilai de baogao wenxue" (Reportage since the Beginning of the War of Resistance), which is, significantly, an introduction to another anthology, *Zhandou de suhui* (Sketches of Battle).[55] Yi Qun in his summary of reportage history minimizes the contribution of the League of Left-Wing Writers and makes it appear that *baogao wenxue* was from the outset inextricably connected with resistance against Japan; moreover, he gives such a full account of Chinese war reportage that this article became one of the central sources for later constructions of the reportage canon.[56] Finally, like Hu Feng before him, Yi Qun is explicitly concerned with adopting critical standards by which reportage can be evaluated with a view to pushing the genre on to greater heights.

The stage of critical assessment can be said to have culminated with Lan Hai's (Tian Zhongji's) 1947 *Zhongguo kangzhan wenyi shi* (History of the Literature and Arts of Resistance in China), and indeed this work represents the advancement of reportage into the canon of modern Chinese literature.[57] Unlike the critical treatments just discussed, Tian Zhongji's account places reportage literature into a comprehensive narrative of a period of modern Chinese literary history, leaving clear implications about its importance relative to the major genres of fiction, poetry, and drama as well as other forms such as filmmaking, musical composition, and folk crafts. Tian's account also consolidates existing accounts of Chinese reportage history as well as adding substantial new information, making its narrative more lucid and comprehensive than past works.

In this light it can be seen what a relatively small step it was for reportage to be included in Wang Yao's seminal 1951 *Zhongguo xin wenxue shigao* (Draft History of New Chinese Literature), a comprehensive account of more than fifty years of modern Chinese literature, and indeed in virtually every subsequent literary history of the modern period.[58] As Zhang Yingjin observes, the organization of Wang's text reflects the orthodox Marxist emphasis on strict historical periodization as the overriding category of literary history, under which equally rigid formal categories are subordinated. Wang's account is divided into four historical periods (1919–27, 1928–37, 1937–42, and 1942–49), and under each there is an initial chapter on historical background, followed by a chapter on each of the four major genres of poetry, fiction, drama, and prose. However, there is some variation in the treatment of prose in each historical period: the first period's prose section is devoted exclusively to *sanwen* (literary essays),[59] while the second discusses various forms, including *zawen* (satirical essays), reportage, and *youji* (travelogues) in addition to *sanwen*. In the third and fourth periods (wartime and civil war literature), reportage has moved to the head of the prose section, followed by *zawen* and a third, miscellaneous section that includes *sanwen*, *xiaopin* and *suibi* (familiar essays), and *youji*. It is apparent that beneath the symmetrical veneer of Wang's historical typology, the category of prose is rather unstable, as is the position of reportage within it. Wang Yao's contribution to the formation of the reportage canon is in providing the first extensive narrative of the development of reportage in China through different historical periods. At the same time, when it is compared to previous treatments of the genre's history mentioned above Wang's account begins to show the effects of uncritical borrowing and accumulation that have made reportage's history increasingly opaque as it becomes richer and more complex.

Even after the publication of Wang's account, reportage did not entirely come into its own in the Chinese Communist literary institution, and it made no further advances toward the center of the canon for the rest of the 1950s. The most significant event for reportage history in the 1950s was the introduction of the at times socially critical Soviet *očerk* ("sketch"; *texie* in Chinese) by Liu Binyan and the debate about whether socialist reportage ought to extol or criticize.[60] Otherwise, writings on reportage from this period were little concerned with the preservation or assessment of past works of reportage, focusing rather on contemporary works, issues of veracity, and definitions of the genre, questions more about future of reportage than about its past.

The final phase of reportage's journey into the heart of the Communist canon was inaugurated in 1963. In March of that year, the editorial board of *Renmin wenxue* (People's Literature) and the Zhongguo zuojia xiehui (Chinese Writers Association) invited thirty authors for the first nationwide conference on reportage literature.[61] Although the conference was primarily oriented toward promoting reportage writing and co-opting at least a watered-down version of the critical stance established in 1956 by Liu Binyan's *texie* (oçerk sketches), the conference coincided with the preparation of a number of anthologies of reportage literature, including the three-volume *Baogao wenxue xuan* (Selected Reportage Literature, 1963–64), *Chuntian de baogao* (Reports of Spring), and *Budui baogao wenxue sanwen xuan* (Selected Literary Essays and Reportage from the Troops).[62] Also, the massive editorial project that culminated in the 19-volume *Zhongguo baogao wenxue congshu* (Compendium of Chinese Reportage Literature) seems to have begun in 1963 or shortly before.

In a *Wen shi zhe* (literature, history, philosophy) article in 1963, Tian Zhongji (whose *History of the Literature and Arts of Resistance in China* I discussed above) writes of himself and several others spending over three months "scanning over one hundred magazines and newspapers, more than 70 anthologies, altogether about three thousand works of reportage literature and feature articles from the May Fourth period to Liberation" for a new, comprehensive, and critical anthology of Chinese reportage to be entitled *Texie baogao xuan* (Selected Feature and Reportage Articles).[63] Although I have not been able to determine whether this anthology was ever published, we do know from Tian Zhongji's article that the editorial team completed a selection that fell within the planned length of 150,000 Chinese characters—the length of a single volume. Tian also discusses many (probably most) of the selections the committee made, which included previously anthologized works, new selections that were later included in the 1983 *Compendium* (ZBWC), and a few selections that do not appear to have been included in the later work. Another interesting aspect of his article is his criticism of previous historical accounts of reportage literature: "Few past literary histories had sections covering representative works that were reliable. When we checked the content, we discovered that many references had been perfunctorily included without [the authors] ever having seen the original work" (763).

Tian's selection of the term *texie baogao* for the title of the collection, moreover, shows that by 1963, *texie* (feature article), a term that had been associated with reportage since the 1930s, had vastly increased in importance. Moreover, its meaning had changed when Liu Binyan adopted it as a translation of the Russian *očerk*, and Liu's own controversial *texie* from 1956 had added much to *texie*'s conspicuousness. However, this consolidation of different forms into a single category, whether we call it *texie baogao* or *baogao wenxue*, opened the possibility of discussing reportage as a distinctive literary form with stable characteristics over time rather than just as a transparent record of discrete historical events and experiences.

The will to consolidate actually went over the head of reportage by 1979, when the *Zhongguo xiandai wenxue shi cankao ziliao: Sanwen xuan* (Research Materials on Modern Chinese Literature: A selection of Literary Essays) appeared.[64] Here works identified as reportage before and after this collection are mixed without comment with travelogues and familiar and satirical essays. Lin Fei's later coverage of reportage in his 1980 *Zhongguo xiandai sanwen shi* (History of Modern Chinese Literary Essays) follows suit in principle by placing reportage under the general rubric of prose literature, but he is careful to sharply distinguish reportage as a distinctive subgenre and he describes it in much the same way as past accounts. Moreover, Lin, like many of his contemporaries, has dropped the term *texie* as a generic category, perhaps a reflection of an anti–Liu Binyan backlash at the time. *Baogao wenxue* makes an odd sibling to *zawen* (satirical essays) and especially forms like *xiaopin wen* and *suibi*, which are traditional terms for forms that are in practice more like the English "familiar essay." The issue of whether reportage belongs in a general category of "prose literature" has never been resolved, principally, I would argue, because there is no consensus as to whether prose literature itself is a tenable category and if so whether it is to be defined in terms of content or form or otherwise.

The overall process of the institutionalization of reportage reached its culmination throughout the 1980s. In 1980, of the first Chinese journal since the 1930s *Wenyi xinwen* to be devoted to the research and creation of reportage literature, *Shidai de baogao* (Reports of the Times, later *Baogao wenxue*), was established. Research organizations like Huang Gang's *Guoji baogao wenxue yanjiu hui* (Society for the Research of International Reportage Literature) and Yin Junsheng's *San S hui* (The Three S Society) mushroomed.[65] Finally, in 1987 the first scholarly monograph devoted to the history of modern Chinese reportage, Zhao Xiaqiu's *Zhongguo xiandai baogao wenxue shi*, appeared.

It is this canon, whose conscious formation began after the War of Resistance against Japan and may be said to have reached completion with the publication of the *Zhongguo baogao wenxue congshu* (Compendium of Chinese Reportage Literature), begun in 1983, that forms the basis of my investigation. Through a close reading of representative texts in this canon, I reconstruct the artistic conventions of reportage from its beginnings in China up to the mid-1960s, by which time Liu Binyan's *texie* had introduced fundamental changes into the genre.

WHERE IS THE ART IN REPORTAGE?

I will leave the presentation of the specific techniques used to the following chapters, but they fall generally into the categories of narrative verisimilitude and the "characterization" of events, environments, and collectives rather than individual characters. Verisimilitude in Western narrative poetics is usually understood in connection with realistic fiction as a resemblance to lived experience that makes the fiction plausible; surely it is quite a different matter when applied to the narration of "actual events." Verisimilitude is in fact rarely discussed in relation to nonfiction literature because of the prevalent but erroneous assumption that nonfiction narrative is not constructed or arranged as fictional narrative is: true stories are supposed to tell themselves. However, in reportage it is precisely in the verbal/artistic construction of the event (even if actual) that the writer imparts the tendentious message to it. At the same time, the conventional *belief* that the message is inherent or immanent in the event is an important feature of the aesthetics of reportage: reportage only "works" when it is understood to be about "real people and real events" (*zhenren zhenshi*) and approached with a rigorous fidelity to observation and the facts. This belief is enhanced by the use of techniques such as the frustration of narrative closure and deliberate artistic "roughness" to create a reality effect.

Once alive to the artistic dimension of reportage, the verisimilitude that is the very vehicle for its effect of veracity, it becomes possible to distinguish types of reportage in formal terms. "Form" in this sense can no longer be categorically opposed to content. The form of each subgenre as I define it consists of the literary realization of the setting in which the action takes place; it cannot be discussed separately from it. The work's social space is described or defined precisely in terms of the distinctive physical contours, structure, atmosphere, and dynamics peculiar to the social situation depicted—world cities and natural landscapes articulated by international conveyances like the train and the ocean liner in travelogue; the streets of Beijing and Shanghai for the reportage of political demonstrations; the "factoryscape" (as I will describe it) for labor reportage; the battlefield, refugee camp, and hospital for war reportage; and the socialist work site (whether agricultural or industrial) for socialist reportage. From these physical contours, structures, atmospheres, and dynamics emerge characteristic moods, rhetoric, and narrative situations. Similar to the way in which Mikhail Bakhtin's notion of the "chronotope" defines the intersection of time and space in works of European fiction, these settings both spatially and temporally define distinguishable types of reportage. As a feature of Chinese reportage literature, I refer to this technique as the *literary construction of social space*.[66]

The literary construction of social space—an adaptation of Henri Lefebvre's concept of "social space"—indicates a two-layered activity: (1) the social process by which the spatial environments of human activity are produced,[67] and (2) the depiction of these environments in literature and art. The spatial environments of human activity encompass more than the physical contours of the spaces in which human activity takes place; they include the subjective perception of those environments by their inhabitants. Lefebvre's concept of social space embodies the dialectic between the physical environment and our perception of it. The second layer is closely related to the first in that artistic depictions are not passive reflections of these environments but play an important role in the production and reproduction of social space itself.

Before I go further I need to clarify what I mean by "space" in order to rule out a number of conventional definitions. First of all, social space is not an empty, limitless void; it is the act of a human community inscribing itself through social activity upon a natural space or (more often) an existing social space. It features its own topography and atmosphere, and a particular kind of space is definable by its contours and other physical characteristics that are sensed and expressed by those who live and work within it. It is in this sense that the environment or landscape in which action occurs (or is imagined) is socially produced. The contours of space shape the character of the action, the historical/social situation, and vice versa: action, like perception, is in a dialectical relationship with the landscape.

Second, social space and its literary construction are not static, not an inert dimension of the physical universe, but a *dynamic* product of human activity that is constantly changing, constantly being elaborated. Literature is neither the only nor the principal producer of social space; architecture, agriculture, and all other kinds of building and reshaping clearly play the major role. But so do public policy, human organization, labor, and transportation. The acts that produce social space are often but not always direct physical transformations of the environment; just as often they are intellectual and creative processes that in turn condition and shape such physical transformations. Literature is such a creative process and, as a form of human activity, also takes part in the shaping of social space. Moreover, creative and intellectual processes can shape people's perceptions and conceptions of their environment without *needing* to physically change it. What is written about a place can not only lead to changes in its configuration but also in reconstructing the version of the physical environment readers carry with them in their minds. I will provide examples of this in the ensuing chapters.

Third, the *literary construction* of social space is not "spatial" in the physical sense but generates the perception or impression of a certain type of landscape with the medium of language and the techniques of literature, including metaphor, connotation, and description as well as emotional and rhetorical coloring. It is not delimited by the physical world, but there has to be an impression of resemblance for the sake of verisimilitude, particularly in reportage: literary landscapes are chosen as much as they are created. Writers can appeal to readers' memories and imaginations—making "spatial allusions" as it were—to assist them in the mental reproduction of their spaces. And, unlike the exhaustive, three-dimensional Cartesian model of physical space, the literary construction of social space need not be, and in fact cannot be, exhaustive: it is characteristic of the literary construction of social space to be selective, to highlight certain features of a given landscape to give it its characteristic and unique quality, and to emphasize the nodes of its dynamic relationship to the people acting within it.

Unlike strictly intellectual disciplines, literature continually makes reference to the experience of the body. The body as a vehicle of perception is linked to the physical topography of social spaces and also becomes a vehicle for identification with and opposition to others around it. The landscape inscribes the perceiving body just as the perceptions shape and highlight the topography of the landscape. This is a crucial point underlying the interpretations I offer in this book: because the body in reportage is the vehicle through which the dynamic transformations of social space are perceived, and the features of the physical environment expressed in each work bear the mark of the author's subjective reaction to each unfolding situation, the body itself becomes part of the continuum of social space. If there is a three-dimensional relief map that we can describe as the social space of a work of reportage, more often than not the perceptual landscape of the author's or narrator's body and mind forms part of that topography.

I classify works of reportage here according to types of space, but that does not mean that the social space constructed in a given reportage work is homogeneous. Nicos Poulantzas has pointed out that no single mode of production exclusively inhabits any particular society— rather, in each society there coexists a variety of layered, intersecting, or interlocking modes of production, at some points resonating, at some points clashing in dissonance.[68] Social space corresponds to a mode of production somewhat like signifier to signified; it is a concrete manifestation of a mode of production. Thus, a given society manifests a variety of layered, intersecting, or interlocking social spaces, and it is often the points of friction or interference patterns among them that make for interesting literature.[69]

In addition to the landscape topography of social space, this complex heterogeneity is manifested in the form of the crowd: the dissonance referred to sometimes arises between the crowd (or a group within it) and highlighted features of the topography (environment). Existing theory on crowds and their literary manifestations tends to assume they are made up of persons who are individuals first and only partake in crowd psychology as an overlay to their individual personalities.[70] This assumption leads to the conclusion that crowds are inherently homogeneous and their behavior tends to follow predictable patterns. The interests of the crowd can only be distinguished from those of individuals. Chinese reportage from the 1930s, however, illustrates crowds made up of members of different, sometimes adversarial groups. The tensions among these groups suggest a more complex model for understanding the crowd experience from within. Like different types of social space—the imprint of different dominant classes in different eras on the human environment—the groups that compose a crowd cross and interlock, so that individuals within the assemblage may act or feel alternately or simultaneously as an isolated individual, a member of one or more groups (a class, an ethnic group, or a group defined by social function such as the police), or a member of the crowd as a whole. Just as members of constituent groups may define their interests and identities out of a relation of tension with aspects of the urban environment in which the crowd congeals, so they define themselves and struggle in relation to tensions with and attractions to other groups around them.

I do not wish to argue that there was conceptually nothing like the "individual" in Chinese culture—much has been written on this subject and at any rate, even if there were no individual, that would not be the point.[71] Nor do I mean to imply that individual persons are not discrete entities or that it is possible to have some kind of "collective consciousness" outside that individual experience. People are of course physically separate from one another, and their experience is mediated through their discrete bodies and a unique set of experiences that distinguishes them from one another. Identification with collectives as it is represented in literature does not imply mystical or metaphysical connections between people; what it comes down to in literary expression is how the choice of identity functions to contextualize experience. By looking beyond "individualism" as a context for the interpretation of reportage, I am not negating individuality but rather questioning the common assumptions that there is no possible perspective other than the individual and that the individual is a world unto himself or herself who can, if he or she chooses, carry on an existence completely separate from "society." While the social embeddedness of the individual is now a theoretical commonplace, in many corners of Chinese literary studies individualism still hinders our ability to see the value of reportage with the same eyes as those Chinese writers who were attracted to it in the 1920s and 1930s. Common notions about the individual that prevail despite theoretical developments—that he or she is self-sufficient and can be at odds with society and even "the world" and that individuals' particular rights and interests can rival those of groups and society as a whole in importance—are not universal truths but historically and culturally distinctive conceptions. These notions belonged to systems of thought and belief that the Chinese were aware of and confronted early in the twentieth century, notions that some embraced and others rejected but all looked upon them as something alien. Even if those Chinese who embraced the ideology of the individual also took on its rhetoric of naturalness and universality, that in and of itself does not make the individual any more natural or universal.

KINDS OF SPACE IN CHINESE REPORTAGE

Looking at the table of contents, one might think that I am simply categorizing Chinese reportage by subject matter. However, my readings of reportage works (most of which were republished in the abovementioned anthologies) have led me to a spatial typology based on the literary construction of social space described above. Each type is defined by the landscape or "social space" it conveys. In chapter 1, I present Chinese travel literature from the turn of the century to the 1930s. Travel literature is the most important link between late imperial prose and modern Chinese reportage. The examples I discuss are not reportage in the form it finally takes in the 1930s, but they exhibit many key features that define the genre. Like other types of reportage in the following chapters, modern Chinese travelogue can be distinguished by its particular type of spatiality, yet this spatial mode is not defined by a fixed environment. While travel is a movement through space, the space moved through is rarely depicted: modern travelogue consists of a series of locales articulated by scenes in trains, ships, and later airplanes. I begin by discussing late Qing dynasty journals of world travel written by literati, especially government officials on diplomatic missions. This leads to the crucial transitional figure of Qu Qiubai, whose narratives of his journey to the Soviet Union in 1921–22 became an integral part of the textual legacy of the May Fourth movement and blueprints for the methodology of the yet to emerge genre of reportage.

Chapters 2 and 3 describe two different types of urban reportage—the reportage of public demonstrations and labor reportage—which represent two distinctive types of urban social space. The first begins in the May Fourth movement with the narration of student demonstrations and dramatizes the streets of Beijing and Shanghai as a stage for the enactment of collective historical dramas. An implicitly shared theatrical paradigm functions to structure events, highlight certain "actors," and impart meaning to the spatial position and direction of movement; it is a particularly clear example of how social space can be produced in literary terms. The form emerged in the 1920s, but works like this continued to be written through the war. Although no celebrated pieces of this type emerged and many of its authors are anonymous or otherwise unknown, well-known writers like Mao Dun, Zheng Zhenduo, Ye Shaojun, Zhu Ziqing, and Ding Ling contributed striking examples.

The second type of urban reportage, labor reportage, is more conspicuous because it flourished in the early 1930s when the word *baogao wenxue* (reportage literature) and synonyms like *wenyi tongxun* (artistic dispatch) first came into use in China, the reportage genre was actively promoted by the League of Left-Wing Writers, and prominent writers began deliberately experimenting with reportage as an artistic genre. Labor reportage dissects the environments of labor—factories, mines, slums, public kitchens, and so on—which I refer to collectively as the factoryscape, and their dialectical, dehumanizing relationship with the bodies of workers. Dramatist Xia Yan's "Baoshen gong" (Indentured Laborers), the most celebrated work of prewar reportage, meticulously details a day in the life of a teenage rural girl in one of Shanghai's numerous textile mills. The girl's plight is illustrated almost entirely in terms of the configuration and textures of the factoryscape and its operators as a semiotic simulacrum of capitalist exploitation. I also discuss similar works by Ding Ling, Peng Zigang, Lou Shiyi, and others.

Chapters 4 and 5 concern the impact on reportage of the War of Resistance against Japan (as World War II is generally referred to among Chinese). The war allowed reportage to greatly expand its range of content and become a principal mode of written expression in the war period. Chapter 4 presents reportage from the early months of the war that dramatizes the transformation of peacetime social space into battlefields. These works combine writers' bad consciences about their often ineffectual roles in the war effort with terrifying images of wounded bodies both in the field and in hospitals as vehicles for visceral emotional involvement in the war. Chapter 5 deals with later works that illustrate the war's expansion of the spatial compass of reportage to include vast landscapes of mountain ranges and rolling plains. Many of these spaces were being experienced by writers for the first time, and because of the thematic focus of wartime literature these landscapes and battlefields often became media through which these writers could project and illustrate their own emerging national identity, beyond ethnicity to geosocial belonging, to bringing one's body into the continuum of the national landscape.

Finally, chapter 6 illustrates another important ramification of the literary culture of war: the emergence of socialist culture and consciousness through intellectuals' encounters with both agricultural and industrial change in practice. I will also be illustrating the process by which reportage got caught up in the Communist cultural machine in the elaboration of a utopian space that was imagined as much as it was experienced. These utopian landscapes, which became a literary commonplace in the People's Republic of China after 1949, were not invented by the Communist Party but have their literary roots in the experiences of intellectuals deliberately roughing it in the 1920s and 1930s.

The social space realized by writers from within the Communist cultural organization in the Yan'an base area and the People's Republic afterward—usually configured as landscapes of agricultural or industrial reform (communal farms and factories or major construction/exploration sites)—exhibit a peculiar aesthetic of their own if you are willing to look beyond their conformity to literary policy. The Party's cooptation of the reportage genre had by this point severed the aesthetic and informational functions of reportage. Politically uncontroversial reportage, in other words, became principally concerned with the effective employment of artistic techniques, while the first critical reportage written within the socialist system deliberately abandoned the artistic pretense and, it would seem, the entire legacy of reportage in China. This bifurcation occurred in the Hundred Flowers Campaign of 1957 with the publication of Liu Binyan's "Zai qiaoliang gongdi shang" (On the Bridge Construction Site), but since the "orthodox" branch continued to develop until the eve of the Cultural Revolution I follow it up to that point (1966) with the publication of the legendary collective reportage on the self-sacrificing county Party secretary Jiao Yulu. The other, critical branch of reportage has been dealt with already at length in English and insofar as it explicitly defines itself in theory and practice as nonliterary falls outside the scope of this study.[72]

This study, the first comprehensive exploration in English of Chinese reportage before the Cultural Revolution, necessarily only scratches the surface. I only discuss a fraction of the easily available materials, not to mention rare materials such as publications from the various Communist base areas during the war. I have deliberately chosen to focus upon forms and texts of reportage characteristic of the genre's most essential aspects before the Cultural Revolution: the textual practices leading up to the explicit adoption of the genre in China and the heyday of its development in the 1930s and 1940s. Whole studies could be done on other areas I only touch on here, such as nineteenth-century accounts of world travel, twentieth-century domestic and international travel literature, collective reportage projects, and civil war and Korean war reportage. Even socialist reportage in the 1950s and 1960s could be dealt with more comprehensively. I only hope this study will be sufficiently interesting (or disappointing) to inspire such further inquiries.

ONE

Travel: Writing a Way Out

One of the first treatments of Chinese reportage in English, Yin-hwa Chou's 1985 article "Formal Features of Chinese Reportage and an Analysis of Liang Qichao's 'Memoirs of My Travels in the New World,'" boldly asserts that Liang's 1903 travel essay was the origin of Chinese reportage.[1] Chou's article was an important first step in filling out the historical background of reportage in China and linking it to fundamental concerns and methods of modern Chinese culture.

Liang Qichao visited over twenty cities in Canada and the United States over a ten-month period "1. to examine the conditions of Chinese living in America; 2. to study the socio-political establishment of the United States; and 3. to solicit financial backing for the 'Protect the Emperor Society.'"[2] *Travels in the New World* records Liang's efforts on the first two matters. Structured by his travel itinerary, Liang's text provides extensive statistical information on Canadian and American societies and the place of Chinese immigrants in them, alternating with copious analytical commentary and polemics on the part of the writer. Although Yin-hwa Chou's brief formal typology of reportage provides a sound basis for further investigation of the genre, her explication of *Travels* reveals these expository aspects much more than it sheds light on the genre's status as literature.

Chou argues that Liang's piece is a conscious and unprecedented transformation of the traditional travel essay. She divides the latter (following the Zhongguo congshu zonglu) into the categories of jijing (landscape descriptions) and jixing (chronicles of journeys), emphasizing the aesthetic and anecdotal qualities of both. The differences Chou attributes to Liang's travel essay are that the narrator has become "a highly self-conscious, reflective and judgmental commentator dedicated to methodical information-building" and that Travels has "a deliberate narrative and conceptual framework," which she further analyzes as "braided narrative—a preliminary itinerary substantiated by historical information, sociological statistics, and analyses, but with a minimum of descriptive passages." Chou cites Liang as explicitly dissociating this text from traditional travel narratives, emphasizing his exercise of a "citizen's obligation to contribute what he knows to his motherland with the hope that it will benefit, however slightly, our immature society" (213).

Chou's argument holds as a distinction of Liang's Travels from traditional travel narrative but fails to mention earlier such divergences, such as Xu Xiake's geocultural survey of China,[3] Gu Yanwu's socially and politically engaged travel notes,[4] and numerous late Qing narratives of foreign and domestic travel that preceded Liang's yet shared his narratorial stance as an engaged commentator acting as the conscience of the Chinese nation at a time of crisis.[5]

Moreover, Chou's treatment of Travels fails to establish it as a prototype of a genre that she herself defines quite correctly as "a consciously artistic narration of a series of factual events" (202). While Liang as a late Qing literatus includes a small amount of scenic description and poetry, Chou makes it clear that he is exerting efforts to keep artistic embellishment to a minimum, preferring to dominate the text with an abundance of facts organized into thematic exposition. Though taking the outward form of a travel memoir, Liang's text is essentially discursive and expository. If anything, it is consciously nonartistic.

The difficulties Chou thus encounters have a number of significant implications. Foremost among these is that Northrop Frye's distinction between "ornamental" and "persuasive" speech, upon which Chou bases her typology of reportage, fails to explain how persuasive speech (or writing), as opposed to ornamental speech, can be regarded as literary or artistic. In fact, Frye's discussion of literary expression strongly implies that it is not, and this conflicts with Chou's assertion that reportage is a literary genre. As a result Chou's typology of reportage, while succeeding in categorizing different kinds of reportage narrative, fails to demonstrate how any of them are literary. By characterizing reportage's literary aspect as a veneer of subjective ornamentation Chou renders reportage's literary quality trivial and superficial, and Liang's *Travels* seems to bear this out.

However, in defining the *Travels'* divergence from traditional travel narrative in terms of a self-conscious, judgmental narrator and a "deliberate narrative and conceptual framework," Chou approaches a more essential aspect of reportage's literariness—the verbal and figurative construction of a new kind of subjectivity for the expression of historical experience—that Frye's definition of *literary writing* as a "hypothetical verbal structure that exists for its own sake" is unable to account for as literature. Reportage is literature because it makes historical events, facts, and persons symbolic of abstract processes and in this very process creates a narrator who perceives events and social phenomena in this way, not as an individual or generalized human being but as one who primarily and collectively identifies with the Chinese nation. The historical nature of this subjectivity, particularly its close association with the historical and intellectual problems of modern China, as well as its indebtedness to a cultural tradition that has developed literary subjectivity not as the internal world of an autonomous individual but as an unspecified yet cultivated form of collective experience, is precisely what make reportage inaccessible to Northrop Frye's purely formal taxonomy.

Apart from missing the special subjective foundation and historicity of reportage, Chou's account glosses over the complex relationship between the modern travel essay and reportage as such. As Chou shows, the modern departure from the traditional travel essay was in evidence in China as early as 1903 and was particularly common in the early 1930s; it was a recognizably distinct form of writing practice before the notion of reportage was proposed in 1930.[6] Moreover, reportage was initially conceived in the 1930s narrowly as agitational reports on labor conditions; only in recent decades, with the compilation of comprehensive anthologies of reportage, have certain works of the modern travel essay form been included in the reportage canon. Thus, there is no reason to suppose that modern travel essayists associated what they were doing with the emerging reportage form, even after it became a prominent part of the literary scene in the mid-1930s.

However, insofar as modern travel essays resemble reportage they are illustrative of reportage's essential aspects. The writers I discuss in this chapter express their conscious divergence from traditional travel narratives clearly in terms of explicit discussions of method that could serve as guides for the writing of reportage. Their comments on method rarely concern travel as such but rather deal with society, culture, direct authorial engagement, and the author's quest for solutions to China's historical predicament through immersion in social life and the expression of that immersion and its consequences as a distinctive form of literary practice.

THE TRANSFORMATION OF TRAVEL
LITERATURE IN LATE IMPERIAL CHINA

Travel literature is unique among the types of writing I am discussing in that in China it is an explicit response to a familiar, traditional form: *youji* or "records of journeys."[7] Since the earliest times there have been records of travels real and imaginary in both the orthodox and lesser literary canons. The well-known *Shanhai jing* (Classic of Mountains and Seas) is structured explicitly as a record of travels outside the borders of the known world, and Qu Yuan's *Li Sao* (Encountering Sorrow) can be read as an extended cosmic journey. Medieval landscape poetry such as that of Xie Lingyun (385–443) features a distinctive travel component, and travel makes a conspicuous intervention in Chinese narrative with the rich and varied "journey to the west" (*xiyou ji*) tradition, based in part on the factual seventh-century journey of the Buddhist priest Xuan Zang (596–664) to procure the Mahayana corpus.[8] The travel essay as a specialized activity, in which the practice of writing is intimately involved with the experience of travel, found perhaps its earliest extended treatment in the Song dynasty travel diaries of Fan Chengda (1126–91).[9]

Once *youji* became a distinctive literary genre, writing about travel developed into a form of sophisticated aesthetic appreciation that fit into a repertoire of literati leisure activity, including antique connoisseurship, calligraphy, painting, and poetic composition. In works of the traditional travel essay, the landscapes and communities described either become the passive scroll upon which the writer paints his or her refined and highly trained emotional expressions or a repository of curiosities and exotica that the reader can enjoy as a form of leisurely amusement. In addition to providing a rich context for social interaction among the traditional literati, such activities aimed to evoke moments of aesthetic transcendence and spiritual rejuvenation.

By the late Ming dynasty, Xu Xiake (1586–1641), one of the best-known and certainly most prolific of travel writers of late imperial China, devoted most of his energies to renovating the travel essay tradition. Xu was concerned far more than any of his *youji* predecessors with accurate empirical (specifically geocultural) knowledge assembled through travel and observation; he created an unprecedented, new way of writing about places linked in spirit to the interpretive revisionism of *kaozheng xue*. Xu Xiake's work is encyclopedic; he was clearly not concerned with producing belles lettres. However, Xu has something important in common with modern Chinese travel and reportage writers as well: an obsession with truth manifested in the actual, the accurate account as an (occasionally uncomfortable) antidote for popular myths and fantasies taken as truth about places, peoples, and environments.[10]

Gu Yanwu (1613–82) is another late Ming/early Qing transition figure whose travel essays played an important role in his contribution to intellectual history but who is utterly ignored by literary historians. Even more than Xu Xiake, Gu Yanwu has in common with later writers of travel essays, even to the present day, a sense of cultural crisis. In his case it was a perception of the practical and social problems that were being ignored or exacerbated by the reigning philosophy of neo-Confucianism, particularly its idealist strains. Immanuel Hsü points out that Gu "traveled widely in North China and studied the practical problems of geography, frontier defense, farming and trade. From his geographical investigations he drafted two treatises based on practical applications: *On the Strategic and Economic Advantages and Disadvantages of the Counties and States of the Empire* . . . and his *Local Geography.*"[11] Few other than Hsü have linked Gu Yanwu's emphasis on textual research with the pragmatic empiricism of his travel essays. In this light, we can see Gu making an important connection between text (the Confucian classical corpus) and landscape (the culturally saturated territory of China), and his approach to both puts emphasis on vigorous exploration and the support of intellectual positions with empirical evidence.[12]

The kind of investigative, geographical travel essays of writers like Xu Xiake and Gu Yanwu diverged from and even directly critiqued traditional travel literature for its reliance on stereotyped diction and imagery and unconcern with true conditions or whether the writer had actually visited the place described. These voluminous and less aesthetically inclined works openly criticized and overturned misperceptions and distortions of actual conditions that had been propagated within that tradition as well as investigating a wide variety of anthropological, social, economic, and military issues. It is significant that such travel essays and their writers were closely aligned not only with the *kaozheng xue* (evidential studies) critique of late Ming neo-Confucian idealism but also with the Chinese cultural nationalism that characterized the Ming loyalists of the early Qing (Hsü, *The Rise of Modern China*, 114). While there were reactions against and revivals of the School of Evidential Studies (*kaozheng xue pai*) throughout the Qing, one way or another it conditioned the intellectual climate of the entire dynasty. Adherents did not always, like Xu Xiake and Gu Yanwu, advocate personal investigation of social conditions as well as textual research, and indeed many of the prominent late Ming neo-Confucians were highly engaged social activists. However it was applied, though, the spirit of the movement continued to be an outward-directed adherence to the facts and a determination to overturn baseless assumptions as opposed to relying on subjective judgment.

In the late Qing dynasty, in part because of the increasingly conspicuous presence of Western powers in China and throughout Asia, written accounts of foreign travel began to appear in significant numbers, and by the end of the nineteenth century such accounts, written largely by ambassadors and ministers, were legion. Because of the legacy of evidential studies and also because of its unprecedented international scope, late Qing travel literature bears a resemblance to that of European writers in that the writer's journey itself arises from a passion or need for knowledge and the quest for knowledge about the world through personally observed, actual conditions is conceived as a liberating historical force.

Travel writers' persistent interest in cultural comparison encourages them to view every detail of their journeys, from events the writer may consider to be of great historical importance down to their most minute observations, as symbolic of cultural difference. These observations are frequently expressed in an evaluative context, and the writer takes on the responsibility of accepting or rejecting the phenomena he or she observes on behalf of China. In this sense, the allegorical dimension of late Qing travel literature consists in offering the individual's actual journey as a surrogate for China's journey into the modern world, observing other cultures and accepting or rejecting them in a piecemeal fashion.

An interesting illustration of how dangerous it could be to harbor doubts about China's cultural superiority during the Qing dynasty is Guo Songtao's (1818–91) record of his mission to London and Paris (1876–79).[13] Guo, a young minister with an established reputation as a pro-Western agitator, was sent on the European mission under the supervision of an older, much more conservative minister, and the diary often records the friction between these two men as well as their contrasting reactions to the welter of modern Western intellectual and material culture to which they were exposed. A portion of this diary published by the *Zongli yamen* (Office for the Management of the Business of All Foreign Countries, established by the Qing government in 1861 to manage foreign affairs, particularly with Western countries), in which Guo boldly asserts that the West "also has a two-thousand-year-old civilization," caused such a stir in the prevailing conservative faction of the Qing government that, according to Zhong Shuhe, Guo was recalled from diplomatic duties, the printing blocks of his book were destroyed, and there was a ban placed on existing copies. Ten years after Guo's death in 1879, an imperial order was carried out to disinter and mutilate his and Ding Richang's corpses to "avenge the realm." Liang Qichao mentions Guo's travelogue in his "Wushi nian zhongguo jinhua gailun" (An Outline of China's Evolution in the Past Fifty Years), and it is likely that his *Travels in the New World* was influenced in theme and method by Guo's work, among others.[14]

Late imperial travel accounts share with modern travel literature a sense of China in crisis and an overriding concern with the question of its "way out" (*chulu*) of the predicament or dilemma posed by the insistent economic, religious, and military incursions of Western countries in the nineteenth century. For many, significantly, answers to these questions lay on a road out of China, a literal way out, the way of foreign travel and study. Thus, those who became best known for this kind of writing (Kang Youwei, Liang Qichao, Wang Tao) were also those who were the most committed to Westernization and what at the time were the most radical kinds of cultural revolution.

The distinction I am making between traditional Chinese travel literature and later developments of the genre is thus based on their differing projections of cultural identity. By turning *kaozheng xue*'s impetus toward investigation outward into the world at large by the end of the nineteenth century, Chinese travel literature had clearly become a vehicle for cultural critique. While a number of modern works should still be classified as *youji wenxue* and partake more of the aesthetics of connoisseurship than they do of reportage aesthetics, the early modern foreign travels of ambassadors and intellectuals, culminating in works like Liang Qichao's *Travels in the New World*, were more direct precursors of modern Chinese reportage.

Like their nineteenth-century predecessors, twentieth-century Chinese writers of foreign travel essays have been (and often still are) concerned with foreign societies, political systems, and even methods of solving everyday practical problems as *possible alternatives* for China. These writers seek neither spiritual enlightenment nor refined enjoyment; their foreign travel and especially the act of writing about and publishing it are intimately tied up with a consciousness of themselves as the eyes and ears of China. In other words, modern Chinese travel literature is characterized by its writer's posture as a representative of and contributor to Chinese culture. In the process writers of travel literature, like writers of other kinds of reportage, manifest in their works a consciousness that is not primarily individual but cultural and collective.

QU QIUBAI: BEYOND THE "GATE OF DARKNESS"

In 1921, Qu Qiubai set out on a difficult rail journey from Beijing to Moscow, which he documented in the widely read travelogue *Exiang jicheng* (Journey to the Land of Hunger).[15] According to the opening passages of his account, his decision to visit the Soviet Union was not a matter of curiosity or even a journalistic urge to keep abreast of world events. Qu felt compelled to go as a stage in his own personal spiritual development and as a necessary gesture in the unfolding of the modern Chinese nation. Indeed, these two impulses were one, for Qu was by then attempting to engage himself fully with the modern Chinese nation, so that what he experienced and learned would become the knowledge of the nation itself.

Ambitious as his hopes for his journey were, Qu was careful in his considerations about how to write about it. He was sure that he did not want to write a "dry travelogue," which in his words consisted merely of descriptions of political and legal structures and laconic accounts of major figures and events (i.e., the sort of thing Liang Qichao had written), and equally sure that what he wanted to accomplish would not fit into existing categories of writing. To Qu understanding a nation meant "understanding its heart," immersing oneself into its social life to the degree that one's very feelings and private contemplation would yield to readers the subjective experience of that nation's people.

Tsi-an Hsia's Gate of Darkness, still one of the most influential accounts in English of leftist literature in China, includes the most extended treatment of Qu Qiubai's travel essays available.[16] Part of what makes Hsia's exposition compelling is his rhetorical adoption of the same vivid repertoire of images that Chinese writers themselves tend to use to symbolize modern China's historical struggle. In this context, China is enmeshed in a mythical, romantic drama of the clash of the forces of darkness and light. Most readers are familiar with Lu Xun's images of the stifling, iron house and the gate of darkness; the popular image of China as a sick man that Lu Xun himself relies on when he explains his conversion from medicine to literature; and Qu Qiubai's extended meditations on the metaphors of atmosphere, color, and madness to depict the cultural condition of China in the midst of the May Fourth movement. While it is instructive to recognize the artificiality of these images as illustrations of modern Chinese society and history, it is also important to remember that the popularity of these images in the minds of modern Chinese endowed them with their own historical agency. They conditioned the identity (especially insofar as that identity is collective and national) of both those whose actions helped make history and those writers who documented that history in the form of literary works, newspaper articles, and even historical studies.

Most influential modern Chinese writers have succeeded insofar as they were able to tap into this larger collective text of shared images, integrate it further and more convincingly with observed reality, and realize it more vividly and sensually than other writers. These habits of thought and writing are a significant part of what makes commentators insist on Chinese reportage's classification as literature rather than a type of journalism: casting current events and historical and social forces in the form of vividly realized images created by the writer in his or her very process of observing contemporary events and persons. What makes reportage literature so illustrative of modern Chinese cultural history, in sum, is its ability to mobilize all of the imagery that had been developing in this collective drama of the modern Chinese nation in the timely narration of contemporary events and persons.

Qu Qiubai, writing two of the earliest yet still greatest works of Chinese reportage literature, *Exiang jicheng* (Journey to the Land of Hunger) and *Chidu xinshi* (A Personal History in the Red Capital), elaborates at great length the intimacy with which he conceives his spiritual journey to be bound up with the fate of the nation. As a summary of the content of these two works, T. A. Hsia's chapter on Qu Qiubai is more than adequate. However, Hsia's thesis that Qu's commitment to socialism was misguided and tragic, the dichotomies Hsia thus establishes between individual dignity and revolutionary zeal and abstract theory and the realities of life, and especially his identification of Marxism or communism with "abstract theory" seem motivated more by a determination to indict communism than to shed light on the works under discussion. For if Qu Qiubai emphasizes anything in these two works it is the inadequacy of abstract theory as a solution to the problems of human existence: Qu repeatedly stresses the need for contemplation to be integrated with lived, social experience. It is not a question of discarding either theory or reality but the necessity of integrating them in practice. Qu's journey and his writing are meant to realize such an integration.

T. A. Hsia's approach and agenda render a number of significant aspects of Qu's work silent. First, while we are shown Qu the frustrated individual, the frail intellectual cast into physical misery and fitfully complaining about it, we are not shown the Qu who struggles to *deindividuate* himself, to render even his petty annoyances meaningful for a community of Chinese not necessarily limited to his readership. In Qu's arduous effort to wrench cultural meaning from every episode he encounters, we see some of the earliest steps in the literary forging of a collective modern Chinese mentality, one that is not limited solely to the individual (nor does it represent, at the other extreme, the "human condition" independent of time and space).

Second, Hsia insists that Qu Qiubai's zeal for the Soviet Union and international communism is contradicted by his depiction of the suffering, poverty, and vocal dissatisfaction with the Soviet government with which he is continually confronted. Hsia's only explanation for this is that Qu's account is governed by sincerity and candor. But considering the goals Hsia attributes to Qu of glorifying the revolution and the Soviet Union, why should Qu write in such a self-defeating vein? As I read *Journey to the Land of Hunger*, Qu defends Soviet Communism against accusations of theoretical inconsistency by stressing that it is a method that directly engages existing problems without the benefit of a necessarily clear-cut, internally consistent blueprint.

Finally, and most importantly for my purposes here, Hsia fails to discuss the *form* and *method* adopted by Qu in these two works, upon which Qu repeatedly lays emphasis as an attempt to integrate concrete observation with theoretical principles, indeed to develop a mode of cultural understanding that is grounded almost entirely in concrete observation. It is this failure to take Qu's explicit concern with methodology into account that leads Hsia to interpret the unpleasantness in these texts as a sign of Qu's inability to transcend his status as a latter-day literatus and the naïveté of his idealistic belief in Soviet socialism, which he had drawn from "books."

It is the form itself, and the works themselves, that are Qu's solution to the challenge set up by Hsia as a dilemma or contradiction: it is precisely in *rendering* concrete experience into literary images, narratives, and descriptions that Qu comes to understand life in the Soviet Union. Rendering the poverty and suffering of the victims of Soviet bureaucracy and corruption demonstrates his investment in Marxism as he understood it at the time: as a practical method rather than an abstract theory. In later leftist formulations of the method of reportage as well as in political pronouncements of all kinds right up through the 1980s, emphasis is placed on unflinching attention to concrete realities, regardless of how much they may shake one's faith in abstract principles and of how great the failures to do so have been.[17]

As the titles of these works—*Journey to the Land of Hunger* and *A Personal History in the Red Capital*—indicate, Qu Qiubai's physical journey to the then still young Soviet Union is profoundly intertwined with a personal spiritual journey in which he painfully and with great difficulty tries to illuminate the possible future of China. In the words of the opening passage of *Journey*, it took years of spiritual struggle to lead him finally to his conviction to travel to Soviet Russia.

> I succeeded in creating a worldly "idealism." I wished to venture out with resolution, to seek a realistic solution, a real knowledge in a certain area—and not for myself—knowledge and thought cannot be privately possessed. Moreover, the atmosphere of the years of my youth made me willy nilly into a "stoic," accustoming myself to hardship in my daily life and seeking simplicity and thrift in my eating and living circumstances. Although these are my idiosyncratic developments as an individual, they created in me a will to go to Russia— and to take upon myself part of the burden of the development in thought in the era of China's rebirth. (ZBWC I.2, 32)

In other words, the outcome of years of spiritual self-cultivation is his desire to go to Russia and realize his "worldly idealism." By worldly idealism, Qu means a metaphysical understanding of the human condition that is fully immersed in the realities of contemporary social life. This is not only an intellectual position but the basis upon which he chose to experience his journey and record it as he did, in a form virtually indistinguishable from the yet to be discovered reportage. In his words, "Abstract social ideals like *truth, beauty,* and *goodness* cannot swoop down from the sky like a flying warrior—therefore, I take my own philosophical concepts and extend them to these actual examples; subjectively speaking, all truths—from material economic life to the spiritual life of the mind—are intimately tied up with 'actuality'" (46). Images of light, color, and eyesight proliferate in the opening section and pave the way for the author's experience of the visual landscapes of his journey as packed with moral and historical significance. Qu's consciousness is continually manifested in the concrete and vivid vignettes that form the substance of this double journey.

The opening section of *Exiang jicheng,* for example, is indebted to images of the modern Chinese spiritual crisis already in circulation by 1920 in both traditional-style and new fiction such as that of Lu Xun. Not only does he describe the tenacious hold of traditional Chinese culture in the form of atmospheric images of darkness, sweetness, passivity, and inaction but he describes his own perception of the "red light" of hopeful, revolutionary change disingenuously as "perhaps" being "the words of a madman."

> The red blossoms covering the earth, stained with the blood of battle, shine forth with a red glow like that of the sunset or sunrise, shimmering brilliantly. To me [this red] is at least a little more vibrant than the "black" in darkness. Moreover, to suddenly be confronted with light after being in the dark for a long time, it is impossible to avoid being dazzled with spots before our eyes, and natural that at first we can only see red. But the essence of light, I feel, is not in the color red. It has to gradually turn around and in the end will regain all the colors natural to our sense of sight—perhaps these are the words of a madman. (14)

Qu is particularly attentive to his method of observation, contemplation, and literary realization of events, and his thoughts along these lines could well have served as a primer for reportage composition in later years.

> My feelings on being in close contact with social life in comparison with "diplomatic" investigations has led me to a conclusion:[18] if it is an investigation of *major figures and events* for no other purpose than negotiations of political diplomacy, or a social investigator with a "love for abstractions," then conversations, visits, and interviews with important figures would be quite enough—besides, that is the duty of "news reporters." However, if besides all this one wishes to attain an understanding of actual social life, to understand the intimate and hidden depths of the meaning of human culture, or even the value of human existence and the spiritual and material aspects of the structural relation between the individual and society, it would be better for an unqualified "person" to immerse himself in the society he wishes to investigate, to express his views as he makes his observations, and to place them as much as possible in an *objective* position,

only then can what he gains satisfy his own desires . . . thus I decided from here on to pay close attention to my own goal of contemplating the answers to the questions of human existence, and as for my duty as a "news reporter" all I can do is to try my best—within my capacity—to fulfill it and leave it at that. (66)

Clearly, although his contributions were originally published as installments in a newspaper column in Beijing's *Chen bao*, Qu is distancing himself from the role of a journalist and, though with great humility, justifying his concern with nonjournalistic observations insofar as he is "immersed in the society he wishes to investigate," by claiming that only they, and not concentration on major persons and events, can give clues to the most fundamental questions about the nature and value of human social existence.[19] It is noteworthy that these thoughts arise on the journey into Central Asia, just as Qu is beginning to develop feelings of disdain for the Chinese bureaucrats with whom he is forced to interact daily on the train, precisely for their being too abstract or too specific in their concerns and "typically Chinese" in their selfishness and lack of professionalism (67–68).

The desire to integrate everyday life experience with an all-encompassing worldview that takes in the extremities of philosophy and religion inflects Qu's vision of Marxism at the time: his philosophical meditations, frequent especially in the opening sections, are focused precisely on the importance of discourse being connected with physical reality in order to be significant and understandable. This theme has a double function in Qu's text of grasping communism as it is practiced in the Soviet Union and at the same time affirming the formal and thematic approach he is taking in so writing. Qu's insistence on the concrete becomes an apology for the form of his unusual text: unlike any other book on socialism, his will be able to convey the immediate experience of life in a socialist nation.

Indeed, Qu Qiubai seems to devote more energy to articulating his ideal than to carrying it out, but there is in evidence a powerful will to innovate in his actual narratives and descriptions. For example, Qu's landscape descriptions are much more saturated with emotion and symbolism than was typical in traditional travel literature and landscape poetry. These descriptions are in fact a distinctive feature of *Exiang jicheng* overlooked by T. A. Hsia and other English-language commentators on the work.[20]

Qu's landscapes are much more thematically alive, dynamic, and forward looking than their traditional counterparts; they are animated by social and historical elements and unabashedly anthropomorphic. As his train winds through Siberia, the frozen waves of Lake Baikal and the immense forest and gigantic trees on the nearby plain are described at great length but almost uniformly as symbols of powerful life forces caught in an almost hopeless struggle against the merciless and violent forces of nature: "The ice waves close to the shore protrude and arc toward one another like steep cliffs and strange rocks—I wonder what fierce winds impelled these waves of 'freedom' to rise up, when suddenly a fierce and solemn cold caused them to be frozen here, beyond the cunning schemes of the rising winds that made the waves—but they still have their ferocious, willful, and stubborn ugly demeanor" (71).

Such description partakes of traditional Chinese techniques and language, but by identifying the waves with freedom Qu seems to imply that his main concern is with the conditions of life in the remotest parts of the Soviet Union (life in Moscow is reserved for *Chidu xinshi*), and his lengthy landscape descriptions vividly reflect at least what he has come to feel and understand about that life: "Our old tree, with the remnants of ice and snow, supporting them with its last ounces of strength, accumulating weakness and loss from the furthest reaches of antiquity, not to mention the red tongues' tips just brushing its rotted branches and trunk. If it happens to split apart, the inner strength of the power of spring in which it is so confident takes this chance to burst forth boundless and beyond capacity, and among the rotten roots suddenly rises up new, crisp, fresh, and green tender sprouts, which will suffer the trials the old tree has not yet encountered" (77).

The feeble hints of life Qu observes in the forbidding wastes of Siberia are for him signs of power of endurance, the power to overcome the ponderous weight of the past and the relentless buffeting of the storms of the present. In the context of Qu's momentous journey, these natural images take on a social, historical significance; they call to his mind the peasants of the Soviet outback struggling against nature and history.

If *Exiang jicheng* narrates Qu's journey, *Chidu xinshi* (A Personal History in the Red Capital) elaborates his sojourn in Moscow and St. Petersburg.

Formally, the latter work differs in its almost complete lack of landscape or environmental description, its experimentation with different literary forms (particularly the generous inclusion of translated and original poetry), and the relative richness of conversations and vignettes illustrating Qu's eventful stay in Moscow. Qu's exposure to Russian art and literature (both prerevolutionary and Soviet) have a marked effect on both his language and the very style of his presentation.

For example, note the language with which Qu registers his strong impression of a futurist art show: "Here I suddenly discovered crudely forceful and bold strokes; the creations of the futurists give one's spirit a pleasure that turns into excitement, yet mixed with some irritation: crude, hard-edged shapes, impressions of perversity within harmony, an air of dramatic rage, expressions of anxious excitement and abruptness, but all in all leaving me with feelings of freshness, brightness, dynamism, and timeliness."[21]

What is exciting to Qu here is the discovery that art does not have to be pleasant to be an effective vehicle for evoking emotion. He clearly associates specific shapes and colors with the emotional reactions they engender in him as a viewer. This experience affects many of his later experiences in *Personal History*, including one of the best known, his first glimpse of V. I. Lenin at a political rally: "When the electric camera flash burst, a large shadow of Lenin's head was cast over the words *Communist International, Workers of the World Unite,* and *The Union of Soviet Socialist Republics* on banners behind him, creating a marvelous picture set off by the red silk background—giving me yet another new kind of feeling, an astonishing symbol" (116).

Qu is fascinated here with a particular visual image that must have looked like a futurist painting with its bright colors and contrast, its sharp angles, and its technological detail. Qu's adoption and generalization of the futurist imagination is part of the spirit of playful experimentation that distinguishes *Personal History* from *Journey to the Land of Hunger*, observable in the author's poetic forays and dramatic treatment of mundane vignettes.

As is well known, Qu Qiubai, after joining the Communist Party, had a stratospheric yet disastrous political career on its Central Committee (ultimately as secretary-general) while he chaired the Social Science Department at Shanghai University in the late 1920s. After attempting to return to the life of a cultural activist, he found that his political failures continued to haunt him, and after a brief period of leadership with the League of Left-Wing Writers and a stint as director of education in the Jiangxi Soviet, he was arrested in May 1935 by the Guomindang and executed on June 18 of that year.[22]

Judging from the regrets he expresses over his political career in his "Duoyu de hua" (Superfluous Words), written in prison in 1935, it may well have been the few years after he was removed from the Communist Party leadership that were the most fulfilling to Qu Qiubai. It is through his accomplishments as a cultural activist, championing the "massification" (*dazhonghua*) of the modern Chinese language and its literature, that Qu's contribution to modern Chinese culture can be felt most deeply. Although the language of *Journey to the Land of Hunger* and *A Personal History in the Red Capital* is hardly "proletarian," Qu Qiubai's later concerns with mass literature and the simplification of literary language can be seen as an extension of the concern evident in both of these works with forging both a social practice and a mode of consciousness through which he as an intellectual could identify with the modern Chinese nation as a whole and help propel it into the future.

ZOU TAOFEN: TRAVELING THROUGH GLOBAL CRISIS

Also among the most widely read works of nonfiction in modern China, the travel essays of Zou Taofen (1895–1944) are a search for solutions to China's historical predicament. By the early 1930s, adventurous newspaper and magazine correspondents were being assigned long journeys (domestic and international) and publishing accounts of them in serial form, later to appear as books. Zou Taofen had already established a reputation as a publisher by editing such magazines as *Shenghuo* (Life) and *Dazhong shenghuo* (Mass Life), both of which had a wide circulation.

Zou's voluminous *Pingzong jiyu* (Notes of a Wanderer) and *Pingzong yiyu* (Recollections of a Wanderer) take the form of an evaluative comparison of the societies of Europe, America, and the Soviet Union.[23] Zou departed on his two-year journey in 1933, in part to avoid capture by the Guomindang and in part at the bidding of the editor of *Dagong bao* (L'Impartial) to bring the social life and political trends of Western Europe, the United States, and the Soviet Union home to these readers in

his idiosyncratic, intimate style.[24] His account was published in installments in *Shenghuo zhoukan* (Life Weekly) until the magazine was closed
down by Nationalist authorities in late 1933 and then in its reincarnation
as *Xinsheng zhoukan* (New Life Weekly). Later contributions were compiled into three volumes published by Shenghuo chubanshe (Life Publishers) in 1934 and 1935. A fourth volume on his subsequent travels
in the United States was first published serially in *Shijie zhishi* (World
Knowledge) and later in book form as *Recollections of a Wanderer*.[25]

According to an informal survey conducted by Olga Lang in the 1930s,
Zou's travel essays trailed in popularity only behind the essays of Hu Shi
and Lin Yutang among urban student readers (Gewurtz, *Between America
and Russia*, 7). Zou's weekly, *Shenghuo zhoukan*, in which *Notes of a Wanderer*
began to be serialized, had already broken all circulation records for a
Chinese periodical, and the popularity of Zou's hardworking, sincere,
and amiable character is voluminously documented in letters to the editor of that magazine, many of which praise the travel essays explicitly.
Moreover, by the time *Recollections of a Wanderer* came out, luminaries like
Zhou Enlai also sang its praises.[26]

For Zou, writing about other societies consisted of a practical,
double-edged critique of both idealism and empiricism. Like Qu Qiubai,
Zou was concerned with the fate of China, and he perceived every country he visited as a proving ground for a different approach to the problem
of modern nationhood. Zou evaluated each in terms of the effectiveness
of its approach to a wide variety of concrete situations and problems.

In the conclusion to her 1975 study on Zou Taofen's travel essays,
Margo Gewurtz reflects on the relationship in travel literature between
politics and factual narrative: "The point has been made repeatedly
throughout this analysis that the travel books were, or at least appeared
to be, concrete, factual, first-hand evidence of how such otherwise abstract concepts as capitalism, fascism, and socialism were realized in
actual practice, and what that practice meant in terms of China's needs.
Almost by definition, travel books as a genre made concrete those abstractions hitherto known as 'China' and 'the West,' and that has been
and continues to be the source of their power on both sides of the historic encounter between East and West" (147–48; emphasis in original).

Gewurtz focuses on Zou Taofen's travel essays as an intellectual his-
torian, amply demonstrating his embodiment and development of the

consciousness of revolutionary youth in the first half of this century in China. She is particularly interested in Zou's choice of travel literature as the form in which he preaches his message, emphasizing how it manifests young intellectuals' passion for outside knowledge and the importance of bringing back a clear message about the path China should follow in the face of what was widely perceived as impending annihilation. As such, Gewurtz's book provides an invaluable contextual basis for any further study of Zou Taofen.

I am more concerned here with travel literature's methods of observation and expression than with its particular intellectual and informational content, and in this respect the present discussion can be linked to the preceding one on Qu Qiubai. Both Qu and Zou Taofen organize their travel plans and their writing around a pilgrimage to the Soviet Union as a real, working model of what can be accomplished in China. This they have in common with Hu Yuzhi's also influential 1931 work, *Mosike yinxiang ji* (Impressions of Moscow).

Unlike Hu, however, Qu Qiubai and Zou Taofen are particularly attentive to their methodology of personalized, concrete narration and description and its political implications. These writers invest considerable energy in the revelation of historical truth in actual examples, and this is what sets them apart from both the cynical/critical flaneur and the newspaper journalist with his or her vaunted rigorous fidelity to objective facts, regardless of their interpretation.

In the first volume of *Notes of a Wanderer*, which was written in London in the winter of 1933–34, Zou is explicit about his method and aims as a travel writer: "These 'notes' are just scattered papers of 'jumbled scribbling' (*laza xielai*), but when this reporter is observing and investigating, when he is taking up the pen to narrate, two problems often surge to the forefront: *the first is, what are the major trends in the world? The second is, what is the way out for the Chinese nation (Zhonghua minzu de chulu)?* . . . These two aspects obviously are closely related" (ZBWC I.4, 13; emphasis in original). Thus, "observations" and "questions" are put on two separate levels; they serve as signifier and signified, respectively.

The first volume narrates Zou's excursion by ship from Shanghai to Venice, then by train to Paris and by ferry to London. Written on the road and with little time for reflection, the first volume of *Notes of a Wanderer* vividly demonstrates Zou's desire to be observant. In France and England, he devotes a considerable amount of time and energy to analyzing the educational and publishing industries as well as how recent political events reveal the fundamental characteristics of these two countries' political systems. In short, the installments that comprise the first volume, some of which appeared in *Shenghuo zhoukan* before it was closed down in December 1933 by the Guomindang, were written before the author had time to discover what sorts of themes might bubble up unexpectedly and directly from his experience on the road.

After leaving England, however, Zou stopped writing for three months, and the second volume consists of his collected impressions of those months, this time only about 60 pages. Zou was no longer sending articles to *Shenghuo* since it no longer existed. In this, as well as in the third volume and *Recollections of a Wanderer*, Zou keeps the format of entries the same (a laconic description of the section's content as a heading, then four or five pages of writing), but the last two volumes are much more substantial, 250 and 230 pages, respectively.

In his introduction to the third volume, Zou's comments go some way toward explaining the rambling, overstuffed quality of his prose as well as the increasing size of each volume: "I originally planned to write 100,000 characters, but I got to 120,000 before I was finished and there was so much more material I wanted to write about, the more I wrote the more excited I got. . . . In the past two weeks I have been writing all day as well, hurriedly finishing 180,000 characters before I could force myself to submit the manuscript" (ZBWC I.4, 211).

As mentioned above, in the introduction to the first volume Zou starts out with the questions: "What are the major trends in the world?" and "What is the way out for the Chinese nation?" In the introduction to the third volume, he begins to answer them: the Depression, massive unemployment worldwide "is not a population problem, nor a problem of resources or technology, but a problem of social organization, . . . a problem of the increase in productive capacity becoming incompatible with social systems in which the tools of production are privately owned" (3:212). Zou's interpretation of fascism is that it is a newfangled way of using force to keep wealth and power in the hands of an elite minority (where it had always been), a solution that is in fact unconcerned with social problems, though it manipulates them to its own benefit. By claiming that Europe only has "two roads"—socialism and fascism—

he is proclaiming the historical bankruptcy of capitalism, implying that fascism is taking over the role of capitalism in the future. Thus, "Internationally, it will speed the coming of a second world war" (3:212) and "*The complete liberation of productive capacity is the only way to go*" (3:214; emphasis in original).

In the opening pages of volume 3 of *Notes of a Wanderer* (3:217–30), the five-day voyage on a Soviet steamship across the North Sea to Leningrad provides Zou and the other passengers with an opportunity to examine the Soviet system, including its imperfections, in microcosm. Zou devotes an entire section to the physical arrangement of the ship, meticulously comparing the first- and second-class quarters to the third class in which he was sleeping, trying to figure out why, while equalizing things to a degree by allowing all passengers the run of the ship, the Soviets nevertheless maintained a hierarchy of decks in increasing order of luxury. Subsequent sections show the curious passengers (not only Zou) interrogating the captain and crew about every detail of their lives and work, including their pay, relative status, relation to their organization, what happens if something goes wrong, and so on.

Zou taps into the vitality and sexual energy of youth in his depiction of the political differences on the ship. The "rigor mortis group" (*siying pai*) are all in the first-class cabins and keep their distance from "our gang of kids" (*women zheban* "*haizi men*," 3:223), whom Zou describes most vividly in their incarnations as attractive young women engaging in physical activities such as tennis and sunning (3:224). Through his close friendship with the American students on the ship, Zou gains the opportunity to join the American National Students' League educational tour (for the economic and other advantages of being in a group).

Zou's subsequent observations of the Soviet Union are colored by the zealous enthusiasm with which the American students have infected him. While the ship to Leningrad provides Zou with a microcosm of Soviet social organization, the streets of Moscow Zou observes on a three-hour bus tour of the city offer him a physical manifestation of the Soviet Union's newness and its overcoming of class distinctions.

Old Moscow—the Moscow of philistines, nobles, landlords, and priests—was gone; the new Moscow—the Moscow of laborers, the Moscow that is the central "laboratory" for hardworking social-

ist construction in all areas of politics, economics, and culture—
emerged before us. . . . What attracted my attention the most were
the roads, buildings, parks, and boulevards in the process of construction everywhere I looked.

What our public bus was driving on was a wide, smooth, asphalt
road flanked with rows of shade trees, not an unusual sight in Western Europe. But when we thought of how in European countries such
fine roads can only be seen in areas in which the bourgeoisie lives or
often visits, but cannot even be dreamed of by millions of laborers
in their hovels, and when we thought of the vast difference between
the roads of Czarist Russia and those constructed after the October Revolution, the feelings evoked by the scene were quite different. In the Czarist era, there were only narrow, filthy, mud lanes in
the areas frequented by Moscow's laborers; of course, there were no
sidewalks. Only in the center of the city were there a few streets said
to have been fashionable, and they were the exclusive precinct of
aristocrats, landowners, and capitalists; workers would have never
dared approach them, so there was never any fear that there weren't
enough! Besides, the streets were twisted and complex and difficult
to improve because of the corruption and obstruction of powerful
landowners. After the revolution, all this corruption and obstruction
was swept away, and so there were many roads that were straight-
ened and broadened according to new plans. According to statistics,
in 1931 there were 650,000 square meters of new roads constructed
but by 1932 there were more than 1,000,000. Also, within the road
construction crews, they have "socialist competitions" so that they
can build more and better roads faster for their own capital. They
hope that by the end of the second five-year plan the streets of Moscow will all be as smooth as glass. (ZBWC I.4, 246–47, emphases in
original)

One striking and (as will be shown) prophetic aspect of this passage
is the way it explicitly ties social progress and social relations to spatial configurations. Beyond the fact that under feudal or capitalist rule
workers are relegated to filthy and small spaces, their roads are without sidewalks, "twisted and complex and difficult to improve." These
are the concrete, spatial manifestations of the upper classes' economic

and political repression of the proletariat. Under Soviet socialism, however, urban spaces are cleaned up, rationalized, and democratized. The former aristocracy and bourgeoisie would no longer have wide, tree-lined boulevards all to themselves, and the new spacious avenues would be straight, flat, well paved, and easy to maintain inexpensively. The suggestion of hyperbole in this passage is echoed and amplified throughout Zou Taofen's experience of Soviet Russia, and indeed it seems to condition his observations. During the same bus tour, which ends up at the Kremlin, Zou is struck by the workers at *Pravda*, the central Soviet news agency.

> As our bus passed in front of the *Pravda* building, we saw a long column of workers, four in a rank, marching out of the building. There were both men and women, at least two or three hundred, with clean, well-coordinated steps, full of energy, singing as they walked. When I asked the tour guide, I found out that it was the workers of *Pravda filing off to the exercise field on their break.* On that day we happened to see quite a few such columns of men and women workers, singing as they marched, and their vigorous spirit and attitude attracted the interest and attention of the "gang of kids" in the bus. In the bus we would suddenly hear a guy yell, "Look! Over there! It's another one!" and then a gal would yell "Hey! There's another group coming over there!" When the groups marched close to us, our bus would stop to let them pass; when they saw who we were, a bunch of tourists having a look around, they happily raised their hands and called out to us, and we were fighting each other to wave and call back. I thought to myself how these folks, who would all be slum dwellers in another country, had something quite different here! (ZBWC I.4, 248–49, emphasis in original)

Clearly this is quite a different Soviet Union than that depicted in *A Personal History in the Red Capital.* Indeed, Zou by this point and for the rest of the narrative adopts the tone of overweening optimism for everything he sees, which had also characterized Hu Yuzhi's visit to the Soviet Union three years before.

However, it is significant that Zou registers puzzled annoyance at some aspects of his tour. In one episode, his expensive German camera is stolen from the coat check at the Hermitage in Leningrad—he discovers the loss only later because his camera bag had been returned to him empty. Neither the museum staff nor the police was willing to take responsibility for the theft, and Zou singles out this lack of responsibility as a repeated source of frustration (3:238–39, 244–45). Similarly he points out having to wait in line everywhere he goes and the sluggish service in restaurants and shops, particularly in Leningrad.

Zou is also cognizant, especially in the earlier chapters of *Notes of a Traveler*, volume 3, of the multiply mediated nature of his experience in the Soviet Union, particularly how the Intourist travel service (established exclusively for foreigners) and the Summer University in Moscow, also for foreigners only, seemed to create a less than authentic, beautified Soviet face especially for foreign consumption. Throughout the dozens of chapters that follow, narrating visits to all manner of new and experimental factories, hospitals, sanatoriums, agricultural communes, electrical stations, and so on all over the western half of the Soviet Union, Zou finds himself continually comparing his own experiences and living conditions to what he is able to observe of the actual lives of Soviet citizens, often finding significant differences. These considerations invariably arise from Zou's concrete, personal experiences, and, although he takes pains to make excuses for the negative aspects of life in the Soviet Union, he, like Qu Qiubai before him, makes no attempt to conceal them or his irritation.

Ultimately, however, although Zou Taofen was interested in demonstrating the applications and manifestations of theories, social forces, race, and other abstractions through concrete examples, his accounts of these examples are on the whole lacking in concreteness. This is particularly evident in his final excursion to the United States, in which almost all of his observations are short on description and long on polemic. Perhaps just having come from the Soviet Union he felt confident that he was armed with a sufficiently rigorous theoretical framework to interpret everything he saw "correctly" and with a conspicuous, even excessive, internal consistency. Theory is no longer being tested against concrete application or observation but rather conditions the very act of observation itself. Thus, all he sees are "fat capitalists," "benighted," "forlorn" workers, and the "contradictions inherent in a capitalist society." This is borne out by Margo Gewurtz's demonstration that Zou lifted his "analysis" of American society almost verbatim from pamphlets published by the American Communist Party, which he picked up in a "workers' book shop" in New York (*Between America and Russia*, 43).

One significant respect in which Zou's account of the United States differs from those of European countries is that he is no longer concerned with national character and its relationship to the physical environment. In the first volume of *Pingzong jiyu*, in which Zou describes his initial European travels, he had been interested in Belgium and the Netherlands in their precarious strategic position between France and Germany and how this situation had conditioned the personality of the people of these countries to be resolute and fearless, particularly in battle. Zou's enthusiasm for the Soviet accomplishments in reconstructing their cities (particularly the roads) in a more egalitarian fashion can be read in this way as well. In America, however, Zou reflects little on how the country became what it is and whether there may have been a relationship between the physical environment, the existing social organization, and the character of the American people. Rather, for Zou America is first and foremost a symbol of capitalism, and so all the people and events he observes become mere incarnations of established Marxist-Leninist categories. I interpret this as a weakness in Zou's account of the United States, and to a lesser degree throughout his series of travel essays, because all he seems to be accomplishing by traveling is witnessing what he already "knows" to be the case: his account of America could easily have been written without traveling there. Thus, travel and travel literature are not as much a learning process as was the case with Qu Qiubai.

Gewurtz interprets this abstract quality in general as arising from the fact that the volume on America was less of an "eyewitness" account and, more importantly, because in the United States he was the guest of the National Students' League ("our gang of kids"), with whose members he had spent the summer in Moscow, and not the network of Chinese friends, fans, and acquaintances that had structured his European sojourns (*Between America and Russia*, 32). Moreover, this may have had something to do, as Gewurtz argues, with the fact that by the time he wrote *Pingzong yiyu* Zou was in a much more polemical and agitational mood than when he started the series; indeed, he wrote much of the final work in prison, having been jailed by the Guomindang for organizing militant anti-Japanese activities. Thus, the sense in which Zou viewed the content of his writing about a foreign country as being crucially relevant to the solution to Chinese problems was already highly intense at this stage.

As to whether it was an "eyewitness" account or not, Zou was definitely in America and was free to write of his personal experiences as vividly as he had elsewhere. And if one were to argue that it lacks the concreteness of the earlier volumes because it was written retrospectively in China it must be pointed out that the second and third volumes of Notes of a Wanderer were both written after he had left the countries described in them; in those cases, vividness and specificity were preserved in the notebooks he kept while traveling.

Taken as a whole, Zou Taofen's travel essays manifest an increasing conflict between his investment in historical truth and the material he presents as its manifestation. There is a gradual abandonment of critical scrutiny of his surroundings to a point at which, by the time he arrives in the United States, he is willing to accept others' interpretations of that society without question. Moreover, this abandonment goes hand in hand with the increase of his anxiety over the historical situation in China. In other words, the problem Zou initially wished to solve through the introduction of voluminous concrete examples must increasingly be dealt with by way of abstract polemics.

Zou Taofen's work in the end must remain at the fringes of what I am classifying here as reportage literature. There is a marked lack of imagery throughout Zou's prose, which makes him more akin to Liang Qichao in his Travels in the New World than to Qu Qiubai's text: Liang and Zou are less concerned with forging new kinds of experience and subjectivity than with conveying information, as much as possible, and interpreting and commenting on it in relatively abstract, analytical terms. Nevertheless, Zou Taofen's positioning of himself as the very consciousness of modern Chinese radical youth as he moves throughout the Western world from one country to another, successively evaluating the various possible paths China could take, is very similar to the prevalent subject position of reportage literature. This consciousness forms the basis of the metonymic dimension of such writing and thus also of its status as literature.

FAN CHANGJIANG: LANDSCAPE AS GEOSOCIAL TEXT

At about the time that *Notes of a Wanderer* appeared in print, another prominent journalist named Fan Changjiang (1909–70) was traversing northern and western China observing relations between the Han Chinese and other ethnic groups, the problems of achieving national unity, and the threatening encroachments of the Japanese along China's northern border following their occupation of Manchuria. Also a major journalist, Fan's works are comparable to Zou Taofen's in scope but quite different in content: his *Zhongguo de xibei jiao* (China's Northwest Corner) chronicles the author's dangerous journeys to the edges of China's war-torn wilderness to places many of his readers had never seen or heard of before.[27] While not explicitly using his journeys as a search for answers to China's pressing social and political questions, Fan Changjiang, like Qu Qiubai and Zou Taofen, perceived and interpreted all of his experiences on the road, down to the most "trivial" daily activities, in the allegorical light of the Chinese national crisis.

Fan's travels, largely by horse and on foot, took him all over western and northwestern China. He often observed very shocking and disturbing manifestations of the economic and political crises faced by China at the time, especially ethnic discord between Han and local minority groups and the threatening incursions of the Japanese army across China's northern frontier as it attempted to drive a wedge between the Soviet Union and China. Fan's encyclopedic perspective and concern with overturning common misperceptions links him to the tradition of travel literature as a form of knowledge established in late imperial times.

Though neither a novelist nor a poet, Fan must be credited with a seminal contribution to modern Chinese literary culture. Not only is *China's Northwest Corner* fine nonfiction writing but it contains a great deal of firsthand information and cultural lore on local areas in northern Sichuan, Gansu, Qinghai, and Ningxia Provinces. He adds immeasurably to the popular knowledge of regional cultural issues and racial conflicts in the Chinese hinterland, providing detailed reports of economic exploitation and military repression from "the ground" and a vivid unraveling of the rugged terrain of China's wild west. Fan accomplishes these things in an unadorned, unsentimental language of simple elegance. He gives us the modern Chinese west with ready echoes of late imperial, medieval, and even ancient history, representing as well as almost any writer a modern Chinese worldview that encompasses China's cultural heritage.

Fan begins *China's Northwest Corner* without fanfare or self-introduction, much in the tone of a tourist, explaining how he had originally planned to make a tour of western Sichuan (not, like Zou Taofen, to resolve China's historical crisis but rather seemingly just to have a look around). Because a friend happened to be going another direction, however, he "by chance" gained an opportunity to head north to Lanzhou instead (13). In short, he takes pains at the outset to assert the casual arbitrariness with which he set out on his journey.

Maintaining this tone, Fan describes the sites around Chengdu he visits during the period before he set out, laying stress on leisure, romance, and pleasures traditional and modern, but at the same time everything is quickly contrasted with the surrounding poverty of the peasants, the imminent Japanese invasion, economic imperialism, and local corruption and exploitation. As the irony of Fan's initial tone subsides, his distinctive mode of "tourism" emerges, and what unfolds before us is rugged countryside in every imaginable state of emergency. The following is an example of how the concern with embodied economic, racial, and national suffering emerges from beneath the shell of leisure.

> I stayed one day in Xindu, then returned to Xinfan. The two towns are about 35 li apart, and the scenery is quite nice.[28] But once you encounter the human world of this area, there is nothing that does not leave you despondent. The Chengdu Plateau is so rich, yet the villages along this road are disgracefully run down. The coolies all smoke opium. Because they are poor, they are for the most part forced to spread a tattered bamboo mat on the ground, lay down, and partake. There are many among the peasants who have this habit. Of the people you run into on the road, the ones with filled-out faces and

strong, healthy bodies make up scarcely half. Who is behind it? Who has made things this way? Sooner or later, the people of Sichuan will know. (ZBWC II.1, 15)

Fan's party (the other members of which are conspicuously absent from the narrative) travels largely by horse, occasionally by truck or bus, and sometimes even on foot, into the mountains north-northwest of the Chengdu Basin, along the banks of the Min River up through Songpan and on into eastern Gansu. The countryside in these areas is inhabited mostly by Tibetans but with a substantial Han Chinese and sinicized Tibetan population in the cities and towns. Fan observes the drastic social and economic changes brought about by militarization (i.e., the chaotic mix of remnant warlordism, clashes between Communists and Nationalists, and the incursions and threat of Japanese troops), adding a rich layer of complexity to the strategic/historical mapping he has already given the area.

In addition to contemporary economic and political contexts, Fan's mode of "tourism" also includes reconstruction of ancient battles, events, and persons upon visiting the sites associated with them. It is in this sense that Fan's journeys are interpretive; he reads the landscapes and social phenomena he encounters in multiple contexts (historical, social, economic, cultural), emphasizing the multivalence and ambiguity of observed reality. At the same time, all of his multiple contexts point to the same general crises and the particular political positioning from which he writes the texts. Fan is skillful as a reportager, as he embeds his political convictions within the landscape itself so that he can dig it up and discover it there as a tourist.

Fan's attitude toward the hardships of travel is worthy of note because most other writers who were thrown into similar situations went to either of the extremes of constantly complaining of their misery, to the degree that one wonders what they are doing in the wilderness in the first place,[29] or completely ignoring discomfort, as in works by writers who accompanied military units. In the latter, while there may be mention of the reporter's trials, they are always accompanied by affirmations that discomfort does not matter when soldiers are risking their lives and the very existence of China is at stake.[30] Fan, however, integrates the difficulties of his journey into the thematics of his narrative. One never gets the feeling that he is weak or ill suited to the rigors of travel through uncharted areas. Rather, the difficulties of the road itself are always vividly juxtaposed to the horrors he encounters. Fan is truly an explorer and his journey an expedition, especially as he sets out in the beginning of *China's Northwest Corner* from Chengdu through the forbidding and almost impassable mountainous landscapes of northwestern Sichuan into Gansu and all the way to Lanzhou.

In *China's Northwest Corner* we can see how modern travel literature focuses on the transformation of landscapes; Fan is attentive to the landscape only insofar as it has been worked on, particularly by armies before and after battle. The significant markers of a scene are the traces of the strategic exploitation of terrain or the ruins of an ancient or recent battle. Having set out on his journey to Lanzhou, he observes the northwestern Sichuan towns of Jiangyou and Zhongba primarily in terms of the physical transformations wrought by the pro-Communist warlord Xu Xiangqian.

In the thirty li from Zhongba to Jiangyou, the roadside is covered with the marks of war. In the mountains to the west of the road, there was no place without some kind of fortification; of the peasants in the countryside, a large portion was conscripted by Xu Xiangqian, while the rest had fled, and there were very few who returned home. In the villages it was silent, with scarcely a wisp of smoke from a stove. In the hills about ten li east of Jiangyou we discovered the great mountain-encircling fortress Xu Xiangqian had used when he besieged Jiangyou. The main roads had layer after layer of obstacles; in the winding curves of the mountain paths, earthen bunkers had been established at regular intervals. The surrounding fortress itself was made of bamboo poles, pine, and cypress branches woven into a stockade. In the more than thirty li around the mountain, there wasn't a single crack you could crawl through. A traveling companion familiar with military matters looked at this array and let out a sigh over Xu Xiangqian's abilities as a strategist and how quickly the Sichuan army was bested by him.

Jiangyou is a small city, overlooking the Pei River seven or eight li to the east and surrounded on the north and west by tall mountains, most significantly Mount Guangwu. When Xu Xiangqian surrounded

Jiangyou, a brigade of Yang Xixuan's Sichuan army was trapped inside the walls but defended it for more than a month without giving in. From the point of view of terrain, the defense of this city was no easy matter. At the time, Xu's main camp was on Mount Guangwu, and a certain gentleman from the county seat led me to the top of the main gate to have a look at the configuration of Mount Wuguang. From there I could see that there were over a dozen densely situated trench formations stretching from the foothills to the west of the city all the way up the mountain. Although by now most had been disabled by the Sichuan army, their traces were still easy to discern, discouraging any prospective attacker from ascending the mountain. (ZBWC II.1, 18)

This is typical of innumerable descriptions in Fan's major travel essays and newspaper articles from the war period; the strategic focus demands reference to the unique terrain of a particular place. Each city and town poses its own problems of defense, and the viewer easily alternates between the perspectives of attacker and defender.

Fan Changjiang sets himself apart from other chroniclers of war's transformation of the landscape of China by viewing scenery as much as possible through the eyes of a strategist rather than a victim. Less militarily indoctrinated observers (who would come to write much reportage during the war against Japan) tend to be obsessed with destruction, horror, and suffering as such, often oversimplifying the military complexity of war by implicitly or explicitly blaming the enemy for all such destruction and suffering.

This strategic dimension of Fan's hermeneutics of landscape is further enriched by historical and literary allusions, digressions that are anything but superficial. Fan's initial foray into the mountains of northwestern Sichuan is accompanied by an extended meditation on how the great Han dynasty and Three Kingdoms generals like Liu Bei, Zhuge Liang, and Deng Ai appear not to have known that the Min River afforded access to the Chengdu Plateau. This provides a context for his wonderment over the tactical insight demonstrated by Xu Xiangqian's entry from that northwestern direction, as he easily unseated Tian Songrao, whose corrupt administration of the area in recent years becomes the butt of Fan's ironic barbs (16–18). Similarly, as he traverses the Wei River valley west of Chang'an, Fan cites several poems by the Tang dynasty poet Du Fu that attest to Tibetan might in the area and associate its terrain particularly with the strategy of ambush (80–81). Like Xu Xiake at the end of the Ming dynasty, Fan Changjiang is testing his reading knowledge of the territories he explores against his personal experience, with experience and observation ultimately prevailing over book knowledge. Unlike Xu Xiake, however, Fan unfolds multiple layers of human landscape to great artistic effect. With his strategic emphasis and poetic and historical allusions, Fan adds new layers of richness to the literary experience of war, and avoids becoming sentimentally obsessed with the suffering of the victims of battle, while at the same time maintaining a full emotional engagement with China's position in a larger perspective of military struggle.

Fan's further travels through the mountain towns and villages of northwestern Sichuan gradually reveal the desolation and degradation of a once flourishing region due to the cruelties of war, corruption, and racial discord. Many places once known to him as bustling market centers reveal themselves as deserted ghost towns, often inhabited only by destitute women in tatters and with little or no food. Otherwise, the majority of the population consists of decommissioned or deserted soldiers opportunistically plying the trades of merchants and innkeepers in the absence of their conscripted owners. "Poverty" often takes the form of scarcity of food, as in the following passage.

> It was close to dusk; the evening wind that began blowing was too cold to bear. Our companions all caught up, most wrapped in blankets as if against a severe winter. Luckily, we later found a thatched hut two or three li into the Yellow Dragon Temple complex, with no walls, chairs, tables, or any kind of furnishing. But there was a dilapidated heated bed (kang) already covered with sleeping soldiers, and what was even more wonderful was half an oil can that could be used as a pot for cooking rice. The hosts were two little girls, each about ten years old, their tattered clothes barely covering their bodies. When asked about their parents, they said they had died in the fighting. To eat their fill they rely on that can: when someone passes through, they use the can to fix their meal, and these two poor girls might get to eat the leftovers. (29)

The ironic power of this image of destitution flows from an implied comparison of the exposed hovel with a roadside inn, suggested by the working *kang*, the sleeping soldiers, the "kitchen" provided by the oil can, and the two girls in tatters playing the role of hosts. The literary technique of ironic comparison underlies Fan's critique of many of the communities he encounters transformed by war, with opportunistic soldiers acting as merchants and traders in the absence of shopkeepers gone off to war, meager scraps of rotten bread being fought over by dozens, and the desertion of what used to be bustling local markets.

Fan Changjiang often juxtaposes such images of abject poverty, economic collapse, and widespread starvation with reflections on the meaning and vanity of life inspired by his experiences of those living and dying at the extremes. Such reflections often emerge in quiet moments when the author is left alone with his thoughts, as in the following passage, which was written in the same wayside hovel as Fan kept watch for wild animals late into the night: "When it was my turn, I draped a quilt over my shoulders, a gun in my hand. I looked up at the starry skies and listened to the whistling wind, straining my eyes to search the darkness in all directions. By now my thoughts were running freely, darting to the east and west, and I began to deeply feel the insipidness of life. People who run about and toil their whole lives are especially driven by the necessity of survival but at the same time it doesn't have any special meaning, thus simply acting out of the necessity of survival is the real meaning of human life" (29).

Fan's encounter with a makeshift graveyard the following day seems to have been designed to inspire him to expand at great length along this line of thought. As in the above passage, Fan's philosophical reflections are carefully intertwined with his description of the immediate environment so that each enhances the other.

There were quite a few rock piles alongside the road, the graves of passersby who had died on the mountain peak. The pounding midday sun baked them, releasing the occasional whiff of rotting corpses. I wonder what men and women lost their lives here. If the dead were conscious on this clear and quiet mountain and could think back on their scurrying and toil while they were alive, trying to figure out what the purpose of an entire life of busying about might have been, they would probably burst out in laughter. Many suppose that it is "money" they are hurrying after in this society. Those with money can dress well, eat loads, live in splendor, possess a charming wife, boast of their brilliant hometown friends, and even control others and pass their fortune on to their children and grandchildren. Those without money strive for this, and those with money also strive for this, seeking better, more perfect, richer lives. Pretty-sounding ethical terms that circulate from day to day are all ways of speaking that deceive the ordinary masses but aren't enough to shed light on life's true nature and are inadequate to resolve or respond to the above-mentioned facts. Why, after all, do people strive for these things? Suppose life were perfectable, where would be the meaning in that? If, for example, these sojourners who died on the mountaintop all ran gold mines in Songpan, became millionaires, and returned to Chengdu in all their glory, enjoying only the finest products, everything they consumed imported from New York and London, what would it all mean? What is the essential difference between dying suddenly on a desolate mountaintop and being placed in a crystal casket on a famous mountain? Even if the dead were conscious, they probably would still be at a loss to answer this reporter's questions. If only people would work hard to maintain, continue, and spread survival; that is the essence of life. (30–31)

Such reflections are often intertwined with the military and historical dimensions mentioned above, as can be seen in the following passage inspired by Fan's encounter with remnants of the Nineteenth Route Army of Shanghai Incident (January 28, 1932) fame.

The army stationed here is an old unit of the 19th Route Army, very active in construction; their accomplishments in the cleaning and repair of roads and the construction of simple parks are remarkable. According to what a certain officer told me, after the Fujian debacle there were a lot of lower officers and soldiers of the Nineteenth Army who retreated to Guangdong; after transfer to Henan, retraining, and restructuring, only 10 or 20 percent of the original officers and soldiers remain. It has only been four years since the January 28 incident; who could have known then that some of the soldiers and officers who fought in the fierce battles of Zhabei, Hongkou, Jiangwan, and Wusong, after the Shanghai cease-fire treaty, and the Fujian incident, would be reorganized in Henan? How much more unlikely it seemed that they would end up fighting in the soaring mountain peaks of Sichuan! The changes of human fate seem inscrutable, but if you analyze each event in terms of its environment there is a thread by which to follow the relations of cause and effect: under certain circumstances, certain results are inevitable. Although not every detail may fall into place, you can't fail to discern the overall pattern. (23–24)

Such metaphysical reverie is never truly abstract in *China's Northwest Corner;* Fan constantly weaves his thoughts tightly into the textures of the observed environment. Environment, both physical and cultural, provides the "thread" through which the patterns of cause and effect that render events meaningful can be discerned. Apart from underlying Fan Changjiang's whole mode of observation, this interpretive scheme emerges with particular clarity in certain instances. For example, Fan pauses to critique the common notion of mountain "ranges," *shanmai* (literally "mountain arteries"), noting that despite the way mountain ranges are commonly spoken of, "originating" in some spot and "flowing" in a certain direction like a river is completely flawed from a geological point of view: mountains are merely the high places left behind by geological processes like erosion from rivers, shifts in the earth's crust, and volcanic eruptions (62–63). Similarly, his experience of flying over Gansu and Shaanxi Provinces prompts him to attack the notion of a Shaanxi-Gansu "plateau," as it is clear to him that the area in question is neither level nor without mountain ranges (78–79).

This will to correct geocultural misunderstandings takes on more social significance in his critique of roads. Being conspicuously human transformations of the environment, roads are central to Fan's symbolic landscape. The section "Some Observations on the Xi'an-Lanzhou Highway" (69–73) is an extended examination of the highway's social and economic geography and a multifaceted critique of enthusiasm and interest in the project common along the east coast. His target is not only the poor quality of the recently constructed, government-funded highway but the expensive, shabby restaurants and inns established along the way and the unreasonable power and irresponsibility of the bus drivers arising from the highway company's monopoly over bus service. Fan contrasts this example to that of Zuo Zongtang's substantial contribution to the economic/geographic development of the northwest in the previous century, represented especially well by his wide, tree-lined Xinjiang highway (85–86).

From military strategy ancient and modern, to concrete human tragedies unfolding before the reporter's eyes, to philosophical and historical reflections on the meaning of life and the vagaries of fortune, and even the critical interpretation of his environment's topography and the current language used to describe it, the physical landscape is always the text from which Fan's considerations arise. Fan's human geography makes space significant by superimposing complex layers of meaning onto his account of each place, from the ancient campaigns of Deng Ai to variations in local customs, current warlords' territories with strategic analysis, economy manifested in variations of available food, the dress of local people, and transportation and communications conditions. The cumulative effect of this layering is to render the *place* as it unfolds in Fan's account as rich and complex as any other literary figurative structure such as plot or the exploration and analysis of character.[31]

It is clear that Fan Changjiang's travel essays are very different from those of Zou Taofen and not only because he writes of domestic instead of foreign travel. Fan's text strikes me as definitively literary insofar as it creates a hermeneutic of observation by means of which the landscapes that surround him become overdetermined signs, limited only by the extent of the observer's knowledge and his or her ability to make meaningful associations. Fan's text is in this sense more akin to Qu Qiubai's travel essays, though Fan has attained a higher degree of refinement in his nonfictional art by maintaining his concentration on the landscape as a figure that in all its details manifests a complex and urgent social and historical situation. It remains for me here to situate these modern travel essays in relation to the concurrently emerging reportage tradition.

If we view these texts as symbolic structures in addition to their primary function as repositories of information, the actual journeys these authors take are signifiers, and the signified referent (or destination, to borrow the trope of the journey) is China, specifically, China's future.

Even in the case of foreign journeys, as I have pointed out in relation to these writers' late Qing predecessors as well, the purpose of the journey and especially of writing about it is to answer certain questions about China, indeed, to point out a reasonable historical "direction" for China to pursue.

In the process, however, whether implicitly or explicitly, the solution lies in the process of immersion within the investigation itself. For both Qu Qiubai and Zou Taofen, the value of their socialist destination lies not in its specific answers to practical and larger issues, but in its method of penetrating to the level of concrete conditions and working with them. In the case of Fan Changjiang, he is content with eloquently articulating the problem, impressing its urgency on the reader, and overturning prevailing myths. Finally, in all cases, the act of writing itself necessitates the writer's identification with China as a nation or a people; the position of the solitary, contemplative individual simply does not lend itself to the task at hand. As a result, the specific observations, experiences, and reflections of these writers become the very fabric of a collective consciousness of modern China, not independent visions but discrete strands in a growing, multivocal master text that narrates the nation.

While none of these writers explicitly identifies with the genre of reportage, all of these aspects of the relationship between experience, writing, consciousness, and China are fundamental to the reportage approach as it coalesced within the literary journals and reportage anthologies of the mid- and late 1930s. These travel essays were widely read at the time, and reportage writers undoubtedly identified with the subject positions they express; their language of engagement and urgency and the diffusion of the private self within the vagaries of contemporary events pervaded public discourse and much literary creation, including fiction, poetry, and drama as well as reportage.

The following chapters, each elaborating a distinct type of modern Chinese reportage, will demonstrate this commonality between the consciousness of the modern travel writer and the reportager. However, it will also become quickly evident that reportage is fundamentally different from travel literature. The inclusion of the works I have discussed in this chapter in the canonical *Zhongguo baogao wenxue congshu* (Compendium of Chinese Reportage Literature) is problematic, particularly in the case of Zou Taofen, whose travel accounts become increasingly removed from the author's concrete experiences and whose thematic concerns often depart from addressing Chinese conditions to extol the social order of the Soviet Union.

The contribution of modern Chinese travel literature to Chinese reportage, particularly in the respect that Chinese reportage differs from that of other cultures, is seminal. I have treated these works incompletely, and there are a number of other influential travel essays that could be explored with these issues in mind. My aim in this chapter has been to recognize the affinity between travel literature and reportage and to begin to demonstrate a way of reading that draws out the artistic aspects of nonfictional texts as a foundation for my literary treatment of reportage in the chapters that follow.

TWO

Public Demonstrations: The Mise-en-Scène of History

Compared to other landscapes of modern Chinese reportage, the city is clearly demarcated and circumscribed; particular locations are easy to identify and thus have a much more vivid impact on readers familiar with the territory. In dealing with the Chinese reportage of the city, I adopt a performative or theatrical paradigm to elucidate the particular kind of space in which these narratives are played out. This is useful in dealing with the reportage of student and worker demonstrations in the spaces of the metropolitan city. This chapter is the first of two devoted to urban space; here I will be dealing with texts dating from 1919 to 1935 that are specifically concerned with the narration of public demonstrations.

Public demonstrations are themselves "performed" theatrically, and there is usually a heterogeneous crowd of spectators present, analogous to the theatrical audience.[1] Moreover, they often converge upon meaningful places, which often become the stages on which tragedies are enacted. This theatrical structuring of space functions as a medium through which urban space-time is realized explicitly as a system of signification, a running allegory in which concrete actions and events are continuously read as convulsions in the fate of the nation. A theatrical paradigm for the reportage of urban struggle accounts for the particular use of both space (organized to permit ritual and other performative activity) and time (accelerated, scene-driven, dramatic, and emphasizing the explosive succession of selected, critical events). The authors of texts on urban struggle *dramatize* demonstrations in a fuller than usual sense of the word; they are in a sense writing plays retrospectively, after they are performed. The work of reportage becomes the completion of the "script" through the author's witnessing (and even participating in) the event and his or her depiction of the performance, from the speeches and marching to the confrontation with authorities; the dramatic dialogue of ultimatums and exchanged threats; the vivid, climactic scene of violent suppression; martyrdom of demonstrators; and the spectacular technology of political repression.

The author's triple status as part of the audience, participant in the action, and writer is emblematic of the vague distinction between performer and audience in this type of performance, calling to mind Antonin Artaud's notion of a "theater of cruelty" in which all of the metaphysical dualities that characterize classical theater are broken down and the performance becomes pure action rather than representation.[2] Despite my emphasis on epic qualities and performative exaggeration, this vision of theater is one sense the opposite of Bertold Brecht's "epic theater," in which actors consciously and critically *distance* themselves from the characters and actions they portray. As depicted by the reportage writer, demonstration turns upon highly significant (heroic or villainous) gestures and utterances, a stirring and epic action on the stage of the city streets.

Finally, the published work remains a script insofar as its readers may be prompted by it to go out and perform similar "plays." This open-ended quality of true-life narrative as theater is an important distinguishing feature of reportage: the text's connection to the real world via the veracity of its subject matter is met with a reader's response that is connected to the real world via the text's lack of aesthetic closure. The moved reader is motivated by the text to act. In contrast to the *catharsis* of classical theater, which resolves tensions within the system of the text or performance, here the reader or audience is called upon to resolve tensions that are real in society to complete the system of the work.

The May Fourth incident of 1919 and the events that followed inspired a new wave of progressive journalism opposing the government's concessions to Japan and other foreign powers as well as bad working conditions and inhuman management practices in foreign-run mines and factories. Among such works, the article "Yizhou zhong Beijing gongmin de da huodong" (The Great Citizens' Movement in Beijing This Week) stands out for the vividness and specificity of its narrative treatment of what has become one of the most celebrated events in modern Chinese history.[3]

The Beiyang government had been preparing to sign the Treaty of Versailles after World War I, which, among other things, ceded Germany's rights and possessions in Shandong Province to Japan over China's protests. The cabinet ministers who advocated this passive policy, Cao Rulin, Zhang Zongxiang, and Lu Zongyu, became the targets of a student demonstration on May Fourth protesting the agreement. Many of the participants in the demonstration ended up beating Zhang and burning Cao's house. The government's detention of the radical students aroused further, much larger demonstrations nationwide, strikes, and business shutdowns that eventually forced the Beiyang government to release the students and dismiss Cao, Zhang, and Lu from their posts on June 10.

The anonymous "Great Citizens' Movement" sets the narrative context by recounting the meetings of various organizations and the development of thwarted plans to demonstrate on May 3 (National Humiliation Day, *guochi jinian ri*), then the initiative proposed by the students of Beijing University to demonstrate on the following day at Tian'anmen. The third section of the text focuses, however, on an impassioned yet laconic narrative of the demonstration and its culmination in a march from Tian'anmen to the home of Cao Rulin in order to confront him.

> Once they arrived in front of the Cao house, everyone cried in unison "Traitor!" The house was surrounded by over two hundred patrolmen, who held their ground. Then everyone began using their banner poles to loosen and knock free roof tiles, and the patrolmen, military police, and special agents moved to one side. Several students leaped, heedless of danger, over the walls and into the compound, then broke

the doors down. Everyone rushed in, hitting things and looking for Cao Rulin, shedding tears as they ransacked. Some policemen wept as well. They caught Cao Rulin's father, his younger son, and his concubine Su Peiqiu, as well as another thirty-nine-year-old woman. These they released without a beating, while Cao Rulin continued to elude capture. That morning, Cao was with Lu and Zhang at a reception at the dean's compound. Someone warned Cao not to go home, but he said "What do I have to be afraid of?" and he went home with Zhang Zongxiang, at which time they encountered this scene. Everyone grabbed Zhang Zongxiang and beat him bloody and senseless, his skull showing through his broken scalp (ZBWC I.1, 359).

The selection of details in this passage and throughout "The Great Citizens' Movement" is calculated to justify all of the demonstrators' actions. The demonstrators' shedding tears as they ransacked and the spectacle of the police patrolmen weeping along with them ensure that the violence in which they are engaged is not simply chaotic, mob violence but a solemn, patriotic act. Here tears are a sign of rebellious, nationalistic outrage. The demonstrators' seriousness of purpose is exemplified as well by the fact that the procession as it set off from Tian'anmen was led by mock funeral couplets "mourning" the "deaths" of Cao Rulin, Zhang Zongxiang, and Lu Zongyu and cursing their posterity for eternity (359).

"The Great Citizens' Movement" also carefully notes that the physical violence was directed at these three men and no one else, not even Cao's closest relatives. Thus, the shedding of tears and of blood are tied directly and exclusively to the nationalist political aims of the demonstration and divorced from any other personal or individual considerations. Maintaining the emphasis on emotional intensity and unity of purpose even in the most anonymous collective action marks the first step toward the development of collective subjectivity in documentary narrative, which would later be elaborated in reportage literature.

In a discussion of fictional realism in the May Fourth period, Marston Anderson observes the active promotion of a "literature of blood and tears."

For realists the new fiction could authorize itself only through authors' rigorous moral efforts to purge their consciousness of all modes of self-involvement that might inhibit their capacity for so-cial engagement. The curious blend of liberation and constraint that resulted from this formulation was given metaphorical expression in the repeated call by Zheng Zhenduo, Mao Dun, and others for "a literature of blood and tears": the new fiction was to possess the pal-pable reality of fluids exuded by the body. But significantly the fluids to which the expression refers are released only when the body is physically wounded (blood) or when the spirit is bruised by empa-thy (tears). The metaphor would seem to suggest that self-expression becomes possible only within a context of injury or loss.[4]

In the documentary essays of Mao Dun, Zheng Zhenduo, and Ye Shengtao published in *Wenxue zhoukan* (Literary Weekly) during the May Thirtieth demonstrations in 1925, this initiative is put into practice per-haps even more clearly than in the fiction of the time. These texts can be treated collectively, as they were published more or less as a series, treat-ing different aspects and scenarios of the course of events, and because all of the authors were active participants in the movement.[5]

Emerging within the lengthening shadow of the May Fourth move-ment, May Thirtieth was a more labor-oriented movement organized by the Communist Party in Shanghai and directed at the Japanese and other foreign governments rather than the Chinese government. At this time, *movement* (*yundong*) was understood to mean a series of organized protest demonstrations and their attendant speeches and meetings. On May 15, 1925, Japanese employees of a Japanese-run textile mill in Shanghai killed Gu Zhenghong, a worker in the factory who was also a Communist Party member, and wounded several other Chinese workers. On May 30, around two thousand students demonstrated and spread propaganda in the international settlement, calling for assistance for Chinese workers and the recuperation of the foreign concessions; one hundred or more of them were detained by international police. Soon thereafter thousands of people gathered at the police station on Nanjing Road demanding the release of the students; British police opened fire on the pretext of the crowd's unruliness and menace, killing twelve and wounding dozens. This led to subsequent strikes and demonstrations all over the country on a scale much larger than the May Fourth movement, but in the end May Thirtieth led to little improvement in the situation.[6]

Rather than utilizing the newspaper, several Literary Association (Wenxue yanjiu hui) veterans who had come of age in the May Fourth era published short articles in the journal *Wenxue zhoukan* describing their own participation in or observation of the demonstration, including Ye Shaojun's "Wuyue sayi ri jiyu zhong" (In the Driving Rain on May 31), Mao Dun's "Wuyue sanshi ri de xiawu" (On the Afternoon of May Thirtieth) and "Baofeng yu" (Rainstorm), and Zheng Zhenduo's "Liu yue yiri" (June First).[7]

A striking aspect of the *Wenxue zhoukan* essays on the May Thirtieth movement is that there is little narrative treatment of the central events themselves; they are structured rather as impressionistic meditations or soliloquies on the significance of the events as the writers visit the sites of their occurrence. Blood takes on a potent significance as a symbol of the demonstrators and their sacrifice, with which the authors establish a dynamic, sensual relationship. Ye Shengtao wrote, for example: "I rushed to the Old Sluicegate (Laozha) detention center gate to pay my respects to the bloodstains of our friends; I wanted to lick those bloodstains clean with my tongue and swallow them into my belly. But they're gone, not a bit left! They've already been sprayed away by the enemy's water cannon, already trampled clean by rotten-hearted passersby. Washed away, too, by the demonic, arrowlike, driving rain!"[8] Zheng Zhenduo develops the connection between blood and water cannons more completely than the others, following the blood all the way to the sea: "Nanjing Road has become a slaughtering field. The blood of the victims is splattered for yards in all directions over this most glamorous of oriental avenues, staining the gray road a reddish-purple. But after several washes, the blood on the street follows the red-dyed water into the gutters, into the Huangpu River, and finally into the ocean, gone without a trace."[9] Ye Shengtao is more optimistic, viewing the blood as having "penetrated the earth for good," from which the vengeful "flowers of blood" will bloom (22).

The water cannons, street cleaners, and the thunderstorms of May 30 and 31 clean away what for these writers is the precious and sacred trace of the demonstrators' sacrifice. Water thus becomes a sign of forgetting, the opposite of tears, which are the sign of realizing, remembering. Mao Dun begins "The Afternoon of May Thirtieth" in disbelief at the ease of forgetting: "Who would believe that only half an hour ago, beside this towering 'housewives' paradise' took place an intense living drama, unprecedented in its tragedy?[10] Millions of 'Fight for Liberty' banners were flapping, millions of 'Down with Imperialism' shouts were resounding: how many brave youths spilled their hot blood, staining this gray earth red?! Who still remembers the firing of rifles into the dense crowd right here?! Who still remembers how the men of advanced civilization took off their false masks to reveal their true faces of cruelty and evil?!"[11]

These texts indicate the urge to document history among these writers and others dedicated to overcoming the apathy of the public and the distortions of the bourgeois press. Also indicative of this trend is the establishment of the *Gongli ribao* (The Truth), a newspaper devoted to sympathetic and thorough reporting of the May Thirtieth movement. As Vera Schwarcz puts it, Zheng Zhenduo, who oversaw the editing of the paper out of his Shanghai home, wished to put the truth about May Thirtieth in print "to counter his own fear that the massacre was a mere 'play staged on a live podium.'"[12] *The Truth* was supposed to provide a perspective both sympathetic to the movement and faithful to the facts. In this way, as much as in formal terms, the documentary essays inspired by the May Thirtieth movement formed a basis for reportage literature, which would be articulated explicitly a few years later.

The difficulty with the mainstream press at the time, which in this case may be said to have been represented by *Shen bao* (Shanghai News), was less that it failed to tell "the whole truth" than that it failed to tell "nothing but the truth." Perusal of *Shen bao* from May 31 and June 1, 1925, reveals a cacophony of competing versions of the events of May 30 presented side by side, chiefly in the local news section. The fact of twelve dead, most of whom were students, was not disputed, but the conditions under which the British police opened fire on the crowd differ with every version. For example, the police version and those of some newspapers indicate that a volley of empty-chambered warning shots was fired and a clear announcement made that if the crowd did not disperse the officers would have to begin firing upon them (in the police version, moreover, many in the crowd were shouting "kill the foreigners" and trying to physically wrest guns from the hands of the police; the crowd is repeatedly described as being of a "xenophobic nature"). The student version and those of some newspaper reporters and other organizations claimed that the firing began suddenly and arbitrarily as soon as the crowd converged at the detention center where students were being held in custody.

In addition to all these reports, groups of merchants and certain business concerns placed advertisements, some to mourn the deaths of the students and others to warn the citizens of Shanghai "not to go outside except in an emergency; if you are walking on the street, do not stop to watch what is going on or applaud and cheer, and by no means do anything violent." Finally, Shen bao's editorials are strongly emotional about the tragedy and yet noncommittal about its significance or what to do about it, perhaps out of a desire not to offend its foreign advertisers.

What Vera Schwarcz describes as the "exhilaration," even "fetishizing" of blood, on the part of May Fourth veterans seeking new identities in a much more violent China must be counterbalanced with the sheer terror expressed by Zhu Ziqing later the same year in his "Zhizhengfu da tusha ji" (Record of the Massacre at the Government Building). Then an instructor at Qinghua University, Zhu took part in a protest against the Beiyang government's pro-Japanese policy. The demonstration was not a march but a rally in front of the government's administration building on the east side of Beijing. Terror is given shape in the panicked scattering of the students under the nonchalant yet relentless gunfire of the guards, as well as in Zhu's at once intimate and anonymous baptism in blood.

> Suddenly the ranks [of students] began to scatter, and many people began to run away in all directions. Someone shouted loudly and repeatedly, "Don't anybody leave, it's nothing!" waving his hand. The leader of our Qinghua group also waved his hand and yelled, "Qinghua students, don't leave, everything is all right!" . . .[13] Just when the Qinghua leader finished calling out for the second time and I saw the crowd scatter for refuge—one squad of guards had already loaded its rifles! I quickly ran forward a few steps and dove to the ground beside a group of people, but before I could get down two people rushed behind and in front of me, pressing close to me. I couldn't move; all I could do was crouch.
>
> By this time I could already hear the pi-pi pa-pa of the guns. It was

the first time I had ever heard a gun in my life, and at first I thought they were firing empty chambers (I had forgotten that I had just seen them load their guns). But a minute or two later, there was hot, red blood dripping on the back of my hand and my jacket, and I suddenly realized that a massacre was taking place! . . .

The one bleeding above me didn't make a sound right up to the time the sound of the first volley died away and we got up to run away. This was the descent of death, and his silence spoke of death. When I thought about it later, it was really frightening. Who was that above me? . . . Only later when I was running away did I realize how much blood there was on my head and on my hat . . . all his! He bled for more than two full minutes, and all that blood flowed onto me. . . .

The first round of gunfire took four or five minutes, many volleys altogether; the commander was using a whistle: one whistle and they fired a volley, one whistle followed immediately by another and the sound of guns stopped. The sound of that whistle was sad and shrill, but with an almost regular rhythm; you could tell how relaxed the commander was! Later I heard another eyewitness say that he even used his sword to point out where to shoot, and it was always toward the greatest concentration of people! Another witness said that at the time there were people standing on the government building dancing about with glee![14]

The area in which the massacre took place is a small plaza surrounded with high walls and with few routes of escape, and thus Zhu's narrative underlines in the most excruciating detail how the circumscribed spaces of the city play a role in the technology of violence.

The sound of gunfire had not yet ceased, and the eastern gate was stuffed solid with people. I could vaguely discern dozens of people crouching and squatting below; we pushed and shoved, crowded our way in, struggled, and clambered right over them. By then reason had lost all functioning, and I was [climbing over living bodies] calmly, as though there were nothing odd about it. I was pushed upright and backward several times, and in the end I had no choice but to lunge forward with all my strength. . . . This gate was the border between safety and peril, a gate of life and death, so no one dared relax and step back for even a second. (ZBWC I:1, 46–47)

The impetus of Zhu's piece, like the *Gongli bao*, is to uncover the distortion and lies in newspaper reports of the slaughter: "The next day when I read the newspapers I felt that, apart from one or two exceptions, just about every paper's report was full of discrepancies from the facts. Whether they were the distortions of hearsay or deliberately changed for other reasons, I have no way of knowing and no desire to discuss at length. All I wish to tell is what I saw there with my own eyes and heard later with my own ears: behold the brutal savagery of China on the eighteenth of March in the twenty-sixth year of the twentieth century!"

This idea of a true, corrective version is crucial to reportage literature; it permeates statements like Zhu's and those of many other writers within their texts about what they are doing. There is the newspaper version or versions, which may be influenced by the government or financial interests; there is the version provided by hearsay, which is consciously or unconsciously partial and unreliable; and then there is the elusive "true" version, which is based in the minds of these writers not on scientific objectivity but on a faith in and loyalty to the truth immanent in events to which only the eyewitness has privileged access. Moreover, the truth of a version is implicitly based on the judgment of "the people," not authority, private interest, or the individual but the citizenry as a collective witness. The mission of reportage is often expressed in terms of a critique of bourgeois journalism, which is seen as exploiting sensationalism to sell papers and as deceiving itself into thinking it can be objective when it is actually serving the common interests of warlord or Nationalist governments and large capitalist concerns. Reportage literature and its immediate precursors, such as the texts discussed earlier, present themselves as being self-consciously interested, narrating events explicitly from the point of view of the oppressed and taking as a matter of course the premise that no narration can be disinterested.

THE EMPOWERMENT OF THE COLLECTIVE BODY

"The Eruption of the Crowd"
In "Beyond Realism: The Eruption of the Crowd," the final chapter of his *The Limits of Realism*, Marston Anderson describes how in the 1930s, one of the most conspicuous ways Chinese fiction grew away from the para-

digm of realism was through the replacement of the individual character as protagonist by the crowd: "The real protagonist of much of 1930s' fiction is no longer the individual struggling to achieve a critical perspective on a chaotic social environment, as it had typically been in the 1920s, but a special kind of crowd, abstractly conceived yet possessed of an overwhelming physical immediacy."[15] Anderson goes on to observe that "the crowd's ethical motivation is never imposed from the outside but emerges in its collective consciousness and finds expression in its disparate and anonymous voices. . . . This diffusion results in a theatricalization of the critical message: the narrator steps aside and lets his characters speak for him. In fact, the theatrical nature of such scenes is often already evident in the behavior of the crowd itself" (187–88).

In fact, as I have shown, this narrative practice has roots in the 1920s, and the association of the crowd and its collective subjectivity with a theatrical narrative space is the basis of the "chronotope" I examine here.

One thing the narratives of urban struggle have in common is the depiction of the violence of cruel, well-armed authorities against innocent, patriotic, unarmed demonstrators (Zhu Ziqing, Mao Dun, Ye Shaojun). The image of the British police, rendered in full stereotype as blond haired, blue eyed, and pink skinned,[16] embody the dispassionate cruelty of imperialism; there is less attention paid to them as particular men than is paid to their weapons and the mechanical relentlessness with which they use them. This leads on the part of all of the authors to reflections on violence that lead in the direction suggested in "The Great Citizens' Movement," to the abandonment of passivity and nonviolence and the embrace of violence as the only path to justice: "Their clubs hitting human flesh made me think I was hearing someone say 'Surely there must be some other, more peaceful way. . . . We have an oriental, spiritual culture; why avenge such trivial humiliation and harm to our bodies' — Peaceful way! It may be a nice-sounding phrase, but sadly it has no place with a people who are beaten and killed for no reason! What is the meaning of a peaceful way in the mouths of people who are beaten and killed? If they're not peaceful to you, what can you do?"[17]

Mao Dun arrives at a "new belief" in "an eye for an eye," which is the conclusion of many of these writers when they are confronted with the spectacle of ruthless, mechanical violence; the texts reach closure in the belief that the Chinese are not ultimately powerless in the face of such an enemy. Ye Shaojun expresses this belief through a stylized image of the modern Chinese collective hero: "I was taken aback by their faces. I've never seen such grave faces; some were like the soaring peaks of Kunlun, faces of such gloomy anger, as if carved by bolts of lightning. The soft and shining color of youth was completely faded and shadowed, replaced with the aged strength of heroic northerners. Their eyes spewed forth all-consuming fire, and their tightly pursed lips hid teeth that could chew living beings to death. Their noses fear neither the stench of blood nor of dead bodies; their ears do not fear cannons or the roar of ferocious beasts. Their flesh is nothing less than tempered steel armor.[18]

A year later, Lu Dingyi's report of the memorial activities for the anniversary of May Thirtieth expands the scope of the destructive power of the Chinese masses, depicted with a new level of enthusiasm and strewn lavishly with exclamation marks:

The people all poured into the street, like a flood gushing onto Nanjing Road from all directions! Traffic came to a standstill! . . . Slogans shook the heavens, and before long the road was packed solid! Small businessmen brought out stools and gave speeches in front of their shops! Apprentices, workers, all of the city people challenged the armed guards at the Chamber of Commerce, rocks and pieces of wood flew upon them from all directions! Someone started smashing up the trolleys! . . .

By now the imperialists were trembling! They never thought these fearless "lowly *Chinamen*" would make such a ruckus. . . .

Around Zhejiang Road, it really got out of hand; all they could do was bring in a fire truck and spray, and the traffic was stopped there, too. On Edward VII Road some foreigners weren't allowed to drive through; they were forced out of their cars and chased away by the blows and shouts of hundreds.

It went on like this until eight or nine o'clock at night. All the trolleys from Edward VII Road to Markham Road were smashed! Stones and broken tiles were constantly flying on the street, and the imperialists didn't dare fire a round to the end!

One clerk said to me, "Today I was finally a man!"

There was a worker siezed by a policeman who was going to beat him; he shouted "What day do you think this is? I beat you! You don't get to beat me!"

Oh! May Thirtieth, great May Thirtieth! The day I can be a man! The day I beat you![19]

Even when reading "The Great Citizens' Movement" narrative from 1919, one senses a profound historical rupture when confronted with the spectacle of the exalted government minister Zhang Zongxiang's wounded head and the capture and release of Cao Rulin's concubine by the anonymous crowd identified only as "students." In Lu Dingyi's piece, the sense of empowerment following upon such a rupture is explicitly expressed in the words of the worker turning against the policeman ("I beat you! You don't get to beat me!"). Here, the mob, the crowd, the masses, are identified with the Chinese people (*Zhonghua minzu*) in contradistinction to imperialist invaders and treacherous Chinese authorities. Imagining violence in this way is psychological empowerment for the writer and reader in a world where most violence flows in the other direction, and it is one of the early steps in the development of "posthumanist" themes in reportage that directly attack liberal humanist as well as traditional Chinese values. This is only the beginning of imagining the masses (within the urban context) as a righteously unruly collective subject. In the early 1930s, when the proletarian literature and cultural movements were in full swing, this imagining struck out in new directions.

"Laobosheng lu" (Robison Road) is a narrative of a strike and series of protests against a Japanese cotton mill in Shanghai in the wake of the Mukden Incident (the Japanese occupation of Manchuria) of 1931. It is one of the surviving texts of the Worker Correspondents movement promoted by the League of Left-Wing Writers and presented as a transcription of a "wall newspaper" (*bi bao*, factory or office news pasted on a wall or written on a chalkboard).[20] Formally, "Robison Road" resembles a newspaper report, as it is divided into short sections with headlines and subheadings in much the same way as contemporary local reports appeared in *Shen bao*. However, the rhetoric and dramatization of the events shows the clear influence of the student movement texts examined above. The entire text extols violence against the Japanese overseers and security forces as well as other foreign and Chinese police.

The text begins in media res with over ten thousand workers, students, and citizens gathered beneath the Robison Road clock tower in western Shanghai for an anti-Japanese rally.

> By 10:55, the number of people was growing quickly, and a group of workers rushed over to the lawn across from Ma Pei Road on Ferry Road, giving speeches in groups; just at that time Okura, the Japanese head of security for Factory Four passed by and had the gall to gang up with the 161st Sikh police unit and the 292d Western police unit to interfere. The Western police were forced onto a corner of the lawn by the crowd, crying for help; the Sikhs, seeing the westerners in trouble, escaped along Ma Pei Road. As for the Japanese, they were left alone with much more than they could handle. They escaped into the Putai Tobacco Shop at the intersection of Robison and Ferry but were immediately dragged out by the mass and got a good beating in front of a certain fabric shop. In no time, shouts of "Down with Japanese Imperialism" and "Down with the Japanese" (*Dongyang ren*) shook the heavens and the earth; those security guards normally flirted with the women workers and harshly shook down workers at the Factory Four gate, but now one shout and everyone descended on them, beating them half to death. The women workers couldn't get in close, so they wildly threw pieces of rock and tar from the road. (53–54)

This violence goes on, emphasizing the fear and cowardice of the Japanese factory managers ("shitting in their pants" [54]) and the fierce, vengeful indignation and physical power of the crowd.

An important difference between this report and the sort found in newspapers like Shen bao is that, while the content of the mottos and specific incidents might be similar or identical, the protesting crowd as an agent of action would invariably be depicted in newspapers as a chaotic, arbitrarily destructive force to be put in line with increasingly harsh police measures, while the labor press depicts the power of the crowd as directed and measured, unruly only in the sense that its righteous power cannot be controlled by the police. Another important difference is that at the end of the first section, or "article," there is a direct call to workers for specific action (to strike, not to let anyone go to work, to arise, resist, and stay together as a group under the clock tower [54–55]).

The next section dramatizes the Japanese intensification of the battle in the afternoon by calling in their troops. Two armored cars, four motorcycles mounted with machine guns, and over forty soldiers, with several machine guns set up at the Gordon Road intersection, all spell the desperation and potential cruelty of the Japanese, which is only fuel for the growing crowd's fury. The crowd runs over to the factory's Japanese staff building a block or so away and smash the entire front wall of the dormitory, "the Japanese scurrying away like mice with their heads in their hands, with the slower ones kowtowing and begging mercy from the workers!" (55). But two trucks full of Japanese marines charge at the crowd without warning, bayonetting two workers. The concession police, "anxious to demonstrate their loyalty to imperialism, pulled out their clubs and beat countless women and children workers . . . [while] at the roadside officers of the Chinese Public Security Bureau idly watched these beastly foreign soldiers doing their killing, not only failing to aid their compatriots but later actually helping the foreigners suppress the protest . . . by preventing the crowd from escaping, making it more convenient for the Japanese to massacre them" (55).

Many other texts, of course, are driven by humanitarian concerns similarly fleshed out in concrete action, particularly during the war against Japan, but this radical moral iconoclasm, informed to a large extent by Leninism, is particularly prevalent in reportage and is closely related to the construction of collective subjectivity that characterizes the development of the genre. One rarely or never sees, for example, violence carried out by particular individuals against the authorities arising out of circumstances in their personal lives; rather, it is always depicted in the form of a counterattack by a whole class or nation represented symbolically by a given crowd on the street against authorities who are already violent, exploitative antagonists. Thus, no matter how graphic the depiction of violence against the authorities, there is never danger of pity for the person in authority as victim because he is never shown in the light of his common humanity. "Humanity," in fact, is not assumed to be "common" and is not a salient characteristic from the posthumanist point of view of the aroused masses.

After a few additional follow-up news items, "Robison Road" closes with an interview with one of the wounded that exemplifies the Marxist-Leninist approach to journalism in action: "Yang's thigh had been punctured by a Japanese bayonet, and now it was bundled up in a sheet but with fresh blood oozing out, an unspeakably pitiful sight. From his left eye to the corner of his mouth, a Japanese boot had left a bruised, bloody scar. His right index finger broken, he was constantly moaning in pain. This correspondent wiped some of the blood from his face, gave him a bowl of cold tea, and he began to regain some of his spirit" (57).

The wounds on the worker's body are no mere unfortunate accident of fate; they are read by the writer as the cruel inscription of Japanese imperialism on the bodies of the Chinese working people. The relationship between the reporter and interviewee is not simply one of information exchange but commiseration, tenderness, and hatred for a common, palpable enemy. Moreover, part of the worker correspondent's duty, beyond gathering information, is to educate and act as a moral guide, even to the interviewee.

Q: Now that you're injured, what do you plan to do?
A: . . . Even if I hadn't been hurt, I'd still go hungry, now . . . I guess I'll just starve to death.

With this, his parents and all the children began to cry bitterly, and the conversation comes to a standstill.

Q: Have you joined the union in the factory?
A: Union? Why should I? They aren't going to fool me again. When I was working in Yangshupu we paid union dues until the whole family was starving, and my woman and I argued till we were blue in the face — the union organizers all became managers; I won't be their obedient son again.
Q: You can't lump everything together like that, what you're talking about is probably a "Skin the People Party" union;[21] unions like that are no good. We have to organize our own union. Do you know about the Red Union here?
A: No. (Looks at the reporter in anger) Hey, did that union send you? I'm not talking to you. I haven't even got any food; what business have you got coming here?
Q: It's because we've got no food that poor people have to unite. Take today, for example; if we weren't unified, if we hadn't organized, those Japanese would have really been brutal.

Note how the roles of "question" and "answer" have reversed; Yang, the ostensible focus of the text, has to make room for the reporter's lecture and does little but agree with the reporter for the rest of the interview. The juxtaposition in "Robison Road" of the epic confrontation between the laboring masses and the armed forces of imperialism on the one hand and the quiet interview in the wounded worker's hovel on the other is made to look arbitrary by the slapdash urgency of the wall newspaper format, but it is also emblematic of the frequent juxtaposition and even superimposition of the personal and public characteristics of reportage literature.

The masses in "Robison Road" are powerful and destructive, but they speak only through their acts and slogans; when their thoughts are revealed, they are benighted and hopeless, in need of awakening. But collectives in the reportage of the city are of many different kinds and develop complex relations with one another. In addition to heterogeneous crowds on the streets witnessing one spectacle or another, activists who try to lead them or channel their power are themselves a collective body: as a protest march moves along the road, they may try to bring onlookers into their ranks. The marching collective may be changed in its constitution by newcomers from the watching procession, who have thus assumed a new collective identity. The police and army in urban reportage also act as antagonistic collectives, though sympathetic individuals among them may be driven to tears by the rhetoric of the marchers. Marginal groups such as foreigners shouting slogans with heavy accents or reporters holding cameras and notebooks are the bit players of the urban drama, and they highlight the functional character of collective identity, each collective being defined by the role it plays in the unfolding of events.

The City as a Stage for Historic Confrontation
The reportage of the December Ninth movement of 1935 consolidates the tropes of brutal victimization with those of the emergence of collective power, creating a more stylized dramatization of the struggle over the space of the city. The students of Beijing are portrayed more explicitly than before as the heroes and martyrs of the nationalistic cause of resistance.[22]

The focus of the movement—the demonstration of December 9—was a student march of about two thousand to the Xinhua Gate to deliver a letter of protest to Gen. He Yingqin, criticizing the He-Umetsu agreement (which established a Japanese-backed puppet government for all of North China), and then to the legation quarter headquarters of the East Hebei Autonomy Council to confront Yin Rugeng the chairman of the puppet council. Another such march, this time reportedly almost eight thousand strong, occurred on December 16, and sympathetic demonstrations were organized with varying degrees of success in other large cities throughout the country. In short, like May Fourth and May Thirtieth, December Ninth was a student-led movement protesting Chinese acquiescence to the Japanese invasion of China and the first such demonstration to occur in Beijing for three years (Israel and Klein, *Rebels and Bureaucrats*, 87–88). The similarity of the situation to that of May 1919 added to the passion and symbolic significance of this movement. Most of the reportage on these events appeared in January 1936 issue of Zou Taofen's magazine *Dazhong Shenghuo* (Mass Life), while two pieces by Chen Huangmei describing the response in Shanghai appeared in the January 20 issue of *Haiyan* (Petrel).[23]

The spatial configurations of Beijing (and other places involved) take on an explicitly strategic importance in these texts, as apparently well-informed security forces manage to control the demonstration through their control over gates and narrow passages. Moreover, sites of confrontation such as the Xidan Arch and the Xinhua and Xuanwu Gates are sanctified by the rituals of heroic speeches, vocal confrontations with officials, and the shedding of student blood.

Blood, as in the May Thirtieth movement texts, is a galvanizing, electrifying image through which the reader can associate his or her own body with the unfolding of history and the reawakening of national consciousness. The December Ninth reports combine images of actual bloodshed with a rhetoric of powerful, destructive, natural phenomena such as volcanoes, earthquakes, and tidal waves as images of the potency of the awakened Chinese masses. Insofar as the collective subject can identify with volcanic magma and the waters of the Yellow River as readily as with blood and tears, the distance between the feeling body as a trope and the physical landscape of the Chinese nation is closing.[24]

Interestingly, the impetus for the December Ninth demonstrations may in large part have been the "false" demonstration said to have been staged by Japanese-backed capitulationists in the beginning of December: "Xinhua Gate—in the past, it was the main gate to Zhongnanhai in the imperial palace; now it's the gate to the Juren Tang.[25] Several days ago, a group of hired delegates of the puppet 'North China People's Autonomy Association' came here to petition 'Commissioner He,' demanding 'North Chinese autonomy,' and the police politely did exactly as they said. Today the Xinhua Gate is closed; many troops are stationed in the parapets, and several trucks mounted with automatic rifles are lined up outside, while beyond the gate there are bayonet tips as far as the eye can see."[26]

The scene is thus set in the anonymous "The Furious Volcano Erupts" for the confrontation at Xinhua Gate, which is one of the climaxes of the December Ninth movement as it is constructed in these texts. Such climactic confrontations are the primary organizational units of the narratives of urban struggle; they are opportunities for the writer to dramatize nationalism and patriotism in the form of collective theatrical speeches and gestures as well as violent conflict and the victimization of the innocent and unarmed.

The demonstrators finally deliver the petition to a committee delegate who appears before them after hours of waiting at the gate, upon which one of the student organizers declares the petitioning process over and calls upon all the participants to begin their demonstration. This elicits a string of extravagant metaphors from the narrator: "This was a peal of spring thunder sweeping over the oceans, throwing huge waves in all directions. Immediately, the sounds of slogans, shouting, cheering, singing, and the flapping of banners . . . joined together in an unprecedented symphony of national liberation, performed with great solemnity. . . . This torrent of thousands was like the Yellow River bursting through its banks, rushing and tumbling down onto Western Chang'an Avenue" (361).

In their lengthy march through Beijing, the procession is often detained by police, but the students lecture them about how they, too, are Chinese and the land about to be lost to the Japanese is their land as well, making many policemen shed tears like the police at the Cao house during the May Fourth demonstration. The situation becomes violent during the procession's confrontation with Song Zheyuan's Twenty-ninth

Army near the latter's headquarters at Xidan.[27] Soldiers and police nearly defeat the demonstrators not only because they are armed but because they are in control of the space. Significantly, the first to fall victim are women.

> As the procession was nearing them, suddenly a group of soldiers rushed over to surround them in an attack formation. A woman carrying a large banner was injured and fell, as did many others; people trampled them as they fled. Police who had been hiding in alleyways poured out into the street with clubs and whips in their hands, beating and arresting everyone they ran into; the procession scattered and fled in all directions. Some rushed into shops, but the police followed them right in; others escaped into alleys but were quickly ferreted out by the police. Quite a few were being led away with their hands behind their backs by plainclothes police, although they were wounded and bleeding, and quite a few were being restrained by two or three officers, still shouting slogans as they were being taken away. Empty-handed students were hardly a match for armed soldiers, and many people fell with wounds, their fresh blood spattered on the snowy ground.
>
> Blood—blood is the seed of vengeance, planted in the fields of people's hearts. (363)

This final, aphoristic reflection on blood is one of many that punctuate this text, becoming a means of artistic structuring; another way in which the imagery of blood is advanced in the December Ninth texts is through the strange and arresting spectacle of blood in snow and ice.

The ensuing passages resemble some of the most disturbing battlefield reportage of later years, dramatizing the retreat of a large part of the group in fear and the determination of the remaining men and women, "almost all of whom were scarred by now," to reorganize, helping the seriously injured to hospitals. As they continued on to later, even more cruel stages of the demonstration, "they were like the losers of a cockfight, short a few feathers but still strutting with pride, crowing heroically" (363). This spectacle attracted the participation not only of onlookers on the street but of many of the students who had given up and begun to return home.

With the support of many newcomers from several schools, the reconstituted procession made its way to the legation quarter to protest the Hebei-Chahar Political Council (the puppet administration of the North China Autonomous Region, whose chairman was Yin Rugeng). In all of this the special significance of violence in a collective context is emphasized in two aspects: the images of blood shed by members of the group evokes not only fear but indignation; furthermore, this indignation, which belongs properly to the collective (fear and self-preservation belonging to the individual), actually reinforces the physical unity among those who remain in the group.

This is not a claim that those who identify with the collective are somehow more heroic than those who do not; rather it is a statement about the nature of collectivity itself, its relative independence from the survival interests of any particular individual but also its vulnerability to fragmentation and division. The power of the collective is imagined in the most extravagant terms under conditions of unity, often dramatized as the physical joining of bodies: "The students marched shoulder to shoulder, arm in arm, as intimate as brothers and sisters, unified like a giant to use the strength of one heart in a mass of ten thousand to resist the turbulent storm they faced" (365). But when the firepower of the oppressor is sufficient to scatter the marching collective the group is atomized into individuals and its unifying consciousness ceases to exist.

As they pass Beiping University (Beida), several students rush in to seek more support ("because, though many were participating, there was no central student mobilization"); in their cries across the campus, they call upon Beida students to "rekindle the May Fourth spirit" (364). In fact, a whole section of the narrative is devoted to the movement's "bringing Beida's glorious May Fourth spirit back to life," the effect of these calls on the campus being likened to a match being thrown onto a mountainside and starting a wildfire. By the time the procession reaches the third gate there is a group of students awaiting them inside: "One student was holding up a bamboo pole in which was clasped the cardboard cover of a large hatbox with the characters for 'Beida' painted in black. This was the school banner the group had improvised in their haste, and the Beida students gathered together to advance beneath this flag."

Later, the procession advances along East Chang'an Avenue, making its way to the International Relations Building, where the Hebei-Chahar

Political Council was headquartered. Here they encounter a crack detachment of military police from the Twenty-ninth Army, blocking their way with several fire trucks arrayed in the intersection before them. The police have flooded the street in front of the blockade and created a thick sheet of ice, while the sidewalks on both sides are crowded with police. Hoses are attached to fire hydrants, swords have been drawn, and the policemen are grasping at their clubs. Here, again, we have the elaborate construction of a scene of critical confrontation, this time one of pure violence rather than a show of force and a dramatic verbal exchange.

While the leaders of the procession are trying to negotiate with the police, the fire hoses are opened on the marching students; at the same time, policemen rush in from both sides. There follows a litany of the impressions left by the scene.

By this time the procession had fallen apart and started to retreat, many falling to the ground, many trampling over them. But at the same time countless others ran straight into the spraying, cold water and blows of clubs to fight with the police. The grappling of hand on hand, the impact of rifle butts on flesh, the tumbling of banners and white-brimmed police caps, the police chasing the crowd, the chaos of the violent clash, the indignation of the groups near and far, the shrill cries of the women students, the frightened screams of the children, the enraged cursing of citizens, the shouts of youths, the splattering sound of rushing water, the running of the water pump, the attack yell of the police . . . all of these sounds composed a solemn and tragic symphony of the Chinese nation performed on this historic avenue of the ancient city of culture.

A woman's arm was broken by a blow from a rifle; she fell with a cry to the ground. Several students ran over to help her, but the police kept coming and beating them. Fortunately an old man hollered "Can't you see she's down? What are you beating her for?" and the police finally stopped, running over to another crowd of students. The students at last helped her up and rushed her amid the confusion into the safety of an alleyway.

One student slipped and fell, hitting his head on a telephone pole. Blood was flowing, but the police were still beating his rear with a rod.

Another student was running at top speed, carrying a torn banner with two plainclothes policemen close behind; he frantically stormed into Ligu yanghang, a foreign company, but was pushed out and fell down three flights of stairs. The agents rushed forward and snatched away his flag, forcefully dragging him away. (366)

Many foreigners are taking pictures and filming from the windows of the tall buildings on either side of the street, while a Japanese spectator appears to be enjoying the scene: "There was a short man wearing a Western suit, carrying a small camera; just when the police were about to turn the hose on him, he bellowed '*Baka yarō!*' [Idiot!] and the police immediately turned the hose away. Some more people rushed over, talking to him and flashing their teeth in broad smiles. He took a few pictures and walked away, satisfied. Several agents ran up to him with both hands full of banners of all different colors, smiling and nodding to the short one with the satisfaction of victory" (367).

The scene of the aftermath of this most dramatic confrontation after the students had retreated and the police had left is followed again with an aphorism on blood: "At dusk, the avenue quieted, the street covered with ruined banners, shreds of clothing, lost shoes, flattened skullcaps . . . [while] piles of paper shreds flew in a dance with the bone-chilling evening wind. The water that had been spouted onto the street had already frozen into a river of ice, and upon that ice river were spattered stains of fresh blood. . . . Blood—blood is the sprouting of resistance to Japan, growing on the terrain of our ancestral land" (367).

The Penetration of the Campus
In Wang Rujuan's "The Hot Blood Converges in Torrents," this close association of nationalist fervor and blood running in the streets is reinstated in the general imagery of rebirth characteristic of the December Ninth movement.[28] The text is framed as a letter from the author, a Northeastern University student, to Zou Taofen, the editor of *Dazhong shenghuo*, reporting specifically on the activities of the university contingent. The first few pages are polemical, figuring the events only on the most abstract level, but then Wang focuses on the specific activities of students in early December of 1935. The text as a whole thus bears a striking structural resemblance to the "Great Citizens' Movement" nar-

rative of the May Fourth demonstrations. The beginning section concludes with the assurance that the students of Beiping, though faced with formidable obstacles and lack of moral support from their May Fourth generation instructors, have not lost the "indignation in their hearts and the fervor to save the country, . . . they are so furious they are shouting at the top of their lungs and leaping into the air, in such agony that they shed tears of pain! Their hearts have ignited like raging fires! All are certain that one day this great volcano will erupt" (388).

On the morning of December 9, Xizhi Gate was closed, preventing the Yanjing-Qinghua contingent from entering the city walls. The well-informed police were thus controlling the situation by sealing off points of entry and exit and thus closely circumscribing the movements of the students. The narrative turns to the Northeastern University contingent, which was already within the city making their way to the Xinhua Gate.

Here the author observes that all of the women students were in the marching ranks: each rank was made up of four students holding hands, and the women were all in the inner two files. This observation is interesting in that it is the implied physical vulnerability of women that makes their very presence in the demonstration an act of courage, while it is the same vulnerability that supposedly confines them to the inner files, with the men on the outside protecting them. This image of women in reportage demonstrates a tendency common in modern Chinese narrative (both fiction and nonfiction) to position women in the active space of revolution and yet exploit traditional gender associations to signify and dramatize ostensibly genderless or "masculine" qualities and themes.

After narrating a confrontation with security forces in much the same way as the text above, Wang skips past the ensuing events of the ninth "because they have already been reported several times" (perhaps in the newspapers), turning instead to developments at Northeastern University over the next several days, which involve more intimate collective confrontations. The students are holding another general meeting in the school auditorium on the tenth to evaluate the movement and decide on further action when they are interrupted by the school's head administrator ("the general secretary") and a struggle, both verbal and physical, ensues.

Not long after the beginning of the meeting, as the chairman was making his report, the general secretary *stormed over to the auditorium in a fury* with the dean and some security guards. The lookouts at the doors tried to hold him back and talk with him, but *he kicked them aside.* The chairman interrupted his report and said to the general secretary: "We are holding a meeting; if the general secretary has something to say, I have to consult with the students."

"What is this 'we are holding a meeting'?! Holding what meeting?" the general secretary said as he pulled the chairman from the stage; but the chairman struggled back to his position and stood up next to the general secretary and in a voice choked with tears said: "General secretary! Surely you have not forgotten your old motto of 'regain the lost territory'? The Northeast has been lost for four years now, and now all of North China is about to be lost as well. How can we go on settling for momentary peace!? All of the students of Beiping have risen up to save the country, and we Dongda students are all northeasterners who've lost our provinces and our homes; if we don't act, how can we face others . . . are we still human? Our actions honor Dongda, honor the Northeast, and are to your credit as well. You, too, are a homeless northeasterner, and there is no shame in that!" The chairman then asked the assembly, "shall we have the general secretary speak?" but *the students all cried out in unison* "we don't want to listen! Down with the traitor!"

"Who said that? Seize them, seize them!" the general secretary ordered the dean. The dean immediately made for the back of the auditorium to capture students, but the pickets at the doors persuaded him to stop. The students were bursting with grief and indignation; some of them cried out in tears, "Don't forget we are a conquered people!" and "The general secretary is a northeasterner too!" (392–93)

The general secretary experiences two levels of confrontation: direct confrontation with the chairman of the student organization, characterized by the use of logic and rhetoric, and the general confrontation with the student "body," mediated at times with shoving and kicking and negotiated on a verbal level through threats and ultimatums. The student chairman's appeal to the general secretary's sense of shame

has some effect, but seeing that the students were not prepared to con-
cede some of their demands, he left, warning them not to "be manipulated by a minority." The general secretary is thus portrayed as an anti-
Communist Japanese puppet who blames the whole movement on the
Party's machinations. The writer, while not saying anything about the
specific politics, takes pains to insist that it is a broad-based nationalist
movement.[29]

We see portrayed here a real sense of awkwardness as the Communist Party tries to appropriate and channel general nationalist feelings:
to anti-Communists, this is exploiting the innocent for political gain,
but to the Communists, as well as the students they organize, it is not
simply a political strategy (though it is that as well) but a solemn, patriotic duty. The recuperation of this and similar texts in the production
of the reportage canon in the 1980s is again an attempt to credit the
Communist Party for all the dramatically nationalist and anti-imperialist
acts of modern Chinese history. This is important because it contributes to the effort to appropriate and channel the emotional subjectivity
of nationalism (the exclusive source of tears in this text; class struggle
and revolution play no role whatsoever). If reportage were to concentrate solely on class struggle and the plight of the proletariat, it would
forfeit the powerful emotional appeal of such nationalist narratives.

That day the students boycott class, demanding the release of the
students who had been arrested the day before. The following morning
before dawn the campus is occupied by military police, and what follows is an unprecedented invasion of private space that, more than ever,
foregrounds the political significance of spatial mobility.

It must have been about five in the morning; as soon as the lights
went on in the dormitory, paddy wagons had pulled up to the school
gates, and more than two hundred armed police, led by the campus
sentries, headed straight for the dormitories, where they occupied the
entrances, not allowing any students to enter or exit. Then the sentries searched every bed according to a name list; most of the beds
were empty, so they ransacked all their suitcases and boxes, throwing
books and things all over the place. Although the student organizers
were ready for them and were not captured, there were nevertheless
six students incarcerated. The name list for this raid was written on

Northeastern University's official stationery, with over thirty names on it; the police were assisted by the campus sentries, and the workers and staff of the entire university had been mobilized to search the grounds for students trying to hide. It was obvious who was behind all this. (394)

Unlike the anonymous text ("The Furious Volcano Erupts") examined above, which remains in the city and dramatizes the violence in the streets, Wang's narrative moves inward to the campus dormitories, showing how students who had more or less complete freedom of movement a week before had, because of the demonstration, lost mobility by degrees to a point at which they were being actively searched for in their own beds.

From here the narrative illustrates the increasing militarization of the campus situation; the campus is put under "emergency martial law" the next day, and students are restricted in their movements to their dormitories, classroom buildings, and the library. Student organizers who had escaped the dragnet are forced to operate outside the campus; then comes an order that students who boycotted class for another day would be demoted to "self-supporting auditors" and expelled if they continue to boycott.

At this point, Wang writes, the students hold yet another meeting, resolving to demonstrate in front of the administration building, demanding that arrested students be released, that the police be expelled from the campus, that the student organizers at large not be arrested, and that the school not further hinder patriotic student activities; if the demands are not met, the students will personally drive the police off the campus and occupy the school themselves. Almost surprisingly, the general secretary agrees to their demands (perhaps, as the author suggests, because he felt he was losing control of his low-paid military police force, which was made up entirely of northeasterners who were beginning to be influenced by the students' speeches). The text thus ends on a victorious note, Northeastern University having won "the freedom to save the country" (jiuguo ziyou).

In this reportage of urban confrontation, the emotions of workers and students who take part in demonstrations are given much more attention than those of other collectives. This is because of the positioning of the narrator; just like the spectator in the street, the narrator is to choose which collective identity to assume and more often than not will choose that of the marchers. The emotions that run through this collective body are generally negative: fury, indignation, hatred. The protest march as a body can only take joy in two things: the failure of the police to stop them and the spread of their influence within the crowd of spectators, manifested in the chanting of slogans, with the students or part of the crowd joining them in the march. Everything else is an obstacle that must be overcome with cold determination. Protest marches are often organized in response to the deaths of other protesters or strikers, and so images of blood and violence are common in these texts. The more blood spilled on the streets, the more furiously the protesting body's blood boils in its members' veins.

There is an interesting exception to this narratorial positioning as a member of the protesting body in Lu Fen's (Shi Tuo's) "Qingyuan zhengpian" (Main Account of a Petition Demonstration) and "Qingyuan waipian" (Apocryphal Account of a Petition Demonstration).[30] Rather than identifying himself with the protesting students, the narrator becomes part of the crowd of spectators, looking at the protest with apathy and some disdain.

The author's use of irony in these texts makes it at times difficult to see that he actually advocates resisting Japan, at least until the end of "Main Account." In a postscript to "Apocryphal Account," the author claims that the former work is "a true record of what actually happened and thus doesn't count as fiction," while the "Main Account" expresses the "true soul of the demonstrating students."[31] "Apocryphal Account" provides us with a panorama of the Beijing streets as an anti-Japanese demonstration is moving through them, with vividly caricatured shopowners, urchins, and hoodlums arguing with each other, whiling away the day, and making fun of the marchers. Slogans such as "Down with Imperialism," which in the narration of public demonstrations are normally given the aura of sacred mantras that shake the heavens, become just so much annoying background noise in another average day in the life of Beijing, and even the butt of ridicule as urchins mock the marching students and their sloganeering and a puzzled shop-keeper (unconsciously?) puns on *imperialism*, transforming it into *imperial pig-concubine*.[32]

In the "Main Account," the tone is more serious but still bitterly ironic, as the narrator relates the making of a demonstration, from the secret meetings of the student organizers to their handling of the crowd of students at the campus rally and the emergence of the crowd itself as the vanguard of the movement. The moment at which the crowd thus emerges as agent and not the passive extras in a cast of thousands is the same moment at which the reader comes to realize what has been wrong with the demonstration from the start and why the narrator is so clearly cynical: the organizers are a clique of self-important, depraved youths sponsored by the Nationalist Party (Guomindang). After one of the origi-nal organizers (referred to throughout as the "Little Cossack") loudly criticizes the meager turnout of women for the protest, he is wrestled to the ground.

> The Little Cossack had been thrown down. He quickly leapt back to his feet but couldn't escape a hand from behind, which grabbed his hair, his hat flying into the air. The sound of the crowd's voices rained down a confusion of every imaginable humiliation on him.
>
> "—beat him to death, the shameless . . ."
>
> "—spy! Shameless bastard, Nationalist (*guojia zhuyipai*) running dog . . ."[33]
>
> "—Beat him, beat him, beat him! Throw him in the urine trough!" . . .
>
> He [described up to now as a foppish dandy] had been trans-formed into a common hooligan; he was just like a wounded jackal, howling angrily from his ragged throat. Amid the crowd, he leapt and bumped his way through the jubilant excitement; finally, he ran away in defeat, utterly dejected.
>
> In this anarchic scene, the raised judge's stand for athletic com-petitions found new uses in the eyes of the clever.
>
> Someone climbed upon the high perch amid the waves of wild shouting, and stood upon it like a great man ascending the stage to

give a speech. The difference was that when great men speak, they always pause for a moment after they ascend the podium, looking around them once before they play at their great, uncommon diction. This is perhaps one way of conquering the little people—a gesture to frighten the audience into awe. The one who climbed up did the sweeping glance, but he began talking without pausing first. Of course, he had his reasons; he had to act on the spur of the moment. But in the end he achieved the opposite of what he was trying to do. The boiling blood of the crowd was hardly sympathetic to his efforts. Before he got to open his mouth, the sea of waving heads fired at him like bullets. . . .

"—I know who you are, Fang Gang! You have the gall to show your face, you dog shit, you betrayed your classmates!"

"—Down with the Nationalists! Down with the shameless terror squads!"

"—Down with XX Party's lackeys . . ."

The pretty face on the observation seat was thus immediately pushed off.

In fact, all of the responsible "directors" were scattered and overthrown; they were left with nowhere to turn and no way out, running around and bumping into each other. It may have been early winter, but by now their backs were soaked with sweat. But of course they always have their clever ways. (146–47)

Nevertheless, the procession gets under way and marches off campus, but soon it is confronted with another voice.

Unexpectedly, there was an assault on the glory of the demonstration: several people, people who weren't all that remarkable looking, leapt up from one side of the procession, waving clenched fists and jumping all over, yelling at the top of their lungs,

"—Hey! Students! We're all clearheaded people, everybody knows that what we're out to do is protect the freedom of the Chinese nation. Our vast, all-seeing eyes are not about to be covered up with narrow, impotent patriotism!"

"—Students! Think about it! Imperialist running dogs, and the little clowns fed by imperialism who betray the Chinese people, are they going to be able to handle the difficulties before us the same as we are? Of course not! Their background, their past activities, are proof that tells us it's just a foolish game they're playing . . ."

"— Students! No matter what, we must be clear about our duty; we must not, under any circumstances, surrender to capitalism!"

"— The demonstration is — "

Before he could finish, a guy like a rabid dog with a "director" ribbon across his chest cried out:

"Beat him, beat him! Down with the red hoodlum . . ."

And again there was a commotion; the procession began to fragment again toward the other side. Part of the people responded, but the rest just quietly held their ground. (148)

The procession is then brought back into unity by one of the original organizers and manages to move on under slogans of ethnic unity like "General —— will accept our petition" and "he won't betray us because he is Chinese, like us."

Thus, this text illustrates the sensitivity of the imagined crowd to the conditions under which it will march in unity: clearly some words and actions split the crowd, while others bring it together. This is the mass at its most heterogeneous: ideologically somewhere between communism and fascism, led by students, but, unlike the image of the December Ninth demonstrations, not saturated with the collective will of the students as a social force. That the commonsensical and at the same time ethno-nationalistic ("General —— will listen to us, after all, he's Chinese, too!") will to proceed over and above political differences is embodied in the multivocal, almost reluctant unity of the mass.

This basically unified but discursively divided heterogeneous crowd is elaborated further in other texts. In Ding Ling's "Duo shi zhi qiu" (An Eventful Autumn),[34] for example, the action does not follow any single group but jumps all over the city of Shanghai over a period of time, focusing on many different groups. Invariably, however, the stage remains the streets.

Ding Ling's reportage from the early 1930s, of which "An Eventful Autumn" is a noteworthy example, illuminates what for many commentators seems to be an inexplicable transformation in the famous writer's career.[35] Inattention to reportage as a form of literary creation has led to the impression of a hiatus of several years throughout the 1930s in

Ding Ling's creative output, followed by her reappearance as an indoctrinated if outspoken participant in Yan'an cultural discourse during the war years.[36] In fact, Ding Ling was an active member of the League of Left-Wing Writers, making significant contributions to its literary initiatives, and then went on to organize the Northwest War Zone Service Corps (a traveling theatrical propaganda troupe) before entering Yan'an's inner cultural circle. Thus, her engagement in reportage practice and collective cultural mobilization forms a little-discussed bridge between the Shanghai writer who explored the ennui and sexual frustration of the independent urban educated woman and the increasingly loyal member of the Maoist cultural coterie.

"An Eventful Autumn" illustrates the growing instability of Shanghai after the Mukden Incident of September 18, 1931, with student demonstrations, incidents with police, the city government's attempts to harness and diffuse the tension by holding mass rallies, failing, and finally instituting a "volunteer army training program" to placate the demand for military action without actually deploying troops. The text is theater on a grand scale, like an "epic" film. Ding Ling makes effective use of posthumanist techniques, often advancing the narrative with the anonymous and broken (self-interrupting) commentary of onlookers and sympathetically portraying the use of verbal abuse and violence in dealing with official figures perceived as the "running dogs" of imperialism. Students, workers, the anonymous crowd, police officers, and government officials are all represented as collectives but in sensuous, vivid, and concrete detail, sweating, fuming, shouting, dying. Marston Anderson's comment that narratives of the crowd "do not provide a single perspective through which to focalize the reader's view of the crowd" (185) is especially appropriate here, as it is made in reference to Ding Ling's short story of the previous year, "Shui" (Water).

The text begins, as do many works of urban reportage, with a lavish, impressionistic picture of the bustling Shanghai streets. The arrival of news of the Mukden Incident is dramatized by the appearance of newspaper boys hawking the extra edition on the streets. The narrator dwells on how through the paper the news travels into the hearts and bodies of the masses of people on the city streets, reemerging as debate as contending, anonymous voices react to and interpret the news, which finally spreads into the countryside via telegraph and telephone. This is only the first example of how Ding Ling manages to "flesh out" abstract or intangible processes and connect them directly to the thoughts and feelings of onlookers and participants. In contrast to Lu Fen's ironic text, Ding Ling takes pains to vividly realize everything that is positive about the movement to resist Japan, to incorporate the collective heart of the nation in the various, multivocal groups that make up a city. The sum total of the clamor and commentary of these groups, in turn, is a critique of and physical resistance to the Nationalist government's desperate and deceptive attempts to harness or squelch the unruly upsurge of protest.

The students are still depicted as the indisputable vanguard of national salvation, with the masses explicitly referred to as "ignorant lambs" in parts 2 and 4. Part 2 illustrates the subjectivity of student activists and their complex relationship with the common people:

They forgot the pain in their feet and legs, forgot how dry their throats were; beneath the autumn sun, they walked some distance, then walked farther. They forgot to eat lunch—something else filled their bellies. Here time became more meaningful. At times like this, people feel especially fulfilled, affirming the word *survival*. Looking down upon those simple faces, faces covered with tears of fury, they felt a kind of truly inexpressible, solemn feeling. They felt as if they'd wronged the people in the crowd because they themselves were literate, educated, enjoying all kinds of rights and privileges; for so long, they had neglected these people, and this had reinforced their own well-being [at the expense of the others]. They were used to looking down upon them, yet they were so simple and pure, so full of the sympathy of humanity. (90)

Ding Ling's crowd, made up of "unschooled laborers, poor people, and children," is receptive to the speech makers, shedding tears, eager to hear more, relating their message to their own experiences (worker speech is almost invariably tagged with obscenity in this and many other texts): "Fuck their mothers! I can believe those Japs are that vicious; isn't our factory run by a Jap?" The crowd's thirst for knowledge is expressed in its startling questions hurled at the speakers: "What's a colony? What is China?"

Part 4 dramatizes the attempt of the student demonstration to go to Nanjing (then the capital) by train as a street scene around the railroad station.[37] The railroad company, afraid of reprisals, does not help the students. The scene and action are rendered in a montage of spectators' voices, often replacing the narrator.

"Hey, those kids are something! They couldn't go to Nanjing, so they just went and beat up the stationmaster . . ."
"The way it looks, they'll have to let us fight Japan sooner or later. Even if those students beat up a stationmaster or a general, they're doing it for the good of the country, after all."
"All they have to do is mobilize and there's nothing to fear from Japan—China has millions of troops! Hmph, recruiting and buying horses year after year . . ."
. . .
The northern railroad station became crowded again.
"Are you still going to Nanjing? . . ."
"They're back, the petitioners are back . . ."
"By the looks of it, they didn't make it after all. . . ."
"Ha ha, ineffectual intellectuals! . . ."
"Hmph, they did beat up Wang Zhengting. . . ."
"And got a scolding from headquarters, . . ."
"As soon as they got to Nanjing they sent troops to keep an eye on them, . . ." (103)

These spectators are not purely passive commentators; their interest in what the students are doing has to do with shared feelings of disrespect for government authorities and fear and hatred of Japan. Their approval of the students beating up the stationmaster is typical of a crowd as depicted in these works (particularly of the labor voice in the crowd), but again it is tempered with a higher justification ("it is for the country, after all"), much like the tears of the police in the texts treated above.

In the absence of student leadership, and confronted with a *government-organized* public rally, the crowd talks back and acts out its frustration. In part 3, which dramatizes the disintegration and overthrow of a government-organized anti-Japanese rally, the students are absent from the vanguard, leaving the crowd, dominated by worker voices, to move in and fill the space. The narrator as the perceptual center of the scene is located within the crowd, in which it is much easier to hear the heckling voices around her than the speeches being given by public officials "in their pretty white suits." As a voice, the narrator is vastly outnumbered by the voices of the crowd.

What begins as cursing and heckling at the government speaker's empty talk rapidly becomes threats impossible for the speaker to ignore. He retreats from the podium. Others on the dais try to calm the crowd, but it is precisely the word *calm* that is making them angry; desperate officials plead with the crowd, saying that there are foreigners watching and not to make fools of everyone. Finally, the official speakers climb down from the dais and the rally is taken over by the crowd; there is a series of speeches of the sort students were giving in part 2 about Japanese brutality in the Northeast, how the streets of Changchun were "rivers of blood" rushing around "mountains of bodies," and so on. The emotional intensity and graphic nature of the rhetoric indicates the sincerity and truthfulness of speakers who belong to the crowd.

The narrator's relationship with this emerging crowd constitutes a major avenue of exploration of collective subjectivity in reportage, and this relationship is mediated more often than not through a concretiza- tion of national consciousness, not the abstract concept of nationhood but an ethnically defined nationality involving a more visceral conscious- ness of belonging than mere membership. The oft-repeated slogan "We Are All Chinese" expresses a sometimes desperate faith in the unity of the nation against the threat of foreign invasion, despite violent division within.

Though not explicitly called "reportage" at the time, most of the works discussed in this chapter possess all of the attributes character- istic of reportage literature discussed in the introductory chapter. The appearance of these works indicates the consolidation of the indige- nous strands that informed reportage in China; reading them as a group leads to the conviction that even without the direct influence of foreign models something like reportage was bound to emerge as a distinctive form in China at this time. Failure to recognize this has led to the prevail- ing view in Western scholarship that reportage is in the final analysis a foreign genre imported into China.[38] Such a view cannot help but under- estimate the significance of reportage as a form of cultural practice in modern China.

As the above examples indicate, the role of public demonstrations and student activism in the early development of reportage literature cannot be overestimated. The "Great Citizens Movement in Beijing This Week" is one of the earliest commonly recognized precursors of reportage, and the first wave of impressionistic documentary narrative came in the wake of the May Thirtieth (1925) demonstrations, which also involved student organization, participation, and sacrifice. Similarly, throughout the 1930s writers of reportage focused closely on the activities and demonstrations of students: "From the 'Great Petition of Northern and Southern Students in the Capital,' in response to the January 28 incident, the painful struggles of young students continued to leave their record as spotted bloodstains on the reportage tradition."[39]

The emphasis placed upon documenting demonstrations with eyewitness accounts can be linked to the general tendency to conceive of modern Chinese history in terms of significant dates: May 4, May 30, September 18, January 28 and July 7,[40] to name only a few of the major ones, are flashpoints of modern Chinese history not only because of a Chinese uprising or a Japanese attack that occurred on the date in question but because these incidents were perceived as the explosion of a volatile *combination* of historical themes, such as national humiliation, cultural pride/patriotism, and imperialist and capitalist exploitation of Chinese labor, that were constantly active, especially in the imaginations of intellectuals. In short, it is the symbolic richness of such events that make them memorable.

Such incidents would often become newsworthy precisely because of immediate public outcry in the form of a demonstration. Activists would "read" the event (e.g., the killing of Gu Zhenghong that sparked the May 30 Movement in 1925) and interpret it in the larger contexts of imperialism and national shame. Through their interpretations and the demonstrations inspired and organized by these activists (which then becomes a historical event in its own right and takes on new meanings), the event is sanctified and packed so densely with meaning that the mere mention of the date can evoke strong emotional reactions and vivid memories as well as accounts of the events involved and their historical significance.

Reportage as a writing practice emerges precisely from this way of perceiving events. Many reportage writers took an active part in this process of making history, at least up to the end of the 1930s, both by participating in demonstrations and by writing articles that could influence readers to demonstrate themselves. The efficacy of such making is not confined to discrete events; the more this process is repeated, the more the tradition of focalizing history by stressing certain dates reinforces itself. This becomes evident in the use of an already significant date as the occasion for a demonstration (May 4 has repeatedly served this function throughout the century) or the recalling of a whole string of dates of "national humiliation" as rallying cries.[41]

This periodizing and shaping of history by privileging certain events is one aspect of the view of modern Chinese history that underlies and informs reportage creation throughout the decades of its formation and development. The dates themselves become an essential part of the symbolic language through which the writer places his or her own text in the shared narrative of modern Chinese history. Reportage texts in turn derive their value for readers, and especially for anthologists, from their contribution to this shared narrative.[42]

The theatrical analogy I suggested early in this chapter is not meant to trivialize the actual demonstrations or the authors who recorded them as "mere theatrics" but is intended to draw attention to the sacred and ritual implications of this kind of perceiving and writing. As a modern tradition (without entering into the older tradition of peasant uprisings here) the political demonstration in China was in a sense made sacred by the May Fourth demonstrations. As the reportage of later demonstrations shows, the invocation of the "May Fourth spirit" is an integral part of the ritual. Political demonstrations in which participants are killed are quickly followed by demonstrations of mourning, which are in some cases revived in anniversaries.[43]

What is the basis of such a ritual? What is the authority to which demonstrators appeal in resistance to regimes they reject? I suggest that it is the idea of the Chinese nation itself that is sacralized and transcends the authority of any particular government. The nation is in this sense constructed not as a concept of territorial sovereignty but as the living collective spirit of the "Chinese people" (Zhonghua minzu).[44] Those who are martyred are martyrs to the cause of the Chinese nation; they gave their lives to the Chinese people. Violent suppression by the authorities is equivalent to violent suppression of the Chinese people as such and thus constitutes treason, or more accurately *sacrilege*. It is armed with this sense of sacred mission for the nation as against the government that students especially, but also workers and others, go out and demonstrate, knowing that they may be killed or seriously injured.

The urban social space under discussion involves the dramatization of violent struggle among collective actors in the name of saving the nation from imminent peril; "the nation" exists on a simultaneously visceral and sacred level, with an authority separable from and superior to any government. Specifically, the public demonstration is figured as a scene of spectacular violence with specific subjective effects on the onlooker. The victims of violent government suppression are identified with the imperiled nation on both the figurative and literal levels (this coincidence of the figurative and literal is peculiar to reportage). The spatial aspect of the "chronotope" is realized not only in the theatrical staging of propagandizing, marching in the streets, and suppression of such demonstrations but in the struggle for control over urban space.

The spectacle of bloodshed engenders rich subjective reactions: fear, outrage, even a kind of exhilaration in the writer, who invites the reader to participate in these reactions. This is typical of the general anticathartic aesthetic of reportage whereby one is agitated by the work of art rather than purged of emotion (how successful reportage was in this respect, however, is impossible to determine). Violence is not condemned but solemnly accepted as a responsibility, even a sacrament.

The victims of government and foreign suppression strike back, at times with ritual solemnity and tears in their eyes, at times with festive abandon. The process of striking back coincides with the emergence of the collective as both a physical body and a special kind of subjectivity. The collective emerges from the heterogeneous crowd and wields power through violence and willful unruliness. As has been said, all of the "actors" in the drama of urban struggle are collectives, but the writer positions himself or herself with one group, either a unified phalanx of demonstrators or among the heterogeneous crowd of onlookers.

As a physical body, the collective has the capability to pass in and out of existence at will. This is demonstrated when, at a prearranged signal, students scattered throughout the bustling crowds of Nanjing Road suddenly form into tight, marching ranks, shouting provocative slogans. Whether thus tightly bound, holding hands, or as a huge, amorphous mass of workers, as in "Robison Road" and Lu Dingyi's "May Thirtieth Anniversary," the unified collective is powerful and capable of substantial destruction. However, when security forces, also efficient and powerful collectives, are able to mount superior technologies of violence against the demonstrators the latter collective is forced to scatter, passing temporarily out of existence. Not being tied to the life of a single body, the crowd is nevertheless capable of resurrection and in fact becomes enraged and more powerful at the sight of bloodshed within its ranks (in contrast to Zhu Ziqing, who is consumed with his personal terror at the spectacle of slaughter).

Gender plays a suggestive role in this type of reportage. Marginalized in this public, national drama, women are nevertheless carefully situated in thematically sensitive positions (such as in the inner files of marching students). The activism or nonactivism of women, moreover, is often a matter of much more salience than that of men. In following chapters, the representation of gender will be similarly thematized by the increased yet often silent presence of women in central positions in the texts. As more of the later reportage is written by women, moreover, the dynamics of gender become more complex. Nevertheless, as I will show in later chapters, reenvisioning socialist culture requires careful examination of gender, precisely because it seems to have been willfully silenced or erased.

In the next chapter I will treat another kind of reportage of urban struggle, one that depicts labor conditions in the confined spaces of textile mills and mines. While violence occasionally erupts in physical confrontation between actors, it is more often manifested as the ongoing, systematic exploitation of workers in factories and mines managed and run both by Chinese and foreigners. Nationalist themes also surface here, but are not as salient and even at times seem to come in conflict with the effective elaboration of the labor situation. Nevertheless, industrial reportage is closely linked to the depiction of public demonstrations we have just examined, particularly through the dramatization of the invasion and control of space by those in political and economic power.

THREE

Labor Reportage and the Factoryscape

As was discussed in the introduction, the history of reportage in China begins properly with its adoption in 1930 by the League of Left-Wing Writers as a new form of literary expression that had achieved success in Germany, Japan, and other countries as part of the broader proletarian culture movement. Reportage was associated closely with the Worker Correspondents Movement (Gongren tongxun yundong), which was originally an initiative of the cultural wing of the German Communist Party intended to encourage workers to write of their experiences and expose inequitable factory conditions as one of the goals of literacy education and political indoctrination.[1]

Reportage gave professional writers and journalists an opportunity to participate in the Worker Correspondents Movement as educators and mobilizers but also by rendering their understanding of the experience of the industrial worker in literary form. One of the main goals of the League of Left-Wing Writers was to develop and engage in just such a movement in China. Some pieces by actual workers were published in league journals, but works on labor conditions by experienced writers and journalists dominated league publications throughout the early 1930s, further prompting a wide variety of writers to contribute to what eventually developed into a wave of labor reportage during the early

1930s. Thus, reportage emerged in China in the context of leftist literary mobilization, and creative writers' organized but voluntary immersion in the milieu of industrial labor provided them with rich new creative resources and the potential for developing a fuller consciousness of and identification with the struggles of common people.

Beginning with the Worker Correspondents Movement, investigative reporting on labor conditions helped writers develop techniques of expressing consciousness through the elaboration of the industrial environment (what I will call the "factoryscape") and narration of concrete vignettes within that environment. The process of revealing the factoryscape itself enters the text, and, as an expression of the writers' own attempt to penetrate the experience of the working class, becomes an integral part of the consciousness expressed.

BEHIND THE FACTORY WALLS

Accounts of labor conditions emerge from prisonlike spaces tightly circumscribed by gates, factory walls, long banks of machinery, and tiny living quarters, thematizing the organization and control of space in a more fundamental way than in the reportage of demonstrations. In the city, as we have seen, the gate becomes a test of one's mobility, and measures for limiting mobility can be read as intrusions on one's political and economic rights and even one's national sovereignty.

In the reportage of labor conditions, just as in the reportage of public demonstrations, the imagery of physiological response is the central device through which history is mediated and made concrete. Here, however, acts of violence are not conspicuous scenes of public struggle that appear in the newspapers, but day-to-day, institutionalized violence that most readers would rarely have thought about, much less experienced themselves. As in other forms of reportage, the narrator serves as the sensory and emotional medium through which this otherwise inaccessible experience of violence is made available to the reader.

One of the earliest texts to decry the cynical calculation of the value of human life in the system of industrial production is "Tangshan meikuang zangsong gongren da canju" (The Tragic Burial Alive of Workers at the Tangshan Coal Mine, 1920).[2] In this investigative report, two students visit the scene of a mine collapse two or three days after it occurs.

"The Tragic Burial Alive" does not actually explicate the system of labor extraction and exploitation, only the capitalist and imperialist roots of the tragedy manifested in the crass calculation of the value of human lives. The "bare facts" are disposed of in the first sentence: "At 9:00 A.M. on October 14, [1920,] there was a marsh gas explosion in the 'new vein' of 'sublevel 9' of Jiudu Alley at the Tangshan coal mine; the sound was deafening, and five or six hundred people were killed" (363). In fact, the explosion is not what "The Tragic Burial Alive" is about at all, although it is what brought the writers to the scene; the text is about the fact that the Belgian mining engineer hired by the Mining Bureau (which operated the coal mine) must have known of the danger of an explosion but sent the miners back to dig anyway.

This kind of disregard for the workers' welfare is emphasized through comparison and irony. When the writer attacks the rumor that the explosion was caused by workers smoking in the mines, he points out how strictly the workers are forbidden to bring matches and tobacco into the mine shafts, being physically searched each time they enter and punished if they are found to have any: "This is not out of concern for the lives of the workers but to protect the Mining Bureau's mules" (364). In terms of replacement cost, mules are more costly than human laborers, and as a result management is more concerned with the mules' welfare.

The text concludes with a disturbing image, which links the above with economic realities: "Someone said to me: 'When they took the unconscious workers out they were all smiling. When they were treated, some of those who were saved began to cry. It looked as if death were preferable to life for them; otherwise, why should they be smiling in death and crying in life?' Someone else said, 'In a way, that Belgian engineer . . . did those workers a favor sending those who lead a life of misery to the paradise of death" (365).

More specific accounts of how peasants are attracted into indentured and contract labor are given in later texts, such as Cang Jian's "Kuanggong shouji" (A Miner's Notebook, 1932) and Li Qiao's "Xi shi ruhe liancheng de" (How Tin Is Smelted, 1937), while others are concerned, again, with Shanghai textile mills.

"A Miner's Notebook," presented as the actual words of a coal miner, is representative of the Worker Correspondents Movement's initiative of bringing the voice of the proletariat into the world of culture. In it, a miner describes, with little of the melodrama of urban leftist writers, the circumstances under which he came to work in the mine, his economic relationships with his labor contractor and management, and specific instances of the mine's institutionalized cruelty to laborers. Like "The Tragic Burial Alive," this text also dwells on the cheapness of workers' lives, noting that the mine elevator is reserved for coal while the workers have to crawl and climb in and out of the mine. Fire and explosions, made to seem dramatic in the earlier text, are a frequent occurrence.

> Sometimes there's a fire in the shaft. Why? No one really knows, but every time there's a fire a lot of people burn to death. If people are killed in a fire, it's not a big deal to the mining company people. If a fire starts in the mine, for sure the first question they ask is:
> "How many of the animals died?" Only later do they ask: "Anybody hurt or killed?"
> This is because if one of the animals is killed the mine loses eighty or ninety yuan, but if it's a person they only have to come up with at most forty yuan in compensation.[3]

Part of the reason for the low value placed on human life is the plentiful supply of indentured labor. Most factories and mines described in these texts employ two kinds of worker. The first are legally hired workers, who are as a rule paid on a regular basis, allowed to organize to a certain extent, and in general treated as Chinese law of the time required. The other workers, who are the focus of industrial reportage and are represented as the majority, are called "indentured" or "contract" laborers (baoshen gong or baogong); they are portrayed as the property of the factory and have no rights whatsoever on its premises.

The key to the various forms of indenture is the contractor (baogong tou), an independent agent paid by factories to collect labor in his home village or county. The prospective worker either directly contracts with the agent or (as is more often the case) is presented by parents or relatives in exchange for a sum of money. Here the demand for female labor power coincides with the perception of unmarried daughters, especially in poor families, as primarily an economic burden; the ready cash available through indenture was often irresistible.

In "A Miner's Notebook," the narrator voluntarily contracts with the agent, not realizing that the latter would not pay him cash wages, only giving him poor-quality rice and grain. The company pays wages to the contractors and is not concerned with how the agents treat the workers: "We only have direct contact with management after we die" (135). Caught in this set of relations, the worker observes that "as our blood dries and our flesh withers, the contractor's belly gets fatter" (136).

More vivid images of the meager value placed on the worker's body appears in Li Qiao's "How Tin Is Smelted" as the narrator elaborates the consequences of illness in a Yunnan tin mine.[4]

> If you get sick and you happen to have some money, you can go out onto the street and seek the help of pharmacists, who hang shingles reading "This or That Hall" or "This or That House" (but in reality have no medical knowledge). If you don't have money, all you can do is go into the mountains and dig up some roots you know nothing about and eat them. Some actually saved their lives that way, but most have already gone blind from the dysentery. If you don't eat the right roots, then you're really in trouble! You won't die immediately, but as soon as you get really sick, the boss will have someone drag you outside the dormitory door: it's against the rules for people to die in the dormitories. Now, if you're sick and tossed outside the dormitory, even if you are lucky enough not to be eaten by dogs you will surely freeze to death in the high mountain winds. (350)

THE RHETORIC OF UNMASKING

Most labor reportage is concerned less with particular events and more with the unmasking of inhuman conditions in factories and unfair or even brutal treatment of workers, and this rhetoric assumes the concealed and insular nature of the factory environment. As a result of this strategy of exposition, the texts treated here make much more use of description than narration. Works of labor reportage are often divided into topical sections, collectively oriented toward the elaboration of a system, its spatial manifestations, and its physical and spiritual toll on workers rather than a course of events. However, such descriptive elaboration is almost always concretized by the insertion of miniature narratives within the topical structure.

The significance of the space- and system-oriented iteration of labor reportage lies in its implication that in the process of industrial production workers are treated as quantifiable commodities, their well-being and their very lives valued purely in terms of their labor power and the economic cost of its extraction. Thus, the image of industrial machinery appears in labor reportage not only as the distinctive feature of the environment in which workers live but as an analogue for their mode of existence. The industrial concern and the society in which human relations are increasingly influenced by industrial production are imagined as an extended machine; the actions of management and consumers are as "dehumanized" as the restricted movements of the workers themselves. Exploitation is thus represented not as evil managers willfully abusing workers but as the tragic extension of the purely economic logic of industrial capitalism.

Labor is portrayed as almost hopelessly hemmed in by cunning and airtight management methods on the one hand and the impenetrable insularity of the factory or mine on the other. The remoteness of the factory from the outside world is illustrated vividly, for example, in Lou Shiyi's encounter with the gates of a textile mill in "Fangche de hongsheng" (The Thundering of the Looms, 1933): "Beside a huge, tightly shut, and locked gate was a tiny open door just big enough for one person to pass through. At this pass were standing the imposing figures of a Sikh guard, a Chinese policeman, and a plainclothes man with dagger-like eyes staring at our group as we emerged from the car. If it weren't for the thundering of machines faintly emerging from behind, I could almost believe I had arrived at the Bastille, full of political prisoners, or a medieval castle; but in here capitalist production was taking place on a massive scale, the sweat and blood labor of thousands."[5]

Here the writer depicts the factory's insulation in terms of the massive wall that surrounds it and the analogous impenetrability of the numerous guards at the gate. Significantly, Lou compares the factory to a prison (the Bastille, full of wrongly imprisoned inmates who gain their freedom through political revolution) and a medieval castle, encouraging readers to contemplate the function and significance of various kinds of walls.

Another, less concrete barrier is elaborated in the woman reporter Peng Zigang's account, "Zai jiqi pangbian" (Beside the Machines,

1936).[6] Though a journalist, Peng's literary inclinations are indicated by her membership in the Chinese Association of Writers and Artists (Zhongguo wenyijia xiehui, Zhou Yang's 1936 attempt to replace the defunct League of Left-Wing Writers) as well as in her figurative approach to investigative journalism.[7] "Beside the Machines" is an account of her visit to the Yufeng Textile Mill in Zhengzhou, which she describes as being one of a few remaining purely domestic textile concerns.

After repeatedly being prevented from entering the factory, Peng is escorted into a reception room. A manager explains that the secrecy is meant to protect trade secrets from Japanese plants so that domestic production can still compete in the hostile environment of the Japanese industrial invasion. Peng attempts to draw him out with questions about sources of raw cotton and sales routes, but he gives perfunctory answers and claims ignorance of specific details, apparently affirming the principle of industrial secrecy. Then Peng turns the conversation to labor, unexpectedly drawing revealing comments from the manager: " 'What is the labor situation like? Is there organization? There must have been activity in 1926 and 1927, around the time of the Revolutionary Army's northern expedition?' . . . First he shook his head, then spoke haltingly: 'Yes, it was pretty aggressive then; there was a union. Before long, though, it was quiet again, and we changed to women workers; now the plant is 85 percent women.' Then he added, 'They're very docile, you know, easy to control' " (464).

Peng's text then unfolds, penetrating the smoke screen of protectionism thrown up by the manager, revealing that the factory is in fact also hiding the working conditions of the women laborers. Although the manager answers all of Peng's questions about conditions, her tour of the inside of the factory (against the manager's wishes) is punctuated by one discovery after another of the untruth and exaggeration of the manager's claims.

All of Peng's observations upon entering the factory illustrate her surprise at the prisonlike regimentation and institutionalized distrust of the workers, reflected in the very arrangement of the factory space. She is confronted upon entering with the photographs of workers who had been punished for stealing factory property and learns that all of the workers are body searched at quitting time every day. She notes also that the "word of the day" tacked on the bulletin board for literacy education is *arrest.*

Peng's visitor's pass must be stamped by the supervisor of every workshop she passes through; the pass here signifies the restricted mobility of the workers as well as Peng's restricted access to them. As she tours, she notices how the workers seem almost to be controlled by the machines they operate and how the environmental conditions—the noise and the steam heat—are at the limits of human tolerance.

First, we entered the coarse yarn shop, where the cotton blossoms are made into coarse cotton yarn. The whole room was filled with the sound of machinery, so loud that we couldn't hear each other talk. In this air filled with cotton fiber and oil stench, each woman worker was in charge of a whole line of machines, jumping back and forth and calling to each other; they would gasp this suffocating air for twelve hours or more before getting any rest. [Though a few of them stood out because they were wearing printed cloth blouses,] no matter how pretty they seemed, no cloth could hide their emaciation; very few had any life in their eyes, most of them having been withered down to a deadly sulk. (467–68)

Here the exposition develops from the hostile physical conditions of the shop to their effects on the bodies and souls of the women who work there. The stifling environment reflects the factory's greater concern with productivity than with the health of the workers; it is sufficient to keep them alive at the edges of human tolerance. Long months or years of constant occupation with the large banks of machinery wither the women's bodies and obliterate any trace of liveliness from their eyes. The printed blouses some of them wear stand out in ironic contrast, seeming to mock in their superficial liveliness the workers' deadened expressions.

Children in the factory, whether engaged in labor, studying in the factory school, or languishing in the decrepit nursery, are a source of continual astonishment for Peng Zigang. As she continues her unauthorized tour of the mill, the spectacle of a workshop staffed almost entirely with children causes the writer to reflect on their lost childhood: " 'There are so many children!' The reeling shop was staffed almost entirely with children, and pitifully young ones at that, by the looks of them at most eleven or twelve years old, their little hands nimbly flitting about the spindles, joining threads, mounting spools, and working with a seriousness that permitted not the slightest hint of a smile, with a decidedly adult air about them. They don't know that in another world even children older than them still get away with being naughty to their doting mothers" (468).

Mirroring the women in the previous passage, these children are depicted as having lost their social identity and become lifeless extensions of the machines they operate. Emphasis is placed upon the difference between the world inside the factory and the world outside, in which normal human relations obtain and children can be "children."

Many of the children Peng encounters in the Yufeng Mill are the children of workers, trained in the factory school. From their parents' point of view, educating their children in the factory rather than sending them outside to a regular school can potentially supplement the family income; from the factory's point of view, "knowledgeable workers can increase production." However, Peng suspects that really knowledgeable workers could also cause trouble for the factory, so the education provided was carefully designed to discourage independent thought and serve the factory's interests.

Peng's revelations about the fate of children in this environment multiply when she is confronted with the nursery.

I entered the "nursery" with great anticipation; the man this morning had told me they had toys, cookies, and knowledgeable nurses there.

The smallish room was stuffy with the stench of sweat and urine; along the walls were thirty or forty "sleeping baskets"—you could hardly call them cradles. Babies were lying in them without covering, some asleep, some bawling away, some just quietly laying there as if accustomed to neglect, their little eyes wide open; what they all had in common was thinness and frailty, just like their mothers. In the whole nursery there were just two women, older and more ragged than the workers, watching over them. A lot of the babies' faces were covered with bright red sores as big as beans.

"They've been to the clinic?"

"No, they were only bitten by bedbugs!" a woman said, with a dull, sidelong glance. (470)

Here even infants show signs of deadening and dehumanization, and the harsh conditions of the shop floor are reproduced in the form of filth, squalor, and neglect.

Apart from the seriousness of the problem of child labor from the perspective of social justice, images of children in almost any context tend to work effectively on readers' emotions. The use of children in all kinds of reportage may be compared to the similar use of images of women; the emphasis on their victimization reflects not only the actual prevalence of such victimization in modern Chinese society but an underlying assumption that whatever unhappy fate may befall a man becomes much more outrageous when it happens to a woman or a child.

As Peng moves throughout the factory, the place reveals itself increasingly as a cruel parody of the outside world, complete with school, nursery, and a cafeteria that gives Peng further food for thought. In the following passage, Peng observes how the economic disciplining of the body enters the ideological realm in the form of mottoes hung on the cafeteria walls, and she playfully associates these exhortations with physical nourishment. She notes that

> there were some decorations on the wall—couplets surrounded with painted flowers:
> "Every inch, every fiber of yarn must be made into cotton goods."
> "You're not poor if you have no money;
> You are poor if you have no job."
> "The cost of every speck of damaged raw material will come out of your pockets." . . .
> No doubt these serve as an aid to digestion. (469–70)

The picture painted by this text is of a carefully sealed environment with a self-perpetuating system of labor exploitation: the managers have found through experience that women workers are not only "more docile" to start with but they can work them to such extremities that they will have no strength or imagination to organize or resist.

By paying the workers less than they are supposed to and keeping them on the verge of collapse, the factory has made the women oddly dependent on the factory for their survival: their only means of improving their lot is to work harder and faster (they are paid for piecework, not by the hour). Peng Zigang illustrates this through the revelation of a series of dismaying spectacles of exploitation and poor working conditions, an unmasking of the hell behind the high factory walls that is a common trope of labor reportage.

Peng's description of the workers, lifelessly yet nimbly repeating mechanical gestures, suggests that they themselves have *become* machines. Every detail of their lives, from their work to their education and nutrition, is shown to mechanize them, to maximize their contribution to production in an entirely physical and economic manner. This trope is central to virtually every work of factory reportage; it envisions the factory or mine as a huge machine, of which both labor and management are mere fleshy components.

"LOW-MAINTENANCE MACHINES":
IMAGES OF INDENTURED LABOR

The condition of indentured labor is depicted in more intimate terms in a work by Xia Yan (Shen Duanxuan), "Baoshen gong" (Indentured Laborers).[8] Xia Yan's Japanese textile mill in Shanghai is the logical extreme of the capitalist industrial concern; every act of brutality, every subtle manipulation of the workers' meager scraps of food, sleep time, and space is calculated to maximize labor output at minimum cost. Throughout the reader is continually drawn back to the exhausted, malnourished women's bodies, represented especially by Lu Chaibang (Reedsticks), as the by-product of this economic struggle.

> It's already the middle of the fourth month in the old calendar, quarter after four, as the morning star gradually disappears behind the slowly moving light clouds; some creatures in honeycombed chambers are already beginning to stir.
>
> "Roll up your bedding! Time to get up!"
>
> A man wearing leathers out of season shouts irritably.
>
> "Lu Chaibang! Get the fire going. You mother— . . . Still lying down? You little pig!"
>
> Downstairs in the seven by twelve foot dormitory, sixteen or seven-

teen "pigs" are lying every which way. His powerful shouting creates a commotion in the air packed with the stench of sweat and shit and dampness, as if he'd poked at a bees' nest: yawning, sighing, looking for clothes, accidentally putting on someone else's shoes, confusedly stepping on others' bodies, calling, and peeing in a pot only inches from someone's head. The feelings of modesty girls all have when they reach maturity have already become dulled among these creatures called "pigs." Half-naked, they arise and open the door, fighting for the toilet with their pants in their hands, and, turning their bodies slightly away, they change their clothes in front of the man.

He ferociously kicks one of the "pigs," who is getting up a little slowly, then turns and, standing on a stairway less than two feet wide, starts yelling at another group of creatures upstairs.

"I'll give you a good beating! Still not up? Lazy bugs! Are you waiting for the sun to climb up the mountain?"

Tousled hair, bare feet, buttoning their blouses as they go, some sleepy-eyed "lazy bugs" come down from upstairs. The water taps are crowded with people, using their hands to splash some water on their faces. Lu Chaibang tries hard to bring the porridge water in the big pot to a boil, but the gray smoke coming out [of the stove] makes her cough hard. Fifteen or sixteen, apart from the boss there are probably not many who know her real name; her arms and legs are as skinny as reeds, so everybody calls her Reedsticks.

This is a dormitory at Dongyang [Tōyō] Textile Mill on Fu(———) Road in Yangshupu.[9] The rectangular dormitory area is tightly sealed with a red brick wall and split into two long, thin parts by a cement alleyway. Divided evenly like pigeon lofts, there are eight rows on each side, five houses in each row, altogether eighty two-story houses. In every dormitory house live on the average thirty-two or so "lazy bugs" and "pigs." Thus, apart from their contractor bosses and their families, and the errand boys in their leathers, the guards, and so on, there are about two thousand of these "pigs" living within the walls of this dormitory area, who, wearing tattered rags themselves, do nothing but produce fine cotton fabric for others. (265)

I quote the opening passage at length to show how it moves abruptly from the intimate ruckus of rousing the workers to a description of the neatly arranged, tiny houses into which they are crammed. This sets the tone for Xia's sustained ironic contrast of the suffering, biological reality of the workers' bodies with the cold, hard, physical environment and system of labor relations that imprison them. The author enhances this contrast with an equally ironic treatment of the language that permeates the factory: the words of workers, management, agents, and overseers, whether euphemistic or derogatory, are often set off with quotation and question marks to emphasize the pathetic predicament of the indentured laborers.

The economic significance of the control and manipulation of space is spelled out in the narrow confines of the everyday activities of the workers.

> After the downstairs sleeping pads, worn quilts, and such are gotten out of the way, the two tables that hang sidelong on the walls are put in their places. A dozen or so bowls and a handful of chopsticks are carelessly tossed onto the table, and whoever's turn it is to make the rice porridge brings in a pot full of gluelike gruel and sets it in the middle. . . .
>
> There are only two benches—actually, if there were more there wouldn't be enough room for all the workers to eat porridge; once they swarm in and manage to get a bowl, they tilt their heads and catch the gruel dripping down the sides of the bowl and scatter back outside, standing or squatting in the gate or on the path outside. The chance to get seconds, apart from special occasions like the boss's birthday or payday, is rare, and when it's your turn to scrub the floor or dump the latrine, you might not even get one bowl. If the pot is empty before the hungry workers have filled their bowls the first time, the boss scrapes off some crust and leftover porridge from the pot, goes to the faucet and runs some water over it, then uses the greasy hands that had just preened her hair to stir it up, angrily thrusting it in front of these cheap, low-maintenance "machines." (268)

In comparison with the opening narrative passage, this more iterative account of the daily lives of the workers shows how easily the text alternates between these two prose modes.[10] Some commentators describe

"Indentured Laborers" as a narrative of one day in the life of a Shanghai cotton factory. In fact, reportage tends to break down the distinction between narrative and iterative exposition, as it is written to emphasize the typicality of the specific instances cited.

Part of the power of both passages lies in their illustration of the factoryscape's encroachment into the entirety of the workers' lives, including their sleeping, washing, eating, urinating, and defecating. This encroachment is manifested in the minute rationing of all material needs, from food and clothing to tables, benches, and piss pots, and all are unified by the extreme economy with which space is allocated. The daily displacement of sleep space by eating space at a precise time demonstrates the rigor with which these laborers are physically coerced through each moment of the day. Ironically, it is the human body's ability to tolerate extremities of abuse and malnutrition that allows it to be viewed as a "low-maintenance machine."

The multiply sealed factory environment becomes a surreal realm in which civil law is replaced with economic law and overseers brutalize workers (conceived as organic machines) with impunity for the benefit of the balance sheet, which is the ultimate arbiter of behavior.

The body of the indentured worker belongs to the contractor, so she doesn't have the least bit of freedom to "do" or "not to do." Their daily wages are pure profit for their contractor, so even when a worker is sick you can be sure the boss will step in on behalf of the company and use fists, clubs, or cold water to force her to go to work. Take Reedsticks, mentioned above, for example (actually, every indentured worker may have an experience like this): once on a very cold morning, Reedsticks came down with a serious cold and stayed in her "bed." The place where they sleep must be given up early for morning mess, but on that day Reedsticks really couldn't struggle herself up. Aware of her predicament, she cleverly dragged her body over to the corner of the room and shriveled into a clump, making her best effort not to take up space. But in this kind of dormitory they aren't about to let you make a precedent for lying around nursing an illness. In no time an odd-jobber came over. The people who do this kind of work are usually relatives of the boss-agent or local thugs who have a little pull, so in a place like this, where the arm of the law doesn't reach, they have the power of life and death. Reed-sticks had long since lost her voice, so she used gestures to say she hadn't a bit of strength and begged for pity.

"You're faking! I'll give you a cure!"

With one hand he grabbed her hair and ferociously pulled her up. Reedsticks' arms and legs were still dragging on the floor like squid tentacles with suckers. He gave her a kick in the legs and, of course, the second and third kicks weren't far behind. But then the odd-jobber stopped suddenly; later they were saying that because of Reed-sticks's "revealingly" (*lugu de*) jutting legbones, he had hurt his toe![11] The odd-jobber lost his temper and grabbed a basin of water that another worker was using to wipe off the table and dumped it over Reedsticks's head. This was winter, and a cold wind was blowing out-side. At this unexpected dousing, Reedsticks involuntarily leapt up, and the boss lady, rubbing her teeth clean by the doorway, laughed out loud:

"Look! She was faking after all! See how easily she got up: cured with a dunking of cold water!" (269–70)

By depicting cruelty against workers like Reedsticks as motivated en-tirely by concern over profit and loss, labor reportage serves as a popu-larized Marxist critique of capitalism. It depicts corporate managers and their minions in their treatment of workers as habitually abandoning familiar (humanist) moral standards of behavior, regarding the welfare of the worker's body only insofar as it benefits the company and being insensible to injury and death when health and life become expensive to maintain. Physical abuse and oppression visited upon workers come not from the evil or malice of their overseers but from the cold logic of the larger machine of which they are all a part. The cruelty is not per-sonal, nor does it represent some tragic, universal aspect of the human condition; it is a systemic cruelty, experienced collectively.

The factoryscape as it is manifested on the shop floor is constituted by material substances and arrangements that lead to specific subjective effects. Xia Yan analyzes the three worst aspects of working conditions in the mills, illustrating each vividly: noise (so loud that supervisors have to use whistles and hand gestures to communicate with the workers), airborne cotton fibers ("the little fibers float through the room like malicious demons, getting into every little crevice, their hair, their nostrils, their eyelashes, even their pores"), and humidity ("steamers are used to maximize the elasticity of cotton yarn to keep it from breaking in the machines, making such a fog that you can scarcely see your hand in front of your face, also aggravating the hundred-plus-degree heat and quickly infecting any little sores a worker might have" [272]). Thus, the beating of workers, particularly indentured workers like Reedsticks who cannot leave, is only the outward, spontaneous expression of a violence that is visited upon them systematically every day through the very conditions under which they work.

However, beating is also explicated as an economic measure.

> In a textile mill, there are usually three ways to punish workers for damaging goods: beating, fining, and suspension. Now, to the bosses who own the indentured workers, of course the latter two alternatives are not very attractive. Fining will reduce their own profit; suspension will not only mean lost wages but they still have to provide meals for the worker. So the bosses opt for beating without hesitation. Every time there is a holiday like Duanwu, Double Nine, or New Year's, the agent brings gifts to the *namowen* ["number one," the factory overseers], abjectly begging them:
>
> "You have to help me out, do me a favor: if there's trouble with my girls, just beat them! I don't care if you beat them to death, just don't fine them or suspend them!" (273)

The desperation with which the agents protect their labor supply route is also figured as brutality.

> There was another whose name escapes me. She couldn't stand this kind of life, and over a long period of time, during fifteen-minute breaks in the morning, she secretly got an outside worker who was studying at a remedial school to help her write a letter to her family; the stamp was probably also provided by that sympathetic worker. For a month there was no response. She became anxious, hoping that maybe her father would come to Shanghai to take her back. But the return letter was in the boss's hands. One day at quitting time, when she returned to the dorm, the boss and two odd-jobbers were standing at the door, scowling with anger. The grabbed a fistful of hair,

kicked and threw her, and exploded with a blast of indistinguishable curses.

"You stinking whore! You're a smart one, aren't you, cutting off my village supply route!"

"Pig, three meals a day have made you delirious!"

"I'll beat you to death, make you an example for everybody!"

"Who wrote the letter for you? Talk, speak up!"

The blood and pitiful cries stunned the whole dormitory house; everyone was trembling—it seemed she really was serving as an example. After they tired of beating her, they hung her up all night in the boss lady's attic. All night there was no other sound but the woman's near-death whimpering. Holding their breath, with their eyes wide open, tens, hundreds, thousands of slaves sighed over their fates. (276)

There are many pieces on the textile industry for which much or even most of the labor power is provided by women.[12] Moreover, the investigation of labor practices that forms the raw material of most industrial reportage is almost always mediated by women, even when the text is written by a man. Xia Yan published an article in *Funü shenghuo* (Women's Life) five months after the publication of "Indentured Laborers" in which he describes the process of gathering information for the project.[13] We learn that Xia was able to enter the factory with the help of a worker there, introduced by a young ex-college student who was teaching at a remedial night school for workers. In his description of these two women, we see that Xia is most impressed with their "capability" (*caigan*), which to him is all out of proportion to their age and appearance.

> V. was small and short, with the kind of long, thin eyes common among the intellectual class. At an age when other young misses who had been pampered since childhood regard films and love letters as their most important daily lessons, she was already a resolute fighter on the career front who supported herself with her own labor. . . .
>
> Sitting there with her was a student from the night school, Ah T., who also worked at Tōyō Mills; she was one of the hardest working contributors to "Indentured Laborers." She had the straightforward

simplicity of the working class, but what I found most surprising was that behind this simplicity was hidden an extraordinary ability to improvise according to the demands of the moment. When she took her fifteen-year-old sister and me, with some trepidation, to "observe" the workers' dormitories at the mill on Fu(———) Road, we hadn't agreed beforehand upon a story about our relationship, but as soon as she strode into the back door of the agent with whom she was familiar she pointed to her sister as if she had it all planned and said to the boss:

"This is someone from my hometown; she works at Factory Two (then turning her head to me), and this is her "great-uncle," who works at the water and electricity company, . . ."

She played it completely straight, and her sister didn't have any unusual expression on her face; it was the one playing the "great-uncle" who couldn't hide his awkwardness.

"They're having trouble renting their own place, and her 'great-uncle' here thought they might look around this area for a place to put up." As she continued, she shot a glance at me, indicating that I should put in a word or two. That kind of calmness, agility, and cunning was learned entirely through the necessities of real life and work.

But now, sitting face to face in a narrow little room, that rich, creative ability melted imperceptibly into that most ordinary, common, straightforward and simple personality. (74–75)

As in "Indentured Laborers," gender plays a role in the rhetoric of unmasking and the opposition of appearance and reality in this supplementary text. Xia is surprised that such a young woman is supporting herself and volunteer teaching at a night school and that such a "simple-looking" working girl is capable of subterfuge, just as he is surprised in "Indentured Workers" that teenage girls change their clothes in front of men apparently without "modesty," and he passes these revelations along to the reader. Xia's perception is in both cases structured by a tension between appearance and reality, but both for Xia are conditioned by his own ideas about what certain kinds of women look like and how they behave.

As can be seen in almost all of the examples I have cited, the elaboration of the factoryscape in labor reportage is energized by the use of disagreeable graphic images involving sick and brutalized bodies in filthy and hazardous environments. This is set in contrast to the rationalized structure of the factory and the calculating thoroughness of the systems and practices by means of which the workers' labor is extracted, enhancing the overall sense of a hidden yet nearby hell being exposed to the public. The emphasis on disagreeable images becomes even more pronounced in texts that extend the factoryscape outside the factory walls.

Yang Chao's "Baofan zuo" (The Boarders, 1935) represents a reliance on, even fetishization of, vividly graphic imagery.[14] The experience related is of a visit to a boardinghouse for child contract laborers brought by their parents from the countryside to Shanghai. The narrator (an American reporter whose story is retold by Yang Chao) is shocked and repulsed at every turn and transmits her revulsion to the reader through passages like her description of the children huddled around a barren table eating their cold meal.

> Over a dozen girls surrounded the table eating, each with a blue-patterned bowl and a pair of chopsticks in her hands. Some seemed unable to swallow, while others were wolfing it down with abandon, making a constant slurping sound. Their faces: some emaciated, their foreheads and cheeks a jutting triangle, their eyes and mouths sunken pits, really just living skeletons; others seemed quite plump, but on closer look proved to be bloated, like rotten peaches splotched black and yellow. Regardless of whether they were skinny or fat, every one of them had two white gullies beneath their nostrils, with sticky yellow liquid constantly running down them. Even when the sticky liquid dripped onto their rice, they just swallowed it all down together. The blacks and whites of their eyes were difficult to distinguish; all you could see were red balls rolling around in black, tarlike circles. Their twelve- or thirteen-year-old hair was already beginning to gray: cotton fibers and dust accumulated in their black tresses. (326)

The sensations brought about by such a description bring the reader to feel the repulsion of the narrator as she retched (earlier in the account) upon seeing the girls' sleeping quarters, densely infested with fat bedbugs.

The depiction of the girls as dull, unresponsive, and mechanical recalls Peng Zigang's description of the women and children in the Yufeng Textile Mill. However, Yang Chao's text also presents one young girl who was much more conscious and resistant to her predicament, whose enigmatic behavior embodies defiance as well as hope for the working classes.

Another girl was standing alone at one end of the table. Although she had a bowl of rice in her hand, she wasn't eating but rather staring off into space. Several times she put her bowl down, then picked it up again. She would bring her chopsticks to her mouth, chew a few times with effort, then stare off into space again. That mouthful of rice made her cheeks bulge, like two balls, or, together with her jutting forehead and chin, forming flower petals on a blossom. Suddenly, as if with great determination, she put down her bowl and chopsticks and swallowed with all her might, pulled at her clothes, walked over to a nearby doorway, pushed open the door, and took a great stride into the next room, when suddenly some kind of force halted her with one foot outside; then she just stayed there stuck in the doorway like an idiot.

Through the door I could see that there were four or five people sitting around a table, also eating. In the middle of the table were arrayed six or seven dishes, with meat, fish, and shrimp as well as cubes of tofu and green spinach; the rice in their bowls was as white as snow, like the bowls themselves, while the chopsticks in their hands seemed to be ivory.

Just at that instant a sudden shout drew my gaze to the face of a man sitting at the opposite door; he was a mass of oily black ferocity. Ugly enough as he was, he was even more difficult to look at because he was fuming with anger. He made me think of a tiger I had seen in Bengal, India, and I couldn't keep myself from shuddering.

He seemed to notice I was staring at him, but he restrained himself from saying anything, just shooting an angry glance at the girl.

I didn't understand what was going on, but the child immediately went out, trembling, and shut the door. But she didn't go away; one hand was still resting on the doorknob, her eyes in an unremitting stare, and tears began to flow out like water, dripping down on her feet. (327–28)

This pantomime illustrates the exploitation of the contract laborers by their agents in the most concrete terms and partakes in the theatricality I have noted above in relation to the reportage of public demonstrations. The figure of this nameless girl is tremendously significant to the narrator, occupying the center of attention for the entire latter half of the account; she is also the object of the narrator's small intervention into the girls' lives.

Witnessing this scene, the narrator approaches the girl to console her, only to be further shocked by the cold roughness of her hands and the searing heat of her forehead, almost glowing red through layers of soot and grime. Moved by the narrator's pity to a fuller recognition of her plight, the girl suddenly bursts into tears, only to retreat just as suddenly from the narrator to an inconspicuous corner to sob silently. This melodrama consists of strong emotional transactions mediated entirely through physiological responses to physiological states: the girl's nauseous hunger draws her to the forbidden room in which the contractors are feasting on nourishing, even extravagant dishes, but she is held back by the hollering of the "ugly" man, perhaps her contractor. The girl's responses still take place on the deadened, dazed level characteristic of all the malnourished, overworked boarders. However, the narrator's approach, her physical touch, and her weeping bring the girl to life, and she sheds copious tears in response. The emotional intensity feeds on itself, briefly transforming the atmosphere of the entire room.

The dense pathos of this scene, however, is shattered by the factory whistle, at which the girl instinctively stops crying and prepares to go to work as the others also hurry off.

Silence, like the silence of the dead.
Suddenly it was broken by the beastly call of the factory whistle; the whole room came to life, bowls and chopsticks fell to the table. Gruff shouting emerged from behind the door, and the girls ran every which way and were eventually gone.

The one crying raised her head, and when she noticed that everyone was gone, quickly stood up, dried her eyes with her sleeve, and left.

A cold blast of wind from the outer door assailed her, and she instinctively retreated a few steps. Then she quickly covered her head with her arms, bent her waist and drove her body into the wind, staggering as she charged out. She disappeared under the shadow of the four-story factory building.

I strode out of the main gate in a daze, walking on a seemingly endless path. The night sky began to deepen its color. Autumn fog thickly covered the earth; beastly shadows engulfed me on both sides, everything blackening with only the faint glow of a lamp at the horizon. (329)

The girl's practiced, emotionless reaction to the whistle, like her standing stock-still at the doorway of the other dining room, suggest a tragic history of obedience learned through physical coercion, yet the ferocity with which she resists the cold wind coming through the door seems to go beyond the demands of obedience. One is intrigued by the determination with which this exhausted, sickly little girl charges off into the winter afternoon: what compels her so strongly toward the workplace? This question is answered only by the narrator's own silence as she thoughtfully wanders off into the shadows herself, suggesting hope in the conventional image of dim lamplight with which the work closes.

The melodramatic lines of this work converge in the writer's physiological responses to the grotesque horrors to which she is exposed, particularly in the development from retching in the beginning to shedding tears and caressing the girl whose enigmatic movements inspire her fascination. The text bears the mark of reportage in that, rather than directly expressing her anguish and outrage at the sights and smells she encounters at the boardinghouse, the narrator selectively recasts her experience in the form of unsettling images that promise to evoke similar distress (and perhaps tears) from the reader as well.

But in the end it is the disciplined, obedient reaction of the girl, devoid of emotion, that constitutes the real tragedy of "The Boarders." That she can still weep over her own wretchedness (if only briefly) shows how human she is, but that she can *stop* crying and charge off through the winter winds to the factory shows how successful the process of disciplining her into a "docile body" has been. It is the tension between her disciplining and her small emotional reservoir that makes the nameless girl a memorable character.

Ji Hong's "Canguan Zhabei shi zhouchang" (A Visit to the Zhabei Porridge Kitchen, 1937), which depicts a large humanitarian kitchen in Shanghai, also gives the impression of revealing a dark, hidden corner of the city.[15] The author is a female student who visits the porridge line with a classmate. All but a very few of the patrons of the kitchen, who have been waiting in line since before five in the morning, are women and children whose husbands are laid off or sick workers or have already passed away.

Ji Hong's predawn visit to the charity kitchen has already set her apart from many of her student peers. And yet she feels uncomfortable under the stares of hundreds of beggars, out of place. The entire text is driven by the tension in the narrator's consciousness between her own status and circumstances and those of the people who have come begging for porridge: "It was only five-thirty when we got to the kitchen, but as soon as we got in the gate, there were already a couple of hundred people standing within the bamboo railing: hunger and cold had forced them here in the middle of the night. Dozens of astonished gazes fell upon me, and an indescribable discomfort irritated me. I didn't know what I should do, so a worker from the kitchen took me to see Mr. Wang, the kitchen's director" (705).

Ji Hong's conspicuousness provokes a distinctly uncomfortable emotional response on her part, and most of the rest of the text is concerned with coping with that discomfort: " 'Hey, how delightful! A fur coat! It's so beautiful!' The shrill words penetrated my eardrums, and filled me with fear. Although I am just another poor intellectual, in their eyes I'm one of the privileged. Their bodies trembled in tattered clothes, but I wore a soft and warm padded jacket and a coat with a fur collar on the outside; how could I avoid provoking their hatred? I looked for the source of this voice and found a wild-haired woman in her thirties holding a baby not one year old, feeding at her breast. The woman flashed her eyes at me several times" (707).

The organization of space in the kitchen, like that of the living spaces of Xia Yan's Tōyō Cotton Mill, materially reflects the unlimited demand for scarce resources. Moreover, like the factory, the layout reflects the coordination of massive numbers of people simultaneously engaged in productive activity. According to the rules of the kitchen, once you have lined up and received a bowl of porridge you must file onto a fenced plaza to eat, staying there until the porridge is gone before you can leave. This prevents you from jumping back in line for second helpings before others have been served once. Thus, it becomes apparent that regardless of whether the controlled persons are producing (labor power, as in the factory) or consuming (porridge), mass coordination requires strict rules controlling behavior well beyond civil law. The porridge kitchen becomes a factory for consumption instead of production. That the need for such a charity is directly related to industrial capitalism makes it less surprising that the kitchen makes use of such factorylike regimentation.

The porridge kitchen space is surrounded by bamboo fences, and its rules are enforced by laid-off security guards and neighborhood vagrants. The seething crowd is first depicted corralled by this railing.

The crowd got more and more dense, every space in the bamboo lattice filled with heads, old, young, skinny and yellow, crippled, here held in mother's arms, there pushed into the railing, endlessly coming, group after group; who would believe that in a corner of Shanghai, the economic center of the whole country, there would be so many people with nothing to eat or wear! I walked over to them, wishing to understand them more clearly. The air brought with it the smell of their tattered clothes; to use a fashionable phrase, they were so "un–New Life" (*tai bu xin shenghuo*)! But this was probably the stench of sweat and blood that had been squeezed out of them! They didn't ask for it. It is what society has given them. And I, in the same society, having been lucky enough to live in keeping with standards of neatness and cleanliness. How can I despise people who in fact are not allowed to attain such standards! I walked even closer, hoping that in the stench I could find something of the true face of society. (707)

From Ji Hong's contemplation of her own reaction to these disagreeable sights and smells, we can again see the disagreeable imagery at work: recognizing her revulsion to the stench, the author perversely moves closer, hoping to break through the social basis of that revulsion.

The revulsion is socially significant, as the stench is read as having been given to the poor by society. Ji Hong achieves a certain satisfaction in overcoming the peevishness of the privileged.

Mr. Wang and the staff of the kitchen, somewhat like Xia Yan's "V." and "Ah T.," are essential mediators of Ji Hong's visit, legitimizing her presence there and mediating her contact with the porridge eaters. Orderlies keep overzealous beggars from harrassing the visiting students, but even then, by the end of "Visit," the narrator seems to doubt the value of the manager's actions and the whole relief system as a solution to the family and economic problems related to her by many of the women who had come for porridge that day: "Many people thus entreated me; I didn't know what to say to them. I know well that this aid is temporary and passive. These people ought to actively go out and find the path to a permanently better life. But what could I say to them? These thousands of people I see living in hellish darkness, leading an inhuman existence have no one to educate them, no one to lead them to break out of this hell and seek out the path to the light" (712–13).

While thus closing by returning to doubts of her own efficacy in resolving the crisis of industrial poverty, Ji Hong nevertheless obliquely affirms the potential of the lower classes to seek out their own solutions, to discover unknown avenues to power and self-determination.

This affirmation of the working classes' potential to save themselves from ruin emerges much more explicitly in other reports written by Ji Hong in the months leading up to the eve of the outbreak of the War of Resistance against Japan in July of 1937. One such text, "Canguan nü qingnian hui laogong xuexiao ji" (A Visit to the Young Women's Association Labor School),[16] resembles Peng Zigang's reportage on the Zhengzhou factory and Xia Yan's "Indentured Laborers" in its emphasis on the importance of education to factory women but with a much more optimistic tone. This text extols the accomplishments of the Young Women's Association in circumventing factory exploitation by providing alternative living arrangements and a school that encourages self-improvement over subservience. Ji's overall emphasis is on the remarkable receptiveness of the students to a genuine learning environment, despite their fatigue after a long day's work, which is amazing even to her.

This optimistic tone hints at an ambivalence in industrial reportage about how to evaluate the factory as the scene of industrial production. In some of the texts that depict factories and mines as sites of inhuman, mechanistic exploitation the reader begins to wonder whether the authors are opposed to industrial production per se; no alternative set of "reasonable" labor relations is imagined.

However, in Ding Ling's "Bayue shenghuo" (Eight Months of My Life), the relationship between workers and machines is portrayed vividly in a more positive light.[17] In "Eight Months," a printing apprentice tells the story of her apprenticeship in terms of the development of her relationship with the machines with which she works. After eight months, however, the print shop closes down, unable to survive because of its participation in the boycott against Japanese parts and materials. The narrator is left unsure of her chances of reemployment.

The text begins in much the same way as those describing the Shanghai textile industry. The friction between labor and management and the economic vulnerability of workers is portrayed from much the same point of view as in the other labor reports.

> Click-clack, click-clack—in comes a man in a short vest, and another in work clothes (the most lively kind of clothing), then the third is wearing a long robe. Altogether there are over a dozen in this group, made up of people one rank higher (journeymen), two ranks higher (masters), three ranks higher (supervisors), and then the overseers and labor chief. The manager . . . well, you could say he's our number-one master.
>
> "Pigs! Where's the wash water!?" shouts a face full of sleep with a glare of hatred thrown in.
>
> "Dead-beat! The accounts aren't balanced yet, and you're smearing on oil!" said another even more intimidating face, angry enough to eat me.
>
> There are no servants here, so the apprentices have taken on this duty; at each meal working furiously without a break, enduring shouting and shameful cursing, doing what we can to restrain smiles,

frowns, shrinking back hands and feet, reducing the space we occupy to a minimum, trying to avoid being noticed, but it seems that we are just too bad, wrong at every turn, our ears, eyes, mouths, and noses all reasons for complaint. For example, we often hear "Look at those eyes, like a crook!" or "Shut that goddam mouth of yours, okay?" (117)

There is a striking resemblance here to the overseers' treatment of textile mill women in "Indentured Laborers." However Ding Ling's narrator makes an important distinction between the physical scene of labor (the workshop, the machines) and the apprentices' shabby treatment by managers and overseers. Ding Ling's account features a marked physical intimacy between workers and machines and even a lively and (if only to be discovered later) somehow congenial relationship with the journeymen training her. The depiction of the relationship with the printing press is extravagantly anthropomorphic: "The eight of us sleep here, and by our sides soundly sleep thirteen great beasts who can make even more of a racket than we can. Wearing steel clothes, standing on steel limbs, dancing, singing, licking up oil and ink, swallowing up and spitting out dozens of reams, hundreds of pounds of paper" (116).

This imagery is remarkable not only in that it brings the machines to life but in its emphasis on a physical need on the part of the machines that is satisfied by the care given to them by the workers. Thus,

at the stroke of eight in the morning, regardless of whether we have a little something in our bellies, the number-two boss comes mercilessly over to stand by us. We are still wearing dirty clothes that should have been changed long ago, covered with dust and grime. When we crawl over next to the monster, it has slept for a night, but it is actually taking care of us, this great big lovable machine. Yesterday it struggled all day, covered with sweat; the oil we put in all drained away. Ink is splattered all over the place. Sometimes we climb up onto its shoulders, rubbing the rollers, wiping the intricate, paper-eating teeth, while at other times we burrow down under its belly, tightening some screws so the axles don't wobble. Working our way back up, we check the six-inch or four-inch belts—these tough customers can bite off your hands or split your head open—but when we check them they're just insensibly, raggedly hanging there on those shiny steel pullies. If they're damaged (sick) we have to work them over. Beneath our sensitive and agile fingers these things quickly regain their shining spirit, taking on a lively, masterful air, like generals. But we still have to feed them, everyone with a gape-mouthed oilcan pouring a drop of thick brown liquid into every little hole until they are satisfied. (118)

Thus, if the horrors of the Shanghai textile mill can be depicted by transforming the looms' operators into machines, Ding Ling accomplishes the humanization of the workshop by transforming machines into lively, needful creatures.

The eventual, untimely closing of the print shop (the only narrative event in this otherwise entirely iterative text) is depicted as a betrayal of the apprentices, the masters, *and* the machines themselves by the incompetence of the management or owners. The effect of this event on the narrator is a reevaluation of the eight months of sweat and pain in the dim, close workshop as a lively, fulfilling experience far superior to the desolation of winter unemployment the narrator subsequently faces. In the end, Ding Ling's apprentice realizes that behind the constant friction and playful cursing between apprentices and masters lay a genuine and at times congenial working alliance.

FACTORYSCAPE AND THE SCENE OF PROLETARIAN CONSCIOUSNESS

The Worker Correspondents Movement was initially a strategy on the part of the League of Left-Wing Writers to unleash labor as a social and historical force by guiding workers into the cultural realm, giving them a more conspicuous voice in literary journals, magazines, and newspapers. The movement itself was quickly overshadowed by the attempts of writers such as those discussed in this chapter to tap into the subjective experience of the worker and to reconstruct the workers' world on their own terms. The trend of labor reportage extended beyond left-wing literary circles to include more moderate writers like Ji Hong, who wished less for social revolution than for industrial reform centered on worker education. This is an example of how the initiatives of leftist literary institutions, including the cultural apparatus of the Chinese Communist Party, even when they did not dominate artistic production, did have a significant influence on the literary scene.

Writers of labor reportage, whether under the auspices of leftist organizations or not, brought many of the hidden inequities and cruelties of the experience of labor to public attention and provided tentative solutions to these problems. Xia Yan, for instance, in his article "Reflections on 'Indentured Laborers,'" tells of how his investigation of the legality of the system of indenture resulted in a discovery that the system broke a number of existing laws; he implies that if civil law were able to extend its reach into the autonomous factoryscape labor relations could be improved greatly. Peng Zigang's and Ji Hong's emphasis on education represents another tentative solution, imagining education as a means to workers' self-empowerment. However, Ji Hong notes that workers' lack of time and energy was a real obstacle to such a project.

In the end, no comprehensive solution is suggested for controlling the exploitative nature of existing industrial relations. Violent solutions, represented to some extent in the previous chapter, are most often subsumed into the theatrical struggle for national self-determination; only rarely does reportage depict violent labor struggle purely in terms of workers' self-liberation.[18]

Chinese labor reportage is literary insofar as it constructs a vivid factoryscape symbolic of capitalist exploitation and class struggle. The factoryscape includes not only the physical factory environment but the extension of the factory's spatial logic into other social spaces (such as educational and living spaces and venues of social service for the unemployed) that manifest the industrial transformation of the modern social environment in general. This spatial critique of industrial society extends even outside the city through the description of the system of indenture as a pipeline through which labor is cheaply and deceptively extracted from the impoverished countryside. Thus, the factoryscape is the basis of the symbolic structure of labor reportage as a form of literature as well as the basis of the expression of consciousness in these works.

A formal consequence of this method of investigating and reporting on labor conditions is the predominance of a rhetoric of unmasking, penetration, and awakening that builds upon the literary critique of bourgeois journalism discussed in chapter 2. What is unmasked or revealed in these works, however, is not the falsity of bourgeois journalism but the entrenched, inhumane system of labor supply and extraction characteristic of Chinese industrial production in the 1930s.

The elaboration in reportage of this system is approached primarily through (1) the description of the system of labor indenture (which is a revelation in that such illegally supplied labor represented the majority of the labor force in the Shanghai textile industry) and (2) the manifestation of the cruelty of industrial production to workers in the particular arrangements and control of industrial space, from the factory floor to workers' living quarters, factory schoolrooms, and even charitable services provided for the unemployed outside the factory.

In "Reification and the Consciousness of the Proletariat," Georg Lukács discusses time in the factory in a way very reminiscent of M. M. Bakhtin's definition of the chronotope. In his words,

> time sheds its qualitative, variable, flowing nature; it freezes into an exactly delimited, quantifiable continuum filled with quantifiable "things" (the reified, mechanically objectified "performance" of the worker, wholly separated from his total human personality): in short, it becomes space. In this environment where time is transformed into an abstract, exactly measurable, physical space, an environment at once the cause and effect of the scientifically and mechanically fragmented and specialised production of the object of labour, the subjects of labour must likewise be rationally fragmented. . . .
>
> The internal organisation of a factory could not possibly have such an effect—even within the factory itself—were it not for the fact that it contained in concentrated form the whole structure of capitalist society.[19]

From a slightly different perspective this sense in which the entire environment of the industrial city manifests the inhumane, exploitative nature of industrial production is reminiscent of Foucault's account of the emergence of the "disciplines" manifested in the spatial arrangements of military camps, hospitals, and prisons in *Discipline and Punish*. Foucault suggests that the arrangement of the industrial factory follows closely that of the prison and military camp. In both cases, the arrangement of space reflects the division of labor, hierarchical division of units, and the isolation of persons at the bottom of the hierarchy in such a way that they can be watched by their superiors but cannot easily interact with one another. The point of the spatial emphasis is that the inhumanity depicted is not limited to the conscious cruelty of evil individuals but is characteristic of social organization and control in modern Western culture, of which industrial capitalism is only a part.[20]

As a pervasive formal foundation of modern society, the rationalized, disciplinary approach to spatial arrangement penetrates into the consciousness of the whole population — including capitalists and managers as well as laborers — so that all are dehumanized and the agency of cruelty is diffused into the system itself. While systemic exploitation can be read in the configuration of factory space, it becomes much more dramatically evident in the listless faces and withered bodies that are the by-product of that exploitation. Foucault finds that in the classical age (eighteenth-century France in this case), "The human body was entering a machinery of power that explores it, breaks it down, and rearranges it. . . . Thus discipline produces subjected and practiced bodies, 'docile' bodies" (182). It is in the sense that such spatial arrangements and worn-down bodies suggest a crisis in the history of human relations that their elaboration in a reportage text can be seen as metonymical with respect to the proletariat and the world in which they live, in other words, as literary. At the same time, on the functional side, reportage attempts to intervene in this crisis by promoting the awakening and mobilization of workers, largely through literacy education and union organization, to discover and create ways out of their roles as passive and dispensable implements of industry.

Factoryscape is at the same time an unprecedented reconstruction of the experience of the industrial laborer, an experimental foray into the expression of proletarian consciousness that is nevertheless mediated through the consciousness of the reporter.[21] Mediation is consciously struggled against as reporters attempt to immerse themselves thoroughly in the everyday life of the worker, attempting to bring the voice and subjective experience of the worker to the reader intact. However, the mythical ideal of immediacy is never attained in these texts, as the writers rely on melodramatic uses of their own discomfort, disgust, and repulsion to strengthen the sense in which the human subject chafes against the cold, rationalized factoryscape.

The critique of the factoryscape is complicated, moreover, by writers' identification with China's modernization. Reconstructing proletarian consciousness requires not only the expression of the awareness of exploitation but also the affirmation of the industrial laborer as an active participant in modernization. This affirmation entails the possibility—perhaps even the necessity—of a positive relationship with the factory environment, with coworkers, and even with management. Workers as such must on some level wish to engage in industrial production for the strengthening and economic self-determination of China, and thus industry per se cannot be attacked head on. This is a difficulty because it suggests that it is not the structure of industrial production that is exploitative, once again raising the question of what should be overcome by the proletariat. Ding Ling's "Bayue shenghuo" (Eight Months of My Life), the last piece discussed in this chapter, is evidence of this dilemma, as the writer imagines a warm, positive relationship between worker and machine.

The factoryscape elaborated in the labor reportage of the 1930s, like the theatricalized space of the reportage of public demonstrations, becomes literary in its investment of observed physical space with social and historical meaning. This is accomplished through the writer's observation of an immanent formal system (the economic logic of industrial capitalism) manifested in the particular configuration of social space of industrial production and his or her illustration of the human consequences of that system through the recounting of specific instances of cruelty, with emphasis on the subjective experience of pain and suffering brought about by the system.

Such accounts are often made melodramatic by emphasizing the plight of women and children in the factoryscape as well as through the copious use of graphic images (bodily fluids, disagreeable smells) to sharpen the edge of the systemic critique. This subjectivized intervention vivifies the rationalized, quantified character of the experience of labor as manifested in the physical arrangement of industrial space as well as the crass commodification of labor manifested in the hidden pipeline of indentured labor that extends into the rural countryside.

The widespread unmasking trope of labor reportage problematizes the theatrical perception I spoke of in chapter 2 as a paradigm for the ontology of reportage because it clearly distinguishes the staged (false) from a more compelling reality that it reveals. But this act of revelation is also staged—presented to the reader visually through selective emphasis on details (the writerly equivalents of makeup, costume, and stage properties). This tension recalls Brechtian theater, in which audience members are repeatedly reminded of the falsity of the theatrical performance and the social reality they must return to after the performance.

In labor reportage, the staged illusion is always the false mask of industrial factories in China as bastions of national wealth and power, or even a form of material resistance against Japanese economic and military invasion, and the work of the reportage text is to defamiliarize this mask, to tear it off and look upon the unsettling, ugly reality behind it. This is particularly evident in Peng Zigang's "Beside the Machines." However, like the defamiliarizing and alienating techniques of Brechtian theater, this unmasking is also staged, a dramatic gesture that reveals yet another mediated representation. It is the unique convention of reportage as well as documentary theater and film that what is revealed behind the mask of illusion is conventionally taken to be social reality, not a representation. This convention, the tenability of which is rarely questioned in discourse on reportage, is responsible for its special anticathartic effects and can be linked to the agitational aspects of Brechtian theater.

There are important similarities between Chinese labor reportage and that of the public demonstrations examined in chapter 2. Primary among them is the use of the body with its attendant world of immediate sense experience as the fundamental symbolic medium for the expression of historical consciousness. Xia Yan's use in "Indentured Laborers" of the starving, ailing, and much abused Reedsticks as the living text upon which the harms of capitalist industrial exploitation and indenture as a system of labor supply are written is perhaps the most successful example of this widespread trope.

Moreover, labor reportage provides an alternative approach to the symbolic interpretation of space: if the reportage of public demonstrations theatricalizes the cityscape, labor reportage commodifies the factoryscape. This is evident in the painstaking detail with which many writers describe the allotment of factory space (including the living and eating space of the workers) as a sign of the relentless obsession with profit of industrial firms and its invasion of the dignity and rights of their laborers. In more than one text we have seen workers in trouble attempt in vain to escape harm by minimizing their encroachment on the highly valued space of the factory: sick workers are punished for taking up space without providing labor.

Indeed, insofar as the factoryscape penetrates the worker's body, the body itself is also commodified. The system of indentured labor becomes a favorite target for reportage writers not only because it is perceived as unjust but because it implies that the worker's body does not belong to him or her but to the factory. This loss of personal sovereignty can be depicted in vivid and shocking ways (such as the disposal of dying workers on the mountainside described in Li Qiao's "How Tin Is Smelted" or the oft-repeated motif that contractors of indenture prefer to work their charges to death rather than fine them for shoddy production or grant them sick leave), and this particular form of labor commodification lends itself well to the sensationalist proclivities of reportage.

However, the penetration of capital into the worker's body manifests a spiritual invasion as well: Peng Zigang's loom operators' gestures are so swift and mechanical that the reader begins to suspect that they have lost their souls and become machines. In Yang Chao's "The Boarders," the children in the boardinghouse are also more or less depicted as automatons, mindless of even their own sickness, and yet one of them is driven, as if by a force beyond her control, to transgress the boundary that separates their eating place from that of their overseers.

The urban environment created in the reportage of both public demonstrations and labor conditions exemplifies a stage in the development of the myth of national awakening, resistance, and revolution. The reportage works considered here, whether anthologized or not, are not an "official" version of the myth, but they exhibit features that persist in official and institutional rhetoric about modern history on mainland China to this day and thus belong to the formation of what in Gramscian terms could be called the "historical block" of Chinese socialist culture, a system involving interdependent cultural, political, and economic institutions as well as works of art.

This technique of expressing social experience through a combination of environmental description and bodily sensation rather than through the techniques of psychological analysis and internal dialogue common in fiction would form the basis of the reportage of war discussed in chapter 4. In the latter case, however, the consciousness brought to literary expression in the reportage text is no longer that of the proletariat but that of the Chinese nation itself. The most obvious reason for this is the outbreak of war with Japan, but the dilemma of proletarian consciousness in a historical environment increasingly suffused with nationalism (illustrated most vividly in Ding Ling's "Eight Months of My Life") was also a significant contributing factor. While thus marking a return to the nationalist concerns of the reportage of public demonstrations, war reportage advances reportage's aesthetics by more fully integrating the experience of the body with that of the environment, figuring China's physical territory as an extended body into which the writer projects his or her subjective experience.

FOUR

War Correspondence I: Terror and the Wound

Modern warfare is a vast and violent transformation of space. The immediate physical consequences are massive human loss and the destruction of railroads, bridges, and buildings, but this destruction manifests itself in consciousness also as the redrawing of national boundaries, the wiping out of familiar institutions and landscapes, and the emergence of new social orders. For the civilian, daily life is suddenly saturated with a sense of emergency, social relations are pushed to extremes, and opportunities constantly arise for both heroism and treachery. For the soldier, war casts him or her into an entirely unfamiliar environment—the battlefield—and a strict, ostensibly rationalized set of predetermined social relations. These aspects of the dynamic, imaginative landscapes of war are the substance and driving force of war reportage, and they will be the focus of my attention in this and the following chapter.

During the war against Japan, China's human geography as expressed in literature and popular discourse was divided into separate regions— *lunxian qu* (occupied areas), *da houfang* (the rear or interior), or *bianqu* (border areas—remote Communist bases), each with its own atmosphere of emotion, conventions of description, and thematic concerns. The flight of most writers out of the two hubs of the Chinese culture industry (Beijing and Shanghai) as they fell to the Japanese made the literary landscaping of these regions possible, creating a "geopoetic" of modern China at war that would become conventional up to the present day for remembering the war experience. The mere mention of occupied areas, the rear, battle zones, and the border areas works strongly on the emotions and imaginations of those who lived through the era. More than simply two-dimensional zones on a strategic map of China, these geographically malleable regions persisted as discrete states of mind, alternatively signifying decadence, unthinkable atrocity, or "good, clean living" and idyllic encounters with peasants and soldiers in the expanses of the Chinese countryside. Such impressions were as much the product of the reportage and other types of literature emerging from all of these areas as they were of actual experience. The resulting subjective "regions" are geographically fluid; their boundaries move, they overlap and often they encompass one another. This is particularly evident in the case of the Communist base areas, which until the late 1940s remained discrete pockets scattered over a large area of China within occupied areas, battle zones, and the rear. Nevertheless, each region has its own distinctive social space and emerges in discourse and art as a discrete form of consciousness expressing a distinct category of experience.

I will show, for example, how the image of Shanghai changes when the metropolis is transformed into a battle zone. Not only are there drastic physical changes, but the narrator's treatment of light, and his or her perception of buildings and other physical objects and people as well, is markedly different than when Shanghai was the scene of the reportage of public demonstrations or labor conditions. Likewise, parts of the Chinese countryside, though physically unchanged, take on different aspects when they change from being part of the rear to being a battle zone and then part of the Communist bases or occupied areas. The same mountainside may change from a feature of an imagined landscape painting into a tactical configuration and then suddenly become a horrific pile of corpses or a bucolic paradise.

This remapping of China arose not only from natural geographical features but also from levels of technological development, lines of communication and transportation, and the new strategic implications brought about by the use of aircraft and tanks in battle. Bombings, for example, elicited fascination because air raids were still a new phenomenon in the late 1930s. Not only did they inspire awe for their high-technology destructiveness, but this kind of battle reinforced the idea of viewing China as a contiguous, physical body, a topographical, organic unity that could be broken into pieces, "nibbled away at," or otherwise invaded and injured by outside forces. Whereas for many the only relevant geographical distinctions had been "local and national" or "urban and rural" and "China" had been perceived as a limitless conglomeration of famous places connected by roads, rivers, or canals, now the nation was increasingly imagined even on the popular level in terms of strategic geography. A country town might take on unprecedented significance because it lay at the junction of major railroad lines, and ancient cities full of historical significance (Luoyang, for example) often do not play any decisive role.

For example, Taierzhuang, a tiny town in southern Shandong on the bank of the Grand Canal, became a conspicuous example of this phenomenon, indeed, a microcosm of China at war, because it was the site of an early Chinese victory. The victory enabled many war correspondents from all over the world then covering the war from nearby Xuzhou to personally visit the site, creating a major "media event." Taierzhuang's military importance at the time lay not in its being located on the bank of the Grand Canal but rather because it lay directly in the path of Japanese troops advancing toward Xuzhou from the southern coast of Shandong Province. The town was transformed through its coverage in reportage into a monument to the bloody battle to defend it. For all of the writers who came to Taierzhuang, although the town had been nearly flattened, its ruins still offered a rich and tangled mess of symbolic objects.

As our truck crawled over the railroad tracks, we all gazed upon the completely demolished town.

"That's Taierzhuang's south railroad station; it used to be three stories high, but this time it was hit by heavy bombing, so there's only one story left."

We all followed the direction of Mr. Lin's pointing finger with our eyes; although the station was largely blown up, that solid, heroic posture was just like that of a courageous warrior protecting China.[1]

Correspondents like Xie Bingying extracted rich significance from everything they observed around Taierzhuang, from objects with stories behind them like the crippled remains of six Japanese tanks that tried to simply roll into the town, unaware that the otherwise poor defenses featured flat-trajectory cannons that stopped them all immediately, to alternately self-evident and enigmatic symbols such as a Japanese flag, tattered in a heap of rubble in a bombed-out building, the skeletons of soldiers ("bones like 'dry sticks'") picked clean by hungry dogs, and an old woman weeping over the loss of her son and utterly unreceptive to the reporter's feeble attempts to console her. All of these speak to the enormity and significance conferred upon the battle, which, partly through these kinds of writings, came to be widely perceived at least on the popular level as a turning point in the war.

WAR AND REPORTAGE

War correspondence is perhaps the most familiar type of reportage literature to European and American readers, especially during and after World War I and the Spanish Civil War, when reportage works and newspaper articles by Henri Barbusse, Aldous Huxley, George Orwell, and Ernest Hemingway circulated widely and were translated into many languages, influencing both the fiction and the drama of the time.[2] The war correspondent cut a romantic and even glamorous figure, daring to risk his or her life by relentlessly pursuing the front line to convey the horrors and exhilaration of battle. This was no less the case in China than elsewhere.

The outbreak of war in July of 1937 was not a surprise to the Chinese. Activists had been publicly demanding a military confrontation with Japan since at least 1931; Japan had already occupied Manchuria and had been advancing troops through northeastern Hebei Province over the previous six years and was attempting to extend its sphere of influence over Mongolia as well. In a broader sense, since the Opium Wars of the mid–nineteenth century, every generation was touched by military conflict in some region of China, whether as a result of internal uprisings, contention among warlords, or attack and invasion from the outside.[3] However, there was no precedent for the outpouring of reportage that accompanied the War of Resistance against Japan. Nor did the conclusion of that war stem the tide of reportage texts: reportage remained the principal medium outside the newspaper for documenting the civil war of 1945–49 and the Korean War of 1950–53.

I use the term *war reportage* to refer to literary nonfiction works that explicitly illustrate the war and its effects. This includes both battle narratives and other kinds of texts whose subject matter and themes are a direct result of war, such as those covering refugee camps or hospitals for the wounded. At the time, only a few such works were explicitly referred to as "reportage" (*baogao wenxue*); they usually appeared as "dispatches" (*tongxun*), "sketches" (*suxie*), or "reports" (*baogao*).[4] Their unification under the category of *baogao wenxue* is a later development, one of the consequences of the process of bringing reportage into the socialist literary canon.[5] After outlining the context of China's wartime field of cultural production, I discuss two major types of Chinese war reportage. The first, which I will deal with in this chapter, features the urban intellectual's shock and confusion immediately following the outbreak of the War of Resistance against Japan in July 1937. Chapter 5 is concerned with the second type, which arises from the experience of moving into and through the countryside, developing relationships with new environments, and renovating literary images of the rural landscape and the peasant. Both types of war reportage feature visual images as vehicles for expressing or constructing consciousness. They differ in that the imagery discussed in the former type mediates historical experience primarily through the body as a figurative paradigm, while in the latter the physical landscape becomes the favored medium for the expression of historical experience. This is only a difference of emphasis, however, as both types of war reportage tend to rely upon a *linkage* of the body with the physical landscape as the figurative basis for a collective (in these cases, strictly national) consciousness.

Reportage and the Material Conditions of War

The widespread adoption of reportage as a form of literary expression during the War of Resistance is usually explained in terms of adverse material conditions in the publishing industry: publishers, universities, and public and private cultural institutions were forced by the Japanese occupation of Beijing and Shanghai to move into the interior cities of Hankou, Chongqing, and Guilin, leaving behind most of their printing equipment, libraries, sources of paper supplies, and a large portion of their markets and constituencies. Under these conditions, newspapers and low-budget magazines came to dominate the publishing industry in the interior, forcing still active creative writers to adapt to the editorial demands of such media. According to reportage historians, *baogao wenxue* was merely an available form exploited during the war for reasons of material convenience.[6] An equally decisive factor was the public obsession with military developments; creative writers shared this interest and were aware of themselves as potential reporters. The rapidity of changes made forms of writing that require contemplation and revision (particularly fiction and poetry) unmanageable; for an active writer, the alternatives were either to simply report on events or to more fully elaborate on the experience of war, providing readers with both new information and the unique strengths of a literary perspective and the employment of artistic techniques.

But arguing that reportage was popular merely because it was impossible for creative writers to write anything else provides little sense of the genre's own momentum and its distinctive characteristics, and fails to account for its conspicuous presence in modern China both before and after the War of Resistance. Although departure from cultural metropolises deprived writers of the ideal environment for "serious" literature, it was also true that the new environments through which they fled, settled, and resettled were a constant source of imaginative transformation and enrichment.[7] Travel over long distances enabled writers to remold their national consciousness in the form of a diverse, broad, and yet bounded topography. This instability and diversity was as exhilarating for writers as it was a hardship; it forced them out of what was still habitually an isolated lifestyle and closer to "the masses" than they had generally been throughout the 1920s and 1930s.

Moreover, precisely because of the disruption of the publication and cultural industries, writers' organizations were fast becoming larger and more important, providing financial assistance to poor and ailing writers during the war years. The All-China Resistance Association of Writers and Artists (Zhonghua quanguo wenyijie zangdi xiehui, est. 1938; abbreviated hereafter as Wenxie), for example, began by 1940 to hold symposiums and raise funds to aid ailing writers, improve libraries, and establish a foundation for literary scholarships and grants. By the end of 1944, when Wenxie officially brought its fund-raising campaign to a close, it reported that the scope and duration of the campaign far exceeded the planners' expectations and observed that many contributors and organizations would be continuing such activities independently.[8] Such organizations not only acted as a support network for writers in difficult times; they actively mobilized writers in literary campaigns, and reportage was one of the principal vehicles of both the coordination of writers' efforts and their creative expression.

Wartime Literary Journals

Due to many writers' and editors' desire to continue their work and contribute to the war effort as well (expressed in creative works as well as editorial articles), a number of new journals mushroomed in the first eight months or so of the war. Journals like *Fenghuo* (Beacon Fire), *Qiyue* (July), *Wenyi zhendi* (Literary Battle Line), and *Kangzhan wenyi* (Resistance Literature),[9] quickly became as prominent as such prestigious prewar literary journals as *Xiaoshuo yuebao* (Short Story Monthly), *Wenxue* (Literature), and *Xiandai* (Les Contemporains).[10]

The case of *Fenghuo* reveals the motivations for and manner of literary activities in the rear (*da houfang*). In a note inaugurating the first issue of *Fenghuo*'s brief earlier incarnation (*Nahan*, or Battle Cry), the editorial committee explains how the magazine was formed through the cooperative efforts of four influential Shanghai magazines that had been forced to close down as a result of the Japanese occupation.

> With the outbreak of the war in Shanghai, the four magazines *Wenxue*, *Wencong*, *Zhongliu*, and *Yiwen* are temporarily unable to publish. The staff of these four companies all take this to be an extraordinary time, wishing to do our utmost under adverse conditions for our loyal and courageous soldiers and officers at the front and righteously indignant people in the interior, to marshal our meager writing abilities and let out a battle cry to help give a show of strength, and to consolidate our collective power, so we have cooperatively organized this little magazine. If we can rely on support and generosity from all sides to provide us with manuscripts, woodcuts, and cartoons, we would be deeply grateful. However, because we are all covering the

costs of paper and typesetting for this magazine ourselves, editing and writing must all be done on a volunteer basis. As for outside contributions, we cannot provide any remuneration other than a copy of the issue in which the piece appears. We respectfully request your valuable suggestions.

—Colleagues of the *Nahan* weekly[11]

Fenghuo came out irregularly during September and October of 1937, and the next issue did not appear until May 1, 1938, when the magazine was resurrected in Guangzhou (Canton). From there it began to appear every ten days, but soon the issues again were published farther and farther apart until the magazine closed down on October 11 of the same year. What had been until the fall of 1937 influential literary journals with the financial resources to independently print relatively large issues and still pay their writers were now forced to pool their resources even to maintain a volunteer operation. On the other hand, *Kangzhan wenyi*, part of Wenxie's well-organized cultural institution, and *Qiyue*, Hu Feng's self-supporting journal, led a healthy existence throughout the war years, appearing regularly until the Japanese surrender in 1945.

The contents of these journals are a testament to the unprecedented importance of reportage literature after the outbreak of the war. While the first issue of *Nahan* consists mainly of five or six polemical essays from such famous writers as Ba Jin, Xiao Qian, Li Liewen, Hu Feng, and Mao Dun, it also includes reportage works. With the third issue (upon which the journal took the name *Fenghuo*), there appears one "sketch," and various other forms of reportage appeared in increasing numbers throughout the life of the journal. The first issue of Mao Dun's larger *Wenyi zhendi* features three works of reportage in comparison with one piece of fiction, five poems, three reviews, and a number of miscellaneous items. Unlike the bare-boned *Fenghuo*, *Wenyi zhendi* features woodcuts, photographs, and cartoons. Later issues average about 40 percent reportage titles.

Kangzhan wenyi (est. May 4, 1938, in Hankou) has only one piece of reportage in its first issue, but that is partly because there were two feature articles on the nineteenth anniversary of May Fourth and the rest of the journal was taken up with news of Wenxie affairs (there is also only one piece of fiction). *Wenyi zhanxian* (est. February 16, 1939), edited by Zhou

Yang, was published in Yan'an for the border area readership that did not have access to these other journals of the interior. It features many of the same contributors and works as *Wenyi zhendi* and *Kangzhan wenyi*, but it has a separate reportage section, located after fiction and theory and before poetry. The first issue published four pieces of reportage, four short stories, two critical articles, five poems, an interview with an American reporter, two cartoons, and a woodcut.

Qiyue was edited by Hu Feng, who to many embodied the most liberal literary thought within the leftist camp at the time. Like Mao Dun, as a literary critic and an editor Hu was quickly interested by literary journalism, evidenced in his 1935 article "Lun suxie" (On the Sketch) before the genre exploded in popularity in the following year. In the article Hu, like many others, accounts for the existence of the sketch (a form of reportage) in terms of historical and artistic necessity: "Life in a dramatically changing society makes writers, in addition to their creative work, unable to resist occasionally using sketches (*sumiao* or *suxie*) to critically record social phenomena occurring in every corner." For Hu, unlike *zawen*, "'sketches' are critiques of social phenomena expressed or hinted at from the aspect of imagery." Sketches and *zawen* "cannot replace creation, yet they fulfill a function that creation cannot immediately fulfill."[12]

As reportage increased in popularity, Hu Feng's interest in the genre became more serious, and after the outbreak of the War of Resistance he began to conceive of reportage more as an independent literary genre with its own unique mode of figuration. In a 1937 article, Hu emphasizes that the unique strength of good reportage is that it allows the writer to express his or her emotional engagement with factual events through the narration of those events without necessarily distorting them. In other words, this emotional investment is as essential to the literary integrity of factual narrative as factual accuracy itself.[13] Reportage literature would become one of the central literary vehicles of Hu Feng's wartime journal *Qiyue* (July). With *Qiyue*, Hu hoped to avoid the tendency toward stereotyped and romanticized reactions to the war, promoting writers and works that he felt carried on the legacy of Lu Xun, relentlessly pursuing and exposing the dark side of Chinese social life. Because of Hu Feng's editorial discernment and his attraction of some of the most talented writers of the time, *Qiyue* made some of the most significant and lasting contributions to wartime reportage in China.[14]

In sum, journals that appeared in direct response to the war promoted literature as a unique and necessary contribution to the war effort. The frequency (weekly or biweekly instead of monthly) and editorial emphases of these journals encouraged the contribution of forms that quickly conveyed the subjective experience of rapid wartime social transformation, and thus reportage, which had reached a peak in popularity in 1936, came to increasingly dominate their pages in the early years of the war.

Collective Reportage

The popularity of Mao Dun's 1936 collection *One Day in China* led to an impressive tradition of "one-day" works that continued at least until 1956.[15] *One Day in China* was a collection of nearly five hundred articles solicited from ordinary readers as well as professional and amateur writers, each a tile in the mosaic of Chinese experience on May 21, 1936. Although some (especially scholars of reportage) call this a "reportage collection," reportage is only one form amid many, including diary, drama, fiction, conventional journalism, and statistical information. Nevertheless it was inspired by the same spirit of drawing close to the pulse of everyday life that inspires reportage, in addition to being one of the most innovative and widely read publications of the 1930s.[16] While the anthology form was not a new way to present the genre and quite natural to a form that thrives on short pieces, the more careful artistic editing of reportage anthologies in general (as represented by Liang Ruiyu's *Living Record*) and the unique form of "collective reportage" (such as *One Day in China*) emerges and develops into an art form of its own. Like literary work groups, the one-day format of collecting a large number of short personal narratives from people from all walks of life, including many with no literary background, was a convenient way to mobilize reportage production, creating a massive document commemorating a historical event or a particular geohistorical situation.

For example, in Shanghai more than a year after its 1938 occupation by the Japanese, some progressive writers and journalists who remained in that city produced *One Day in Shanghai*. From two thousand manu-

scripts totaling four million characters in length, the editors Zhu Zuotong and Mei Yi selected about a quarter, still a work of impressive size.
The topic was not a particular day selected in advance but anything that
occurred in the year following the August 13, 1937, invasion of the city.
Even more than *One Day in China*, *One Day in Shanghai* is organized in a distinctively chronotopic fashion, dividing the experience of the first year of
Shanghai's occupation by the Japanese into time-space categories saturated with emotion. Abstract chronological and geographical divisions
were both ruled out as "stiff" (*aiban*), and what results are divisions
of "content" that incorporate both space and time and are rich in the
emergent "battle zone" rhetoric.[17] The four major divisions, "Huoxian
xia" (Under the Firing Line), "Kunan" (Agony), "Fenghuo shan shang"
(On the Beacon Hill), and "Xuanwo li" (In the Whirlpool), are divided
into such suggestive (chrono)topical chapters as "Lingkong de zhandou" (Battles in the Sky), "Benbo" (Surging Waves), "Sheng de zheng-
zha" (The Struggle for Life), "Rexie de benliu" (The Rushing Torrent
of Blood), "Gudao fengjingxian" (A Landscape of the Solitary Island),
and "Quchong yang de yiqun" (A Maggotlike Bunch). The chronotopical
character is made even more evident in the editorial committee's "Ben-
shu bianji jingguo" (On the Editorial Process).

What a great, heroic, and epoch-making year this year in Shanghai
has been! To fight for the freedom and liberation of our country,
the Chinese people have finally used military might to attack military might; to protect the justice and peace of humanity, they are not
afraid to use war to annihilate war! Tens of millions of Chinese soldiers and the three million patriotic citizens of Shanghai, without regard to political affiliation, occupation, age, or gender, are all standing together on a single battle line, using boiling hot blood to write
the first glorious chapter of the history of their own nation's war of
resistance. And the enemy's brutality, the shamelessness of traitors,
the debauchery of decadent youths, the hesitation and depression of
"small people in great times," which set them off, combine to form a
wonder world the likes of which Shanghai society has never seen. We
decided to publish *One Day in Shanghai* only because we wanted to use
the strength of numbers to paint this complicated and diverse reality
as a scroll of flesh and bones, to make the people of China and the

world, as well as our children and grandchildren, recognize the true face of the August 18 War of Resistance.

BAD CONSCIENCE AND THE GRAPHIC IMAGE

As can be seen from the inaugural statement of *Nahan* and the preface to *One Day in Shanghai*, art was being maintained under adverse conditions, not for its own sake but to make its own unique contribution to the war effort. The editorial rhetoric of these and other publications, stressing that everyone must make their contribution through the activity to which they are best suited, and using increasingly militarized categories to imagine cultural activities, demonstrates that writers perceived the war as an opportunity to redefine their mode of social intervention. In his inaugural statement for *Wenyi zhendi*, Mao Dun speaks metaphorically of "constructing battle lines, coordinating firepower," "observing enemy activities so as to launch a decisive attack," and "investigating spy activities in the rear in order to wipe them out as well as tempering our weapons and carefully organizing strategies" as the major concerns of cultural mobilization during the war.[18] In a number of works, writers seem to be reassuring themselves that it is alright not to grab a gun and run to the front lines, that art in and of itself can be an intimidating weapon of national resistance. One of the consequences of this is the persistence to the present day of imagining reportage especially as a weapon and its practitioners as "scouts" and "cavalry."

Without reading war correspondence, one might jump to the conclusion that it consists of romanticized narrations of battles and relief work written entirely to boost morale, depicting heroic figures and models of personal sacrifice for the nation and the people. There are indeed a number of works of this type. Writers eager to engage in the war effort took pains to make themselves witnesses and storytellers, either embodying battlefield experience themselves or immortalizing the heroic exploits told to them of soldiers or well-known generals. However, there is a surprising prevalence of self-consciousness and irony in reportage during the early months of the war, and there appears in many of what later were considered to be influential and representative texts a variety of aberrant narrators who are self-conscious, guilt ridden, paradoxical (firsthand accounts in which the narrator plays no role), displaced (borrowing the voices of others), or alienated. These particular responses to the horrors of war are gradually sublimated as the editorial and political demands on reportage writers urged them to find new ways to mediate the terrors of destruction and violence.

Many intellectuals had been writing about and discussing "revolution" for more than a generation, but until the War of Resistance few were actually placed in a permanent state of emergency and danger, much less dislocated from their metropolitan homes and forced into the interior, the countryside, or the battlefield. The experience of war was for many an opportunity to experiment in a transformation of consciousness. This was accomplished through actual immersion in the struggles of common people, the kind of immersion leftist intellectuals had been talking about and experimenting with unsuccessfully for at least ten years before the outbreak of the war. The tragedy of war gave leftist writers the opportunity to align this integration with patriotic concerns rather than specifically leftist ones, both strengthening their sense of collective belonging and adding to the centrality and influence of the reportage form.

As in previous chapters, I attend here to the forms of consciousness in reportage not only as a matter of internal dialogue and direct expression of emotions and thought but even more as a way of rendering space, of reading the environment and its atmosphere as something already charged with meaning. Much more so than in the forms of urban reportage I have discussed, the narrators of war reportage emerge as voices acutely aware of their own presence and the complex relationships among themselves, the reader, their environment, and the events they relate. Before turning to the works of the War of Resistance itself, I will discuss an earlier work, Shanghai shibian yu baogao wenxue (The Shanghai Incident and Its Reportage, 1932) as representative of the basic figurative conventions of war reportage.

The Dead Woman

The transformation of the city into a battlefield is more than the introduction of fire and smoke and the destruction of buildings; it is the destruction of the social significance of the urban objects and places on which the reportage of urban struggle (discussed in the previous two chapters) relied for its shrill theatrics of confrontation or the dissection of capitalist exploitation. The spaces of war, at least as they are represented in Chinese war correspondence, are demarcated by fluid battle lines, trenches, and bunkers that are often indifferent to the peacetime significance and functions of buildings and squares. They become targets for bombs, obstacles for tanks, cover for soldiers. Hand-to-hand combat or close engagements that take place in and around buildings (xiangzhan, "alley battles") rarely identify or describe their environs in peacetime terms. Indeed, urban space in wartime is little more than a convoluted extension of the embattled landscape of the countryside, a landscape whose broader vistas hold, as I will show, considerably more interest and significance for the reportager roving through it. For him or her, the embattled or fallen city has become like a bad dream, a place to be longed for nostalgically but one that cannot be visited again because it no longer exists.

As early as the Shanghai Incident of January 28, 1931, Shanghai began a transformation in works of reportage from an urban metropolis to a battlefield. In the pioneering reportage collection The Shanghai Incident and Its Reportage,[19] this transformation manifests itself as the emergence of a new mode of perception, with a treatment and organization of space much different from what we have seen in either the theatrical reportage of public demonstrations or the more iterative, systemic critiques of factory conditions: "The flourishing, majestic metropolis of Shanghai: Nanjing Road with its resplendent lights; the mysterious lanes of North Suzhou Road; Avenue Joffre, with the tranquility of a southern song—amid the sound of mortars, under the silver wings of iron birds, have all changed their color, changed their normal condition. The air has become desperately anxious, as if crises lie in ambush at every turn: at any time a bustling metropolis can turn into a war zone."[20]

The Shanghai Incident and Its Reportage consists of twenty-nine reportage-like newspaper articles on the Shanghai Incident assembled by Ah Ying (Qian Xingcun). This was the first anthology published under the rubric of baogao wenxue (reportage literature).[21] The language of Shanghai Incident expresses an inflated sense of historical moment and a conscious effort to beautify or impassion the battles with rhapsodic admiration for the heroism of the troops of the Nineteenth Route Army. The greater portion records stories told to the reporter by soldiers and officers who witnessed the events under discussion; the reporter sets the scene in each with a paragraph or two of either elaboration of the personal circumstances that led to the interview or a landscape description such as the one quoted above.

The articles vivify the sudden outbreak of war in Shanghai by narrating reporters' personal experiences as they travel near the front lines or visit relief workers in hospitals and on the streets. There was no plan to write in this way or to produce a collection; the appearance of such articles in different newspapers suggests a spontaneous interest in this sort of writing as a supplement to what are referred to below as "dry newspaper reports."[22] Leftist cultural activists like Ah Ying were no doubt inspired by the emotional investment revealed by the writers of these works, and their resemblance to the much heralded and as yet little practiced form of reportage (first promoted by the League of Left-Wing Writers about two years before). Reading the preface to *Shanghai Incident*, one can sense the editor's enthusiasm at the literary opportunity provided by the Japanese attack for the development of this genre.

The significance of this battle of resistance is immense, expressing the Chinese people's anti-imperialist tide of fury, gravely illustrating the importance of fighting the capitulationists. Apart from those capitulationist running dogs of imperialism, who betray the welfare of the Chinese nation, there was no one who did not give his utmost in this ferocious struggle.

Writers were no exception. Regardless of their social class, except for those who directly serve imperialism, all writers took part in these battles, engaging in both organizational and writing activities. As for writing activities, the greatest volume took the form of news reports resembling the form of *reportage*. Using this form, so well suited to the narration of the episodes of this incident, writers communicated the facts about every aspect of the January 28 Incident's aftermath. Among these short works of theirs are reflections of the progress of the war, panoramas of several major battles, conditions within the line of fire, civilian activities in the rear, and sketches of rescue and relief as well as all kinds of other events. . . .

Generally speaking, there are two ideas behind the editing of this book; the first is to commemorate this great event, so that young readers will be able to understand all the various activities that took place throughout the course of the incident more deeply than by skimming dry newspaper reports. The second is to make young readers able to understand the importance in our times of this *reportage* form and to study it thoroughly, although of the works collected here many fail to take up the mission of reportage literature; their class consciousness is extremely problematic, and they are only formal approximations.

Let new, powerful works with correct consciousness that are better able to act as models of reportage literature continue to come forth! As long as writers and readers continue to work hard, this hope will not be difficult to realize. We hope that in the very near future we can have much better books to offer to our readers. In short, *reportage literature is the newest form of literature, a form with limitless potential for agitation [guli]; young readers must not forget that it must be studied and must be practiced.*[23]

Clearly, it is as important to Ah Ying that this collection promote experimentation with the reportage form as it is that it should serve as a document of the incident itself. Although such emphasis is unusual, it is indicative of the importance in leftist literary circles of promoting the genre at the time. Moreover, the direct appeal to young readers and class consciousness reveals the editors' moral and political concerns. This was not peculiar to reportage; if one can judge from book prefaces and magazine editorials, it seems that by the 1930s editors of all kinds perceived their audience as made up of impressionable high school and college students and felt compelled to play a paternal role, selecting and arranging the contents of their publications in such a way as to optimize their moral influence.[24] Despite the paternal overtones of this approach, iconoclastic young readers searching for radical answers to the question of China's "way out" (*chulu*) eagerly read these publications.

Notwithstanding reporters' frequent exuberance over the courage of soldiers and citizens uniting to fight off the powerful enemy, there is already in *Shanghai Incident* a distinctive self-consciousness emerging on the part of the war correspondent. In "Bu pa si de tongzhimen" (Fearless Comrades), the reporter takes great pains to assert his colleagues' courage and yet remains aware that their bravery is in a different class than that of the soldiers themselves. War correspondents "dart back and forth in a forest of guns and a hail of bullets, with those silver-gray iron birds above our heads wildly tossing horrible bombs from the sky; with the merciless enemy artillery fire before us, sweeping over like strings of pearls, we seem like dogs in a hunting park, charging toward our object in the most dangerous line of fire, seeking out our quarry. . . .

"However, if you wanted to compare the fearless spirit of the three of us with that of the hardy lads on the front lines, we would die of shame. We may say, 'we are fearless comrades,' but we have not yet had an opportunity to face the enemy and fight to the death" (117–19).

Beyond this, another reporter, in "*Qianxian yi pie*" (A Glimpse of the Front Line), writes of how living with soldiers gives him privileged access to their inner lives and the atmosphere of battle: "In ten days of life in the war zone, I have had a taste of this kind of life they live, I understand them, I am able to see through to the despondent and courageous moods in their inner hearts. This kind of despondency and courage is nothing like what people safely situated in the rear shouting slogans could possibly imagine. Unless you have personally had a taste of mortar attacks and charges, the solemn sacrifices of our Nineteenth Army are impossible to understand!" (53).

In effect, the reporter is affirming the distinctive value of reportage as a literary form: its ability to bring to the reader the human experience of witnessing newsworthy, even historic events. At the same time that he is telling the reader that the experience is "impossible to understand" for people "safely situated in the rear," he is also providing such readers with mediated access to this experience. This is accomplished through the interpenetration of the reporter's abstract understanding of the historical and military significance observed scenes with his or her emotional reactions and physical sensations.

In "Si nüren" (The Dead Woman), another of the *Shanghai Incident* articles, the lines of historical consciousness, emotional engagement, the transformation of landscape, and graphic violence converge on the corpse of a woman encountered in Zhabei. The article's introductory passage establishes a close relationship between the landscape and the human body, brilliantly illustrating the mixture of physical sensation, emotion, topography, and tactics that would characterize most battle narratives in war correspondence for the next generation.

Ever since Saturday when the enemy began their general attack, we could hear the sound of distant artillery fire, fierce and desolate, carrying massively threatening power as it roars from the north, breaking through the night air to invade the foreign settlements and making our hearts race, so that even our breathing is stifled to suffocation. Indeed, the enemy has already commenced its general attack, a pitiless and merciless annihilation from land, sea, and air; in their brutal and destructive path there is nothing but cries of terror and blazing fire, from Suzhou Creek to the Yangtze River. Those ponderous hammers of theirs are just now pounding our central division at Jiangwan, and everyone knows this means that if they concentrate on breaking through the central division's line then our left and right flanks at Zhabei and Wusong, in order to maintain contact, would have no alternative but to give up the positions for which they shed their blood and painfully retreat twenty kilometers with cannons, planes, and infantry in three-dimensional pursuit.

A Thirty-li Wall of Iron
Hanging high in the sky are the smoke signals of destruction; sleeping eternally on the battlefield is the Shanghai-Taiyuan line of congealed blood and tears. Fragmenting bombs are exploding all around, and the very air is trembling. Deathly black artillery smoke curls upward and blows into the foreign concessions, into our hearts! We silently wait, anxiously gazing into the distance, hoping, trembling.

But, although the enemy attacked ferociously, exhausting their tyrannical power of destruction, three days passed and our position was still fixed: from Suzhou Creek to the Yangtze River, thirty Chinese li! A long line drawn of blue uniforms, an impregnable wall of blood and iron! War banners wave on the Songhu line, retreating, advancing, pursuing, while the enemy's steel, cannon, bombs, flesh, and bullets all vanished under the breaking and falling of the flag of the rising sun!

And then, those wounded, cart after cart, are transported along the Shanghai-Taiyuan line, moaning as their broken and wounded limbs pitch and roll with the scattered stones, bumps, and holes of the village roads. Yet they have already fulfilled their mission: Songhu is saved, the smoke of battle gradually clears, and we can see how strongly, heroically, that blue-gray line is flanked by the red of blood. Every gun barrel is fixed on the enemy, forever, in the acrid, rank breeze, under showers of bullets, between rice paddies and graveyards. (120–22)

In these passages and many others, emphasis is placed on the atmosphere of the city under siege, the smell of gunpowder and the thundering of artillery creating a palpable, suffocating anxiety in the air. Moreover, perceiving the entrenched Nineteenth Army as a "blue line" from Suzhou Creek to the Yangtze River seems to superimpose a tactical map of the landscape of Shanghai, and yet we are reminded that this "line" or "wall" is made of flesh or "congealed tears and blood" as well as iron (weapons).

This elaboration of the emotional dynamics of the environment of war relentlessly zeroes in on unsettling, graphic images, particularly human carnage. "The Dead Woman" continues with the narrator's visit to Zhabei, the industrial and working-class residential area of Shanghai that was the site of the Japanese general attack and the fiercest opposition to that attack by the Nineteenth Route Army. During the course of the description, the narrator focuses on the flattened buildings and rubble all over the street, with at first only a passing mention of the human losses: "We walked in by way of Zhongxing Road, passing through many checkpoints held fast by our blue-uniformed men, and arrived between Baotong and Baoxing Roads. What lay before our eyes there was destruction of an astonishing order. We were surrounded by broken stones and bricks, burned pieces of wood, spent shells, bloodied helmets, partially burned sulphur, and half-rotted corpses" (123).

This focus on physical debris is maintained as the narrator is led to the observation post of the regiment he visits to survey the remains of the bullet-riddled Oriental Library (Dongfang tushuguan). Although he is describing an inanimate object, the narrator's rhetoric almost transforms the library into the figure of a wounded soldier, like Xie Bingying's description of the Taierzhuang railroad station: "There, in the light mists and smoke, although it was riddled with bullet holes, without an unwounded patch of flesh, it was still standing proudly" (*The Dead Woman*, 123). The physical environment and objects are bodies in the sense that they are infused with humanity, with social meaning, so that the horror of the crumbling hulk of the Oriental Library, being a symbol of peace and civilization, is not exceeded by that of the corpses lying in the street. Just as the social and the historical infiltrate actual bodies, so, too, the body infiltrates and saturates the landscape as a form of perception, an organic whole, and a source of physical sensation.

The shock of the corpses themselves haunts the narrator until he cannot resist expressing it.

The Dead Woman's Corpse
However, I was unable to sleep that whole night. I could not get them out of my mind. Especially the woman's corpse I saw in Zhabei. Oh, it was terrible! She had burned to death, and her whole body was curled up like a little dog; on her left foot were the charred remains of a high-heeled shoe. I thought she must have been one of those young, so-called modern women, but from her neck down all that was left congealed there on the ground amid that half-seared flesh oozing with yellow fat were some mixed red-brown and black colors. Not to speak of that horrible, woeful face. Ah!

Enemy, enemy! Charge! charge! our comrades in blue!

The next day I went again to the regimental headquarters; recently I have been hearing all over about the enemy's frightening acts, especially how the day before yesterday near Mengjiazhai they used bayonets to kill, kill more than a dozen peasants. Perhaps this is just a common way to die in war, but just imagine, close your eyes and picture it, what a wretched thing it is when a gleaming, icy, sharp blade is forcefully shoved into the chest by a powerful arm, especially when it is stabbing the young, tender chests of babies and women. (124–25)

The repetitive exclamations and direct appeal to the reader suggest that we are much closer here to the emotional center of this text than in the previous passages. Note the particular forms the writer's anguish and hatred take. His exclamation "Enemy, enemy!" follows directly upon his excruciating description of the image of the woman's dead body, an image he says kept him awake all night. He further calls upon the reader to vividly imagine bayonets piercing the chests of women and babies to evoke feelings of terror and revulsion similar to his own. In short, it is in the form of explicitly realized images of graphic violence to "especially" women that rage toward the enemy is aroused in the writer and through which he hopes to arouse rage in the reader as well.

That women as victims "especially" attract the attention of the reportager is significant. For an image of the woman as a mute and passive object of violence had been developing in modern Chinese literature since the May Fourth era as a sign of modern China itself as victim, as we have seen in Xia Yan's "Baoshen gong" (Indentured Laborers). In "The Dead Woman," the writer takes this image to the extreme: the woman becomes a grotesque corpse, and it is precisely the shocking contrast between her half-burned shoe (which reminds the writer of the woman's social existence as a "young . . . 'modern woman'") and the elemental, nonhuman forms and colors to which her body has been reduced that elicits the powerful emotional response from the writer.

Such descriptions are common elsewhere in *The Shanghai Incident and Its Reportage* as well as in texts concerned with documenting atrocities and carnage published after the outbreak of the war. The victims are not always women, but they are always civilians surrounded with symbols of disrupted domesticity, and the bodies of women often form the focal point, described in the most explicit detail. This gendered descriptive habit manifests an association between the image of woman and powerful collective emotions, particularly nationalism, that would persist, as I will show in chapter 6, through the development of the culture of socialism. This association is always mediated by explicit, graphic images that thus serve as reportage's most powerful artistic weaponry, though on the level of representation it robs women of agency—of the choice to be anything but the pathetic victims of cruelty.

This, in sum, is one of the most common ways in which China is manifested in reportage as a body during the early years of the war. The structure of signification is the same as that by which the territorial consciousness of China is imagined as an encroached upon or fragmented topographic whole struggling for reintegration. In either case, the human body is appealed to on some level as a symbolic paradigm, one that can be fleshed out as either the particular body observed or inhabited by the reportage narrator or the extended national body the territory and landscapes of which the narrator travels.

The Rhetoric of Bad Conscience

In contrast to the surge of vivid, emotionally charged newspaper reports of the little-known writers of *Shanghai Incident*, with the outbreak of war in July 1937 several creative writers made names for themselves through their reportage alone, among them Luo Binji, Cao Bai, and Qiu Dongping. This was the first time in the Chinese context that writers became well known entirely because of their reportage.

Writers who came of age in Beijing and Shanghai in the 1930s had rich opportunities for revolutionary engagement in their formative years. Those who found themselves writing reportage literature during the war, though young, were often experienced political activists and had been engaged in one way or another in procommunist military or political activities before the war began. Although the content, themes, and techniques of these writers' works differ, they have running through them various forms of bad conscience, either from not actively participating in the resistance to Japan or, for those who did, from the shame of defeat and letting down their comrades.

These forms of bad conscience can be associated with the anxiety common in May Fourth literature over the intellectual's superfluousness and inadequacy in the face of modernity. Morever, although this guilt is ostensibly inspired by the war's sudden disruption of everyday life, it is also an outgrowth of the existing sense of detachment from the people of China noticeable in the work of leftist writers ever since they began to organize in the late 1920s. This attention to alienation can be read as a critique of the social status of the modern Chinese intellectual, a status that congealed in the educational institutions and literary societies of the May Fourth era. Bad conscience is the first step in a process of self-legitimation observable among intellectuals who consider themselves patriotic and revolutionary: these writers find different ways to overcome their guilt through departure from the ruins of the city into the waiting arms of the Chinese countryside.[25] There, as we will see in chapter 5, these writers take pains to establish intimacy with their new physical surroundings and with the peasants and soldiers they encounter there.

Luo Binji: The Onslaught of Images. Luo Binji's most noted work appeared in the short-lived weekly *Fenghuo* (Beacon Fire), one of the literary journals that mushroomed in immediate response to the outbreak of war with Japan with the avowed purpose of marshaling China's literary forces to unite and save the nation. In works like *"Jiuhucheli de xue"* (Blood in the Ambulance), *"Zai ye de jiaotongxian shang"* (On the Night Transport Line), and *"'Wo you you gebo jiu xing'"* ("I've Still Got My Right Arm"), Luo Binji expresses confusion and fear with startling, uncomfortable images of Shanghai under attack. Ceaseless artillery fire punctuates a cacophony of disembodied voices; bright flashes of light from flares illuminate faces in anguish or lost in shock, set off by the flitting of murky shadows. Above all, Luo Binji's narratives focus on the wounded in various states of incomplete medical treatment, their half-bandaged, still bleeding wounds are complemented by their corresponding states of mental and emotional disarray.

The opening passage of "Jiuhu che li de xue" (Blood in the Ambulance) is indicative of Luo Binji's use of rapid, jagged narrative, unstable visual images, and continually interrupted dialogue to convey the atmosphere of panic and confusion in Shanghai after a bombing.

The ambulance was going full throttle, rushing into the resistance of the air currents, dashing forward almost in flight; the Red Cross flag stuck in front of the cab fluttered violently, too, as if in excitement. Surprised gazes, searching gazes, in row after row flashed past. The ambulance, with the anxious, unceasing cry of its siren, cut through the waves of people like a steamship, and after it went past the people came together again in clumps.

"Where to first?" The driver impatiently honked the horn as he turned the steering wheel.

"I don't kn—" By now I was beginning to feel anxious.

"Dongjiadu, and step on it, the faster the better, Dongjiadu. . . . Did you hear me?!" the small but sharp scout said breathlessly as he anxiously looked ahead.

"No, to the station! Faster, faster!!" Qin, of the first-aid team, waved his arm with the Red Cross armband.

"Halt!"

"What! Get moving! Don't mind him . . ."

"Let's go."

"Halt! There're a lot of wounded here. . . ." A policeman stood with arms outstretched, blocking their way.

"No, wait'll we come back. . . . Come on, let's go!"

"Stop! Stop. . . ." Zhen leaped out of the ambulance; "Quick! Get me a stretcher!"

"Don't panic, you have to stay calm." Just when I had picked up the stretcher, the ambulance's siren started up like a rainstorm.

"Zhen, Zhen! Get back on! Quick! . . . To the station!"

"Stop, stop. . . ." A squad of MPs blocked the ambulance's way, and a sweaty-faced guard took down the ambulance's Red Cross flag.

Finally, Qin jumped down with a stretcher. Zhen lost her helmet when the ambulance's runner collapsed, and the willow branches they were using as camouflage scratched one of her tender cheeks.

"Comrade! Don't panic. . . . Keep calm. Do whatever it takes to stay calm." We flew over to the wall running along the street and, Oh! Blood and flesh were scattered all over before our eyes. I began to feel flustered, though these wounded, already unconscious, were not moaning.[26]

Confusion is conveyed by the ambulance's lack of direction in combination with its speedy zigzagging through the streets. Constant uncertainty about authority is maintained throughout the text. Zhen, the woman who leaps from the ambulance against the wishes of Qin (who at least believes himself to be in charge), responds to the situation without regard to plans or regulations. She "steals" the narrator's stretcher (he is a stretcher bearer) to treat a mortally wounded young mother and her infant (again, against Qin's orders) while the narrator futilely tries to treat a less seriously wounded old woman whose constant invocations of Jesus form part of the confused soundscape of the work. The ambulance pulls out abruptly and the narrator is forced to abandon the old Christian. However, the young mother dies in the ambulance and they are forced to unload her corpse, taking her infant son to the hospital. By the end of the text, Zhen, hardened by the frustration of this experience, vows to quit relief work and go to the front.

Here, as in "The Dead Woman," both the shocking graphic images and the dynamic, progressive forces of the text are embodied as women:

no attention is paid to wounded men, the other men in the ambulance play a reactionary, rationalistic role, and the narrator merely provides a subjective medium for rendering the event and providing it with its atmosphere of highly charged panic. It is in the woman Zhen that the radical decision to go to the front (in contrast to the assurance that it is enough to serve in the rear) is made. The convention of portraying women in reportage as the most explicitly rendered objects of violence as well as those who exhibit the most ostentatious, radical behavior is much more in evidence in wartime than in the years before, which may be precisely because they are perceived by reportage authors as little more than helpless victims in real life.

Luo Binji's "Wo you you gebojinxing" "I've Still Got My Right Arm" narrates in the third person the experience of Jianmin, a worker in a first-aid station confronted with a soldier who has lost his left arm just in the process of regaining consciousness. Unlike the war heroes of later works, especially in those written under the direction of Communist organizations, the image of this one-armed soldier is of a desparate man crazed by the shock of his wound. In the midst of mortar fire and the explosions of flares, he leaps off his stretcher and runs off into the night to the nearest line of defense. The narrator, Jianmin, is powerless to stop him, overwhelmed with the terror of the flares and bombs dropping nearby.

The atmosphere of confusion and shock in "Right Arm" is not noted by Chinese commentators (the piece is signed off "In panic and anxiety"). Zhao Xiaqiu, for example, interprets Jianmin's reaction to the soldier's expression of determination to return to the front ("Jianmin's heart burst into flames, and his blood vessels swelled") as "having his heartstrings struck by the soldier's ringing words" so that he "nervously wrapped his bandages with all the more admiration in his heart." Moreover, while Zhao's laconic summary of the meaning of the text ("The author . . . truthfully expresses this wounded soldier's noble courage and spirit of sacrifice") captures the central theme of the work, it gives little indication of the general atmosphere of panic and confusion that pervades this and other works by Luo Binji.[27]

Luo Binji's "Zai ye de jiaotong xian shang" "On the Night Transport Line," also narrated in the third person, opens with a soldier with a haphazardly bandaged head wound spotted by sentries as he wanders in the wild.[28] Like the wounded soldier in "Right Arm," he is described as being in shock, psychologically overwhelmed, confused, and babbling.

> By now he was completely immersed in a dazed stupor, his conscious-ness and sensations a welter of confusion. Although his legs were still dragging along mechanically and with great effort, he didn't know whether he was walking or still hidden in the trenches. A kind of drunkenness he had never felt before numbed his nerves. Apart from the throbbing of his skull and the muffled waves of gunfire inter-spersed with shelling swirling around his ears, he was conscious of nothing. Even the fact that he had wandered away from his battle for-mation and the words of the regimental dispensary's chief medic tell-ing him "on the road, if you see a truck, climb right up onto it" were completely smothered by the numb, aching mortar wound. (277)

One of the sentries who encounter him in the fields takes him back to the road to help him find a ride to the rear, but many pass him by without stopping, including an overcrowded ambulance and a group of service corps workers rushing through the night. Finally, he is abandoned even by the sentry.

In Luo Binji's reportage, the theme underlying the vivid onslaught of images and words is always clearer than the identity of any of the speakers or their relationships with one another. Beneath the confused welter of images lies an ironic discovery or revelation: in "Blood in the Ambulance" the narrator realizes that those with hope of being saved may be left dying while the doomed are carried off to hospitals. Jian-min's astonishment at the one-armed soldier rushing back to battle is also cast as a revelation. Finally, the dazed soldier in "Transport Line" wanders for hours along a major traffic route on which even an am-bulance refuses to pick him up. The potential sentimentality of these scenes is avoided by their high-impact, high-velocity exposition and Luo's sudden, unresolved beginnings and endings. Rather than directly extolling the heroism and sacrifice of the wounded soldiers or citizens he describes, Luo simply presents them at the extremes of physical and mental endurance, recasting their words and behavior as instinctive, subconscious, and arbitrary.

Second, Luo Binji is skillful in rendering atmosphere as an expres-sion of consciousness. In the nighttime darkness common to all of Luo's works, there is no visible space available to the reader in the text; we are confronted with a rich variety of sounds and visual images only far enough away for a flashlight or flare to illuminate. Luo's interest in transient, artificial illumination underlines the writer's sense of dislocation by lighting things eerily as well as eliminating any sense of safety from air attack the cover of darkness may have provided.

It is significant that Luo Binji's narratives always take place at night; it helps him develop images useful to his themes of shock and despair. As we witness other writers' subjective conquests over the Chinese countryside (not individual conquests but conquests of the collective, the nation), the treatment of light in their reportage continues to determine the subjective character of space and the appropriation of landscape. Works written in daylight provide more opportunity for the subjective appropriation of landscapes large and small. When comparing the use of light and time of day in these nightmarish works with the more optimistic works of later writers, it is possible to discern a relationship in the spatial thematics of Chinese literary war correspondence: the more three-dimensional visual space is illuminated, the more confident the writer is in Chinese victory.

Cao Bai: Breathing in the Nation. Before becoming a writer, Cao Bai was a woodcut artist imprisoned by the Nationalist police for his leftist cultural activities. His portrait of Lu Xun was also rejected from an art contest by Guomindang censors. Lu Xun, after receiving a copy from Cao Bai, urged him to write an account of his experience in prison, in effect encouraging Cao to become a reportage writer.[29] Cao was a central figure in the *Qiyue* group, and his literary contributions to the magazine reflect Hu Feng's ideas on how reportage should be written.

In Cao Bai's most noted reportage work, "Zheli, shengming ye zai huxi . . ." (Life Breathes Here, Too . . .), the narrator self-consciously defines himself as belonging at the rear because he is unwilling to take up arms against the enemy.[30]

> Now that the war has begun, although listening to mortars in my room all day and climbing up on the roof to watch airplanes might be referred to as "life in wartime," it's not the thing to do. At first I thought, this is a time to roll up my sleeves and do something. On

the other hand, that doesn't mean I want to run up to the front lines and grab a gun. I'm not about to grab a gun. Whatever I can do can only be done in the rear.

But that isn't easy either. I ran all over the place, joining organizations, going to meetings, submitting proposals. I talked for days but without result—not a thing. Then I happened to hear a "rumor," told to me as if it were a secret: "There's no way to save the nation!" (*Jiuguo mei menr!*) With this I came to the understanding that in the rear it's not that there aren't things to do, it's just that there seem to be walls built around those things.

But this understanding left a bitter taste.

One day at dusk I bumped into H. with the thick eyebrows. He looked straight at me and told me a heroic story of some monks who usually just count rosaries and chant mantras who put on straw hats and went to the front to help treat wounded soldiers, and then he told me of a charitable organization aiding refugees that had set up a refugee shelter, but that they needed help. As I listened, I grew excited, and immediately decided, "I'm going!" (47)

With his characteristically wry tone, Cao Bai confides his struggle with the issue of engagement. Although he has no illusions about becoming a heroic warrior, this does not temper his determination to "save the nation" in his own particular way. This dramatized decision reflects the author's actual decision to help run a refugee shelter in a closed cinema; Cao Bai's text is the sign of the author's actual social engagement, demonstrating the interpenetration in reportage of the text and the social field. What is "real" about the content of "Life Breathes Here, Too . . ." is not so much the historical actuality of his actions but the author's translation of his expressed determination into historical action.

Cao Bai's most noted reportage appeared in *Qiyue* and was republished in the later collection *Huxi* (Breathing). The image of breathing recurs in Cao Bai's work as a sort of finale to each piece; Cao meditates on the figurative potential of the breathing image, how viscerally it suggests togetherness or unity, how it connotes survival, waiting, and how it suggests death by semantic proximity to suffocation. This emphasis is an example of how the anguished reportage of the early part of the war translated confusion and shock into bodily sensations, the importance of the body in the writing of atmosphere, and the connection of bodily sensation to collective consciousness.

In "Life Breathes Here, Too . . ." after the narrator explains how he came to be working in a refugee shelter he devotes considerable space to his first encounter with a newly arrived refugee. The old man Wang Asan's story gives the reader a vivid awareness of the circumstances that made refugee shelters necessary. The bulk of the text is then taken up with an iterative description of the refugee shelter, often exploiting situational irony (the shelter used to be a cinema) to build pathos and concretize the meaning of *refugee* for the reader.

> Movie theaters are constructed for people's entertainment, not for peasant refugees. The first shortcoming is the lack of windows. A cinema of this enormous size, big enough to accommodate an audience of around two thousand, seems unbearably stifling even with only a little over four hundred refugees. The weather is hot, and in their flight many refugees of course had to take as many of their belongings as they could, so there were all kinds of cases, baskets, and packages. On top of that there were many who brought along their padded coats and jackets, their faces streaming with sweat. Thus, the whole room was filled with the stink of sweat and mildew. (49)

The text goes on in this iterative tone, occasionally presenting brief anecdotes, and ends slowly and quietly with a suggestive, wordless encounter between Wang's son (who wants to run off to the front against his father's wishes) and the narrator and the latter's musing as he watches over the four hundred sleeping refugees late into the night. The beginning and end are held together by the elder and junior Wangs' respective interventions into the narrator's experience, characterized with detailed, tightly focused narrative and an acute sense of time sandwiching the temporally muddy iterations of the daily fabric of the refugee shelter. Japanese bombs rend the narrative through the elder Wang's laconic account of the death of his wife at the beginning and the recommencement of bombardment at the end.

Cao continued to write accounts of refugee work, revealing the obstacles of bureaucratic corruption and sleazy landlords with which his work was constantly frustrated and entangled, thus fulfilling the socially critical mission of writing about the dark side of life in the rear that Hu Feng had assigned the *Qiyue* writers. But subsequent works by Cao Bai describe further changes in the writer's consciousness of social engagement as he moves into the countryside and his work changes from refugee aid to clandestine guerrilla activities. The mildly self-righteous tone of "Life Breathes Here, Too . . ." subsides, and we are presented with subtly expressed manifestations of bad conscience that take the form of petty annoyance at the behavior of strangers, misjudgment of character, lapses of memory, and a sense of remoteness from his own past. These manifestations can be read as refinements of the elsewhere directly expressed awareness of a gap in consciousness between intellectuals and the common people.

At the same time, Cao links this awareness to an unprecedented interest in the description of the environment as he penetrates the villages in the countryside. At the close of "Fang Jiangnan yiyongjun disanlu" (A Visit to the Third Route Jiangnan Volunteer Army), as he leaves the army's base camp and prepares to depart on a small boat, he paints his emotional involvement in the countryside and his guerrilla activities in expressly spatial and visual terms.[31]

> Walking toward the shores of Lake Taihu, the surrounding mountains were undulating as ever, continuous and unbroken, embracing the plain. The sunlight shone so brightly that the lone, mangy-headed Mount Yang gleamed in green and purple. As I looked back, I saw the four chestnut-colored horses captured by the "Third Route" hidden in a thick bamboo grove, neighing. Then immediately before my eyes unfolded a scene of iron and fire, poverty and suffering. . . .
>
> But when I boarded the small boat, I suddenly realized that I had already become a lone horse who had left the herd. The boat was taking me forward. I carefully stood before the porthole craning my neck to catch a glimpse of the white lice and scabies [I had left behind], but where were they now? Those bamboo groves that can hide horses I will never be able to see again, and I will never hear the neighing of the horses. Here are just lonely, barren villages stubbornly lying under the azure sky; there are the black spots of the peasants, slowly moving about on this vast plain. What the rich plain originally promised them was "peace" and "happiness." It promised these to the

homeland, to humankind; but now all that was left behind was an expanse of iron and fire, poverty and suffering . . . only these and nothing else. (96)

As the writer leaves the countryside to return to the "iron and fire" of the battle zone, the objects of his gaze are all transformed into expressions of the self-conscious writer's longings, longings to be integrated into the bucolic scenery, to not have to return to the horrors of war, to be reunited with the herd, to be somehow together with the peasants that are for him "black spots" moving about on the landscape. Just like his gaze at the sleeping refugees in "Life Breathes Here, Too . . ." Cao Bai's doubts and fears are provisionally assuaged by imagining breathing together as one national body: "we must breathe on this plain, consecrating the struggle to eternity, to the victory of tomorrow" (96).

Cao uses breathing as a concrete image of engagement and commonality, shared purpose. He meditates on what people breathe other than air, what symbolic "breathing" might be. Earlier in the same work, he registers longing for oneness with soldiers with the words, "To me, true warriors don't just breathe for themselves as they struggle, but cause us all to *breathe in the struggle*" (95; emphasis added). Breathing becomes a sign of hope in these works, hope of being organically united with the people and soldiers he sees and with whom he works as well as his *inspiration* by the war-torn landscape, his taking in of the atmosphere of war.

The Graphic as Vehicle for Sublimating Terror. I discussed the function of the graphic image in the section on *The Shanghai Incident and Its Reportage* above, but that work was only an early, isolated instance. The graphic image as a thematic vehicle came into its own in the reportage of the rear during the early months of the war, particularly in works dramatizing the treatment of wounded soldiers. Hospital reportage is characterized by the intersection of graphic imagery and the discourse of bad conscience. Works by writers, intellectuals, or students on their visits to wounded soldiers, their relief work to some extent "relieving" their anxieties about their lack of contribution to the war effort, re-create the hospital ward for wounded soldiers as a space for collective emotional transactions as well as a platform on which wounded soldiers can proclaim their courage through their determination to return to the front lines.

In general, when I speak of the graphic, I mean "Producing by words the effect of a clear pictorial representation; . . . conveying all (esp. unpleasant or unwelcome) details."[32] "Unpleasant or unwelcome" leaves room for a wide range of possibilities, but in my reading of reportage this effect is achieved almost exclusively through depictions of harm to the human body, focusing on bodily fluids in particular. In this respect, body-oriented war reportage continues the tradition of a "literature of blood and tears" (*xue he lei de wenxue*) promoted by Zheng Zhenduo and Mao Dun in the 1920s. Moreover, the type of graphic depiction is determined largely by the physical environment described in the work: graphic depictions taking place outdoors in the streets or on the battlefield tend toward dramatic depictions of massive bloodshed and extreme atrocity, while the indoor graphic, such as in hospital pieces, is more often conveyed in lingering, meditative studies of wounds and scars or other unsettling bodily details arising from illness or malnutrition. These types of graphic description play an important role in the aesthetics of reportage, as their unpleasant quality can provoke emotional reactions on the part of the reader.[33]

There are a number of factors that distinguish the hospitalized wound from the untreated or fatal "outdoor wound," of which we have seen several examples in *Shanghai Incident* and the works of Luo Binji. Generally speaking, the hospitalized wound is made more central and conspicuous precisely by being nursed and bandaged, and the writer attends more closely to its symbolic significance. This foregrounding of the wound is accomplished in part by the homogeneity of the hospital environment; the hospital is homogenized by the medical discipline—everyone wearing white, sound reduced to a minimum, smells leveled by the overwhelming odor of disinfectant. This homogenization of the environment contributes to a powerful focus on the rich sensory stimulus of the wound.

The wound, described in minute detail, is an image often realized more vividly than that of the wounded soldier himself. The soldier is covered in white sheets, head perhaps bandaged, equal to all others in the eyes of medicine. His rare moaning fails to distinguish him from his neighbor any more than his far more frequent expressions of determination to rise from his bed and rush back to the front. In this environment, only the wound arrests the attention of the writer, and, although the text may stray from this at length in the retelling of battlefield or life stories, the wound is the medium through which theme and experience converge in a context of physical pain and the graphic image. The writer has gone to the hospital to share his or her self-consciousness and discomfort at the wound, to publicize and nationalize it.

"Hanyang shangbing yiyuan fangwenji" (A Visit to the Hanyang Hospital for Wounded Soldiers, 1937), by the well-known short story writer and essayist Ling Shuhua, can be taken as an example of the norm of this popular subgenre.[34] Ling belonged to an older generation of writers most active in the 1920s.[35] Like many other writers, she attempted to address the issue of engagement in the war effort by joining a service corps (the Wuhan University Wartime Service Corps Women's Work Team, which included Su Xuelin among others) and visiting a hospital for the wounded to bring gifts and comfort the soldiers there.[36] As a result, her text and others like it tend to be structured by strategies for coping with emotional discomfort: "As I was speaking with everyone, in my heart I was thinking ashamedly: I should have gone to this kind of place long ago! Living in our fancy Western buildings, everyone on the street is talking about how pitiful wounded soldiers and disaster victims are (although like everyone else I enthusiastically contributed money to the rescue effort), but do we really know how miserable they are, have we really helped them at all?" (111).

This initial uneasiness is resolved throughout Ling's narrative mainly through the expression of indignation aroused by the poor conditions of the hospital:

Their wounds for the most part had already been operated on and they were now in the stage of rest and medication. More than half of them were wounded by shells and bullets, or had been hit by shrapnel from a fragmenting bomb. The most painful were those hit in the bones of the arm, chest or leg, or the spine; there was danger that the bones were poisoned and would have to be removed. Some such patients had amputated limbs, while others lay in silent agony, their torsos in casts. No doubt they were worrying about their salvaged lives and how they would survive as cripples. Who says the Chinese are feeble? Here we saw two or three hundred soldiers, their painful wounds bandaged, but not once did we hear them moan or curse anyone. . . . (113)

There was a wounded soldier who told me with a bitter expression that he had to have an operation the next day, and my eyes suddenly welled with tears. To have surgery in an ill-equipped place like this, the pain is no less than that of pigs and sheep in slaughterhouses; I have had this kind of experience. (115)

The soldiers' lack of decent weapons on the battlefield and the hospital's lack of proper medical equipment elicits a strong emotional reaction from the narrator, yet despite her revulsion at the condition of the medical equipment Ling paints a picture of herself as kindly and unhesitatingly hovering over the wounded, unfazed by the blood or disagreeable smells. When Mr. Liu, one of the hospital administrators, speaks to the Women's Work Team about the current situation in the interior, he emphasizes the role of intellectuals, saying that "educated people ought now to come out and guide the common people." Ling and the others in the Women's Work Team "all agreed with him completely" (116).

The conventional posture in this subgenre is epitomized in the narrator's conspicuous lack of hesitation; Ling's perception of the demands of her assignment requires her as narrator to overcome her bad conscience, to extend her gaze and imagination into the sickening world of the wound because the soldiers were wounded defending the nation. By thus tying an engaged national identity negatively to physical revulsion, the writer creates an intimately emotional, even visceral basis for this kind of patriotism, one that is also brought to the reader through the elaboration of the graphic image.

Bai Lang's "Wo chiyi de zouxiale futi" (Hesitantly, I Descended the Stairs, 1937) is, by contrast, a powerfully ironic twist on the subgenre of hospital reportage, for which Ling Shuhua's represents the norm.[37] Bai makes no attempt to strike a courageous pose; she is a self-proclaimed coward. She is not, as Ling Shuhua seems to be, simply galvanized by the war situation into an unproblematic, optimistic hatred of the enemy; rather, as was the case with Cao Bai and Luo Binji, the horrors of war assault her anew every day: "I've seen and heard plenty, quite enough, really, but I'll never get used to it. I'll always be staring with terrified

eyes, listening with timid, shrinking ears, seeing and hearing those brutal narrations, often even jumping with a start at terrifying hallucina-
tions" (123). It is these strongly negative feelings engendered by the war
that compel Bai to visit the wounded. Unlike Ling Shuhua, Bai Lang not
only arrives burdened with the bad conscience of one who does not have
to fight, but she makes no effort to conceal the fact that she cannot stand
the sight of blood or her physical revulsion at the hospital smells. Moreover, before she even enters the sickroom, a doctor tells her that visitors
are not allowed to speak to the wounded.

The sight of the ward immediately evokes the (unexplained) tears of
the narrator; she herself is surprised, reflecting that she is "not an emotional person" and that she generally regards soldiers with a mixture of
contempt and fear. But seeing them lying there in the ward, then hearing one let out a long sigh (breaking the convention of never having the
wounded moan), makes her "pores widen," though she "didn't have the
guts to talk to him" (126–27). Gradually the other visitors break the rule
of silence and begin talking to the soldiers, but the narrator at first only
stands aside and watches. She forces herself to look at a wounded hand
"to overcome [her] squeamishness" and then finally begins to make
small talk; the soldier was one of those under Zhang Xueliang's command who was forced to retreat from Manchuria, leaving his family and
home behind enemy lines. But just as he is beginning to tell this, the
"real story," he is interrupted by the reappearance of the hospital attendant.

Anticlimactic as this ending may seem, it corresponds to the mood
created by the narrator: her bad conscience effectively prevents the hospital visit from becoming a meaningful experience. Bai Lang has not
in overcoming her revulsion redeemed herself for not engaging in the
war effort in a more meaningful way. The painful honesty of Bai Lang's
text militates against the psychological tendency to react to the horrors of war with various species of denial such as oversimplification and
abstraction. Rather, the author forces herself to look at the reality of
wounds and grounds her hatred of the enemy in the emotional/physical
reaction to the sight of those wounds. The title refers to her pensive
departure from the hospital ward.

Peng Zigang, in her "Yizhi shou" (A Hand, 1937), takes the palpable

sensuality of this tendency further.[38] Peng, who had written labor reportage (discussed in chapter 3), concentrates her entire narrative on a
seventeen-year-old boy who has not yet received any medical treatment
for massive wounds to his chest and arm. The boy's attitude is much
the same as those of the older soldiers depicted in Ling Shuhua's piece,
adamantly insisting on returning to the front lines, wounds and all, but
it is evident to the narrator and others in the ward that the boy is not
likely to be going anywhere.

The substance of Peng's text is a remarkably vivid, even distracting,
sensual description of the physical reality of the boy's mangled body.
As his blood-soaked jacket, which apparently had not come off for days,
is removed, the narrator remarks at the stench and further reflects that
"of all the things in the world, surely blood has the most complex pro-
fusion of colors" (160). Concentrating on the boy's hand (perhaps, like
Bai Lang, as an exercise meant to "overcome her squeamishness"), Peng
conveys the horror of the rotten flesh and pus as she imagines all the
wonderful, "adult" things that hand has done for army and country, only
to be destroyed at such a young age.

Peng's close attention to the colors of the teenage soldier's blood
actually offers a way to lyricize the horror and revulsion of the sight of
him, to see the bravery embodied in his mangled hand and bloodstained
face. One might say that this is precisely what the hospital visit subgenre of reportage is for—for authors and readers to look straight at the
wounds until they can move beyond them and see the people behind the
blood and bandages.

The graphic image of the wound offers an object whose explicit description allows the narrator to displace her bad conscience and otherwise unmanageable feelings of repulsion. It is the same process by which
Ji Hong drives herself into the disagreeable smells and hostile stares of
the people lined up at the porridge kitchen in chapter 3, only the narrator
is redeemed not only on the level of fellow feeling with the impoverished
masses but on a level of national belonging in a time of historical crisis.
In much the same way as in the depiction of graphic violence and carnage on the battlefield and the street, the writer moves with astonishing
facility from unsettling, graphic images to positive emotions and abstract reveries that are explicitly connected to the nation. This is in fact

the trajectory of Chinese war correspondence, and within a few years the juxtaposition of graphic violence and patriotism would become a cliché. While hospital reportage provided a controlled environment for the displacement and sublimation of terror through the graphic image, this mechanism was by no means limited to the hospital subgenre. As I have shown in the case of "The Dead Woman" in *Shanghai Incident*, vividly realized, gruesome scenes of carnage were a conventional part of the representation of the landscapes of war. There the wound is more than a sign of harm and suffering; it is the sensational, complete destruction of the human body. Other sections of *Shanghai Incident* are structured primarily as inventories of corpses, often contrasting the elemental, inhuman aspect of the remains with the social objects surrounding them and the positions, postures, and juxtaposition of the bodies themselves.[39] Although the space in which these texts unfold is distinct from the hospital ward and the witnesses to atrocity do not explicitly register a struggle with bad conscience, the relationship of the graphic image to the writer's emotional commitment to national defense is the same.

The Terror of the Battlefield
Apart from the hospital wards and smoking landscapes of embattled cities, the other, most significant venue of early wartime reportage was the battlefield. Notwithstanding the rhapsodic accomplishments of the *Shanghai Incident* reporters, the battlefield as an anguished psychological theater was created almost singlehandedly by the *Qiyue* reportager Qiu Dongping. In this section, through a reading of Qiu's "Diqilian: Ji diqilian lianzhang Qiu Jun tanhua" (Company Seven: A Talk with Company Commander Qiu Jun, 1938),[40] I will explore Qiu Dongping's expression of subjectivity and reveal it as a form of collective consciousness with a significant spatial component.[41] There are a number of other excellent battlefield pieces that manifest a similar aesthetic posture, such as Qiu's "Women zai nali dale baizhan" (We Were Defeated There)[42] and Bi Ye's "Hutuo he yezhan" (Night Battle at the Hutuo River),[43] but I will focus on "Company Seven" as a representative achievement.

Qiu Dongping writes of the horror and absurdity of the battlefield from personal experience, with a style and set of concerns inspired mainly by the French leftist writer Henri Barbusse. Translations of Barbusse's stories, reports, and critical writings appeared frequently in late 1920s journals such as *Jixing* (The Deformed), *Wenhua pipan* (Cultural Critique), *Dazhong wenyi* (Mass Culture, est. 1928), *Tuohuangzhe* (Pioneer), *Xiandai* (Les Contemporains), and *Meng ya* (Sprouts, est. 1930) alongside translations of Upton Sinclair and Jack London, providing both a rich set of models and a theoretical framework for reportage practice.[44]

Henri Barbusse wrote of World War I from the perspective of a soldier in the trenches. For Barbusse, soldiers on the battlefield were not fighting machines or unproblematic heroes but individuals with peculiar histories, emotional problems, and personality quirks. His stories often begin long before the war, narrating what the soldier was doing before he enlisted or was conscripted and perhaps the circumstances under which he came to be in the army. Barbusse stresses the veracity of his stories, even claiming that he often did not change them to achieve heightened artistic effect.

> Here the reader will only find what has actually happened. Invention plays no part in these stories; their substance, and even their form, I have taken from scenes that I have witnessed myself, or else gathered from [a] trustworthy source. I have done little or no "romancing," to use a current expression. Sometimes, I have given the crude facts quite plainly; in other cases, I have discreetly covered over details in a thin veil of fiction. I have scarcely ever changed men's names into actors' names.
>
> My hope is that these casual jottings, picked up here and there in our appalling present-day civilisation, may accustom a few readers to the strangeness of truth, and open the eyes of a public opinion lulled by childish legends to the true picture of our xxth Century—a century that may be described as the Age of Gold, of Steel, or of the Jazz Band, but above all, as the Age of Blood![45]

Barbusse's concerns here resemble those of Chinese writers in the late 1920s and early 1930s; like Barbusse, Chinese realists, romantics, and revolutionaries were both appalled and fascinated by the unprecedented cruelty of the modern world demonstrated in the experience of World War I. As discussed in chapter 3, writers like Mao Dun, Zheng Zhenduo, and Ye Shengtao, too, felt that they were confronted with an unprecedented "Age of Blood," and one way they reacted to this feeling was to write emotionally charged accounts of actual events. Barbusse's stress on the "strangeness of truth" is central to the reportage aesthetic as elaborated later by Egon Erwin Kisch. The importance of what the reportager is doing lies not in the veracity of his message but in his elaboration of the astonishing quality unique to the real: "Nothing is more baffling than the simple truth, nothing is more exotic than our environment, nothing is more imaginative than objectivity. And there is nothing more sensational in the world than the time in which one lives."[46]

Panic and chaos are important attributes of Qiu Dongping's texts, conspicuous only by their absence in most later war correspondence. In Qiu's texts the hope for victory and the creation of heroes is problematized by the explicit presence of concretely realized images of terror and chaos. In "Company Seven," for example, the narrator, Qiu Jun, is an inexperienced company commander sent unexpectedly into an almost hopeless battle in charge of the remnants of several disbanded units. The text narrates his increasingly attenuated struggle against panic as the company gradually loses its position in a day of battle and is finally forced to retreat after absorbing considerable losses.

At noon on the twenty-fourth, our front line announced that it had been completely shattered, and artillery fire continued to envelop the second line. We are the third line; we could see the second line (which was now the front line) six hundred meters ahead of us collapse under the enemy's ferocious artillery fire. Scattered troops who had lost all their fighting spirit gathered in clumps in front of us, behind, and on both sides. The accuracy of the enemy's artillery is astonishing; their mortars tightly, relentlessly pursued our retreating troops like moving demons with souls. Having tossed their weapons aside, soldiers covered in blood and mud were madly scurrying in all directions like wolves amid the thick black smoke. The enemy's artillery fire is monstrous, all the more so once it had threatened our formation, forcing the soldiers on the front line to have no choice but to tragically, pathetically disperse in defeat, creating an overwhelming scene the likes of which we had never experienced. It didn't only disrupt our morale; it completely snatched it away. There was no need to wait for the mortars to come and annihilate us; the mere shocking scene before our eyes was enough to shatter our ability to fight. (23)

Qiu describes in painful detail an unavoidable exercise in hopelessness. The hopelessness does not affect his morale, yet he is never unrealistically optimistic. He is actually certain at the outset that he will lose, hoping only to preserve the lives of a portion of his men.

Company Commander Qiu Jun's description of his military school background and his actions and thoughts on the battlefield reveals a distinctive fear of emotion (particularly pleasure) and a complementary obsession with the spirit of military discipline and regulations.

> After we set out from Kunshan, I began a solemn and strange journey. Along the banks of a little creek near Qianmentang, a young, beautiful woman wearing a green dress appeared before our ranks. To all the men I said:
>
> "Halt. Let's take a rest here!"
>
> Chen Weiying, a platoon leader, quietly asked me:
>
> "Why do you want to stop? Let's catch up with her; what could be wrong with walking next to her?"
>
> "This is my own philosophy," I said; "now every time I run across a pretty woman I steer clear because she'll stir up a lot of unnecessary, harmful ideas in me. . . ."
>
> Our special operations officer (*tewu zhang*) brought a phonograph from Taicang, and I made him hand it over to me; I took all of his records and smashed them because I'm afraid to listen to music, too.
>
> I constructed my own path with extreme care, as if I were cutting away brambles and paving with stones—because I want to make myself into a proper soldier, so that I can stand firm on this momentous battle line, on every side I was protecting myself from the poisons of emotion. (20–21)

Qiu Dongping's narrative does not parody Qiu Jun's faults but rather demonstrates how determination and conviction are often built upon very particular experiences and memories (in Qiu Jun's case his relationship with his commander at the military academy). Qiu Jun's straightlaced obsessions are written as understandable, yet flawed, extreme, even neurotic, but they are never harmful to his men. Qiu's recollection includes no mistakes on his part but rather defeat in the face of a far superior enemy when every possible strategy—self-protection, heroic gesture, even suicidal rally—is exhausted.

Qiu's confrontation with military school ethics takes the form of his rethinking the regimental commander's exhortation over the telephone to "stand or fall with your formation!"

The enemy's accurate mortars played a cruel joke on our Chinese army's battle formation. The curved line created by the mortars' impact ruts was a mirror image of the curved line formed by our skirmishers. The dense artillery fire made the ground around us shake differently: it no longer vibrated like a spring but seemed to be dissolving the earth, like eruptions of massive waves in a bottomless sea.

Our regimental commander called me on the telephone, asking me bluntly:

"Can you hold out?"

"Yes, commander, I can," I answered.

"I hope it is perfectly clear to you that this is your chance to do something important and make a name for yourself; you must be deeply conscious of our righteous cause and be determined to stand or fall with your formation!"

I felt as if my commander were speaking directly to my soul; his words (according to the Chinese manner of communication between humans and spirits) should have been written on paper and burned — and I was moved from the depths of my soul by his words, moved to the point of tears. Why should a few such dead, stiff phrases have moved me so? . . .

At eight o'clock in the morning, the enemy launched a general attack on us. The ferocity of the artillery this time was unprecedented; we crouched in our trenches, grinding our teeth, enduring the irresistable weight of the artillery fire. In the beginning, we were calculating the rest of our lives in terms of months and weeks. Gradually it became days, hours, seconds, and now it was thousandths of a second.

"Stand or fall with your formation!" I was calm. I was constantly protecting myself from being cheated by these words. I felt the sentence was entirely wrong: Chinese generals and officers love using it, and I am well aware of the sentence's sacred significance, but I was still afraid that I would be swindled by it somehow. One's "standing" or "falling" was really not an issue here; the guarding of a formation is another matter, which is really more important than one's standing or falling.

My mood at this time was bitter; I deeply hoped that under the unparalleled artillery of the enemy, one-fifth of our men would survive. As for me, the soul of Company Seven, I must live, I must witness with my eyes this resplendent landscape: a landscape depicting how the warriors of the Republic of China leaped forth from shattered and broken trenches and engaged the enemy in front of the formation. (24–27)

The significance of this heavily emphasized battlefield lesson is in the narrator's distancing himself from easy moral and political formulas. Qiu Jun overcomes his spiritual struggle with desire and emotion by recasting the stereotyped relationship with the battle formation ("Stand or fall!") as a projection of his very conscience and sense of responsibility into those very trenches.

Qiu's awareness of the space he inhabits on the battlefield extends into the trenches, his consciousness of his unit facing the enemy in layered, curved lines of defense. Qiu narrates their construction, appearance, and specifications in vivid detail; his intimacy with the trenches corresponds with his paternal or brotherly feelings of responsibility for the protection of his men. The trenches are the only fully realized space in the text, the open space above and around them possessing only a dreamlike, visual quality.

Qiu Jun's identification with the constructed space of the trench formation resonates with further meaning in the context of my discussion of the literary construction of social space. As Qiu imagines it, the battle formation is at once a topographical feature, a piece of Chinese territory, and the extent of his command responsibility, of his very consciousness. In the battle formation, actual physical territory interacts with its cartographic representation on strategic maps, where consciousness is "mapped" onto physical territory. The arduous and tragic process of building the trenches (comparable to his description of his careful "construction" of a path away from pleasure and emotion) is also a process through which Qiu forges a caring, human relationship with his men.

Moreover, the failure of the regiment's mission is woven into the narrative as the impetuous heroism of platoon leaders under Qiu's command, who leap out of their foxholes against orders to charge in hatred of the enemy and thus gradually and inexorably reveal the configuration of the regiment's battle formation to the opposing troops, whose cannon fire increasingly mirrors the actual shape of the formation. In their rashness these platoon leaders have thus forgotten the ultimate tactical importance of the formation's concealed nature and in their acts of heroism betrayed and sacrificed their units.

Qiu Dongping rarely writes in his own voice; dramatic as his own, similar experiences must have been, his most famous texts begin and end with the first-person voice of his interviewee, telling his story in his own words.[47] Thus, while the writer seems to delve into the individual personality to wrench free a somber, humanist tale of the horrors of war, the cumulative effect of doing so repeatedly with different individuals is the author's *self-effacement* as an individual personality. The consequence of this variety of voices is a fragmentary human universe with certain collective truths and emotions brought to the surface by the shared experience of war.

The writer steps back, allowing others to speak through him, allowing, inviting the reader to enter into the narrator's experience, which is We, China, the Chinese nation. This retreat of the writer's personality creates a space of identity, and the narrated experience can be shared vicariously by the reader by virtue of the veracity of the content and the use of the first-person voice: since this really happened, and the narrator really experienced it, its re-presentation in Qiu's text makes this real experience in a mediated sense part of the reader's.

The image of the corpse or wounded body in the context of the War of Resistance becomes a concrete trace of the enemy's cruelty and a sign of the most intimate form of invasion. Carnage and war wounds are fundamentally different from accidental injuries in that they signify the deliberate action of the enemy; it is thus an easy step for the writer (and by extension the reader) to identify with the wounded as a national victim. The war wound, whether of a soldier or a civilian, cements the connection between the personal and national that underlies reportage's characteristic collective exegesis of personal experience.

In Qiu Dongping's account of the terror of the battlefield itself, as in similar work by other writers not examined here, the wounded body ceases to be the primary figurative displacement of terror. Battlefield reportage is instead concerned with the projection of consciousness into the space of the battlefield. In the case of "Company Seven," this is manifested in narrator Qiu Jun's identification with the spatial configuration of his system of trenches. This tactical topography becomes for Qiu the subjective locus of his dual responsibility to the orders of his commanding officer and the welfare of his men, both set against the horrific relentlessness of the advancing enemy's mortar fire.

This figurative alternative to the wounded body takes up a strand that had already been established in *The Shanghai Incident and Its Reportage*, in which the tactical configuration of the Songhu battle line is identified with the flesh and blood of the soldiers who held it and the iron of the weapons they wield. Chapter 5 will explore the development of this emphasis on the physical environment and landscape in the reportage of the Chinese countryside at war. This other facet of Chinese war reportage was roughly contemporary with the works already discussed, but it was written from the perspective of a different set of writers, whose experience of the war was conditioned by their penetration into the Chinese countryside.

FIVE

War Correspondence II: Guerrilla Landscapes

In serving as witnesses of the experience and horrors of war in eastern cities and along the eastern front, many reportage writers made use of a tight visual focus, zeroing in on the graphic image and exploring the possible collective, national meanings of physical revulsion and discomfort. Other writers, however, were striking out into the Chinese countryside on their way to other cities or to Communist-controlled border regions; some accompanied military units as journalists and service corps members or were soldiers themselves. While they often also focus on graphic images, they are primarily concerned with reconstructing in words the terrain they are traversing; the comparative largeness and simplicity of the Chinese countryside; the casual, "lovable" quality of peasants, who are conceived as part of this vast landscape scenery; and the clean, healthy clarity and exhilarating power of the language, behavior, and consciousness of the soldier.

This process as written through reportage is an exploration and an education for reportage writers, who were generally intellectuals forced into concrete action by the war. Rather than serving as witnesses to the war, these writers were increasingly becoming storytellers, passing along heroic exploits told to them by others rather than rendering their own immediate experiences. Apart from the content of the stories themselves, the conventions of storytelling also communicate the emergence of new values and a new form of community among soldiers and peasants.

Rather than attempting to give a comprehensive account of the massive breadth of this latter type of war correspondence, I will instead begin with discussions of some of the concerns, conventions, and assumptions underlying the subjective remapping of China in war reportage and then turn to an extended reading of one of the more ambitious reportage works of the period: Bi Ye's *Beifang de yuanye* (The Northern Wilderness, 1938).[1] In contrast to the works of the previous chapter, this one is characterized more by a tone of narratorial affirmation, brightly sunlit landscapes, and jocular characters. However, the gesture of appropriating the landscapes of the countryside is as much a response to the bad conscience and psychological tensions of the writer's identity as was the explicit graphic image in the works of chapter 4. Indeed, both are specular and spectacular moves by means of which visual images are invested with emotion and identity.

MAPPING THE CHINESE COUNTRYSIDE AT WAR

The tight, suffocating space of the wartime city so well expressed in the reportage of Luo Binji begins to open up in the process of leaving the city; Cao Bai, as we have seen, develops his imagery of breathing most richly during his sojourn in the countryside. Being forced to leave the city is one of the common tropes in reportage in late 1937 and early 1938, reflecting the personal journeys of many intellectuals. The negative feelings of having to leave a place one loves were often displaced by the opportunities provided by the journey out of occupied territory (by rail, ship, or on the road), allowing writers to vastly expand the scope of meanings they attributed to the environment around them, registering differences in emotional atmosphere from one city or another, and watching the countryside become transformed by war.

Like many writers, Liu Baiyu (1916–) describes his departure from the fallen city of Beiping as an event of great moment cast in vivid, sensual images: "The wind blew over from the embattled plains, and I raised my nose, searching for a smell of blood in the wind."[2] As the train pulls away from the city the narrator hangs out the window and yells "Someday I'll return!" Throughout the short narrative, environment and objects express the narrator's emotions and project those of the people he describes. The sight of pompous Japanese soldiers ordering travelers around and a surly Korean bullying an old man out of his seat are among the immediate causes of the mood of indignation that informs the text and is extended into a kind of nationalist fervor.

When the narrator himself is the victim of Japanese oppression, he mixes his hatred for the enemy with a strong sense of shame at his victimization, his weakness, his lack of confidence. These emotions, in other words, are examples of the historicization and/or nationalization of subjectivity. In an example reminiscent of Yu Dafu's narrator in the story "Chenlun" (Sinking, 1921), the novelist Xiao Jun's 1936 account of his journey with his wife from Dalian (Port Arthur) to Qingdao on a Japanese ship integrates or confuses personal emotions and experiences with national concerns.[3] Although it was months before Japan's outright invasion of China, Japanese troops had occupied Manchuria since the 1931 Mukden Incident, ostensibly to protect their numerous and widespread business concerns. Xiao, himself a Manchurian, indignantly moves away from his homeland in part because of this silent invasion of the northeast.

As he is questioned and searched by a group of Japanese inspectors, Xiao's narrator is so agitated that even the question "Where are you going?" makes his "heartbeat . . . irregular." This is an explicitly physiological response to a historical situation: a confrontation between races, between invader and invaded. The relentless interrogation and contemptuous attitude of the inspectors, which the narrator successfully manages to endure, nevertheless gets him so upset that he tells his wife, "If . . . if they . . . come over and bother us again, I'll jump into the sea and feed these dog's bones to the fish!" (413). While such emotional agitation is rare among narrators of reportage, the writer's determination to shoulder the burden of national shame, to let it fully infuse his deepest emotional life, is a phenomenon one commonly sees at least among characters in reportage texts. It is in this way that reportage is able to endow China in the world of the literary text with a body that feels history, both physically and emotionally.

The experience of flight into the interior enhances the writer's awareness of China as a geographical body; the continuous sequence of locales that articulate the undulating, gradually transforming countryside gives the writer the opportunity to register differences in local atmosphere and the extent of the war's penetration into the heart of the mainland. In the pieces signed "Xi Min" and "Shi Ren" published in *Shen bao* in the autumn of 1937, for example, we are repeatedly confronted with an awareness of the vulnerability of the train amid air attacks.[4] On one occasion, the reporter (Shi Ren) finds himself trapped in Nanjing during an air raid. From the people's practiced reaction to this extraordinary situation, the writer reflects on how woefully common such air strikes must be.

While narratives of ship and train journeys provide an enclosed space through which the writer can contrast a tight focus on the behavior and words of fellow passengers with an ever-changing, wide panorama outside the window or porthole, journeys on the open road offer richer allegorical resonance, suggesting spiritual awakening and a heightened sensitivity to historical change. Such readings of the landscape, in addition to providing the reader with a medium for sensory engagement, also create the possibility of the landscape's absorption into the narratorial consciousness, focusing our attention on directed movement through space. The road trope multiplies symbolic or allegorical resonances, from the ancient and ubiquitous arch-image of "the path" or "way" (*dao*) to the more immediate historical problem of a "way out" (*chulu*) for China. Both interpretations rely on the reader's practiced habit of viewing China (both culture and nation) as a sojourner, a human body with whom he or she (as Chinese) can establish a fully empathic relationship. Moreover, these roads in war reportage are more often than not taking the writer away from home to a place he or she has never seen before (the reportage text is driven by the novelty of experience rather than familiar stocks of allusions), and the writer is thus keenly observant of his or her surroundings, carefully selecting concrete details.

These narratives of retreat or deliberate penetration into the Chinese interior echo the paradigm established in Lu Xun's stories of rural return, particularly the series of first-person narratives revolving around the narrator's return to his hometown, such as "Guxiang" (My Hometown), "Zhufu" (New Year's Sacrifice), and "Zai jiulou shang" (In the Wine Shop). The narrator in these short reportage journeys, like Lu Xun's, contemplates his or her identity as the landscape unfolds. Moreover, each event, and the actions and words of each person described, even the very objects of the landscape in these forced retreats into the interior, resonate with historical and national implications: the sense of cultural emergency or crisis brought about by the war, Japanese injuries to China, the suffering of the Chinese people, and the discovery of collective strength and patriotism and hope in a militarized, rural way of life.

Wenxie and the Transformation of Reportage into a Collective Activity
In 1937, after the July 7 Marco Polo Bridge Incident and war broke out in Shanghai on August 13, several of the larger literary magazines temporarily halted publication, and most writers in Beiping and Shanghai were forced to follow the remains of the culture industry into the cities of the Chinese interior, particularly Hankou, Chongqing, and Guilin. Apart from drama, cartoons, woodcuts, and poetry, reportage became the form of artistic production that was published in the greatest volume. Tang Tao writes: "A report of the research bureau of Wenxie [All China Resistance Association of Writers and Artists] given in the autumn of 1938 in Chongqing at the Symposium on Culture states 'we can see from the dispatches from the front that reportage literature is fulfilling a great duty, a duty of conveying the experiences and lessons of struggle to our soldiers,' and that since the beginning of the war 'works with a rather large structure are more and more rare and are largely being displaced by concise and more inflammatory sketches and essays—that is, the forms of reportage literature and *zawen.*'"[5]

The coordination of collective reportage activities by a literary organization was a crucial development in this period that was prompted in no small degree by the war situation. The physical disruption of the publishing industry through forced moves ever deeper into the interior actually had a unifying effect on the increasingly dominant leftist literary scene. Moreover, this unifying effect was manifested in clear transformations of the consciousness of writers.

Most active writers in unoccupied China were brought together in an anti-Japanese effort in early 1938 with the establishment of the All China Resistance Association of Writers and Artists (Zhonghua quanguo wenyijie kangdi xiehui, hereafter Wenxie). The association, headed by Lao She, was better organized than the League of Left-Wing Writers and produced one of the longest-lasting literary journals of the war period, *Resistance Literature* (*Kangzhan wenyi*, published May 4, 1938, through May 4, 1945). The association was much more geographically widespread than the league, establishing branch associations in places all over unoccupied China (chiefly in Sichuan but later also throughout regions under Communist control such as northern Shaanxi and central Hebei).

In the head office, which was established in Hankou and later moved to Chongqing, Wenxie frequently organized symposiums on major issues concerning the association itself and the literary community in general, such as what kind of reading materials to prepare for soldiers and how to organize cultural activities in fallen areas (1939), how to support writers materially during the war (1940), and literary trends during the war (1941). Concern for the welfare of writers, particularly those who were old, ill, or poor, also led to fund-raising and special programs. Related to this were the frequent anniversary celebrations for prominent writers, including the twenty-fifth anniversary of the beginning of Guo Moruo's literary career (November 1941) and the twentieth anniversary of Lao She's (April 1944) as well as the celebration of Mao Dun's fiftieth birthday in 1945. Another of the main concerns of the association was the criticism of writers and trends considered to be treacherous, or at least reactionary, manifested in open letters to Zhou Zuoren criticizing his working for the Japanese puppet government in Beiping (1938) and its angry editorial of the same year in response to Liang Shiqiu's apparent encouragement of literature that had nothing to do with the war.[6]

Finally, and most importantly for the present study, while subscribing to essentially the same literary policies as the League of Left-Wing Writers, Wenxie was more effective in carrying them out. One key factor was the use of organized, collective literary campaigns, especially ones in which a service corps of writers or a drama troupe traveled to the countryside or battle areas to engage in propaganda work and entertain soldiers. This aspect of the work of the association was closely coordinated with the military effort, aided greatly by the activism of certain generals and other ranking military officers sympathetic to the Communist Party (or the Communists themselves) such as Nie Rongzhen, Peng Dehuai, Chen Geng, Sun Lianzhong, and many others. It is a result of this close logistical coordination that the literary work groups were able to pass safely through the base areas and front lines and that a good portion of the reportage to come out of this period consisted of portraits of such military figures.

Wenxie's Writers' War Area Interview Group (Zuojia zhandi fangwentuan) is the best documented of this kind of organized, collective activity. The group was typical of the "literature and arts work groups" (*wenyi gongzuotuan, wengongtuan* for short) that were becoming widespread by the second or third year of the war, especially in the Communist base areas, and would become a standard method of collective cultural organization in the People's Republic. The Interview Group was organized in the summer of 1938 by Wenxie and consisted of fourteen novelists, poets, playwrights, literary critics, theorists, and academics (all of whom were association members), two women and twelve men. Their mission was to set out from the association's Chongqing headquarters for the northern war front in Henan; engage in relief and propaganda activities; interview officers, soldiers, and ordinary people along the way; and, most importantly, give a collective account of their experiences. The main literary production of the Interview Group is the diary "Bi Youji" (Guerrilla Pen), a collective work narrating the experiences of the group over the first two months of its journey. "Women shisige" (The Fourteen of Us, the diary of Bai Lang, one of the two women in the group), also covers the entire expedition and is the best-known work to come out of this project. All of the group's works were published in *Kangzhan wenyi* in late 1938 and early 1939.

The work of the Interview Group is indicative of the status of collective literary organization under Wenxie. Their diary, "Guerrilla Pen," is a telling manifestation of the gap between the articulated goals of literary organization and the at times painful realities of the writer's predicament in wartime. The members of the group were all well-educated, urban writers and intellectuals who enthusiastically threw themselves into an activity that would further the war effort on the cultural front and bring them closer to the Chinese army and the countryside.

Their enthusiasm was seriously dampened, however, by the first several weeks of their journey. Although the tour was carefully planned beforehand, the writers themselves were dismayed by the physical rigors of long-distance travel through the countryside as well as the inclement weather's constant disruption of their schedule. The group was accommodated between each leg of the journey by a different military unit, which in turn would become the subject of their writings. The resulting feasting and sightseeing that punctuate each stop in their travels give the reader an increasing sense of the party as less of a service corps than a tour group. Fatigue and ill health get the better of many of the group's members as they finally arrive at their destination, the eastern front in Shanxi Province, and just when the group seems to be beginning to succeed in its spiritual journey from the city to the front lines the whole project is devastated by the sudden contraction of malaria and death of the group's leader, Wang Lixi.

Literary activities in the base areas, in contrast, were marked by a more or less consistent unity of theme, a unity that was accomplished as much by means of powerful and effective propaganda campaigns as by self-censorship. What is often written off as rigid thought control in Yan'an and the other base areas was to a significant degree a successful attempt to bring talented writers wholeheartedly behind the creation of a new, unprecedented culture that would be the model for China's future.

Guerrilla Consciousness: The Image of the Soldier-Reporter
If the works discussed in the previous chapter depict the emotional environment of occupied cities, the embattled interior, and the nightmarish battlefield itself, the mental appropriation of the countryside I am describing here belongs to the imaginative world of the battle area (*zhanqu*), as distinguished from the front lines seen in Qiu Dongping's works), and the guerrilla-controlled border areas (*bianqu*). Such readings of the transformed landscapes of war were mediated by adventurous reporters and writers who gravitated toward the front lines to convey the experience of the war as it was happening in the richest way circumstances permitted. Due to their daring and the influence of their work, writers like Xie Bingying, Fan Changjiang, Meng Qiujiang, and Lu Ye consciously or unconsciously created images of themselves as cultural warriors that contributed to the literary landscape of war.

In my discussion of *The Shanghai Incident and Its Reportage*, I referred to the image of the war correspondent as a sometimes romanticized icon somewhere between the civilian and the soldier. In part inspired by translated Western works, this image had been cultivated in China as early as 1928 with Xie Bingying's widely read account of her experiences as a soldier in the Northern Expedition of 1926–27, *Congjun riji* (Army Diary).[7] *Army Diary* differs from later war reportage in that the author is not greatly concerned with depicting the atmosphere of a nation at war; rather, Xie Bingying pioneers the reconstruction of the literary image of the woman as an alternative form of social intervention. Xie's self-image constitutes a willful departure from both the passive, victimized woman (as seen in the fiction of Lu Xun and Ba Jin) and the hesitant, "sentimental," and modern woman featured in the fiction of Mao Dun and Bing Xin. Xie's woman soldier is crafted as the embodiment of radical consciousness, the fully engaged intellectual at the forefront of historical change.

Army Diary predates all the works discussed in the previous chapter; I deal with it only now because it illustrates an aspect of war reportage more closely associated with the present discussion: the elaboration of guerrilla consciousness. Since the written expression of this mode of consciousness in China did not really come into its own until writers were fully engaged in organizational and military activities in the countryside, it had little influence on the narrations from the early months of the war. Nevertheless, as I have shown to some extent in my discussion of Cao Bai, it did exist, and Xie Bingying's popular text provided an influential model for writing the transformed consciousness of the fully engaged intellectual.

Chang-tai Hung discusses Xie Bingying in the context of what he describes as a resurgence of the "Hua Mulan" figure in Chinese popular culture during the war, citing numerous plays about historical Chinese woman warriors popular at the time: "Perhaps Xie Bingying (1906–) best personified the indomitability of Hua Mulan."[8] While this was certainly a significant phenomenon that informed readers' reception of *Army Diary*, there is no indication within the text that the author sees herself as recuperating such traditional icons. Rather than alluding to historical woman warriors, whose actions are generally reconciled, at times ingeniously, with conventional Confucian morality, Xie is immersed in the exhilaration of exploring an entirely *new* mode of consciousness. This consciousness is expressed through an emotional and behavioral extravagance and a regrounding of emotional and spiritual yearning within the context of physiological needs and immediate daily experience.

Xie's emotional extravagance is manifested in her construction of herself and other characters as iconoclastic, opinionated, even flamboyant personalities. Using frequent exclamations and expletives and often directly addressing the reader, the narrator gleefully boasts of her own impetuousness in behaviors ranging from hanging out the window of a moving train and grabbing the tree branches moving by to haranguing "backward" peasant women to stand up and demand what they deserve. She also expresses this extravagance by extolling personalities who exhibit similar qualities.

> I made friends with a group of kids; they're the "auxiliaries" for the revolution, but even from the courageous spirit they already have now, they're really the revolution's "young avant-garde." Why do I boast like this? Because there are facts to prove it.
>
> There is a twelve-year-old girl named Zhang Qingyun whose whole family is comprised of herself, her parents, and a little sister. She's a student with unbound feet and short hair. During this reactionary maneuver by S's army, she was wrongfully accused by some wicked woman of working for the Women's Association and so she was captured. Her mother and little sister couldn't stop crying (the father, involved in the peasant movement, was away at the time), but she just bravely said, "Mother! Don't cry! Even if they execute me, I'll shout slogans before I die." At this those bastard criminals said, "Yeah, this is a real revolutionary. Not afraid of death, she doesn't shed tears, only blood." She boldly answered them, "That's right! What's there to be afraid of in death?!" And she happily entered the county jail. With her, there were five in all locked up, and after three days they had executed four of them, leaving only her. She would have suffered the same fate—death—but the county magistrate confirmed that she was just a child, a completely innocent child, so her life was saved. She told me this herself, but then who on this street doesn't already know about it? (17)

In addition to narrating her personal experiences on the Northern Expedition, Xie is exhilarated by the stories of heroism she encounters along the way, and much of her narrative is constituted by such story-telling. By integrating them into a written narrative, these stories gain an epic quality enhanced in part by the narrator's exaggeration and embellishment. Moreover, Xie's account features the description of Zhang Qingyun's external features (her short hair and unbound feet) as emblematic of her social progressiveness. This emphasis on the significance of appearance coupled with narrative concentration on the character's words and behavior demonstrates how the storytelling mode is consistent with reportage's generic limitation to the externally observable. At the same time, the narrator's investment of meaning in external details allows Xie's reportage to convey emotions and themes without delving into the character's own inaccessible emotions.

The mission of the Northern Expedition was to put down warlords and establish the military authority of the Republican government throughout the eastern half of China. The movement was also a "revolutionary" one in that it involved violent reprisals against landlords and corrupt members of the local gentry, many of whom were executed. This is one aspect from which one can see the radical, uncompromising character of Xie Bingying's consciousness; here she derives exhilaration from the unleashed violence of long-exploited peasants. The Hunan peasants "aren't the least bit civil to the local tyrants, corrupt gentry, or the landlords; all they do is beat them to death, shoot them, or run them through. Every day I hear murderous shouting and the sound of guns; even in our little village they took care of eight or nine local bullies' stinking lives; it's really terrific!" (7–8)

Xie then goes on to tell the "funny" and "happy" story of how the chairman of a village peasant association near Changsha asked for a show of hands of all members who agreed to the execution of a certain local bully. After they all raised their hands, a shot rang out and they asked in shock what had happened; it turned out that they had no idea what they were raising their hands for. Xie addresses Sun Fuyuan (this passage is in the form of a letter to Sun): "Ha ha! Mr. Fuyuan, when you read this little story, did you laugh so hard your beard stood on end?" (8). Xie's laughter rings through the text at several points, often highlighting her exhilaration at the unleashed, violent power of revolution.

The narrator Xie constructs is also a devoted writer, one for whom writing is an obsession that often leads her to neglect her own physical needs, but she devotes equal energy to adopting a material simplicity that becomes conventional in later narratives of the countryside. In the following passage, Xie's reaction to the loss of all her belongings combines both elements.

> It's terrible, really terrible! The blanket I brought, the food box, water bottle, and bundling cloth, all lost! These things, except for the bundle, aren't really all that important. Although my water bottle is lost, I can go to my fellow students' and have some tea or spend a couple of copper coins on a bowl. As for losing the lunchbox, I can think of some way to borrow a bowl, but I can only do that when I've got a place to stay; if we have to move, where am I going to borrow it from? In that case I'll just have to let my two empty hands suffice. As for losing the blanket, I can sleep on the floor without any covering. But losing that bundle got me so upset I shed a few tears over my bad luck.
>
> Everything in that bundle was important: stockings, shoes, pants, handkerchiefs—well, those actually aren't that important, there is something even more important: I lost my diary of four days! Ai! Those pages were all written on my lap as I squatted on the ground, they were full of tragic, heroic, happy battle stories, but they're all lost! I can't find even a single one! Ai! Heaven! What can I do? Somebody wanted me to try to rewrite them, but how could that possibly work? All I can do is sacrifice them, make them a revolutionary sacrifice and be done with it. Ai!
>
> As I think back on the record of my life of the past four days, I feel that losing it is more upsetting than losing a friend. . . ! (15–16)

Despite the importance she puts on writing, Xie's priorities are not strictly spiritual; she devotes as much attention to resolving the problems of her water bowl and blanket as she does to lamenting the loss of her diary. These small but necessary objects are part of the experience of moving through the countryside, and may indeed be read as components of the rural landscape itself.

It is precisely this material, physiological component that distinguishes guerrilla consciousness from both the romantic and realistic approaches to writing the countryside. For example, Xie continually makes joking references to her hunger: "It's four o'clock, and my belly's still sunken in like 'anything.' Although in the morning when my stomach ached I had a few mouthfuls of rice, now that my stomach's better and I want something to eat, where am I going to buy something to fill up? Even the jujubes are gone from the pharmacy!" (5–6). Later she laments: "Writing this letter I wrote my belly empty, what am I going to do? Ai! Ai! Sir, buy me some candy, save the children!" (13).

The deceptive simplicity and physicality of guerrilla consciousness as pioneered by Xie Bingying conceal its status (especially in retrospect) as a new way of describing the world and dramatizing social relations. To simply call this a "spartan" aesthetic would rob it of its characteristic jocularity and especially the sensual pleasure its creators derive from the delicate interplay of want (hunger, fatigue) and simple gratification.

The extension of military habits of living, military language, and the paradigm of struggle not only spread through space and social relations but penetrated subjective forms as well, creating a new way of seeing and feeling. Far from ignoring subjective complexity and suppressing inner life, guerrilla consciousness signifies the writer's willing adoption of a simplified, abbreviated palette of emotional responses and metaphors after having been saturated with the various urban neuroses of the romantic and confessional literatures of the teens and twenties. The departure from the cluttered study, the teahouse, and the bustle of complex urban society that had been the modern Chinese writer's environment throughout the 1920s in favor of a militarized rural milieu is reflected on the "inside" with an imagination that no longer derives its metaphors from literary traditions and trends but from the rediscovered landscape of rural China.

In chapter 1, I discussed how the travelogues of Qu Qiubai and Fan Changjiang enriched the youji tradition by consciously inheriting many of its conventions and investing it with a more immediate historical dynamism and adding layers of military, ethnic, and economic meanings. Chen Yi, a famous general and later mayor of Shanghai, is a particularly interesting example of the literary reappropriation of the Chinese countryside in that he integrates the image of the soldier-writer established in part by Xie Bingying into experience of the landscape and its transformation by war. Reading Chen's "Jiangnan kangzhan zhi chun" (Springtime in Jiangnan during the War of Resistance), we witness a process in the general and his men of renewing a covenant of intimacy, not only between a liberating army and the people on whose behalf they are supposedly fighting but with the Chinese landscape, with the sometimes surprising character of a territory that was available to the reader and writer before to a large extent through the poems and essays of the traditional literati.[9]

Chen Yi's narrator often ironically foregrounds the gap between the China of textual tradition and that of immediate experience: "I lay there on a plank in the room that had been flooded with water, exuding the stench of darkness and dampness, and in my heart rose yet another complaint: 'So this is Jiangnan in the rain!' It was as if I had been cheated, because the Jiangnan beneath the brush of literati throughout history was always so picturesque, so utterly different from what lay here before my eyes!" (735). Passages like this signify less an alienation from the unforgiving realities of the environment than from the literature that had led the writer to expect something different. There is an ironic disdain for books in Chen Yi's text; he points out that while the service corps members lament the destruction of their diaries and books by rain (recalling Xie Bingying's plaint of ten years before) the narrator himself gladly discards his soggy library. What is stressed positively is vibrant, physical activity and sensual experience; the lighter side of the heavy rains is dramatized by the laughter and cursing of the troops as they slip and tumble, one after the other, into a muddy ditch and later laugh together at the spectacle of themselves, naked and covered with mud, as they stand around a fire waiting for their clothes to dry (734).

This physical reacquaintance with the Chinese landscape takes place on a subtler level in the unit's encounter with Mao Shan, a mountain sacred to Daoists for centuries. Again, the literary picture as Chen Yi perceived it would have it luxuriant with vegetation. The troops are disappointed as they approach the mountain for the first time, as it appears not only unpleasant but strategically useless. However, the unit moves beyond its initial displeasure, through a process of penetration and identification described in the following passage, to arrive at a new understanding and appreciation.

> The Mao Shan of our imaginations should have been "soaring mountains in a lofty range, dense forests and tall bamboos." How were we to know that when we arrived last year we would see that

on Mao Shan not only were there no trees and flowers but even the *mao* grasses were sparse? Since it wouldn't hide even a single man and horse, naturally it couldn't cover a relatively large detachment, and this made us all very disappointed. Little did we know that after more than half a year of work, when we had familiarized ourselves with Mao Shan's terrain and with the people there, the *mao* grasses of Mao Shan were abundant and thick. There were many mountain recesses and oblique places that could not be seen from a distance. From close up one can see that it's full of deep cavities and could be very useful. It would be entirely possible to rotate several small hidden guerrilla squads within it. Thus, this year's Mao Shan in the minds of our detachment increased in beauty and value. (735–36)

Both the military and aesthetic disappointment at the apparent barrenness of the mountain are gradually shed through the process of entering the mountain and discovering its "recesses," "oblique places," and "cavities." These features, despite the absence of luxuriant vegetation and vibrant color, redeem the mountain both strategically and aesthetically, and this redemption is significantly mediated by a long process of refamiliarization through close, physical work.

Chen Yi's landscape, moreover, is figured as a symbol for the Chinese nation, polluted by Japanese troops. Laughter, the special function of which in the construction of guerrilla consciousness has been noted in connection with Xie Bingying, reinforces this theme of landscape as nation. Chen Yi repeatedly depicts his soldiers laughing at themselves in acts of insignificant folly, perhaps to emphasize good morale in a revolutionary army and to decrease the menace of soldiers moving across the landscape. But laughter also appears in relation to the enemy: one soldier picks up the narrator's theme of reappropriating the Jiangnan scenery by commenting on its perfect beauty—if only it were not cluttered with "those Japanese devils" (736). Presented as a joke, this comment provokes the hearty laughter of all the men. To an extent, this vignette also signifies the morale of the narrator's unit, but the embedded trope of Japanese soldiers as pests invading the serene and beautiful landscape of South China is common to a number of writers of this period and reveals the view mentioned earlier of China as a contiguous whole invaded, diseased, and dismembered by the vagaries of history in the age of imperialism. The reader is infected not only with a sense of emergency (confrontation with a maimed body) but with a palpable sense of something to fight for—a reintegrated China—as an extension or projection of oneself. Indeed, this personal/national "selfhood" is precisely what is created in this process. This China, for both narrator and reader, is one's own body, one's "flesh and blood" on a national scale.

Finally, Chen Yi's troops themselves become part of the landscape as it swallows an unsuspecting Japanese detachment by means of the explicitly landscape-oriented tactic of ambush. Most of the Japanese soldiers escape or are killed, but one who did not falls to his knees after most of his comrades have been killed or have run away and kowtows to the surrounding Chinese soldiers; they have exacted their revenge in this scene for his (Japan's) invasion of the landscape by concealing themselves in it and surprising him. It is the landscape's ability to conceal—its recesses and cavities—that make it useful to the Chinese soldiers, whose intimate familiarity with the terrain gives them an advantage over the otherwise better equipped enemy.

BI YE: LANDSCAPE AS THE CONSCIOUSNESS OF COMMUNITY

Chen Yi's text is typical of Communist or guerrilla accounts of battle zone experience in its projection of the Chinese countryside as a dynamic medium within and through which the Chinese people pursue victory and self-determination. Nevertheless, it is still imagined as something outside the self with which the narrator develops a relationship. For some writers, however, like Bi Ye, the landscape becomes the material of consciousness itself, indistinguishable from thoughts and emotions.

Bi Ye (Huang Chaoyang, 1916–), who was still a young writer in the late 1930s, is representative of a generation of writers whose literary careers coincided with the emergence of reportage in China. The son of manual laborers from rural Guangdong, Bi Ye as a teenager helped his mother work at the local pier. In his high school years he became a student activist, later auditing university classes and began his career as a writer and cultural activist, joining the League of Left-Wing Writers. The outbreak of war propelled him with other students into the northern Chinese countryside to engage in guerrilla activities. Already inclined toward writing reportage throughout the 1930s, Bi Ye arrived in Wuhan in 1938, where he published three collections narrating his military experiences.[10]

In one of these, *Beifang de yuanye* (The Northern Wilderness, 1938), several discrete episodes connect the experiences of three unrelated characters into an unusually coherent structure (for reportage).[11] Moreover, the writer's consciousness of engagement in the nation's struggle for liberation is integrated more closely with the imaginative animation of the Chinese countryside, in effect pulling consciousness farther away from the confined spaces of the city and out into the vastness of Chinese territory and historical struggle. This is a complex, ambitious work that brings into question the limits of reportage as a factual account of events. The writer, himself absent from the narrative, nevertheless gives a rich, detailed account of the emotional and physical environments of both battle and barren wastes as he gradually brings together characters who represent distinct aspects of the experience of war in the countryside. The text, divided into four titled sections, opens with a vivid integration of the sights and sounds of troops moving over the landscape at night with a clear exposition of the strategic context of their movement.

Like a speeding rocket, the comrades threw open their stride, running back into the dark wilderness. . . .

That day, the entire force retreated toward the Hutuo River, drawing the enemy deep into Xingtang, densely surrounded by undulating hills and forests. According to reconnaisance reports, enemy cavalry had already arrived at the line of entrapment—Xingtang. Thus, it was the student brigade, baptized in dozens of battles since it emerged from the bloody battle of Beiping, that was the first to receive the order to counterattack Xingtang.

After the rain, the open fields were slippery; the comrades' shivering, drenched bodies advanced along the field paths. They fixed their bayonets on the tips of their rifles and strapped their packs and ammunition belts tightly to their bodies. The entire brigade gave forth not the slightest sound of life but for the monotonous squishing sound of the mud beneath the feet of the troops.

The night was a vast expanse of blackness. Half the comrades were leaping while the others were sliding because, fearing the enemy might spot their position early, they dared not burn even a horse lantern. At the front of the troops, an old local peasant guerrilla guided them forward. (235)

There are no names, no descriptions of people, nor the kind of self-conscious internal dialogue that characterized Qiu Dongping's battle accounts. The scene is offered for an uninitiated reader, and information is carefully shaped to focus on the experience conveyed as a collective, concrete experience. The reader is partially blind, situated in the midst of the action yet knowing little about what is happening; the spare narration is our only resource for drawing what nevertheless emerges as a clear picture.

This sets the stage for the guerrilla attack on Xingtang from the surrounding hills. Characters like Heihu (Black Tiger) and "the woman comrade" begin to emerge through their distinctive features, behavioral traits, and nicknames. Before the attack is signaled by the raising of a red flag on the city wall, we are made to witness the atrocity of the occupying Japanese soldiers as they drag peasants to death with their warhorses outside the city gate. The attack itself is described in vivid, cinematic detail, with the enemy caught by surprise and finally defeated in a bloody battle outside the city walls. In the final scene of the first episode, one of the most explicitly ritualistic scenes in leftist literature, the victorious guerrillas carry out a "revolutionary sacrifice ritual" at night by the light of bonfire in Xingtang's square.

> Some of the comrades of the transportation team carried from a distance the bodies of those comrades who had died into the square, placing them beneath the very gate on which the red banner had flown during the day. The banner flapping in the night wind looked even more red reflecting the light of the fire. The faces of the comrades who had lost their lives gazed peacefully into the sky, quietly awaiting the revolutionary ritual.
> The general ordered that the warhorses' already butchered carcasses be carried into the center of the circle of people. With a flurry of gunshots, the ritual had begun. . . .
> The guerrillas, peasants, women, and children surrounding the

square all stood at once. In the midst of the general's eulogy, the hearts of the crowd were trembling in sadness.

"You were born in these fields and plains of suffering, and you died for our suffering homeland! You have left behind your comrades, left behind your young wives, left behind your lonely children, to sleep forever here along with the clouds and the grassy plains. . . ."

The general's voice became hoarse. Women in the crowd were quietly sobbing, children were wailing aloud from their mothers' embrace, while the men bowed their heads and sighed. . . .

"We comrades you have left behind who have not died vow to use the bloodied flag flying over your heads to invoke your heroic spirits, to protect the great and broad land, your orphaned children and widowed wives, for a long march in the mountain wilderness! . . ." The general ended this bloody sacrifice with a solemn and resolute tone. Comrades used bayonets to carve off the horse meat chunk by chunk and throw it in the bonfire. The tongues of flame ravenously lapped up the meat, giving off a kind of charred aroma. . . .

Song began to waft up from beside the bonfire, and soon the entire square was undulating with the enormous, wavelike war song. It flew up into the night sky, floated past forests, and flowed onto the barren wastes:

Fight, fight, fight!
Fight for the victory of the new day. (244)

Here the narrator's account blends with the general's eulogy to elaborate the meaning of the soldiers' deaths in the context of the physical territory in which and for which they lost their lives. The coordination of the circle of mourners, the general's eulogy, the placing of the meat on the fire, and the "wafting up" of the song reveals no conscious organization, signifying the integration of the townspeople and guerrillas as a community. The solemn, religious tone of the entire passage is, as I will show in the next chapter, a frequent characteristic of the narration of all kinds of social activity in the Communist-controlled border areas, although in this case it derives directly from the intersection of the social and the military.

The second episode, "Xue zhe" (Bloody Wheelruts), recounts the boy Guier's loss of his family as the Japanese terrorize their village outside

Xingtang. Like the first, this section begins with a lovingly crafted landscape. The emphasis is on plants and scenery particular to the location,
while the features of the landscape seem to gently move and react to
one another: "the little village seeps into the green sea of wild date and
peach trees," mountains "undulate outside the village," and a water-
fall "wavers and beneath the sunlight shimmers white along with the
granite mesas" (244–45). Human figures enter into this bucolic scene
conventionally, as part of the landscape, but they are Japanese soldiers
bringing violence and discord. This kind of aesthetic friction, like Chen
Yi toying with the conventions of landscape description, is a common
means of generating emotional agitation in war reportage.

The focus turns to the village itself; the Japanese attempt, with the assistance of a treacherous local strongman, to enlist the aid of the starving villagers by giving away wheat flour, but when the tactic fails they
resort to violence and atrocity. It is in this context that we are introduced
to the boy Guier, witnessing with him the kidnapping of his mother
and the death of his father in hand-to-hand combat with Japanese sentries. Although the village is retaken by the guerrilla forces, Guier and
his grandfather, now without a family, resolve to take their ox and cart
and join the guerrillas.

The third episode, "Niuche shang de binghao" (The Wounded on the
Oxcart), narrates the guerrillas' narrow escape from entrapment in a
nearby valley. They penetrate the encirclement with great loss and difficulty, and the narrative follows the wounded and ill remnants of the
squad as they advance across a desertlike plain in Guier's cart. More importantly, Guier's slowly emerging grief at the loss of his parents and
grandfather (who was killed in the escape from the valley) is resolved in
the establishment of a new emotional relationship with the lone woman
member of the group, who takes on the role of loving older sister or
mother.

The constant progress across the desertlike wastes, as the night wears
on, slowly focuses on the nameless "woman comrade" as the emotional
center of the scene, softly singing a tragic song of military loss with
Guier's sleeping head resting on her knees. The quiet interplay of this
anonymous, young, yet maternal figure and the undulating, rocky terrain of the dark wastes as a figurative set piece signifies the turning
point in the characters' fortunes. "The Northern Wilderness" will now

be driven by increasing injections of hope, culminating in the unit's arrival in a new, utopian landscape.

The cart group is finally rescued from the wilderness by lookouts from a nearby village, where warmhearted and lively hospitality signifies deep mutual trust between peasants and soldiers. In fact, there is no clear distinction made between the peasants and these guerrillas, who are depicted as peasants who have taken up guns to rush at the enemy with little preparation but great zeal, while the peasants in the village are fully engaged in their own ways in the war effort. The abstract distinction between soldiers and peasants, in short, melts away as they work together through the daily emergencies of the war.

The wounded sojourners in the fourth section ("Wuji de gaoyuan" [The Wuji Plateau]) end up in an idyllic village near Handan in the Taihang Mountains area, described at greater length and in more ecstatic terms than any other place in the narrative.[12] Bi Ye's landscape description here strains to give the venue of this final section the feeling of paradise on earth, a modern "Peach Blossom Spring," and both war and enemy are forgotten. This sets the stage for the arrival of General Zhu, the commander of the whole "red spear" guerrilla operation throughout Henan and Hebei Provinces.[13] His arrival is typical of the great casual warrior, the guerrilla arch-icon.

> The horsemen quickly rode into the village, and one could gradually discern that the horseman who led them had a flowing white beard waving in front of his chest and was wearing a great big, wide-brimmed straw hat, rising and falling with a godlike, martial air on the back of his horse.
>
> When he got to a certain teahouse on the village street, the old man leaped down from his horse, tying the brownish-red steed to a scholartree in front of the door, and saying to the companions behind him:
>
> "You go on to Wu'an City; tell them I'm on my way."
>
> The old man walked into the teahouse, stroking his beard. He doffed his wide-brimmed straw hat, exposing his bristling white hair and his wrinkled, unyielding forehead, his hawklike eyes flashing with light and his square, bronze face radiating a martial divinity. He strode with a steady gait like a lion.

A number of officers of friendly units just passing through here on the way to Handan were sitting around a table, helmets on, having tea. A tall officer among them, as soon as he saw the old man walk into the teahouse, suddenly stood up and shouted to the other officers:

"Attention! Salute!"

The officers simultaneously stood with surprised reverence, bringing their right hands under the rim of their helmets with a military salute to the old man.

The old man, smiling, nodded.

"Hey! That old hero is the chief of the red spears of Hebei and Henan Provinces!" The tall officer said under his breath.

The officers all looked at the old man with amazement and admiration. (269–70)

Soon thereafter, all the characters Bi Ye has been following through the narrative converge in the teahouse to pay their respects to General Zhu, and the text ends, after reminiscing on the general's youthful heroics, with his departure for Wu'an.

One of the most distinctive aspects of "The Northern Wilderness" as a piece of war reportage is the importance assigned to characterization as a technique for writing guerrilla consciousness. In describing Heihu (Black Tiger) and Dayan (Big Goose), for example, Bi Ye is very much interested in depicting their casual, mischievous, and occasionally hot tempers as a somehow more human alternative to the various negative images of soldiers then current in the popular imagination. Black Tiger emerges from the text early in the first episode as an almost larger than life hero: after he is wounded in the forehead in the victorious retaking of the town of Xingtang, woman soldiers pin medals stolen from the enemy on his chest. His homespun, undisciplined familiarity embodies the theme of representing guerrilla/Communist forces as less concerned with discipline than morale and winning battles.

Black Tiger and Big Goose (a younger, sillier version of Black Tiger) are both often depicted in attitudes of ravenous hunger and thirst and the occasional euphoric satisfaction of these desires. For example, the hospitality of the village that takes in the wounded soldiers is realized in the form of great, steaming vats of millet porridge carried into the hut in which the guerrillas have been put up for the night; Heihu and Dayan gulp and slurp it down with such vehemence that tears stream from their eyes from the pain of scalding (261–62). Both characters are frequently depicted as unable to restrain their physical desires, gobbling up all their rationed food at once or guzzling down unboiled water from dirty rivers and constantly flirting with and tugging at village women.

Such earthy revelry is often accompanied by their spirited bursting forth in simple, at times lewd country songs or cursing in humorous, ribald ways as had the heckling workers of Ding Ling's "Eventful Autumn." The dark roughness of their skin, protruding muscles, and veins are often set in approving opposition to the "soft, white skin" of enemy soldiers and treacherous local officials. The idealized, casual, peasant/ soldier image, if one can judge by the frequency of its appearance in wartime reportage, was one of the key textual strategies for resolving the historical problem of soldier/civilian relations that persisted throughout the war and long after. Moreover, the figure of the peasant began to supersede the physical landscape as the paradigmatic vehicle for conveying guerrilla consciousness.

Guier, who enters the text in the second episode through the narration of the loss of each of the members of his family, and the nameless "woman comrade" who befriends him like an older sister are both examples of the reintegration through collective struggle of persons who have been deprived of their normal way of life and sense of identity. On the cart bearing the wounded across the wastes to the promised land of the Taihang Mountains guerrilla base, Guier gets to know the woman (who, like Black Tiger, had been in the Xingtang attack force) by telling the story of his heroic escape from the valley, but he finds himself unexpectedly weeping at the end of his tale.

"Ayah! Little comrade, why are you crying?"

The woman comrade climbed over to the front of the cart and with both arms pulled Guier from the cart shafts, lifting him into the carriage. She used her dirty, oily sleeve to dry Guier's tears, and her soft, long hair to caress Guier's cheeks. She comforted Guier with the tenderness of a mother. This brought all of the sadness buried deep in Guier's heart to the surface: he burrowed his whole body into the woman comrade's embrace, his two trembling arms tightly embracing the woman comrade's waist, and his hot, flowing teardrops were free to soak her long, soft hair. (256)

An emotional structure of maternal comforting is established, apparently fulfilling yearnings on the part of both characters. The fact that the woman is a fellow soldier and not a member of his real family contributes to the macrotextual rhetoric of the collective "family" as the right emotional investment, the biological family as something left behind, whether deliberately or by force.

Black Tiger, the energetic, mischievous, and courageous peasant fully saturated with martial confidence and ability; the nameless "woman comrade," a spirited student dislodged from the city and her education by war yet completely engaged in spirit and action in the guerrilla effort; and Guier, deprived of his family and ordinary peasant childhood and discovering a new identity in the collective life of the guerrilla squad, each typifies a different aspect of the experience of war in the countryside without losing his or her credibility as genuine persons. The convergence of their stories in the difficult night journey across the wastelands, their accommodation by the friendly villagers who save them, and their ultimate arrival in the utopian order of Wuji, where they can finally cleanse and fill their bodies and meet the old guerrilla general, allegorically fulfills the promise or hope for a way out for China, clearing the way for more detailed, joyful celebrations of the idealized order of the Communist bases.

These are very much the "typical characters" (dianxing renwu) demanded by socialist realism. Their literary existence relies on techniques left over from the proletarian literary movement; here they simultaneously represent peasants, soldiers, and the Chinese people as a whole. However, the aesthetics of typicality fit reportage much more comfortably than they do fiction. When the factuality of the subject matter is an assumption against which the text is read, one does not expect the direct psychological exploration commonly associated with the modern fictional character. In reportage, meaning is generated from character precisely from the ability of the character's externally observable qualities to suggest something more general, such as a social group or a historical trend.

In addition to his careful attention to characterization and its allegorical possibilities, Bi Ye is committed to mobilizing the landscape, both as a dynamic, living entity in itself and in communication with the characters he portrays. Vivid and dramatic action alternates almost rhythmically with richly detailed landscape description, and it is through the latter more than the former that Bi Ye fills out the emotional space of the text. Terrestrial features interact with the sky and heavenly bodies through caresses, flows, exchanges of heat and coolness, and color and form pouring up and down distant vistas and in and out of the narrator's and characters' feelings and actions. The sky, the earth, people, and animals are depicted as equally conscious and feeling entities united through the mutual interchange of feelings and physical sensations.

The ox lazily and cleverly brought the cart to a halt under an old scholartree. Everyone was immersed in silent depression, each thinking of the unhappy things that had happened to them. The glistening, reddened eyes of the woman comrade suddenly shed two teardrops, and she raised her head with a start and gazed off into the distant wilds.

The wilds quietly exposed their yellow-brown chest, still exuding an air of dusty heat. In the distance, near the grove of wild date trees full of ripe red fruit, one could make out several pools of still water in which the light of the sun sinking in the west was reflected like tears someone had shed. . . . (256)

The accursed wilderness, wide as a sea, the hot air rising out of the rubble, clogged the whole oxcart with stifling heat. The moon leaked an eerie white light from behind the clouds, and constellations of stars flickered blue in their sparseness, like the eyes of an orphan bashfully peeking at the wide open spaces. A blurry dark shape gradually disappeared behind the cart with the turning of the wheels; perhaps it was a sand dune, a grove of trees, a field of kaoliang. (257)

Far more than Cao Bai was able to accomplish in his parting reflections on the community achieved through the interaction of humans with the rural landscape, Bi Ye realizes the holistic "breathing" of the thoroughly integrated consciousness of the countryside. Bi Ye's text refrains from any kind of verbal abstraction about the themes he expresses; instead, he realizes them in the form of vivid actions and images that communicate directly to the senses and the body.[14]

Chinese war reportage continued to be produced not only up to the Japanese surrender in 1945 but throughout the civil war that ended in 1949, after which it reappeared soon again in great volume during the Korean conflict of 1950–53. These different periods, along with the special kind of war reportage of the border areas throughout the 1940s, each had its own thematic concerns and formal characteristics. Further research on this most voluminous of reportage subgenres is necessary to assess the validity of the generalizations I have made in this chapter, but I do have some observations about these other periods, which situate them in relation to the account I have given here.

All of these later types of war reportage belong properly to the special cultural system created and elaborated in the context of Communist rule and fully within the strictures of the Party's cultural apparatus. War reportage in Yan'an and the other border regions is explicitly concerned with the depiction of the Eighth Route Army as a social and cultural laboratory and model. For example, works by Huang Gang, such as "Wo kanjianle balujun" (I Have Seen the Eighth Route Army, 1941),[15] and "Yu: Chen Geng bingtuan shi zenyang zuozhande zhier" (Rain: How Chen Geng's Troops Fight #2, 1942),[16] are far more concerned with extolling Communist generals and telling the stories of soldiers' education and moral transformation than they are of recounting the historical experience of war.

Further, the reportage of the civil war of 1945–49 provides us mainly with a chronicle of successive campaigns, particularly the liberation of Manchuria and the Southern Expedition, which again tell us more about the emerging rhetoric of Communist cultural institutions than they do about the everyday experience of war or about how civil war may differ on the subjective level from that of resistance to foreign invasion. In my initial reading of civil war texts, I observed no significant difference in writers' treatment of the enemy from that of the War of Resistance, even though the "enemy" was now Chinese.

Finally, the reportage of the Korean War introduces a whole new set of problems, in that the voluminous output of reportage bears the marks of a carefully organized media campaign with specific propaganda objectives. The reportage of the Korean war must be viewed as the product of an already institutionalized reportage genre subject to the immediate demands of the Chinese government at the time. Thus, issues of veracity and historical accuracy would become major obstacles to the serious discussion of these texts, especially in light of contrasting narratives that appeared in the early 1980s from returned prisoners of war. Korean war reportage would thus make a fascinating study, but the issues involved are far removed from the concerns of this one.

There are certain generalizations that can be made about later developments of war reportage in China in the context of the present chapter. The first concerns the above-mentioned movement toward a storytelling paradigm in the war reportage of the countryside. Communist war reportage relies almost entirely on the storyteller type of narrator, and indeed this narrator becomes an overtly *didactic* storyteller from the reportage of the border areas to that of the Korean War. The didactic narrator is characterized by frequent direct address to the reader and especially by the use of strongly suggestive rhetorical questions. This may be manifested most clearly in the title of what is perhaps the most famous Korean War piece, Wei Wei's "Shui shi zui ke'ai de ren?" (Who Is Most Worthy of Our Love?), which goes on to elaborate intimately brutal forms of heroism on the part of Chinese troops engaging directly with the American enemy.[17] The emergence of didacticism in storytelling reportage can be traced to the emphasis on storytelling as a form of education and indoctrination within the cultural system of the border areas discussed in great detail in David Apter and Tony Saich's *Revolutionary Discourse in Mao's Republic.*[18]

Second, Communist writers enthusiastically recuperated the exploitation of the graphic image as an emotional trigger (understanding *graphic*, again, as frequent and occasionally shocking depictions of bodily injury and the flow of bodily fluids). The graphic image was used now mainly as a vehicle for conveying the brutal suffering the People's Liberation Army (PLA) was willing to endure for the success of the revolution and the victory of "the people." This suffering is manifested in the cracked and bleeding bare feet of the PLA troops as they awaited in the frozen winter wastes of the Manchurian countryside the opportunity to descend upon Shenyang (Mukden) and retake it from the Nationalists as well as in the frequent Korean War image of soldiers continuing to struggle though engulfed in napalm flames and covered with blisters. In the previous chapter, I interpreted the graphic image as a figurative vehicle through which the reader could ground his or her hatred of the enemy in physical revulsion evoked by the image, and it is here used in this sense again, showing how the conventions of the very earliest war reportage continued to drive the genre even after the Communist victory.

Finally, Communist war reportage combines the storytelling form with this exploitation of the graphic image to reconfigure the reportage text as a verbal monument extolling Communist generals and the heroism of soldiers sacrificed in battle. Depictions of famous generals such as Zhu De, He Long, Lin Biao, Chen Geng, Wang Zhen, and Peng Dehuai are legion in the corpus of Communist war reportage, and this can be explained in part by the state of reportage practice in the Communist cultural institutions of the time.

Communist reportage, far more than reportage had been previously, was the product of assignments given to writers. In wartime, such assignments more often than not consisted of the writer's visiting military units and interviewing both commanders and soldiers. Communist military leaders were very sensitive to the power of the media image, and thus they were, at least as depicted in many works of reportage, exceedingly accommodating and hospitable to interviewers and culturally oriented service corps in general. Thus, writers assigned to military units found their commanders both very accessible and, by virtue of their fame, often more attractive than other interviewees. Moreover, because of the thematic and aesthetic interests of Communist reportage, numerous interviews served to humanize these generals' images. Emphasis is always placed on the ordinary, common characteristics of these generals, even their charming flaws. The result of this combination of convenience, interests, and thematic concerns is a considerable corpus of portraits of significant historical figures.

The memorializing of soldiers who died in action partakes of both the techniques of storytelling and the disconcerting graphic image. Moreover, unlike all of the war reportage I have discussed thus far, the subjects of these eulogistic texts are almost always named, adding to the memorial quality of the text. Such reportage served or was meant to serve a purpose analogous to that of the public war memorial; the combination of the inscription of real persons' names with the dramatic circumstances of their deaths both enhance the emotional impact of the text and immortalize their sacrifices.

S I X

Socialist Reportage

All of the possibilities realized in the reportage of the 1920s–1940s, from identifying with the collective in urban reportage to physically apprehending the tortuous vagaries of the embattled nation in war reportage, provide a powerful alternative to the individual as the subject of narrated historical experience. And yet this decentered, deindividuated subjectivity possesses an indeterminate identity. While this provided unprecedented possibilities for the rewriting of narratorial consciousness, it was vulnerable to manipulation by the cultural administrative apparatuses of the Communist Party, which claimed authority to pass judgment in the name of the collective body of the nation and demanded unquestioning obedience in return.

Such an appropriation of the collective narratorial subjectivity took place beginning with the utopian discourse of the Communist border areas and extended into the reportage of national construction in the first seventeen years of the People's Republic of China. The result of this invasion was a reportage of unprecedented interiority in which the writer delves deeply into the thoughts and feelings of characters, but the price paid for this renewed moral security was the writer's loss of control over his or her emotional investment in a collective identity.

In the previous two chapters, I explored the expression of the war experience in occupied areas, on the front lines, in the rear, in battle zones, and in the wide-open spaces of the countryside. Reportage from the border areas during wartime, as I have noted, is rarely explicitly concerned with chronicling the experience of war; rather, it is meant to document the unique, unprecedented experience of belonging to border area society. In fact, the language, images, and other conventions of border area reportage resemble the literary productions of the People's Republic of China after 1949 more than they do other types of wartime reportage. The texts of the border areas already belong to a qualitatively different cultural order than that which I have been discussing thus far, one that did not change substantially with the Communist takeover in 1949.

Institutions for the mobilization and organization of cultural activities under the close supervision of the Communist Party were first put in place in the border areas and were the basis for the cultural institutions of the People's Republic. Cultural production within these institutions, reportage prominent among them, manifested a qualitative difference in the expression of subjectivity; the reportage of the border areas offers not only a new set of thematic concerns within the familiar genre of reportage but a substantial change in the structure of experience.

Some of the more superficial conventions of socialist reportage will be familiar to readers: the depiction of warm and congenial relations between soldiers or cadres and the common people (represented by carefully crafted images of the peasant and worker); the cathartic narration and shedding of an ugly, backward past (in the "old" China) to set off the process of education and salvation in the loving bosom of the Party; binary oppositions between the presocialist modern Chinese order and the idealized, utopian, socialist order; the extolling of heroic figures; and a didactic narratorial pose in which the narrator often directly addresses the reader or offers rhetorical questions. For the purposes of this chapter, I will refer to this set of conventions as "utopian rhetoric" to distinguish it from the conventions of critical, performative, investigative, and national-defensive reportage discussed in the previous chapters.

Utopian rhetoric was not new even in the border regions during the Yan'an period. One of the flagship texts of the proletarian literary movement was Rou Shi's 1931 "Yige weida de yinxiang" (An Impression of Grandeur); its expression of the sanctity and ecstasy of Communist social relations and rituals strongly foreshadows the conventions and emotional atmosphere of both border region reportage and post-1949 texts.[1] In addition, the existence of this text and this mode of rhetoric at such an early stage of the development of modern Chinese reportage shows that these later developments were not aberrations or distortions of the spirit of reportage but an integral part of the genre at the point of its importation into China as part of the cultural package of the international proletarian literary movement.

"An Impression of Grandeur" is a description of the secret Congress of Soviet Area Delegates in Shanghai; it conveys to the uninitiated the atmosphere, principles, and methods of such a covert meeting. The rhetoric is grandiose, almost religious. The piece begins with a stanza from the *Internationale* and a meditation on the mood of the committee members as they sing it to initiate the meeting, using the trite yet vivid metaphor of the song being a colorful cloud and communism a great red sail leading them to a paradise of freedom, equality, and classlessness.

Rather than harping on these perhaps all too familiar forms of revolutionary decoration, however, I would like as an entrée into this chapter to concentrate on some of the peculiar subjective overtones and focuses of attention in "An Impression of Grandeur." Rather than attributing them to some idiosyncrasy of the writer, I will show that these aspects of the expression of consciousness and emotion in socialist texts persist, expand, and deepen in reportage written within the Chinese Communist Party's cultural institution from the 1940s to the 1960s. It is difficult to account for the emotional dimensions of socialist narrative without departing from the widespread assumption that socialist literature passively reflects or carries out the demands of cultural policy. Thus, I read reportage even under the direct supervision of the Communist Party as an active expression of experience as much as a passive reflection of policy. The emotional dimension is an outgrowth of the conventions of subjective expression already existing in the genre, and their interpretation demands that we rethink the nature of collective subjectivity in the manner sketched out in the introduction and illustrated throughout the chapters above.

The subjective aspect of socialist reportage is at its most revealing in the treatment of women and love. In "An Impression of Grandeur," for example, part of the narrator's rapture at the heavenly atmosphere of the Soviet Congress derives from the maternal ministrations of a woman who seems to be a kind of secretary: "A woman comrade like an elder sister, with beautiful gestures and sweet warmth and emotion, arranges the purchase and logistics of the things we need and even says 'good-night' to us every evening before we go to sleep." " 'Who would like some *jintan?*' she often asks us smilingly after a long meeting is over" (90).[2] For Rou Shi's narrator, at least, the value of this woman's presence extends beyond providing supplies; she exudes beauty and "sweet warmth and emotion," which becomes an important part of the revolutionary atmosphere Rou experiences at the gathering. Yet it must be noted that Rou's appreciation of the "woman comrade" is represented not as a personal relationship but part of the overall atmosphere of utopian ecstasy at the Soviet Congress. Other participants share his admiration for this or another such woman comrade.

> Everyone is carrying a notepad and pencil given to him by our woman comrade. There are some who are constantly practicing and scribbling in them. During meetings they take notes, between meetings they draw: "Our Chairman," "Our Comrade from Dongjiang," "Woman comrade, you are so beautiful!"—I saw three portraits with these captions in the hands of a Red Army representative; they looked like the kind painted on "flower paper" that you can buy on the street around Chinese New Year. I thought, so this must be what they call "folk art." What the artists study could be based on this—we truly need artists from the masses. (91–92)

"Woman comrade, you are so beautiful!"—the depiction of this beauty, like Rou Shi's own description, is integrated into the iconography of the proletarian movement and thus takes on political significance. The woman comrade is thus neither the object of individual love nor merely an aesthetic decoration; she is construed as a symbol of the Party itself, of the spirit of socialism, which appropriates a maternal role as the basis for strong emotions and a sense of familial identity.

Beneath the shell of conventional images and themes, beneath the tasks assigned to reportage by the leaders of cultural institutions, is the creative expression of socialist consciousness on the part of various reportage writers. This mode of expression is less explicitly prescribed by cultural authorities; it is here that the reportage writer makes his or her creative contribution. It is also here that we can observe the consequences of comprehensive organization on the subjectivity of writers, now conceived of as "cultural workers" (*wenyi gongzuozhe*) so as not to be distinguished qualitatively from the common people.

Especially in Mao Zedong's "Talks at the Yan'an Forum on Literature and the Arts" (although this had always been the main emphasis of leftist literary initiatives), writers were urged to immerse themselves in the lives of the common people so as to understand their hearts and minds. This in itself does not amount to a prescription for what a proper literary consciousness should be, but it does control the conditions under which the writer thinks about how to express experience. Nevertheless, the specific modes of expression remained the creative contribution of the cultural workers themselves. In this process, writers produced a consciousness that seemed to them to coincide with the rhythms of everyday life in the common people.

Socialist reportage inherits the genre's basic characteristics as reconstructed in the preceding chapters: the concentration on external space as the screen upon which a nonindividual consciousness is expressed; the body as the vessel and transmitter of historical experience and as a surrogate for the Chinese nation or people; the open-ended, anticathartic structure by which the reader is invited to participate in the emotional agitation evoked by the text; and the central role of the supposed actuality of the subject matter in driving all these mechanisms. At issue in this chapter are the nonindividual consciousness, reportage's unique contribution to literature, and its fate when concrete experience is subsumed into the cultural production and prefabricated structures of signification of the socialist order.

What had been the indeterminate center or substrate of the consciousness of the event becomes fixed as a form of interiority analogous to that of the private individual in "bourgeois" literature. This development bears the marks of "reification" as defined by Georg Lukács, although in this case it does not take place in a capitalist society. Furthermore, the emergence beginning in the late 1950s of critical, investigative reportage manifests an analogue to Lukácsian alienation that I call socialist alienation, following Wang Ruoshui.[3]

Interiority in the reportage of socialism is centrifugal, rendering public the most intimate emotional stirrings. The extolling of socialism, Mao, the Party, and the spirit of communism is no mere superficial embellishment in these works; in them, the Party has infiltrated the deepest recesses of consciousness, appearing in dreams, lone walks in the forest, and late at night by lamplit study tables, as well as in the workplace and at committee meetings.[4] Indeed, there is no working distinction in these works between domestic "home life" and "the outside world" of society or the workplace; the narrative follows characters everywhere, but the venue of consciousness is always "outside." The Party manifests itself as an emotional resource, a veritable fountain of goodwill and amiable social relations, of determination and strength to overcome insurmountable obstacles, thus representing in innumerable examples the triumph of the spiritual over the material. Such idealism is one of the primary symptoms of reification.

THE COMMUNIST PARTY'S INVASION OF REPORTAGE CONSCIOUSNESS

Mao's Talks and the Rhetoric of the New in Base Area Culture
Mao's Talks at the Yan'an Forum on Literature and Art in 1942 set the stage for the so-called Rectification (*zhengfeng*) Campaign, restricting the scope and attitude of writing by intellectuals under the Communist regime. This process as a foundation for the Chinese Communist Party's history of literary restriction and control has been treated so widely that it need not be reiterated here. For some intellectuals, however, including most of those who began writing reportage after the Talks, it was the beginning of a new era and an unprecedented cultural order.

In treating the organized mobilization of reportage in the border areas, I prefer to follow Bonnie McDougall's little-noticed interpretation of Mao's Talks as an affirmative statement about the nature of socialist literature and the goals of cultural production under Communist rule rather than the prevailing view that its primary purpose was to restrain the critical excesses of more independent writers. Mao strongly emphasized the cultural and historical uniqueness of the base areas and the vast potential for artistic work under these conditions: "Many comrades have come from Shanghai garrets, and the passage from garret to base area involves not just two different localities but two different historical eras. . . . To arrive in a base area is to arrive in a period of rule unprecedented in the several thousand years of Chinese history, one where workers, peasants, soldiers and the popular masses hold power; the people we encompass, the object of our propaganda, are now completely different."[5] What Western scholars in their preoccupation with dissident writers have failed to notice is the willingness with which many (especially younger) writers accepted Mao's call to them: "Revolutionary Chinese writers and artists, the kind from whom we expect great things, . . . must go among the masses of workers, peasants, and soldiers and into the heat of battle for a long time to come, without reservation, devoting body and soul to the task ahead; they must go to the sole, the broadest, and the richest source, to observe, experience, study, analyze all the different kinds of people, all the classes and all the masses, all the vivid patterns of life and struggle" (69–70).

Many believed that in carrying out Mao's cultural policies they were truly creating a new culture, and they devoted a great deal of energy to living with and "learning from" soldiers, workers, and peasants and applying these experiences directly to their creative work. Moreover, they were doing so not out of passive obedience but actively and voluntarily. Finally, positive reportage was not exclusively a response to Mao's Talks; in fact, it had been the mainstream of reportage in the base areas since 1937. Ding Ling's traveling drama troupe and service corps, Xibei diqu zhandi fuwutuan, was the source of a series of publications that included reportage as well as poetry and fiction.[6] As has been evident in the preceding chapters, Ding Ling's reportage throughout the 1930s manifests her deliberate, independent decision to move in the literary direction suggested by Mao's comments even before she left Shanghai.

Writers in the base areas took part in the further expansion and development of reportage by organizing and editing collective writing projects; participating in literary service corps charged with propaganda, public relations, and administrative duties in the field; and through their independent creative work as well. Especially in the years after Mao's Talks, the greater share of their contribution consisted of promoting and participating in a "completely different" culture. In Mao's words, "readers don't need to listen to writers from base areas repeating the same old boring details; they're hoping that writers in base areas will present them with new characters, a new world" (McDougall, *Mao Ze-dong's "Talks,"* 85).

This emphasis recalled a similar preoccupation with "newness" in the May Fourth era reflected in the prevalence of the word *new* in the titles of a large portion of progressive journals (*New Tide, New Youth,* etc.), which also rendered any reference to the "old" politically suspect. The difference here is that, while the May Fourth predilection for the new expressed a yearning for liberation from and an explicit critique of the present, the Yan'an discourse was essentially a propaganda initiative meant to equate an idealized "present" of the base areas with a future for China as a whole. Any association of the old with the base areas was implicitly forbidden in Mao's Talks, and such associations in certain literary works and editorials were in part what motivated Mao to hold the Yan'an conference and initiate the Rectification Campaign.

The difference between these two attitudes toward the new is manifested most obviously in the "new" reportage of the base areas, and well into the 1950s the idealization of the present took the form of glowing portraits of Communist generals, young party cadres, the idyllic life of peasants and workers in the new order of the base areas, and, particularly in the civil war years and in the Korean War later on, the heroic, even epic depictions of battle scenes, troop morale, and congenial relations between soldiers and the people.

Huang Gang in many ways embodies the spirit of the younger writers who implicitly accepted Mao's Talks. Huang entered Yan'an after a brief period of fine arts training in Hankou and received literary and cultural tutelage at the Lu Xun yishu xueyuan (Lu Xun Arts Academy); much of this time was spent in the field with other young writers, traveling to the southeastern anti-Japanese base with the Lu Yi zhandi wengong tuan (Lu Xun Arts Academy Battlefield Literary Work Team).[7] Out of this experience came his "Rain: How Chen Geng's Troops Do Battle #2" and "I Have Seen the Eighth Route Army."[8]

By civil war times, Huang had been assigned to Shanghai, where he published "Tamen shi shenglizhe" (They Are the Victors), which concerns the contribution of women workers to a violent anti-Guomindang labor demonstration in 1946, and "Juelie" (Final Break), which dramatizes the refusal of Wang Chunzhen, the daughter and granddaughter of important Nationalist Party officials, to escape with them to Hong

Kong on the eve of the Communist takeover of Shanghai. Both works explore the rejection of conventional values of family, friendship, and self-interest in favor of the Revolution and the "interests of the masses."[9]

Service Corps and Literary Work Groups
The experience and creative work of these new Yan'an authors cannot be entirely understood without reference to the literary work groups to which they belong. Wenxie's Zhandi zuojia fangwen tuan (Writer's War Area Interview Group), discussed in the previous chapter, was a prototype, but it was organized first in Wuhan, then in Chongqing (then the Nationalist capital), and it was not supervised directly by the Communist Party. In the base areas, these groups were organized more in line with Party policy and were integrated into the educational system and the media.

As early as August 19, 1937, the Xibei zhandi fuwutuan (Northwest War Area Service Corps) was already established in the Shaan-Gan-Ning border area,[10] which included a Correspondence Group charged with interviewing, photography, and publication responsibilities.[11] The Lu Xun Arts Academy was established on April 10, 1938, for the purpose of training "artistic cadres," largely by sending them into the countryside or to the front lines for "internship" (*shixi*); Huang Gang was one of these cadres. While no reportage was produced by this organization during the first year of its existence,[12] by 1940 some of the most noted reportage works of the time were coming out of its Zhandi wengong tuan (War Area Literary Work Teams). For example, Chen Huangmei was a team leader when he journeyed to the headquarters of the Eighth Route Army and Chen Geng's unit of the 386th Brigade of the 129th Division in the Taihang Mountains in the spring of 1939, when he wrote his best-known reportage.[13]

Wenxie also established branches in the base areas at Yan'an (May 14, 1939, electing Cheng Fangwu, Ding Ling, Ai Siqi, and Ke Zhongping as officers) and at the Jin-Cha-Ji border area (organized in July of 1940 by Cheng Fangwu, Sha Kefu, Zhou Erfu, and Yuan Bo).[14] Other groups that were actively organizing literary campaigns in the Shaan-Gan-Ning Area include the Shaan-Gan-Ning bianqu wenhua xiehui zhandi wenyi gongzuotuan (War Area Literary and Arts Work Team of the Shaan-Gan-Ning Border Area Cultural Association) and the Kangri junzheng daxue wenyi gongzuotuan (Literary and Arts Work Team of the Resistance University).[15]

Collective Reportage

In part because of communist cultural organizations' emphasis on all kinds of collective, organized activity, the "one day" type of campaign mentioned in chapter 4 became a significant aspect of cultural mobilization from the Yan'an period through the 1950s. In Yan'an proper, for example, a successful campaign led to the publication of two collections, *Yan'an in May* (1939) and *Life in the Shaanxi Public School*, organized by the Rescue China Alliance of the Shaan-Gan-Ning Border Area Cultural Circles. The first called upon participants to select the most meaningful day in May 1938 as their material and to write it up in a "genuine and lively" way. The second centers on the Public School of Northern Shaanxi, an experimental school established by the Communist Party, its origin, organization, pedagogy, and lifestyle.

The Central Hebei (Jizhong) base area also organized a collective reportage writing campaign in 1941 in which the date May 27 was arbitrarily selected as subject matter to reflect the ordinary lives of people in the area. While there were said to be entries from as many as one hundred thousand cadres, soldiers, teachers, and others,[16] the results were eventually published as about two hundred essays, which survive in three volumes entitled *Guiyu wangliang* (Ghouls and Demons), *Tie de zidi bing* (Our Iron Brothers in the Army), and *Duli, ziyou, xingfu* (Independence, Freedom, Happiness), later published together under the collective title *Jizhong yiri* (One Day in Central Hebei). Tang Tao claims that certain units, "in order to ensure a good piece of news for that day, got approval from their superiors to attack enemy bases."[17]

The vagaries of the text of *One Day in Central Hebei* are fascinating. According to Zhao Xiaqiu, the finished text of four volumes (those cited above plus another, *Douzheng zhong de renmin* [People in the Midst of Struggle]) was mimeographed in two hundred copies. The plan was to send these around for review, complete a final edit, and then publish the collection properly. But just at that time there was an enemy mopping-up operation in the area that took months to fight off. The mimeographed copies (on crude straw paper) languished through the humid summer, rotting on the shelves of a storage room. They were utterly destroyed. At some point in the 1950s, an effort was made to locate surviving copies or manuscripts, mobilizing people through their work units and newspaper advertisements, which succeeded in finding two of the volumes. These were published in July of 1959 by the Baihua wenyi publishing house. In May 1960, a certain Zhou Qi, surprised to see the first two volumes for sale at New China Books in Ding County, immediately sent the full, four-volume mimeographed manuscript he had been preserving for eighteen years to the publisher, and the third and fourth volumes were published in February of 1963.

In an article entitled "Wo shi zenyang baocang 'Jizhong yiri' de" (How I Preserved "One Day in Central Hebei"), Zhou Qi wrote that in May of 1942, with the enemy bearing down on Central Hebei, he left all his things behind to engage in guerrilla warfare but took the mimeographed book with him. In the ensuing years, pressure from enemy troops forced him to move the manuscript from one place to another, in his room, out in the courtyard, in the country, and under ground, finally wrapping it in the driest straw and hiding it in an earthen wall in the fields. Every couple of months Zhou would check on it and air it out. After the Japanese surrender in 1945, he removed it from the hole in the wall only to discover it had gotten wet, so he carefully dried it in the sunlight and put it in a sealed cabinet protected with pesticide, where it stayed until 1959.[18]

Zhou's story, whether we can believe it or not, tells us much about the seriousness and enthusiasm with which the Central Hebei project was carried out. The details of the story also provide a vivid picture of the crude and dangerous conditions under which some of the literary campaigns I am describing here took place. In Zhou's loving hands, the Central Hebei text is almost sanctified as the "word of the people."

This kind of collective writing campaign snowballed throughout the 1940s, resulting in further (but unpublished) campaigns in the liberated areas such as 1943's Weida de yinian jian (One Year of Greatness), 1944's Weida de liangnian jian (Two Years of Greatness), and 1946's Jizhong kangzhan ba nian (Eight Years of Resistance in Central Hebei).[19] The last decisive Communist victory over the Nationalists was commemorated in the 1949 work Du jiang yiri (One Day Crossing the Yangtze).[20] The subgenre resurfaced in 1956 with a four-volume work commemorating the Chinese experience in the Korean War entitled *Zhiyuanjun yiri* (One Day in the Volunteer Army).[21] Unlike much of the reportage published during the war itself by cultural service corps, *Zhiyuanjun yiri* consists entirely of pieces written by soldiers and officers in a literary campaign mobilized within the military administrative apparatus after the end of the engagement. The preface to the work is revealing of the function of reportage in the 1950s after it had been completely absorbed into the Communist Party's cultural institution.

> the editorial committee did not carry out this work independently but coordinated [its efforts] with every unit's work of political training and cultural education, so that the call for contributions was not only not a failure but a great success. Some units combined the writing of *One Day in the Volunteer Army* with their political education initiatives to "maintain our reputation in battle and inherit our glorious tradition"; other units made the writing of *One Day* an important component of their club activities or scheduled it as part of their units' political work programs; some units made writing *One Day* part of their language education, while individuals used their diary-writing time or free time on Sunday. All in all, no one lost any training or work time on account of this, and to a significant degree it [the writing of *One Day*] contributed to training and work.

Reportage, if only for the duration of the campaign, has saturated the very fabric of these soldiers' lives; it has become the content of their education, their form of leisure; it has for some even displaced the writing of a diary. This is the essence and value of what the editor calls "the collective line" (*jiti luxian*), which is the secret behind the successful coordination and execution of such a massive project.

This, like the depth and extent of the "One-Day" campaigns, is another example of reportage's role in the socialist world as a medium for the expression of collective subjectivity. And it was by maintaining emphasis on—indeed, promoting all the more vehemently—the veracity of reportage, its fidelity to "real people and real events," that collective reportage became at least as important to the Communist cultural institution at this point in time as was fiction.

In Yan'an, as the Communist bases developed as much into cultural centers as military strongholds, the minimalist aesthetics of country simplicity that had developed during the war years were deeply influencing what would become the literature of the People's Republic, in reportage as well as fiction, while at the same time writers like Ding Ling and Wang Shiwei were creating the first critiques of patriarchy and totalitarianism among Communist leaders.[22]

Life in Yan'an

The transition to the discourse of the new is seen in its purest form in works describing life in the base areas. Liu Baiyu's 1946 work *Yan'an Shenghuo* (Life in Yan'an) dramatizes the ideals of the new society by projecting them onto the lives of ordinary people, with sometimes unexpected effects.[23] Liu's text is divided topically, moving from domestic life through politics, agriculture, and relations between soldiers and peasants. Throughout, the author uses specific stories, often gleaned from Yan'an's official newspaper, *Jiefang ribao* (Liberation Daily), to develop themes of contrast between the "old society" and border area life and the generally congenial, familial social relations he believes characterized the whole of border area society.[24]

Both of these themes are manifested in the following passage. Note how economic policy and production drives are naturalized through the emotional bonds of a loving family.

> Chang Lanying and Wu Peiye are a young couple under thirty; they used to live in poverty in the Mizhi county seat. In 1941 they moved to Yan'an with their family of six, bringing with them all their hunger. They wanted to go on living, so when they heard the sound of the nearby Weihua woolen mill's machinery, Wu Peiye went there as an apprentice to learn to be a carpet weaver. Chang Lanying asked him to bring back some yarn and began to try her hand at spinning. In short time, Chang Lanying organized her family into the labor process, creating a whole family of yarn producers.
>
> In all of her hard work every day, Chang Lanying's body was thin and weak, and she had to spend time on a child still nursing.
>
> She thinks to herself: "If only I could manage not to waste a quar-

ter of an hour." In this way, she spins a pound and a half of yarn a day, becoming an axle for the whole laboring family. Upon this axle spin the flywheels of all the spindles. Her best companion is her eldest daughter Baozhu; a fifteen year old girl, she can produce a pound. Her second daughter, Yuzhu, eleven, can also put out a half pound of second-rate yarn. Chang Lanying and her daughters have a common motto: no rest until they've met their quota. Around them, the third child moves her short body, doing various chores, sweeping, occasionally carrying some seeds and calling the chickens. The chickens surround her, and she showers the seeds over their heads. Wu Peiye's mother with her white hair is in the kitchen making meals and patching clothes. Wu Peiye? Before the sky is very light in the morning, he goes to the bank of the Yan River to fetch water and bring it back with firewood. Next he shoulders his hoe and goes off into the vegetable plots. Last year he harvested over six hundred pounds of cabbage and pickled several jars of turnips, potatoes, and radishes.[25]

This is a picture of a family whose lives have been renovated by seeking out the socialist order of the border areas and finding both emotional fulfillment and economic security through their engagement in economic production. This family is no longer an "inside" separate from the society "outside"; every moment and gesture of their home life is devoted to activities that contribute to the economic progress of the Yan'an order. Yet their contribution is not imagined as slavish obedience to commands from above (as labor was often depicted in the prewar years) but their own initiative. Thus, their thoughts (as Liu Baiyu represents them) are constantly on how to maximize their intervention in the region's prosperity. Finally, Liu's style renders this family's economic activism as an intimate, lovable activity, for which the image of the youngest daughter happily feeding the chickens becomes a saccharine icon.

In the reportage texts of Yan'an, the sacralization of the present is accomplished through the ritual performance of utopian social relations. This is as evident in the author's account of his own spiritual transformation as it is in the above idyllic family scene.

> "If you stand outside of the collective, you have no way of understanding life in the border areas."

In the past, my philosophy was "You want me to go out? I'd rather light a lamp and read some books; all I want is some peace and quiet. This is my leisure."

But I was a loner then, separated from the life going on around me. Only later did I feel the true meaning of life in the happiness of everyone being together, and I became more outgoing. Like when we go to cultural shows: we've worked all day, had our dinner, and gotten our tickets, and by the dozen we make our way to the hall. Talking and singing, we walk over from the river; from a distance we can make out the bluish, snow-white light shining from the long rows of windows. At times like this I feel everyone dissolving in happiness, like sugar dissolving in water. Once inside, we sit on those benches, smoking cigarettes and telling jokes. Mao Zedong often shows up at these events: when he walks in everyone bursts forth in an endless round of applause. Everyone is ecstatic, and the feelings of the whole company develop along with those of the performance. I have thought at length about how to describe this feeling; I guess it's like a "happy family." This is just the most congenial, big family; everything is all anyone could wish for, joyful and colorful, surrounded completely by my own brothers. Everyone seems to be able to feel my happiness, and I can feel theirs. In this kind of atmosphere one could easily strike up a conversation and be laughing away with a complete stranger. At this year's Spring Festival, I watched almost twenty yangge [traditional-style Chinese New Year musical theater skits], "The Russians" twice and "Forced up Liang Mountain" three times, each time walking back late at night, often with two or three people around the charcoal fire roasting snacks, discussing the show or a particular role, or other imaginings. . . . This change has been very important to me; I feel as if I've lost something, but what? Lyrical, individualistic depression. It couldn't withstand the weathering, the intense warmth of the group. Those feelings that only an individualist can savor had been with me for so many years, but now I've become happy because I'm living in the midst of happiness, eating well, dressing well, working hard, and resting after a hard day's work. I think to myself, let all those depressing thoughts go to hell! They came from the old society, and I'm living in a new society! From then on I began to understand true happiness: the meaning of living in Yan'an resides in everyone's being able to be happy together. In this society, no small group can enjoy itself at the price of the majority's suffering. (22–23)

Liu's happiness springs from losing his self-preoccupation in the enjoyment of the simple things in life and in the midst of a lively group. It is interesting that apart from work and rest the "Yan'an people" Liu envisions while away their evenings enjoying theatrical performances. David Holm has shown that the *yangge* new year skits were appropriated and transformed by Communist cultural institutions for reasons of popularizing policy as well as socializing members of Yan'an society.[26] This is illustrated well in the giddy, carnival atmosphere created by soldiers performing *yangge*: "During the spring festival, troops in every part put on *yangge* plays; the sound of drums and gongs fill the air with joy! Wherever they go, they are surrounded by crowds, and peals of laughter rise into the air. The soldiers on the stage are so happy they dance while they sing. Everyone is mixed together; I take your hand and you take mine and we chatter affectionately. Everyone is clear: this is a lovable bunch of guys that has come here, the good brothers of the border area" (40). The happiness Liu yearns for and has found in Yan'an is thus embodied in the *yangge* performance. Insofar as Liu's own book is also a part of Yan'an cultural policy, it is also concerned with projecting the ideals of Party leaders through dramatic vignettes in which "real people" all play their proper roles.

A central image in Yan'an propaganda is the "labor hero," whose record of superhuman productivity and responsiveness to superiors was the material for almost daily reports and discussions in the *Liberation Daily* throughout the 1940s. The hagiographic glow of Communist biographical reportage is not strictly derivative of Soviet influence but also has precedents in Chinese literary hagiography going as far back as the Warring States period (403–221 B.C.E.) philosophers. By medieval times hagiography, particularly in the traditions of religious Daoism, developed into a well-defined subgenre in which exaggeration and the miraculous were conventionally expected. Confucian hagiography, particularly in the form of popularized moral primers like the *Lienü zhuan* (Biographies of Exemplary Women) would add gruesome physical detail to this exaggeration, rounding out important models for these otherwise modern textual panegyrics.

Like Lui Baiyu's account of the family of Chang Lanying and Wu Peiye, reportage stories of labor heroes are saturated with emotion. The following is Liu's account of one of the most famous of these stars of border area media when he is confronted with his savior, Mao Zedong: "Old Comrade Sun Wanfu from eastern Gansu, when he got to talking about this glorious page in history, stood up from his chair, walked over to Chairman Mao, and tightly embraced him; his spittle-flecked beard trembled with excitement, and he said, 'We have really stood on our own two feet: we have stuff to eat, to wear, our debts paid, our land redeemed, we have cattle and sheep . . . all of this you gave us; without you, us poor devils would be crawling on the earth, unable to stand up our whole lives!'" (29). Here again, the communion with Mao Zedong (who embodies the Party, the "spirit of socialism," etc.) is suffused with intense emotion, and the writer seems to be as engaged in this emotional response as Sun himself. Mao appears in his usual literary guise as a shining savior, affably smiling, indulgently tolerating the physical excess of Sun Wanfu's expression of gratitude. Though cast in explicitly casual, informal terms, this encounter is typical of rituals of affirmation in Yan'an literature, affirmation of the sanctity of the Party's role in renovating the lives of the people, depicted as abjectly grateful, unable to thank the Party and its leaders enough.

What interests me here is the *writer's* emotional participation in the ritual through the act of its narration. In general, Liu Baiyu's *Life in Yan'an* is not only an idealized representation of border area society as a utopia; it is an expression of the writer's exhilaration at belonging to that society, at having shed his selfish individualism to dissolve into its collective subjectivity. These narratives, in addition to providing readers with vivid (if exaggerated) pictures of border area life, affirm the emotional richness of that subjectivity.

"Two New Year's Eves"

Like Liu Baiyu's *Life in Yan'an*, Huang Gang's "Liangge chuxi" (Two New Year's Eves) is primarily concerned with contrasting the human environment of the rear with that of Yan'an and the border areas.[27] Tropes of opposition, mirroring, and doubling permeate the imagery and rhetoric of the entire text. Huang brings the abstract, utopian qualities attributed to the rural and military Communist order down to earth and to the body through concrete and specific instances that typify the essential differences of the two worlds he is contrasting.

The haircut is the master trope through which various themes, images, and characters are brought together to accomplish the contrast. In Chongqing on the previous New Year's Eve, the narrator is alone, apparently enjoying himself but in a way that the retrospective narrative suggests is artificial and immature. The structure of the narrator's experience in Chongqing is constituted entirely of shallow, sensual experiences: having seen an evening film and with the taste of ice cream still in his mouth, the narrator walks swiftly back to his quarters at the hotel in which his company is stationed. Passing a barbershop, he is aware of his reflection in the window and wonders why he is walking so fast. He pauses, taking in the starry, night sky and the atmosphere of the street, and then enters the barbershop for a haircut and shave. He is the only customer, the last according to the barber, who takes more than half an hour to accomplish his task: "After about three quarters of an hour, my cheeks were brightly shining and there was a cool freshness about my eyes. . . . In my room at the inn, the heat from the radiator helped bring warm, wonderful but empty dreams to my New Year's Eve. My quilt was light and warm; the fragrant aromas I had bought from the barbershop filled the room. . . . I felt I was a happy man. I had no worries or bothersome thoughts; I had dreams" (12–13). The narrator dwells on the physical pleasures of having the "whiskers of 1937" scraped from his face, of the fragrant talcum powder, hair oil, and cologne to which he is treated, but already with a consciousness of the superficiality of it all, noting from his reflection in the mirror that his hair "wasn't all that long anyway" and registering the commercial nature of his experience as he pulls out money to pay the barber. All the emotional trappings of human interaction are stripped from this scene of indulgence. The narrator returns to his hotel room and slips under his clean sheets, the warmth of the radiator giving him "warm, wonderful, but empty" dreams, as the "cologne I bought at the barbershop filled the room."

The main difference in the following New Year's Eve, spent in Yan'an, is that now the narrator is "now living among an 'us.' " This crucial difference is manifested in his unfolding of his present haircut experience,

the new barber, and a new kind of "mirror." The contrast of haircut experiences offers the narrator a variety of details bearing rich significance
as signs of a utopian human order.

My hair and beard was many times longer than on the previous
New Year's Eve, but the one who cut them away was not that urban
barber but a comrade of ours. He only took a couple of minutes to
trim my hair, and he didn't pat me with talcum powder, a drop of
hair oil, or a bit of fragrance. At the same time, I didn't give him any
money; cutting our hair is his job, and this job has no commercial
nature. He is a service worker in the Eighth Route Army's Shaan-
Gan-Ning Border Area Camp, one of the Eighth Route Army's rear
servicemen.

Perhaps it is unnecessary to add that if we were able in Yan'an to
find a mirror like the ones in the barbershops outside it would not
be difficult for us to find in our comrade barber's work flaws and
failures to satisfy urban standards. But in the border areas there are
none of those kinds of time-wasting mirrors; here the mirrors reflect
our thoughts and actions—they are our comrades, our honest and
straightforward companions. They have no time or need to pay attention to our appearance, just as my knowing them is not from their
clothing or appearance. (13)

Glass mirrors "reflect" the vanity of life in Chongqing, which stands
for the social order of Republican China; life there centers on external,
superficial concerns, and human relations are more often than not mediated through commercial transactions. Mirrors provide an apparatus
for evaluating and confirming this commercial, sensual focus. By imagining his comrades in the border areas as a new kind of mirror, Huang
emphasizes a different set of values in which "cleanliness" and neatness
of thought prevail over physical beauty. In this text, Huang does not explicitly indicate the source of the standards by which this cleanliness is
judged, but by drawing an analogy with physical cleanliness he natural-
izes it, as though without a rigid set of standards imposed from outside
mutual evaluation and criticism will necessarily lead to the betterment
of all who actively participate.

This faith in the new structure of human relations in and of itself
to transform the members of the border area society into more ratio-

nal, caring, and constructive human beings is typical of what Apter and Saich describe as the environment of the early Yan'an period, before the Rectification Campaign that began in 1942.[28] The function of that campaign was to center the Party as the source of all standards of correctness, extending into the smallest details of everyday life. By creating and, by implication, enforcing a central standard of thought and behavior, the Party (largely through the agency of Mao Zedong) pushes this faith in the structure of border area relations an extra step, making it into a rigid, externally imposed idealism for which Mao and the Party can lay claim not only to moral correctness but, godlike, to the very emotional resources (faith, confidence, enthusiasm) that hold the order in place within the souls of its inhabitants.

"Entertainment" is another point of departure for comparing the two worlds: in contrast to the solipsistic indulgences of the cinema and ice cream, social gatherings in Huang Gang's border area are closely associated with the image of Mao Zedong. We can gather from reportage that Mao habitually slept late, and he made informal public appearances usually at these evening social gatherings, which included ballroom dancing, theatrical performances, and singing. Such an occasion forms the backdrop of Huang's revelation of the ultimate significance of the haircut theme in "Two New Year's Eves."

> Forgive my eyes, comrades; at this moment I saw on comrade Mao Zedong's peasant-style, dark, and steady face that there was a spirit that dared to face any fate, dared to determine any fate, and dared to change any fate.
>
> Just then I noticed his hair; around his ears and in back of his head were the clear marks of a recent haircut; the part where the scissors had cut across horizontally was crude, ugly, inharmonious, showing signs of less than perfect barbering techniques. I began to realize that Mao Zedong's hair and beard were probably also under the care of those rear servicemen who take care of their charges in less than two minutes. (14)

This pivotal observation, which could easily have been the text's inspiration, cleverly links the haircut trope to the leader himself, the embodiment or "surrogate" of the values of the border regions. In so doing, Huang, like many other reportagers in Yan'an, tries to establish Mao's greatness by reducing him to the same material conditions as the writer himself, a common cultural worker. Huang even endeavors to corroborate his evaluation of Mao's haircut by telling a story about a barber like his own who cut Mao's hair without realizing who he was until it was over.

Nevertheless, Mao's rude simplicity comes across as more of a gesture than a necessity. We know that there was a system of grades that entitled leaders to wear different clothes, eat better food, and live in better quarters than common people and low-level cadres.[29] Huang was not necessarily attempting to conceal this grading; rather, Mao's exemplary quality is actually stressed by his studied avoidance of vanity. Many other writers, including Edgar Snow, have commented on Mao's tattered, cigarette-singed, and ill-fitting clothes and especially his apparent neglect of his personal appearance. Huang's observation that the Mao he had seen in pictures "always had long hair" is as representative of this neglect as the shabby haircut that made him difficult for the author to recognize.[30]

Huang's "new" (old) quilt can be read as another sign of the physical neglect attending the emotional transcendence of the border area regime. With this, Huang calls to mind the guerrilla consciousness of the soldier reporter discussed in the previous chapter in relation to Xie Bingying's Army Diary. The narrator's "light" but "warm" quilt in the Chongqing inn is as superfluous as his whimsical haircut, as the room is heated with a radiator. The warmth provided by Huang's soiled quilt in his Yan'an cave attains a spiritual dimension in that the dust and dirt with which it is enriched symbolizes the long road of struggle he has traveled to achieve his new life.

> When I returned to my cave, my classmates were just commenting on how cold the winter is in Yan'an. That night, I walked back to the school through the wilds; the night wind was like being drenched with ice water. . . .
>
> But I felt warm through and through as I burrowed into my quilt. This quilt hadn't been washed for a long time; the dust accumulated from distant travels made it thick and swollen.
>
> However, what I was concerned with was not the cleanliness of my clothing and such but the cleanliness of my thought. Although

my body was covered with lice, my soul was nevertheless undergoing a cleansing. Already I was far away from being a man who seemed happy; I really was happy.

At least I can say that now I am on the road to happiness, along with my comrades and friends as well as everyone like us.

Quickly I fell into a deep sleep, with no dreams. (15)

The three main tropes in this short text (hair[cuts], mirrors, and the moral inversion of body and spirit) establish a field structuring the narrator's discovery of a new form of consciousness. The fragrant yet superfluous Chongqing haircut represents the decadent vanity and superficiality of the city (modern, capitalist) symbolized concretely by the mirror. Unconcerned in the border areas with surface appearances, people cultivate "inner cleanliness" (moral versus physical) for which the comrade/classmate acts as the "mirror." These are mirrors that reflect the mind and heart, which are invisible in physical, glass mirrors. Cleanliness and beauty when applied to the heart are metaphors, and indeed their identification as "inner," to distinguish them from external (actual) cleanliness and beauty, is also metaphorical. The notion of inner cleanliness is as metaphorical as that of the comrade as mirror. Relying on the inside-outside model, what Huang Gang describes in the border areas is a reversal, a turning inside-out, of the body and heart by exchanging the sense-mirror of the barbershop for the heart-mirror of the border areas.

However, the artificiality of this contrast is manifested in the spatial nature of the inside-outside model; the spiritual realm Huang indicates ought not to have a spatial (physical) dimension, but there is no other way to describe it. Although the cleanliness of behavior and thought is supposed to be categorically different and even opposed to physical (external) cleanliness, it still cannot be imagined as anything other than cleanliness reflected in spiritual mirrors, and the author provides no concrete examples, manifestations, or embodiments of such cleanliness. On the level of representation, the implied idealistic spiritual qualities collapse helplessly back onto their material images. The nondialectical rigidity of Huang Gang's scheme prefigures the (socialist) reification of border area thought accompanying the Communist Party's cultural hegemony and opens the door for an unexpected, unintentional parody of bourgeois interiority that we may describe as socialist reification.

"Everybody Is Happy"

After Mao's Talks at the Yan'an Forum on Literature and Art, border area reportage tends to defend and justify the Talks and rectification with anecdotes and examples, and Huang Gang's "Jieda huanxi" (Everybody Is Happy), which concerns the Lu Xun Arts Academy's 150 member propaganda team's folk theater performances celebrating the abolition by the United States and England of the unequal treaties, is representative.[31] Huang Gang, as a student of the academy, was particularly sensitive about the Talks and evidently wished to convey an exemplary attitude toward them. Simpler in technique than others of Huang Gang's texts, the writer's concern—linking Party policy to joy and happiness and happy events to Party policy—is nevertheless the same.

Huang describes the *yangge* performance of the Lu Xun Academy very much as it has been analyzed by David Holm: the troupe roves about Yanshu County from village to village, performing new *yangge* to spread the treaty abolition news, extol the masses, and promote recent Party directives.[32] The new *yangge* replace the lyrics of the old folk theater form with newsworthy content and propaganda, making the folk theater into a kind of news medium for the illiterate, but one that they are supposed to enjoy, one that brings them pleasure as well as information and guidance. Huang points out that the old relations between actors and the public have been transformed as well—the actors now split into groups before or after their performances and have meals with local families, giving the peasants the sense that they are like their own families.

As if inspired by the traditional folk motifs of the *yangge*, Huang explains the new phenomenon in terms of a countrified image: "The Luyi Propaganda Team learns from the people. This learning has only just begun, yet the folks welcome the team onto their own square and understand it fully. Here, song and dance are like the daughter of the masses who has married an outsider with an education and now returns to her mother's house wearing new clothes and saying fresh, new, but easy to understand things—the content is new, but she still has her hometown accent. The irrepressible joy of this new bride, how fond/intimate it makes her relatives feel!" (95). This use of the image of a woman as a sign of the intimacy and emotional richness of the Party's care and regard for the people is strongly reminiscent of that of the "woman comrade" in Rou Shi's "An Impression of Grandeur." Huang's use of the image of the "daughter of the masses" as an analogue for the *yangge* itself is comparable to the *yangge*'s own adoption of a folk form for the purposes of propaganda and edifying entertainment.

REDEFINING LOVE IN SOCIALIST REPORTAGE

I began this chapter with a discussion of the importance of the themes of love and communism as early as Rou Shi's 1931 "An Impression of Grandeur." The process of overcoming bourgeois emotional values is developed with more subtlety in Ding Ling's labor reportage, discussed in chapter 2, which asserted the voice of the awakened proletariat as a reservoir of human values different from those of old China or of the "bourgeois" order of the Republic; I have described these new values as "posthumanist" because of their conscious departure from the humanist norms associated with bourgeois ideology.

"Final Break": Redirecting Love in the Civil War
The theme of critique and displacement of conventional family values achieves new importance in the context of the civil war following the Japanese surrender. During the period from 1945 to 1949, in addition to extolling the military prowess and moral superiority of the People's Liberation Army, many reportage texts illustrated the political awakening of individuals whose personal lives were caught up in the historically momentous and privately essential decision of whether to ally themselves with the Guomindang or the Communist Party.

In Huang Gang's "Juelie: Nanjing Guomindang zhengfu bengkui qian de yimu" (Final Break: A Scene before the Fall of the Guomindang Government in Nanjing, 1949), this decision is embodied in a young woman (which should not be surprising at this point).[33] As the mortars of the approaching Communist troops can be heard in the distance, families loyal to the Guomindang begin to make preparations to escape to Guangzhou or other places on the few remaining airplanes still safely departing from Nanjing. The daughter of one such family, whom Huang names Wang Chunzhen (Pure and True Wang), having come down with a serious case of revolutionary consciousness at school, bitterly refuses to accompany her father and grandfather (both high Nationalist Party officials) and the rest of her family in the flight. Chunzhen's irate father threatens to disown her, and she accepts readily, leaving home forever. The father, it should be noted, is not depicted as a simple, hateful antagonist but as an extremely frustrated parent who is incapable of understanding his only child.

The second part of the story is almost exclusively devoted to Chunzhen's inner turmoil after the break with her father and her ultimate triumph over the insidious remains of familial affection. As she walks through the streets, watching the evacuees' planes flying south, Chunzhen experiences a pang of remorse, which she quickly overcomes by reminding herself of the historical nature of the situation and the historical roles and identity of her parents and herself.

> At this time, the air was full of the sound of flocks of airplanes busily flying south; this is the final flight of the officials of the Chiang dynasty from Nanjing. Wang Chunzhen gazed up at the planes and thought to herself: "That'll be them leaving. My family relations are now over. . . ." Suddenly she thought of how her resolute refusal to flee to Guangzhou must have hurt her parents. Though now her parents can't interfere in her progress anymore, they cannot concern themselves with her anymore either, and she actually softened a bit in her heart, a little "sad." "This is *unhealthy*"—she immediately thought—I can't mourn for these things that are about to be destroyed; why is it I can still feel hurt about my family? She heard the artillery on the other shore of the Yangtze River fiercely firing away, and thought: "Destroy them! All these old feelings! The new life of Nanjing is before our eyes. I can't count on my parents, and my life has entered a new historical era; isn't that cause for happiness?" (107)

What had been objects of warmth and affection have become "things that are about to be destroyed," and Chunzhen's recovery of her composure is accompanied by the sound of the guns of the People's Liberation Army, which she calls upon to destroy her "old feelings." Though a young student, she subjectively adopts the perspective of a soldier; her new feelings by implication partake of the guerrilla consciousness elaborated in the reportage of the border areas, in which the substance of emotional life is identified primarily with the future of the nation.

Chunzhen returns to the abandoned house of her grandfather, and her perception of it is suffused with political consciousness, without a trace of the memory of the years she spent growing up there. She observes that "from its stifling atmosphere, one could already palpably sense the decline and fall of this great house of a high-level official nurtured by a bureaucratic comprador capitalist totalitarian political power" (108). Similarly, her parting memory of her father is untainted by regret, consisting only of the bitterness arising from her political consciousness: "She remembered how when her father left he said he was going to be a teacher; Wang Chunzhen discouraged him, saying, 'Forget about it, don't teach. What the students of today want isn't that old junk of yours'" (108–9).

"Final Break" incorporates the subjective transformation, developed by Huang Gang and others, of border area reportage into the narration of the ponderous decision faced by so many, especially in the cities of southeastern China in 1949, of which historical path to follow. By thus dramatizing the conscious rejection of the Nationalist Party within what might be considered a Nationalist family, Huang Gang does not beautify the Communist path but emphasizes the emotional violence of such a decision. Huang's text, like Wang Chunzhen herself, embodies a forceful, posthumanist rejection of family values.

Mobilizing Love in the Reportage of Reconstruction: "Li Jinzhi"
In the mainland Chinese cultural order after 1949, as some have observed, the emotional reservoirs of romantic love and domestic bliss are displaced by the Communist Party as the emotional core of contemporary Chinese social life.[34] This emotional core is not merely fulsome flattery of the Party and its leaders. It is an almost religious faith embodied in enthusiastic, warm cadres and work team leaders who develop close, quasi-familial relationships with protagonists (very often young women) unattached to their families and in need of guidance and encouragement. More than simply an attempt to humanize the bureaucratic planned economy (or, as Rudolf Wagner argues, to provide a guide for sexual behavior to young people), this penetration of the Party to

the very soul of the people is meant to signify the accomplishment of a radical break with traditional social relations and the abolition of the private emotional life of the individual.

The Party lurks conspicuously in relations between enthusiastic young men and women, the frequent excitement of their close emotional relationships deftly sublimated into realms of revolutionary dedication to learning and progress. Potentially erotic situations in which moments of emotional agitation and bliss are explicitly sublimated to the level of national belonging, class fraternity, and socialist enthusiasm are prevalent in works on industrial development in the 1950s.

In Wen Junquan and Dan Fu's "Li Jinzhi: Ji wufeng gangguan chang de yige nü caozuoshou" (Li Jinzhi: A Woman Technician in the Seamless Pipe Factory),[35] a young peasant woman perseveres through weeks of technical training to learn to operate the main console of a seamless iron pipe factory. The introduction describes the excitement and agitation of this story's main characters on the morning of the opening of the factory, when the woman, Li Jinzhi, is to take the controls and produce the first pipe with the factory chief, reporters, and Soviet experts as an audience. The subsequent episodes retrace the events that led up to the climactic event, beginning with the arrival of a group of peasant women, the resistance of Team Leader Liu to using young women to do a "man's job," the women, especially Li Jinzhi, vociferously opposing his male chauvinism, and his superiors persuading him not to look down on women and to take them on (after all, they were sent by Personnel).

The story then develops with the arrival of the enthusiastic young technical instructor, a Communist Party member named Zhu Weizhi, who has just returned from the Soviet Union unable to contain his burning desire to pass along his newly gained technical expertise. As he begins to teach the women, we are shown from Li Jinzhi's point of view the difficulties they face. Not understanding the terminology or the plant's technology, Li Jinzhi experiences a crisis in the confidence that had recently given her the courage to talk back to Team Leader Liu.

Just when Li is becoming despondent after the first class, Zhu Weizhi appears, encouraging her not to lose faith and carefully going over once again everything he had taught that day. The intimacy of this new relationship is brought home to the reader as the narrator steps back and paints one of the most vivid descriptions of scenery in the text.

The sun had already begun to sink behind the mountains, but the glowing fires of the iron-smelting works lit up half the sky in red; the electric lights all around the construction site suddenly lit up with a glitter like so many sparks. There is no night in all of Angang; night and day, all the comrades are ready at their battle stations. Zhu Weizhi gazed at the majestic beauty of the steel capital's night landscape, then arose:

"That's enough for today; I'll help you review again tomorrow! Don't fret; no matter what the difficulty, us working-class people can handle it!"

Li Jinzhi also rose to her feet; she didn't know how best to thank this young, amiable tutor. Although in her heart there surged a powerful feeling of gratitude, all that was left to come out of her mouth were these words: "Thank you, I've taken up so much of your time!"

A palpable emotional undercurrent is established here that carries the text to the end yet never comes to the surface: Li Jinzhi is strongly attracted to Zhu Weizhi. From there, the narrative of the women's training, primarily from Li's perspective, develops as a fruitful struggle between the unbounded enthusiasm created by Zhu Weizhi and the restraining influence of Team Leader Liu, which is written in terms of the latter's concern over discipline and his fear that the women are expending too much energy learning and aren't getting enough sleep.

Team Leader Liu attempts to exert control by demanding that the women keep to a strict schedule that allows sufficient rest time: "If he couldn't think of a way to make them rest, they would probably fall ill. Thus, every morning when they set off to a practice session he always instructed them: 'Set out on time, and knock off on time; we have to live strictly by the rules!' But it was as if they didn't even hear him, for once the girls hit the machines it was like they were on a date with their lovers: they couldn't bear to leave" (139).

The following passage, which I will quote at length, manages to synthesize the warmth between Li Jinzhi and Zhu Weizhi with this machine love, as well as vividly dramatizing Team Leader Liu's role in the relationship.

That day, Team Leader Liu really lost his temper. Practice time had ended over an hour ago, and Li Jinzhi and Zhu Weizhi were nowhere to be seen. He searched the workshop from top to bottom, but there was no sign of them. Finally, there they were inside the heating furnace. Li Jinzhi was having Zhu Weizhi explain the furnace structure to her. She wanted to be perfectly clear on everything; she looked at the furnace chamber, the bottom of the furnace, and even climbed on top of the furnace to figure things out up there. She was interested mostly in the heat circulation equipment, but she couldn't quite make sense of it. By the time Team Leader Liu squirmed panting into the furnace, there she was leaning nonchalantly on the furnace wall, listening with rapt attention to Zhu Weizhi talking about the function of the circulation pipes, so she didn't even hear Liu's noisy huffing and puffing as he came in. At this, that fully bearded, black face of Liu's became purple with anger:

"What did I tell you to do? You have to set out on time and come back on time, but here you are dawdling away! Do you call this strictly obeying the rules? If you keep going on like this, when we open up the factory, you not only won't be able to work but we'll have to send you all to a rest home!"

Li Jinzhi had long since seen through Liu's "Thunder God" temper: after a bolt of lightning, the sun would eventually show itself from behind the dissipating clouds. This old timer first doubts they can become good technicians, then thinks they can't learn, but then worries that they'll get tired! She hung her head, quietly accepting Liu's lecture, occasionally looking apologetically at Zhu Weizhi, who was standing next to her. The young tutor's face was completely red from blushing; he was someone who demanded seriousness from himself, so now he was surely reprimanding himself in his heart! When Liu's temper finally calmed down, she lifted her long, black lashes, an apologetic smile appeared on her face, and she ran over and grasped Liu's hand, saying "I'm sorry! We won't do it again! Let's go now; we haven't eaten yet!"

Team Leader Liu tightened his face and ignored her, but once they had emerged from the factory and had walked some distance, he called out from behind:

"There's no food left in the cafeteria! After you've washed up come over to my place and I'll have the wife fix you some noodles!"

From ahead, they answered,

"Team Leader Liu, make sure there's a lot. This time we're going to stick strictly to the rules; we'll be there right on time, guaranteed!" and they let out a round of the happy laughter of youth and Liu couldn't help but open his mouth and smile, saying, "after all, they are young!" (139–40)

We are allowed a certain amount of access to Team Leader Liu's thoughts (elsewhere more so than in this passage), and he thus becomes a secondary protagonist. Although his male chauvinism and conservatism tend to alternately dampen and provoke the younger characters' enthusiasm, he is nevertheless adequately self-critical of his temper and attitudes and, more importantly, has a grasp of the concrete realities of steel production from years of personal experience, so his presence is never a negative force in the development of the narrative. On the contrary, his restraining influence is essential to the effective harnessing of youthful energies to the grand project of national construction.

With Liu clearly written as a paternal figure vis-à-vis the relationship between Li Jinzhi and Zhu Weizhi, his reserved condoning of their transgressive educational zeal suggests a father's reluctant acceptance of a charming, capable suitor for his daughter and moreover contributes to the text's overall recontainment or displacement of "youthful energies" from the politically dangerous realm of private intimacy to the "useful" realm of economic or political construction.

This is not the same as saying that texts like this force their characters to *sacrifice* their desires and emotional intensity for the sake of revolution or socialist construction (as has been claimed in readings of socialist fiction). However, the texts, while affirming them, do appropriate and rechannel these energies, recasting them as a collective, public resource ("revolutionary spirit"), depriving their subjects (in this case Li and Zhu) of the autonomy to find private ways to fulfill their desires.

If labor power is reified (i.e., made into an independent thing, taken away from the worker's power to determine its fate) in capitalist society, from this it seems that emotional power is reified in the socialist state: it is abstracted from the concrete context of its arousal, and the worker (almost always a woman) loses her autonomy over the fate of her emotional resources; by investing her emotions in the project of socialist construction (in part through the process of identifying with the interests of the nation), she loses the power to independently determine how her emotions are used and thus (outside of the kinds of text I am reading here) becomes alienated from them; they take on an independent existence, they become usable by others (the Party), and the worker, insofar as she accepts the priority of national construction, is complicit in the process (as is the case with Li Jinzhi).

One evening, after inspecting the dormitory, Team Leader Liu went off to a meeting at the Party branch. By the time the meeting adjourned it was quite late. As he passed the women's dormitory, he couldn't ease his mind, so he went in. Just then, Li Jinzhi was concentrating hard on memorizing new words by flashlight, so even when Liu walked up next to her bed, she wasn't aware of it. The old man quietly stood at the foot of her bed without saying a word and only lovingly patted her sturdy shoulder and lightly brushed back a wisp of hair that had fallen over her cheek, indicating that she should get some sleep, and then left as quietly as he had come. That night, Li Jinzhi cried for the first time. An intense feeling of warmth assailed her: she felt that Team Leader Liu was closer to her than her own father! (140)

The technical instruction was becoming more intense as the weather got hot. The women's enthusiasm for study surged higher every day. In the evenings, Li Jinzhi did as she had since the first day; she went to the open space of the little hill behind the dormitory to review her lessons. Here there was a breeze, the sun began to dip behind the mountains, so this country girl with a poor peasant background, being long used to living and working in limitless expanses of the fields, became very attached to this place. She would also come out here on moonlit nights. Little did she know that beneath the nearby trees the other girls were quietly following her example, moving the battle line of study out under this electric light of nature. Under the bright, clear light of the moon and blending with the surrounding chirping of insects, she thought of new ways of study: she used grass, leaves, stones, mud, and all kinds of things within her reach and arranged them into the forms of all kinds of machines. All the newest Soviet machines they install during the day she used in her own special way to re-create in the sand at night. The next day during the practice session her classmates and tutor would marvel at her familiarity with the equipment and her ability to understand. Everyone said it was a natural talent, that she was clever, but they didn't know how many sleepless nights she had spent on the hill, how much of her heart's blood she had shed!

The harder she studied, the more interested she became. The desire for learning roused vigorously in her heart like the awakening of insects in the spring. A brilliantly colorful and limitless wide world opened up before her: at first she felt as amazed as a child, then later she embraced it with the warmth of a young woman. (140–41)

Here, quite apart from Zhu Weizhi, Li Jinzhi's desire for learning as she recuperates and transforms nature is rendered with a biological intensity akin to what we are more familiar with in descriptions of love. The role of nature in this process is highly significant: Li's identification with the natural environment is linked directly to her background as a poor peasant, which makes her typical of the majority of the new and growing industrial work force in the 1950s. Nature is construed as an important emotional and spiritual resource for peasants, and its transformation is written as a process in which consciousness and matter change mutually and simultaneously.

For Li the best way to grasp the design and functioning of new and complex equipment is to use natural materials to reconstruct models of it in a natural environment. In this way she is utilizing nature in the process of production without taking away from its ultimate ontological priority in her consciousness. However, the significance of nature itself has changed; it has become a "brilliantly colorful," "limitless" new world in which dramatic human and material transformations take place, and yet the apprehension of this transformation is recontained on the level of natural, biological imagery and moreover features a distinctive emotional component in the description of her desire for learning.

The final and most important step in linkages among the worker, nature, and technology is to socialize and nationalize the new subjectivity forming in Li Jinzhi.

For every thing she learned, she gained a degree of confidence and strength. As she thought of how one day she would use her own hands, her own labor and knowledge, to produce large numbers of seamless steel pipes for her country; knowing that she had a share of power in the acceleration of the country's industrialization and the road to socialism, her confidence was all the greater. She became more intelligent, more optimistic, closer and better to others. She often wondered, how is it that she had become this sensitive, this nimble, this able to quickly absorb new things? Her name often came up for praise among her classmates. Not only did she study well herself, but she even began to help others. She studied night and day, yet she did not get tired at all; on the contrary, she had never felt so fulfilled. Her energy was as inexhaustible as the wind or water. She felt there was nothing she could not learn. In these past months, she felt that she had matured; she felt very satisfied with herself inside, like there was a kind of power surging within her that wished to break out of its shell. Sometimes, when she had finished reviewing her lessons for the day and she clearly checked over in her mind everything she had learned, she felt as light as if she had grown wings, as if she could soar off into the blue skies above the top of the blast furnace.

Li Jinzhi's maturity and fulfillment flow directly from her social integration. Her successful technical studies give her a sense of empowerment that is redeemed and strengthened when it is channeled into the enormous project of industrialization and modernization. Here again we are given the image of energy building on itself: the harder Li works, the more energy she has, until she has a surplus, which she channels into helping others. Whether such a consciousness "worked" or indeed even existed outside the writer's imagination is beyond the scope of this study. What I wish to emphasize here are the specific characteristics of the consciousness constructed in these works and especially their grounding in the senses and emotions and landscape.

"Li Jinzhi" ends with the climactic moment that had been suspended throughout the narrative: Li meekly takes her place at the controls and sets in motion the production of seamless steel pipes.

Just a few minutes before the trial hot pressing, the people on the factory floor fell silent; in this extraordinary silence, millions were holding their breath! Suddenly the whistle let out a long cry that startled everyone! Li Jinzhi's heart leaped violently, and she realized that she was becoming panicky and confused. But just then she discovered that the Soviet expert was standing next to her, looking at her with encouraging enthusiasm. His gaze injected power into her like an electric current, and she calmly and forcefully pulled down the control lever.

Just at this anxious moment, Team Leader Liu suddenly shuddered and shot over to the control panel like an arrow. He thought that this way if by chance there was some kind of accident he could take over the controls immediately. But just at that moment, he instinctively glanced at the rollers, and a tube of red hot, brightly glowing steel was just coming out of the coring device and climbing with its searing heat along the rollers to the cooling unit. After a moment, the whole factory floor exploded in cheers. Slogans like "Thank you, Comrade Stalin" and "Thanks for the help of the soviet expert" rolled toward him like a thunderstorm; he couldn't help but raise up his arms and shout for joy along with them.

The cameo appearance of the Soviet expert at the opening and closing of the text is as much a matter of political exigency as of realistic detail and does not contribute to the themes I have been developing here. On the contrary, the tendency of the rest of the text is to locate China's industrial salvation in the transformed consciousness of the worker.

The Moral Landscape of Leadership in
"A Model County Party Secretary: Jiao Yulu"
Along with Lei Feng, Jiao Yulu is one of mainland China's most prominent moral icons.[36] The text that tells his story is separated by more than ten years from those discussed above, but it operates under similar aesthetic conventions. The clearest differences are political and thematic in nature; repeatedly invoking the name and works of Chairman Mao, this work lauds voluntarism in contrast to the pragmatic, technicist focus of the earlier works.[37] Moreover, unlike the other pieces discussed here, Jiao Yulu meets with no resistance among his colleagues, the public, or his superiors; everyone accepts and responds to his leadership and ideas. Finally, there is no sexual tension in this work; Jiao Yulu's complete identification with his work makes him incapable of relating to others as a man, incapable of affirming and acting upon his personal desires.

These differences can be explained in part by the difference in era; the earlier texts were written at a time when the PRC was rapidly developing industry and the economy in its first peacetime, whereas the Jiao Yulu piece addresses (obliquely) the fatigue and despair following upon the failure of the Great Leap Forward and the drought that so devastatingly magnified its ramifications in the early 1960s. Of course, it could not confront these ugly realities head on, so it offers us a story of a highly localized disaster area. One can also discern here the rise of the Maoist personality cult. Jiao Yulu's own story ends in 1964, but the reportage based on it appears in early 1966, just on the verge of the Great Proletarian Cultural Revolution; one can feel this as a reader particularly in the conspicuous emotional effusion in this piece and in the hagiographic rhetoric. Jiao Yulu in retrospect seems to be a real socialist saint molded in the image of Mao. Such effusion and religious ecstasy is not just about glorifying Mao Zedong; rather, it points to areas of emotional excess and repression and the instability of an individual identity created without room for a self. One sees this less in the obvious declarations of theme upon which the overt structure of the text focuses the reader's attention and more in the unnecessary wealth of detail lavished on Jiao Yulu's neglect of his liver cancer, the excessiveness of his parting words with the Lankao cadre in their last meeting and of his dying words to the Party elders who accompanied him at his death, and, in particular, the crucial role that the earth, terrain, and configurations of Lankao County seem to play in Jiao Yulu's vision of himself.

Jiao Yulu's story takes place in Lankao County in eastern Henan Province from the winter of 1962 until Jiao's death in 1964. Jiao is depicted as a county Party secretary who literally works himself to death in an effort to transform a disaster area that had been relying entirely on government aid into a paradise of socialist productivity. The story appeared in the Communist Party's flagship newspaper, *People's Daily*, and it bears some of the characteristic formal features of a newspaper article: the text is divided into nine sections with headings summing up each section's focus that are often also quotations from Jiao Yulu himself.

The text opens with a general description of the county's state of disaster before shifting to a narrative mode to introduce the character. This introductory section is only two paragraphs long, and the reader is struck by the juxtaposition of this objective information in journalese to the highly subjectivized entry of Jiao Yulu onto the scene: the following paragraph is devoted to Jiao's subjective impressions upon viewing the landscape of Lankao County for the first time. This rapid movement from the objective to the subjective is jarring, but it also emphasizes the interpenetration of the two that underlies the text as a whole.

Without hesitation, Jiao Yulu's first act upon arriving in Lankao is to go out and inspect the terrain and conditions in the villages. The protagonist is not a scientist and does not even have a background in technical training, but he is confident that he can just look at the ground and figure out the best thing to do. His attitude reminds one of those scholar-heroes in such Qing dynasty novels as Li Ruzhen's *Jinghua yuan* (Flowers in the Mirror, ca. 1820) and Liu E's *Laocan youji* (The Travels of Lao Can, 1906), whose research in the classics (here replaced with Mao's *Selected Works*) leads them to discover the way out of a river control problem without any specialized technical knowledge.

Jiao Yulu's strength is in confidence, ideas, and vision. He sees an unruly sand dune and says, "Plant some trees, and we'll have a forest here"!; he sees a swamp and says "Plant reeds, grasses, raise fish." Thus, there are two landscapes in this text: the actual crumbling, parched terrain of disaster presented by Lankao and the utopian paradise landscape of Jiao Yulu's vision: "Lankao is a place with potential; the question is to do it, to make a revolution. Lankao is a disaster area; it's poor, and there are a lot of problems. But disaster areas have one advantage: they can temper people's revolutionary will and cultivate their revolutionary character. Revolutionists become heroes in the face of difficulty" (699).

Jiao's conclusion after returning from his tour of inspection, oddly, is not some specific concrete action to be taken with respect to the environmental crises but rather that the first step must be to "transform the spiritual state of the county Party committee." This kind of conclusion is the result of a style of thinking that obsessively seeks a "key" problem underlying the crisis. The solution cannot be complex; it must have one primary solution that will solve all the rest. This key is a spiritual one, and once the spiritual problem has been resolved the material problems will be overcome of themselves. In short, this is a case study in the logic of voluntarism.

Also, Jiao cautions against rash, impulsive action based on subjective hopes alone (which is precisely how we conceive of voluntarism in connection with Mao). "Chasing sparrows blindfolded" and "blindly groping for fish" are used as metaphors for this kind of error. Here, again, the solution is conceived a (hidden) true origin (*dixi*), the sources and consequences (*lailong qumai*, "blood vessel/circulation" image). The idea is to immerse oneself in the details and textures of surface appearance so as to deduce the principle behind their distortion. This spatialized, even corporeal logic relies especially on a conceit of manual contact; the two vivid expressions chasing sparrows and groping for fish concern doing things with one's hands, and the words used to describe Jiao Yulu's own plan of action are also based on a manual metaphor: "He resolved to *feel his way through* (*mo tou*) the natural conditions throughout Lankao's 1,800 square kilometers, to personally go and *feel the heft of* (*dian*) Lankao's triple disaster." Here there is neither a reduction of social relations to a material basis nor a simple bifurcation of spiritual and material but rather a social "theory of relativity" by which the material and spiritual are believed to be mutually convertible, that spiritual energy can be converted into material force or power. The fourth section of the comprehensive report on which Jiao Yulu is working as he finally departs Lankao for the hospital in Kaifeng is provisionally entitled "The Spiritual Atom Bomb: The Material Becomes Spiritual and the Spiritual Becomes Material."

This version of voluntarism is not one that simply privileges the spiritual over the material, for Jiao Yulu's first step in solving the attitude problem in the county committee is to round the members up and take them out to the railroad station late at night to confront them with the spectacle of dislocated peasants huddling in boxcars and the waiting room in their government-issue clothes. The attitude problem is thus a question of bureaucrats being too isolated from conditions on the ground. This highly theatrical gesture, which is emphasized heavily by the narrative, is also representative of the aesthetics of reportage literature since the 1930s, of exposing actual conditions and clearing away the lies of the media and conventional wisdom: the text calls the reader to get out there and open his or her eyes, to viscerally understand the situation by confronting concrete manifestations of social problems within the range of one's senses. Then there is little need to quibble about questions of right and wrong; they become obvious. Jiao's dramatic gesture is effective in awakening the conscience of the committee members, some of whom even shed tears in reaction to what they see.

After shocking the committee into realization of the crisis, a plan emerges to mobilize a team of 120 to conduct a detailed survey of the entire territory, in effect reenacting Jiao Yulu's own tour of inspection in collective form. It is just at this point that Jiao's chronic liver trouble is brought up for the first time in the text. Not long after the beginning of the survey, moreover, weather conditions worsen and there is more rain and flooding, aggravating the crisis, and yet Jiao always takes the lead when weather conditions are at their worst, arguing that these present the best opportunities to observe the various problems with water and earth while under environmental pressure. "During this difficult struggle, Jiao Yulu turned into a village 'man from the mud,' covered from head to toe." As was the case in Chen Yi's "Springtime in Jiangnan during the War of Resistance," being covered in mud conveys a subjective immersion in the landscape and successful amelioration with the environment.

The romantic picture is marred, however, because as the team gropes through the floodwaters, feeling their way with sticks, Jiao "often bends over with pain, his left hand pressing on his liver area." Consumed by his work, Jiao Yulu is not even aware of the nature and seriousness of his illness and seeks no medical attention until he is incapacitated. Standing in the waters, sheltered by others' umbrellas, he draws one diagram after another of the water flow direction. "He went on and on with branch secretary Li Guangzhi, pointing at his diagrams and saying how a river should be opened from here to there and a tributary should be dug out." Jiao took about six months, walking around five thousand kilometers (about thirty a day!), finally collecting all the firsthand data on the three disasters, cataloging and diagramming the eighty-four *fengkou* and sixteen hundred dunes, and made a detailed marsh drainage diagram for all the county's waterways: "The wind and snow came, covering the heaven and the earth. The north wind sounded its shrill whistle, and the snow accumulated to half a foot. Jiao Yulu went out into the storm without so much as a coat, the ears of his cap flapping in the snowy wind. At the time, his liver often pained him sharply. Sometimes when it was really bad he would take a fountain pen and press it hard against the area of his liver. At this time his mind was entirely on other things; with a few young men he would trudge across the piling snows, singing 'Nanniwan' as they marched" (704). (The song celebrates victory over the nationalists in the civil war.)

By 1964, Jiao's liver problem is so bad that people notice that during meetings and work he would stand with his right foot on his chair, using his knee to press on his liver area, and that his bottom jacket buttons were always undone so he could stick his hand inside, clutching his side with his left hand, or put something hard on the back of his chair to press on his side. Eventually the right side of the back of his rattan office chair had a big pit in it from this (707). Jiao is adamant in his resistance to medical care and rest; even when he relents it is only partway. One day, "As the comrades at the commune made their report, they watched Jiao Yulu clutching his side as he made notes." His fingers were shaking, and he kept dropping his pen. As they watched they "fought back their tears, unable to speak." As the struggle against the triple calamity "reached a climax" in March of 1964, Jiao Yulu's liver ailment reached a serious impasse: "As he lay on his sickbed, the tides of his feelings dashed and roared, rushing toward the land that was just now being transformed."

There is a strange correspondence between Jiao's illness and the struggle against the natural disasters. Normally, one would expect such disasters to be likened to illness, so that there would be a parallel between the success of the disaster relief and Jiao's *recovery*. But Jiao's liver ailment is about neglect, the opposite of his salvation of Lankao, and is in part *brought about* by his overwork. Thus, one perhaps unintended implication is that the disasters are analogous not to Jiao Yulu's *illness* but to his *health*: the better the land of Lankao does, the closer Jiao approaches death. Insofar as he is not depicted as being superhuman, the story of Jiao Yulu as told here seems more to be about the man's limitations and how the work he got under way at the expense of his health has to be accomplished collectively by the people as a whole. "The manuscript Jiao Yulu had not finished was completed collectively and forcefully on the land of Lankao by its 360,000 inhabitants." The transformed Lankao at the time of Jiao Yulu's death stands as a kind of fortress, impregnable to the vicious forces of nature that had once brought the county to its knees.

In hospitals in Kaifeng, then Zhengzhou, and finally Beijing, Jiao physically wastes away but constantly demands reports on the Lankao situation. Lankao is more than his home; it is his "work" in every sense of the word. He had mobilized the entire population in an effort to transform Lankao's landscape. Those who visit him are brought to tears by his determination and hopefulness. The Party orders that he not be told that his advanced liver cancer is terminal, but a careless comment from a Lankao colleague visiting him brings it home. "I only have one request after I'm gone; I want the Party to send me back to Lankao and bury me in one of the sand dunes. I might be dead, but I want to make sure you get those dunes under control." Thus, even when he can no longer work at the effort of transforming Lankao, he still wants to commit his body to the very landscape of the place, dramatically emphasizing the physical continuity between his body and that landscape. This physical continuity is also apparent in the expressions Jiao coins for techniques for solving the various problems facing the county: "applying plasters" for covering dunes with clay to fix their position and "applying needles" for planting trees and other plants to fix the dunes; the land of the county is being compared to an ailing body being nursed by the efforts of the people under Jiao Yulu's guidance.

"Jiao Yulu" seems to replace the apparently common sexual or romantic undercurrent of socialist reportage with Jiao's burden of disease and his colleagues and the people's (and the narrator's) strong, tearful, emotional response to the contradiction between his extraordinary kindness and excruciating physical pain. This emotional current is enhanced throughout the text by a hagiographic rhetoric, particularly in the telling of specific encounters with the people of Lankao. As to clues to Jiao's private life, we get only a brief allusion to a son without even a mention of his wife; the only woman depicted in the text is a blind peasant overcome with emotion at Jiao's caring to visit her in a blizzard.

In works like "Li Jinzhi," "Jiao Yulu," and others that depict the subjective experience of engaging in national reconstruction after 1949, the significance of the Party's saturation of consciousness lies in its displacement and replacement of whatever else had been there in the human soul of society or individuals as the source of belief, emotion, and identity, whether it had been parental love, religious belief, money, or knowledge. In the familiar polemical terms of the orthodox Chinese

Communist critic Zhou Yang, it signifies the overthrow of both "feudal superstitions" and "bourgeois humanism." The Party has become the singular principle of human relations; it claims this status theoretically insofar as it is supposed to embody the consciousness of the workers, peasants, and soldiers, especially their goodness. In short, the Party has appropriated the place of what had been emerging as the consciousness of the event, the nonindividual consciousness of reportage.

The mobilization of reportage campaigns was one of the primary and most characteristic forms of social and cultural engagement promoted by the Chinese Communist Party in the areas it governed. Before the emergence in the late 1940s of professional reportage writers within the Party, the collective writing campaign took advantage of an expedient coincidence of the Party's practical needs to propagandize, educate, and develop modes of organized collective activity and the existing momentum provided by curiosity at new lifestyles, enthusiasm, and eagerness to participate on the part of young cultural activists, not to mention the proven popularity of the genre itself (at least as a matter of editorial policy) as a mode of social engagement for both the writer and reader.

One of the results of this coincidence of Party aims and the aesthetics of reportage was the Party's insertion into key structural points of the textual world of reportage. The Party provides the emotional glue for the all-important mission of publicizing idealized relations between soldiers and peasants; the Party is a kind of invisible, enlivening presence at social gatherings. The "spirit of the Party" moves through the concrete actions of common and extraordinary heroes, from Liu Baiyu's industrious mother, who organizes her daughters into a spinning team to help her husband's textile mill compete in the production drive; to the anonymous Korean War soldiers of Wei Wei's "Who Is the Most Worthy of Our Love?" their bodies in flames from napalm rushing desperately to embrace American soldiers, smothering them in flames as well; and finally to the model county Party secretary Jiao Yulu, immersing himself so deeply in the alleviation of triple natural disasters that even after he succumbs to liver illness (which, it is noted, he neglected throughout his years of travail) his dying request is to have his ashes sprinkled on any stubborn sand dunes that have not yet been tamed.

CONCLUSIONS

To return to the concerns raised in the introduction to this study, readers might wonder why a book about Chinese reportage conspicuously avoids the prominent, reform era phase that featured Liu Binyan, Su Xiaokang, Qian Gang, and others. I have pointed out one reason: these works have already been much studied in the West as well as in China, and I wanted to concentrate on what lay behind and before that phenomenon in Chinese cultural history to give the entire tradition of reportage greater resonance. The 1980s writers received much deserved credit for their innovations, or at least the effective application of external models to Chinese conditions. Liu Binyan's works from the late 1950s as well as the late 1970s and early 1980s, for instance, are credited with bringing a samizdat-style documentary critique of socialism from his Soviet model Ovechkin, while Zhang Xinxin's *Chinese Lives* (*Beijing ren*) derives from Studs Terkel's *Working*. However, Liu's critique of corrupt workplaces has numerous *Chinese* precursors in works like Xia Yan's "Indentured Laborers," while Zhang Xinxin's work closely resembles Mao Dun's ambitious 1936 project, *One Day in China*. These resemblances to earlier Chinese leftist works, had they been noticed, would have detracted from the cultural value of Liu's and Zhang's interventions in the 1980s by their association with leftism and the Communist Party at a time when cultural value was measurable in terms of dissidence and subversiveness. The nonliterary character of 1980s reportage and its implicit critiques of Chinese socialism represent a departure from the orthodox socialist reportage tradition so radical that it practically erased the memory of the "orthodox" genre.

The other reason is that I am primarily interested in reportage as a *literary* genre, and 1980s reportagers are virtually unanimous in their conviction that reportage is not literature.[1] In explaining this latter reason, I would begin with a rough sketch of what has become of *baogao wenxue* since the 1980s. More recent works referred to as reportage fall into various categories, none of which feature the controversial critical stances of the 1980s writers. One is what we might call "co-opted critique"—government-approved investigations of social and economic conditions (especially environmental problems and low-level corruption) that are deemed or self-censored as politically safe vis-à-vis the authority of Marxism-Leninism and the Chinese government itself. Such works are what now appear under the heading of "reportage" in major literary journals. This type, though not subversive like 1980s reportage, must be said to be an improvement over the earlier, orthodox texts discussed in chapter 5 (judged by their "actuality" and social efficacy), and indeed they represent a modest triumph for Liu Binyan in that they are a recuperation of the critical tradition of reportage that was one of its most important foundations in the proletarian era of the 1930s.

Another type, which I would call "commercial endorsement" reportage, is a by-product of the commercialization of Chinese cultural life in recent years. Professional writers would be invited to tour the factories of market reform era entrepreneurs and write glowing "investigative reports" for a handsome fee.[2] In contrast to the first type, this at its worst is a cynical abuse of the worst qualities of orthodox reportage (i.e., fulsome praise of the fruits of the latest economic policy, just as was done in "Li Jinzhi") for financial gain. A third, also a commercial type, is what is often referred to as *fazhi wenxue* or "rule of law literature," in which "true stories" of corruption, racketeering, and debauchery become popular pulp literature under the excuse of dramatizing bringing criminals to justice in a society under the rule of law.[3] The market for such literature is driven by readers' voyeuristic attraction to the lurid.

What these very different variations on reportage have in common is the lack of the deliberately literary quality (with the possible exception of rule of law literature), that was an essential ingredient in my working definition of *reportage literature* given in the introduction. This is a legacy of the 1980s, when the prominent reportagers transformed reportage from a literary genre into a communications medium, even when writers like Zhang Xinxin and Liu Binyan made use of certain techniques that had been evident in the literary reportage of previous years such as fictionalization, composite characters, and internal dialogue.

In discussing the emergence of writing as historical engagement manifested in modern Chinese travel essays and May Fourth documentary texts, I emphasized early nonfiction writers' explicit critique of existing forms of literature and journalism. In the case of the travelogue, I argued that influential modern practitioners like Qu Qiubai and Zou Taofen, by linking this critique in practice with an unprecedented particularity and vividness of narration and description and the conscious incorporation of their feelings in the very act of observation, established a practical basis for later theorizing.

In discussing the reportage of public demonstrations, I showed that historical consciousness often manifests itself in writing as a dramatic theatricalization of the struggle for nationhood embodied in scenes of urban conflict. Roles in this drama are not played by individual characters but by groups (students, workers, the police). The consciousness of engagement is realized in the narrator's identification with the protagonist group and elaborated by means of empathic reactions of horror and exhilaration to scenes of graphic violence. This identification is not as an individual member of a group but as the subjective assumption of an identity that is fundamentally collective in nature. Moreover, the group or collective character of the consciousness expressed is enhanced by theatrical arrangement and signification of space.

Space was also a defining factor in the less theatrical worker consciousness of labor reportage. In such works, the consciousness of capitalist exploitation manifests itself as an ambivalent relationship with industrial space and machines. Moreover, the economic signification of the allotment and control of industrial space in factories, as well as living quarters, worker classrooms, and even a public porridge kitchen, can be contrasted with the theatricalized space of urban conflict as an alternative narrative space.

The dilemma faced by labor reportagers (and supposedly workers as well) was that, while the mechanical rationalization of space and the perceived interpenetration of worker and machine were supposed to signify the dehumanizing effects of industrial production, the awakened proletariat was still faced with the problem of imagining a positive relationship with the material environment of industrial production. While this dilemma was not clearly manifested in any single text, it can be observed in the simultaneous existence at the time of different reportage works that expressed one or the other of these two conflicting types of subjective relation to industrial space. The implications of this problem extend to the subject's relation to the entire project of modernity: how would the awakened proletarian consciousness reconcile opposition to capitalism and imperialism (the source of the procedures of modern industrial production) with the will to construct a modern nation (which must make use of its procedures)? While this was a relatively minor issue in the anti-imperialist heyday of labor reportage in the 1930s, it returned, as we have seen, to haunt the reportage of Communist economic policy and the post-1949 reportage of national reconstruction, pushing the expression of consciousness in reportage in unexpected directions.

The outbreak of the War of Resistance against Japan in 1937 drastically transformed the conditions under which reportage was produced by scattering and fragmenting the publishing industry and forcing most writers into new and unexplored environments. But this did not change reportage's primary concern with the problem of engaged consciousness as a basis of a writer's identity. In fact, with an unprecedented number of novelists, poets, essayists, and playwrights now trying their hands at the still new and now unusually popular reportage form, feelings of inadequacy in the face of national peril brought forth the issue of the social engagement of the intellectual as never before.

Following a tendency already established in the genre's aesthetics to rely on violence and other kinds of graphic imagery as a technique for tapping into collective emotions, these feelings of inadequacy were either intensified or overcome with a relentless concentration on scenes of carnage and the wounds of hospitalized soldiers. At the same time, writers more directly engaged in the war effort dramatized the expansion of their consciousness as they mentally absorbed the new landscapes they penetrated as well as their active assumption of new, simpler ways of living, thinking, and feeling, modeled by necessity on those of the soldier and peasant. The exigencies of war forced writers to truly immerse themselves in national struggle and the lives of common people, yielding unprecedented transformations of consciousness that would condition later developments of reportage in general.

Finally, the utopian quality of reportage written about the Communist order, from the wartime base areas to the People's Republic, suggests a reification in collective consciousness when the Party appropriates the multivocal consciousness of the event and thus the subjective vocabularies of identity and engagement. Thus, the Party, the class, the (Chinese) people, and the nation (in that order) are written as the sources of all physical and emotional energy, the source of moral rectitude and humanity. As such they have usurped the role of the "autonomous individual" under capitalism.

One consequence of the Communist recontainment of collective subjectivity is that the reengineered souls of the new proletariat are the testing ground for the development of meaningful connections with the space and machinery of industrial production. Characteristic of this writing is the containment of powerful desires and emotions within an epistemology of material production for the nation. This results in a socialist brand of reification in which the Party and the proletariat become abstractions (like the individual in Enlightenment ideology) sufficient to serve as the basis and source of value and meaning. This reification is accompanied—perhaps even motivated—by a sublimation or displacement of the terror used by the Communist Party to consolidate its authority in the border areas.

With this transformation, the subject matter of Communist reportage manifests an unprecedented and unexpected interiority. Especially in the hero-extolling works of the 1950 and 1960s, the consciousness of the hero is laid before us in great detail as the collective and *typical* interiority of workers, peasants, and soldiers. The event as the intersection of collective social forces and the object, geographical feature, or group of travelers as symbols of the Chinese nation falls into the background.

To illustrate the existence of a literary aesthetic of collective consciousness, I will now turn to an article on reportage by Hu Feng. Hu's interest
in the genre of reportage was complicated by his general dissatisfaction
with the accomplishments of the writers of the time, including realistic
novelists. To Hu Feng, realistic narratives in wartime China, particularly
war dispatches, were plagued with either flat, emotionless description
or abstract polemic without concrete content.

According to Yunzhong Shu, Hu Feng's vision of *Qiyue*'s task was to
provide a social critique in the May Fourth tradition, grounded in concrete, "personal" experience. Indeed, Shu singles out the personal as
the "most important characteristic of *Qiyue* reportage."[4] Putting this
together with Hu's insistence on maintaining the independence of literary journals with respect to Party and government (68–69), one might
infer that Hu Feng was a champion of literary individualism, and indeed
when he was attacked by the Communist Party in 1954–55 it was often as
an "individualist." Even in the 1980s, Liu Zaifu's reappropriation of Hu
Feng's writings on subjectivity was very much concerned with the issue
of the individual at a time when such a concern had a special historical
significance.[5] In all three cases (the Communist Party, Liu Zaifu, and
Shu Yunzhong), though, Hu Feng's emphasis on "the subjective fighting spirit" is strategically misread as a call for a return to individualism to
fight against the collectivism promoted by the Communist Party. Subjectivity is identified with the personal or the individual.

However, Hu Feng as a literary theorist and editor does not seem to
have been particularly interested in the individual, and his writings on
reportage prove this. In the two articles he wrote on reportage, I see
reference to neither the personal nor the individual. By calling for both
more concreteness and more emotional engagement in reportage, Hu
was certainly championing the subjective and critical functions of literature, but there is no reason to equate this with the personal, which could
easily be identified with the individual. Instead, in Hu's most penetrating observation on the reportage method, emotion is supposed to arise
from the *object* of description and narration, not its *subject*: "Without
emotions (*qingxu*), the author will not be able to *penetrate within the object*;
without emotions, the author will be even less able to express the object

he wants to communicate, whether on the level of image, of sensations, or of the mixture of subjective and objective. . . . but *the emotion we want must be presented as an attribute of the object itself,* and indeed be something radiated 'simultaneously with' the object."[6]

In my account of reportage aesthetics, which I believe is consistent with Hu Feng's, reportage cannot possibly be written from the perspective of the autonomous individual. If we conceive of the individual subject as an island of consciousness set in opposition to society and the objective world, then it must be the only source of emotion. If this were so, how could an emotion be presented as "an attribute of the object"? It is only when the realm of subjectivity is released from the conceptual confines of the autonomous and independent individual that the objects of description and narration can begin to take part in the production of subjectivity. I read Hu Feng's extended discourse on the "subjective fighting spirit" not as an attempt to recuperate the humanistic individual subject for revolutionary culture but an attempt to imagine and promote a new and unfamiliar kind of consciousness whose very realization, like Lukács's "consciousness of the proletariat," would itself be revolutionary.

Viewed from the perspective of a critique of journalism, reportage practice is based on a conviction that contemporary reality is neither a welter of quantifiable information—hard facts to be consumed and digested by autonomous individuals in their own private worlds—nor a solipsistic drama of struggle between the individual self and a cold, detached society; it expresses a network of human relations and interactions that take place variously in interconnected political, economic, and personal realms. It is in this sense, I believe, that we should understand the often contested notions that modern Chinese subjectivities are always cast in public, social, and often national contexts; that these contexts are the very fiber of the modern Chinese self; and that often the most acute and powerful emotional responses are elaborated in terms of the self as the Chinese nation in microcosm.[7] Those who criticize such notions argue that they draw attention away from the intimate and private experience of the individual, the ultimate ontological basis of literature. But this "public" self was being produced (whether successfully or not is a separate issue) in an environment that did not take the private, individual self for granted as a mode of consciousness, and the artistic consequences of this textual production of the public, collective self cannot be understood or evaluated in terms of the same set of categories that places the individual at the center of literary creation or takes the autonomous individual for granted.

Such a public or nonindividual consciousness is, like individual subjectivity, a product of the imagination. Identification requires a creative leap from the sense material of experience to notions of wholeness and belonging. I cannot comment on the historical authenticity or comprehensiveness of the experiences reportage mediates in China. However, reportage is in itself an authentic and demonstrably widespread *imaginative* construction and has its own historical agency, just like the economic policies and political campaigns that created the conditions for its emergence.

This public subjectivity as expressed in reportage is imaginatively located not within the individual but *outside*, in the event and in the social space in which it transpires. This is not to say that there is a consciousness outside the person and in the event, only that reportagers *project* consciousness into the event and construe it as an attribute of the event. In the literary ontology of reportage, the event, conceived as the concrete historical manifestation of a moment of change in social relations, has a consciousness, which is apprehended through the reportage writer's experience of the event.[8] Reportage literature in modern and contemporary China at its most characteristic is the attempt to realize the consciousness of the event and communicate that consciousness to the reader.

It is only insofar as the writer partakes in the consciousness of the event that he or she is able to apprehend its human meaning. For the event in reportage is not simply something that happened somewhere to some people; it is the embodiment of dynamic, intersecting social forces with immediate and remote causes and effects and is meaningful (in other words, worth writing about) insofar as the writer can elaborate this discrete intersection as a moment in a complex struggle among individual and collective actors in the drama of social change.

Reportage writers may not literally be transforming consciousness, but they do creatively realize a new, alternative consciousness unassimilable into the familiar categorical opposites of subject and object, individual and society, and theory and practice. It is for this reason that reportage, more commonly than other literary forms, possesses its own historical agency, which is often described as its characteristic "effectiveness" or "operational" quality.[9] By potentially changing readers' minds about social phenomena and historical events, it can influence social action, even though it is rarely an explicit call to action.

COLLECTIVE CONSCIOUSNESS OR COLLECTIVE INDIVIDUALISM?

A dialogue can be established on this point with David Apter and Tony Saich's account of Yan'an culture in *Revolutionary Discourse in Mao's Republic*. Apter and Saich's analysis represents collective identity in Yan'an as something new for members of the community ("individuals") to participate in, created almost single-handedly by Mao Zedong. In their words,

> collectivization in the form of symbolic capital constitutes a fund of power available to individuals that appears to enlarge their powers. It is less a form of entitlement than enablement: it enables *the overcoming of the self through participation in a collective project.* . . .
>
> "Joining the revolution" was made a conscious and deliberate act in which one yielded part of one's persona to the collectivity. This was the first step in a reeducation process in which, through a careful reading of prescribed texts, a form of "exegetical bonding" made each person feel that he or she had transcended individual limitations, had overcome deficiencies, and had therefore gained more from the collectivity than he or she had given up.[10]

The word *individual* is used repeatedly as the subject of the processes of collectivization in the form of symbolic capital and of "exegetical bonding"—realizing community through the common interpretation of orthodox texts. The process of collectivization is portrayed as happening to the individual from outside, a process orchestrated by Mao's tremendous power to forge collective mythology in the form of storytelling. Apter and Saich's breakthrough is to affirm the nonindividual nature of the affirmative consciousness of belonging that characterized the Yan'an order and the pivotal role of Mao Zedong's creation of a collective mythology to engage and direct that consciousness. However, I believe the preceding chapters show that such nonindividual consciousness underlay expressions of identity and belonging in reportage for years before Mao's cultural initiatives were implemented through the Rectification Campaign and Yan'an Talks.

The "individual," as we understand the term (or fail to) in the West, was not something already existing in China that was forcibly transformed from the outside. The history of literature since the May Fourth movement, and, indeed, the conventions of public discourse in general, including speechmaking and journalism, always at some level cast subjectivity as a *collective* identification, and the individual as an autonomous consciousness apart from society was merely another cultural hat to try on, limited in its attraction primarily to Western-educated intellectuals and artists. Collective consciousness as I have reconstructed it here was an already existing component of the modern Chinese cultural field, although the precise nature of the identity in which this consciousness was supposed to inhere was indeterminate until the Yan'an project.

Apter and Saich's model of individuals being pulled into a collective subjectivity by the powerful attraction of symbolic capital (yielding more than the sacrifice of individuality that was invested) neglects this important aspect of modern Chinese culture and assigns too much credit to Mao as the inventor of this mode of consciousness and the orchestrator of the process of collective integration. I would argue that what Maoism had to offer was not collective consciousness per se but an authoritative ethical center in which this consciousness could inhere. Mao's storytelling and mythologizing efforts did not create collective subjectivity but inhabited it and preempted alternative voices. Most importantly, he garnered almost universal acceptance for this in the name of unity and discipline.

Apter and Saich's model cannot account for the sudden turn toward interiority in reportage illustrated in the previous chapter that followed upon the genre's wholesale appropriation by Communist Party cultural institutions. Until the end of the War of Resistance, reportage had been almost exclusively event oriented, out in the open in public spaces and historic events. What little character development there was, as can be seen, for example, in Bi Ye's "Northern Wilderness," emerged almost entirely from external descriptions of facial features, implications in dialogue, and bodily gestures. Characters would occasionally comment on their own feelings, but this brand of interiority had nothing to do with the development of the narrative. On the contrary, I have shown that the expression of feelings and identity are chiefly manifested in reportage before the late 1930s as a mode of physical descriptions of objects outside the individual self. With the advent of Communist-sponsored reportage, on the other hand, there was a sudden obsession with the soul, the interior life, and the close-up character study, dwelling at length on subtle emotional journeys, memories, and dreams. The reason for this is that in the earlier reportage, in its creation and development of a subjectivity emptied of the individual, the individual center was vacant and there was no substrate in public experience for interiority, nor indeed any interest in exploring interiority, which was the proper province of other art forms.

When Mao and the Party occupied the center of consciousness, they provided the cultural worker with an ersatz individual subjectivity whose expression was an affirmation of social progress, allowing there to be produced a whole regime of subjective integration. The illusory nature of this "collective individualism" (Apter and Saich's term) manifests itself in an unconscious parody of the gamut of "bourgeois" emotions and sentiments in the culture of socialism, but with the individual replaced by the Party as the only possible subject, the ultimate source and object of all emotions and sentiments. Familial relationships are displaced by more "genuine" organizational ones (*Life in Yan'an*, "Final Break"); lusts and instinctive drives, when productive, were now manifestations of "Party spirit" rather than a universally shared humanity ("Li Jinzhi"). All drives, powers, and forces are reinvested in the collective project, whether it be war or national construction, rather than the pursuit of universal human truths.

REPORTAGE IS LITERATURE

The preceding chapters demonstrate that, despite recent arguments to the contrary, Chinese reportage before the Cultural Revolution is an artistic form of writing. It can only be viewed that way, however, if we suspend assumptions and prejudices incompatible with a leftist worldview as reconstructed in the introduction. In getting at reportage's artistic dimensions, I have been guided to an extent by Bakhtin's theory of the chronotope, which has in effect allowed me to rethink a number of artistic strategies from the point of view of space rather than individual subjectivity.

Among these the most familiar and yet perhaps the most surprising to find in reportage is the technique of irony. The existence of irony seems surprising in that discourse about reportage tends to stress its authenticity and veracity, while we usually think of irony as a kind of distortion and associate it with humor. Indeed, irony in reportage is rarely humorous. Noting that the first person wounded in a demonstration is a woman is ironic, as is Xia Yan's use of terminology with quotation marks in "Indentured Laborers": the workers are cursed as "pigs" by their foreman, but the squalor in which they live, their loss of sensitivity, and the food they eat all suggest the way pigs live. Qiu Dongping's narrator in "Company Seven" speaks of trying to avoid being "cheated" by his commanding officer's exhortation to "stand or fall with your position," and Fan Changjiang and Chen Yi both remark on the differences between what is said or written about the places they visit and what they are actually like. All of these speak to discrepancies between discourse and lived experience, which is the basic structure of irony, although its effects may range from black humor to absurdity to moral indignation. Without such a juxtaposition of the way things are with the way things are said to be, are supposed to be, or *should* be, reportage would be difficult to distinguish from other kinds of journalism. Comparison is a fundamental, essential aspect of reportage's artistic strategy of cultural critique, conspicuous even in the foreign travel diaries of the late nineteenth century.

These ironies are, especially in the various types of urban reportage, as much spatial as linguistic, drawing attention to spatial positioning as a sign. The symbolic dimensions of spatial irony find their fullest expression in the theatricalization of the reportage of public demonstrations (although they may occur in other types of reportage as well). Theatricalization invokes a complex structural code; spatial positions and relationships take on new significance by virtue of a perceived resemblance to the theater or ritual spaces. When the narrator draws our attention to a stagelike structure, for example, actors and audience suddenly spring into existence by implication and the reader begins to expect suspense and dramatic confrontations. Moreover, when those making speeches or marching are seen as actors, the mechanisms of theatrical representation that determine the relationships between actors and their roles and the audience imply a symbolic, allegorical level on which to interpret the actual events being narrated—I have suggested that this level is usually meant to be read as the nation or the Chinese people. Moreover, the differences that emerge from a comparison with the theater also serve to define and characterize reportage's artistic dimensions: the lack of script and closure, for example, may be connected directly with what I have described as the anticathartic aspects of reportage. Emotions are stirred up but not purged; the text prompts its readers to go out and resolve the tensions themselves.

Another literary aspect of reportage that sets it clearly apart from journalism is the aesthetics of concreteness; most reportage goes to great lengths to vivify narration description through direct appeals to the senses. While generally visual in emphasis, there are numerous examples of explicit reference to smells, sounds, and tactile sensations, particularly in war reportage, which animate not only characters but the physical environment and atmosphere of the places described. Often to achieve the above-mentioned anticatharsis this concreteness is exploited through the depiction of graphic violence or otherwise disturbing graphic images to further agitate the reader. As I have pointed out, by associating the visceral repulsion that can be brought about by such images with certain less tangible things, like national identity or an invading enemy, powerful emotional effects may be produced.

These techniques and characteristics are bound together by the consciousness of collective identity, the artistic aspect of reportage whose interpretation stands the most to gain by the adoption of a spatial paradigm. For this consciousness does not take place within an individual body but rather in a complex field of correspondences between a sensually responsive, feeling body and a contiguous yet topographically delimited landscape. In other words, the ways in which the experiences of the body and the landscape become meaningful are limited only by the conceptual reach of the category of "body": it can mean the singular body of an individual, the collective body of a group of people, the nation as a physically contiguous whole suffering invasion and possible fragmentation, and so on. And because of these resonances the form of identity that binds them or shifts from one to another can project its sensual experiences onto the larger, more abstract bodies and in turn imagine experiencing physical sensations as the nation is invaded, a town is bombed, or a demonstrating group is scattered or fired upon. It is through such associations, as well as through verbal juxtaposition, that national or collective events and experiences are brought home through physical sensations, whether of revulsion or ecstasy. Finally, the theatrical structure of signification reinforces (through an implied connection with ritual) the social and community aspects of this spatial mode of imagining identity.

REPORTAGE AND CONTEMPORARY CHINESE CULTURE

Of all sequences of events during the period extending from 1920 to 1966, the gradual consolidation of literary institutions (the media, including newspapers, literary journals and books, literary organizations and publishing houses, schools and the formation of a literary canon, and so on) under the Communist Party had the farthest-reaching consequences in the history of modern and contemporary Chinese literature. As the preceding remarks show, reportage was not merely a passive manifestation of this process but a tool attractive both to writers for its radical potential to tear the "mask" off of reality, expose the forces at work underneath the experiential surface of history, and move readers, and to organizers of these institutions as a means of simultaneously molding the consciousness of writers and keeping track of their ideology, especially as it is expressed in the selection, rendition, and interpretation of contemporary events.

The alleged literary status of reportage, which is largely attributable to the creative and promotional efforts of Qu Qiubai, Ah Ying, Xia Yan, and Mao Dun, attracted serious leftist writers who were eager to experiment with new forms, especially one like reportage with its potential to galvanize readers politically and establish a dialogue between professional writers (perceived in the 1930s as being overwhelmingly "petit bourgeois") and the "masses"—workers, peasants, and soldiers—who were supposed to be in some sense the beneficiaries of leftist writing activities.

The initially divisive leftist literary camp gradually became unified partly through the efforts of individuals like Qu Qiubai and Lao She, who were more committed to the idea of unity than to certain positions in theoretical and political disputes, but perhaps most effectively through the intrusion of forceful common enemies such as the Nationalist Party and the invading Japanese armies; it was largely through appeals to fear of annihilation by such external enemies that unification was accomplished. Administrative bodies like the League of Left-Wing Writers and Wenxie were the concrete manifestations of this unity (journals could serve as easily to divide as to unite), and they played a particularly significant role in the saturation of reportage into the modern Chinese literary scene. Collective writing campaigns could almost be said to have been the creation of such organizations, having unprecedented consequences for the construction of the writing subject and bringing semi- and illiterate people into the production and reception of literature.

Within the revolutionary base areas during the war against Japan, the establishment of an "entirely new" cultural world, complete with its own characteristic physical environment, a new political regime, a different fabric of human relations, and its own educational and cultural institutions, evidenced itself as much in the reportage produced in this environment as in other discursive and representational media. The consciousness produced (not altogether peacefully) in the base areas would become the mainstream of the literature of the People's Republic of China at least until the Hundred Flowers Campaign in 1956. Rather than being a monolithic stereotype with no variation (as is commonly held), the aesthetics of Communist Chinese literature (as represented by reportage) is, rather, a newly defined zone of struggle and a new milieu of constantly re-created conventions for the narration and rendition of the "new" China.

Ultimately the literary character of Chinese reportage as I have illustrated it here is greater than the sum total of certain literary techniques. My typology based on the landscapes or literary construction of social space in reportage emerged from my readings of the texts I discuss herein and others. It was only after I perceived this spatiality and its substitution for character as a literary structure that I could re-present the genre in terms of this typology. The artistic quality of reportage lay in this spatiality, and it is "leftist" not only because of its critical, interventionist content but because of its replacement of the individual subject with the collective consciousness of these events and social spaces. The radical *form* of reportage thus gave the leftist writer free reign to use his or her imagination in the critical pursuit of the actual. This impulse, already present in European and Soviet reportage literature, underwent a transformation among Chinese writers, who were as motivated to affirm class or national identity as they were to indict social ills, especially during the war against Japan. The subjective spatiality inherent in reportage's aesthetics of historical experience was not an obstacle to such motivations, and so Chinese reportage by the 1940s had become a principal form of literary expression within the Communist Party's cultural arsenal.

Leftist and Communist literary organizations played an important role in cultivating the anti-individualist subjectivity underlying reportage by exploiting reportage as a method of training writers, especially for fictional creation, and assigning or encouraging works of collective authorship. In practice such works and activities may have been manipulated or controlled by certain personalities such as editors, cultural work cadres, or one among the involved writers. But the promise and possibility of collective consciousness and creation, even if specious, made reportage very attractive in this context. On the other hand, the forces of conformity within Chinese socialism, particularly under Mao Zedong, ultimately transformed reportage from a liberating form of leftist artistic expression into an orthodox vehicle for extolling the Great Helmsman and the Communist Party. In this, reportage was no different than any other artistic form and no less literary than it had been in earlier periods. I hope I have shown in chapter 6 that, while it was produced in a highly restrictive ideological environment, socialist literature should not simply be dismissed as formulaic—it has many unique and surprising characteristics, and its close study will surely reveal much more about contemporary cultural life in China. The subjective spatiality, the motivated landscapes of socialist reportage, are still much in evidence in the 1950s and 1960s; however, the open-ended collective subjectivity that characterized the genre in the 1930s, and inhabited those landscapes themselves much more than any individual mentality, had by the 1950s been displaced by an orthodox interiority, a model subjectivity located in specific individuals. Reportage under socialism was losing its hold on "actuality" (*zhenshixing*), and in this sense the highly literary quality of the genre at this point became a burden, detracting from its value. Viewed from the post-Mao perspective of the late 1970s and early 1980s, such literariness in a documentary form (as manifested, for example, in the piece on Jiao Yulu or Wei Wei's Korean War work "Who Is the Most Worthy of Our Love?") bespoke the schizophrenic quality of public discourse during the Cultural Revolution. With this in mind it is not difficult to understand the motivation of the 1980s reportagers in denying the literary qualities of reportage and the general enthusiasm for a rejuvenated reportage that could bring public discourse back in touch with reality. The literary landscapes of reportage had little place here; rather, it was the rhetoric and techniques of actuality put in the service of the communication of information rather than the creation of a new and unprecedented art form.

The time for such truth telling seems to have come and gone. The field of cultural production that conferred value on the discourse of the actual in the 1980s (in fiction as well as reportage) has been altered irrevocably, in large part by the bloody crackdown on the 1989 democracy movement. Since then much more value has been conferred on what is often called "pure literature" (chun wenxue), manifested in a number of different phenomena. Translated fiction from Europe and the Americas is enjoying unprecedented success on today's literary market, and while the market for Chinese literature has shrunk considerably there is a marked tendency to promote avant-gardism, imaginative historical fiction, and essays. Pre-1949 familiar essays by such heretics to the cause of revolution as Zhou Zuoren, Lin Yutang, and Liang Shiqiu are immensely popular and have inspired an unprecedented outpouring of familiar essays by most of the active writers in China. I have been told by publishing entrepreneurs that essays actually sell better than fiction, even when the author is better known as a novelist (Wang Anyi, Jia Pingwa, and Wang Shuo are examples). The essay, even more than Chinese and Western fiction, derives its attraction and value from authenticity, although this authenticity is not the actuality of history but the authenticity of personal sincerity. In other words, even if reportage has lost its value to Chinese readers, those readers are still seeking something authentic, something they are not getting in much contemporary fiction.

NOTES

INTRODUCTION

1 Leo Ou-fan Lee, introduction to *People or Monsters? and Other Stories and Reportage from China after Mao*, ed. E. Perry Link (Bloomington: Indiana University Press, 1983), xiv. See also Rudolf G. Wagner, *Inside a Service Trade: Studies in Contemporary Chinese Prose*, Harvard-Yenching Institute Monograph 5, no. 34 (Cambridge: Harvard University Press, 1992), 147–324. Wagner digs back into the history of the genre but only in the Soviet Union and Europe (following the line of Liu Binyan's influence by the Soviet *očerk* writer Ovechkin back to the Czech reportage promoter Egon Erwin Kisch). Although he acknowledges that the genre was promoted, practiced, and discussed in 1930s China, citing some of the names and works I discuss here, he uses this information only as background for his discussion of Kisch.

2 Wagner, *Inside a Service Trade*, 326–55.

3 See, for example, Hayden White, *The Content of the Form: Narrative Discourse and Historical Representation* (Baltimore: Johns Hopkins University Press, 1987).

4 Rey Chow sketches the ramifications of this in the field of modern Chinese studies in her "Introduction: On Chineseness as a Theoretical Problem," *Modern Chinese Literary Studies in the Age of Theory: Reimagining a Field* (Durham: Duke University Press, 2001): 1–24.

5 Benjamin A. Elman, *From Philosophy to Philology: Intellectual and Social Aspects of Change in Late Imperial China* (Cambridge: Council on East Asian Studies, Harvard University Press, 1984), xix–xx.

6   Richard E. Strassberg, ed., *Inscribed Landscapes: Travel Literature from Imperial China* (Berkeley: University of California Press, 1994); Wen-chiang Ting, "On Hsü Hsia-k'o (1586–1641), Explorer and Geographer," *New China Review* 3.5 (1921): 225–337.

7   Liang Ch'i-ch'ao, *Intellectual Trends in the Ch'ing Period* (Cambridge: Harvard University Press, 1959).

8   Susan Naquin and Evelyn S. Rawski, eds. *Chinese Society in the Eighteenth Century* (New Haven: Yale University Press, 1987), 56–124. Jonathan Spence dramatically illustrates the rise in social prestige of merchants in areas of high commercial and financial activity in the mid-Qing in *The Search for Modern China* (New York: Norton, 1990), 90–94.

9   Naquin and Rawski, *Chinese Society in the Eighteenth Century*, 56–57.

10   Victor Mair, *Anthologizing and Anthropologizing: The Place of Non-elite and Non-standard Culture in the Chinese Literary Tradition* (Durham: Duke University Press, 1992); Robert E. Hegel, *Reading Illustrated Fiction in Late Imperial China* (Stanford: Stanford University Press, 1998), 15–17.

11   Yingjin Zhang, "Narrative, Ideology, Subjectivity: Defining a Subversive Discourse in Chinese Reportage," in *Politics, Ideology, and Literary Discourse in Modern China: Theoretical Interventions and Cultural Critique*, ed. Liu Kang and Xiaobing Tang (Durham: Duke University Press, 1993), 211–42. Xiaomei Chen, "Genre, Convention, and Society: A Reception Study of Chinese Reportage," *Yearbook of Comparative and General Literature* 34 (1985): 85–100.

12   C. T. Hsia, *A History of Modern Chinese Fiction* (New Haven: Yale University Press, 1971), chap. 1, "The Literary Revolution," 3–27.

13   There is a section documenting the debate on revolutionary literature in Kirk Denton, ed., *Modern Chinese Literary Thought: Writings on Literature, 1893–1945* (Stanford: Stanford University Press, 1996), 257–355. It includes essays by Qian Xing-cun, Mao Dun, Liang Shiqiu, and Lu Xun.

14   Qian Xingcun (Ah Ying), "The Bygone Age of Ah Q," in Denton, *Modern Chinese Literary Thought*, 276–88.

15   Leo Ou-fan Lee and Andrew Nathan, "The Beginnings of Mass Culture: Journalism and Fiction in the Late Ch'ing and Beyond," in *Popular Culture in Late Imperial China*, ed. David Johnson, Andrew J. Nathan, and Evelyn S. Rawski (Berkeley: University of California Press, 1985), 360–95; Joan Judge, *Print and Politics: Shibao and the Culture of Reform in Late Qing China* (Stanford: Stanford University Press, 1996).

16   Michael Schudson, *Origins of the Ideal of Objectivity in the Professions: Studies in the History of American Journalism and American Law, 1830–1940* (New York: Garland, 1990). In the unpaginated preface to this published 1988 dissertation, Schudson characterizes the most original argument in the study as his "discovery . . . that journalists began talking self-consciously about 'objectivity' only at the time

(the 1920s) when intellectual life more broadly and changing journalistic practices specifically made reflective journalists aware of how strongly subjective journalistic judgment ordinarily is."

17 Robert W. Desmond, *The Information Process: World News Reporting to the Twentieth Century* (Iowa City: University of Iowa Press, 1978), 44–57.

18 David T. Z. Mindich, *Just the Facts: How "Objectivity" Came to Define American Journalism* (New York: New York University Press, 1998), 64–66, 113–17.

19 Western descriptions of the Marxist-Leninist press tend to focus on its function in the Soviet apparatus of power more than on the theory behind its mode of reporting. See, for example Wilbur Schramm, "The Soviet Communist Theory of the Press," in *Four Theories of the Press: The Authoritarian, Libertarian, Social Responsibility, and Soviet Communist Concepts of What the Press Should Be and Do,* ed. Fred S. Siebert, Theodore Peterson, and Wilbur Schramm (Urbana: University of Illinois Press, 1956): 105–46. Interestingly, David Mindich's *Just the Facts* owns that Marx was said to be critical of "objectivity" as a characteristically bourgeois ideological concept, but he nevertheless cites Marx along with Darwin as a contributor to the Industrial Revolution discourse of scientific objectivity that came to influence journalism as well (106). See John C. Merrill, *The Dialectic in Journalism* (Baton Rouge: Louisiana State University Press, 1989). Merrill is adopting Hegel's notion of the dialectic, not Marx's, and, although the study as a whole is a critique of the tradition of journalistic objectivity, his account of Marxist-Leninist journalism simply reiterates Schramm's.

20 Anthony Smith, *The Newspaper: An International History* (London: Thames and Hudson, 1979), 119–20.

21 Wagner, *Inside a Service Trade,* 326–28.

22 Kisch even claimed that it would eventually overshadow the novel in the twentieth century. See Peter Monteath, "The Spanish Civil War and the Aesthetics of Reportage," in *Literature and War,* ed. David Bevan (Amsterdam: Rodopi, 1990), 72.

23 Wang-chi Wong notes that Qu Qiubai, discussed at length in chapter 1, also came to play a leading role in the Sun Society. See Wang-chi Wong, *Politics and Literature in Shanghai: The Chinese League of Left-Wing Writers, 1930–1936* (Manchester: Manchester University Press, 1991), 39. Wong's scholarly treatment of the Left Wing League largely supersedes T. A. Hsia's *The Gate of Darkness: Studies on the Leftist Literary Movement in China* (Seattle: University of Washington Press, 1968). Hsia's work remains valuable, however, for its discussion of otherwise little known literary works. Leo Ou-fan Lee's *The Romantic Generation of Modern Chinese Writers* (Cambridge: Harvard University Press, 1973), 177–244, also provides a valuable perspective on leftist factions in the 1920s and their interactions.

24 Wang-chi Wong goes on to connect this directly to the campaign to denounce

Lu Xun at this time. He argues convincingly that this could not have been a Party directive and that it had to have been purely the work of the Creation Society (*Politics and Literature*, 20–27). On Fukumotoism, see G. T. Shea, *Leftwing Literature in Japan: A Brief History of the Proletarian Literary Movement* (Tokyo: Hosei University Press, 1964).

25 For a superb anatomy of this problem illustrated with brilliant readings of representative works, see Marston Anderson, *The Limits of Realism: Chinese Fiction in the Revolutionary Period* (Berkeley: University of California Press, 1990), esp. 24–26, 73–75, 200–202.

26 Lu Xun, "Zixuanji xu" (Preface to My Selected Works), in Lu Xun, *Lu Xun quanji*, 4:456; cited in Anderson, *The Limits of Realism*, 87.

27 Anderson, *The Limits of Realism*, 129.

28 It should be noted here that, although reportage was promoted in articles from the 1930s on as a useful exercise for writers to combine writing practice with social engagement, it was never discussed explicitly as a solution to the problems of realism and naturalism. The notion of reportage as a major literary genre that could challenge the dominance of fiction gained currency only much later in the process of establishing a Chinese reportage canon.

29 Wong (*Politics and Literature*) cites the rise of a CCP literary administration from the districts to the central level in 1929 with the establishment of the Cultural Committee as a sign of the Party's awareness of the importance of literary affairs (41). Paul Pickowicz's account of the establishment of the League of Left-Wing Writers distances the league from the Communist Party, but since many league members and officers were Party members it still makes sense to emphasize the importance of the cultural front to the Communist Party at the time. See Paul G. Pickowicz, *Marxist Literary Theory in China: The Influence of Ch 'ü Ch 'iu-pai* (Berkeley: University of California Press, 1981), 92, 98.

30 "Wuchan jieji wenxue yundong xin de qingshi ji women de renwu," ("New Trends in the Proletarian Literary Movement and Our Tasks") *Wenhua douzheng* (Cultural Struggle) SNZWZX, 147–54. The word *reportage* appears in French in the text.

31 See Wong, *Politics and Literature*, 72–74, 100–103. Hu Yepin, along with Li Weisen, Rou Shi, Yin Fu, and Feng Keng, all of whom were writers executed that day along with many others, are known collectively as the "Five Martyrs," and there is convincing evidence that they were betrayed to the Guomindang by Wang Ming or his agents because they opposed the Wang Ming faction.

32 Ibid., 69. It should be noted that after the 1932 reorganization league committees were numerous, short-lived, and often overlapped in duties and activities: "All League members were allocated to a group according to their place of residence. Since they moved frequently, to avoid detection, they might be reallocated to other groups. Each group had a leader who was to hold group meet-

ings. Usually there were four to six members in a group but some were bigger or smaller, with two members only. For the sake of security, only group leaders had the addresses of their members and group members were not allowed to ask for the leaders' and others' addresses. These groups were also found in universities, secondary schools, factories and even among farmers" (75). David Apter and Tony Saich refer to these procedures as a "republic of clandestinity," which formed part of the past of intellectuals later attracted to the Communist base area at Yan'an. See David Apter and Tony Saich, *Revolutionary Discourse in Mao's Republic* (Cambridge: Harvard University Press, 1994), 82–83.

33 See, for example, Yuan Shu, "Baogao wenxue lun" (On Reportage Literature), July 1931, and a column entitled "Gei zai chang de xiongdi" (To Our Brothers in the Factories), that included titles such as "Guanyu chang tongxun de renwu he neirong" (On the Duties and Content of Factory Correspondence, May 1932) and "Guanyu bibao" (On Wall Newspapers, July 6, 1932). For an overview of introductory and prescriptive articles available to reportage writers in the 1930s, see Zhao Xiaqin, *Zhongguo xiandai baogao wenxue shi* (Beijing: Renmin daxue chubanshe, 1987), 116–26.

34 Qu was deeply involved in the central administration of the Chinese Communist Party from 1924 to 1930, ultimately (though briefly) serving as secretary general of the Central Committee (Pickowicz, *Marxist Literary Theory*, 91–98).

35 Benjamin Schwartz, *Chinese Communism and the Rise of Mao* (New York: Harper Torchbooks, 1967), 46–171.

36 Chen, "Genre, Convention, and Society," 91. Chen's observation of reportage's conspicuous institutionalization in the 1980s was one of the factors that inspired this project.

37 The ZBWC is the largest and most widely available collection of Chinese reportage and is the principal source for the texts I discuss in this study. When I cite texts that have been reprinted in ZBWC, I will give their ZBWC citation for ease of access; original venues of publication can be found in the bibliography.

38 ZXWD, 1927–1937; ZXWD, 1937–1949; and ZXWD, 1949–1966, respectively. In each multivolume collection reportage takes up one volume of the whole.

39 Liu Binyan, "Ren yao zhi jian" (Between People and Monsters), *Renmin wenxue* 9 (1979), translated in Link, *People or Monsters?* 11–68.

40 This is the thrust of most studies of 1980s reportage, including those of Xie Yong, Zhang Yingjin, and Chen Xiaomei.

41 Huang Gang, "Baogao wenxue de shidai tezheng jiqi bixu yanshou zhenshi de dangxing yuanze" (On Reportage's Characteristic Contemporaneity and the Necessity of Its Vigilant Observance of the Party Directive of Veracity), BWYZX, 335–382. While on the surface this title smacks of dogmatic bluster, the article strongly implies a critique of the *unreality* of reportage before the death of Mao.

42 Yuan Shu, "Baogao wenxue lun" (On Reportage Literature), BWYZX, vol. 1, 31–33.

43 Kawaguchi Hiroshi, "Baogao wenxue lun" (On Reportage Literature), BWYZX, vol. 2:1182–91. Kawaguchi Hiroshi is the pen name of Yamaguchi Tadayuki (1905–84), a Marxist literary theorist, some of whose writings from the 1920s are translated in the 1933 book Hua Di, ed., *Wenyi chuangzuo gailun* (Elements of Literary Creation) (Shanghai: Tianma shudian, 1933).

44 Ah Ying, "Cong Shanghai shibian shuo dao baogao wenxue" (From the Shanghai Incident to a Discussion of Reportage Literature), in *Shanghai shibian yu baogao wenxue* (The Shanghai Incident and Its Reportage) (Shanghai: Nanqiang shuju, 1932), reprinted in BWYZX, vol. 2, 657–59.

45 Ibid., 658–59.

46 See, for example, "Ruhe xie baogao wenxue" (How to Write Reportage), BWYZX, vol. 1, 34–37.

47 Examples include *Beidou* (Big Dipper), *Guangming* (Brilliance), *Haiyan* (Petrel), *Taibai* (Venus), and *Dushu shenghuo* (Reader's Life).

48 *Wenyi xinwen* (Literary News), as we have seen, is where it all started. Lan Hai (Tian Zhongji) also mentions a journal called *Baogao* (Reports) that was published in Shanghai in the mid-1930s, but it seems to have been lost. See Lan Hai, "Changzu jinzhan de baogao wenxue" (Reportage, Progressing by Leaps and Bounds), BWYZX, vol. 2, 724.

49 *Shanghai shibian yu baogao wenxue; Huo de jilu* (The Living Record), ed. Liang Ruiyu (Shanghai: Shenghuo shuju, 1936); *Zhongguo de yiri* (One Day in China), ed. Mao Dun (Shanghai: Shenghuo shudian, 1936).

50 BWYZX, vol. 1, 51–54.

51 Zhou Gangming, "Baogao wenxue de shidai" (The Age of Reportage Literature), BWYZX, vol. 2, 669–74.

52 Hu Feng, "Lun suxie," in *Hu Feng pinglun ji*, ed. Hu Feng (Beijing: Renmin wenxue chubanshe, 1984), 1:67–69.

53 Hu Feng, "Lun zhangzheng shiqi de yige zhandou de wenyi xingshi," in *Minzu zhanzheng yu wenyi xingge* (National War and Artistic Character), ed. Hu Feng (Shanghai: Xiwang she, 1946), 131–44.

54 For reasons about which I can only speculate, Hu Feng's contribution to the development of reportage in China is generally ignored in mainland Chinese scholarship as well. Great strides have been made toward filling this gap. See Shu Yunzhong's book on Hu Feng's journal, *Qiyue*, *Buglers on the Home Front: The Wartime Practice of the Qiyue School* (Albany: State University of New York Press, 2000), esp. chapters 2 and 3; and Kirk Denton, *The Problematic of Self in Modern Chinese Literature: Hu Feng and Lu Ling* (Stanford: Stanford University Press, 1998). The most influential source of information on Egon Erwin Kisch, Theodor Balk's

article "Egon Erwin Kisch und die Reportage," *International Literatur* 3 (1935), was published as "Jixi ji qi baogao wenxue" (trans. Zhang Yuansong) in *Qiyue* in its October and December 1938 issues (4:3–4). Like Kawaguchi Hiroshi's "On Reportage," Balk's article also became one of the authoritative sources of information on the development of the genre in the West (Wagner, *Inside a Service Trade*, 351).

55 Yi Qun [Ye Yiqun], "Kangzhan yilai de baogao wexue" (Reportage since the Beginning of the War of Resistance). The article also appears in BWYZX, vol. 2, 677–703.

56 Most later accounts, right into the 1980s, simply parrot Yi Qun's inventory, although they may add or drop a small number of references, later accounts reveal their derivative nature by using similar or identical language to describe the texts and also reveal that these later commentators may not even have read them.

57 Lan Hai [Tian Zhongji], "Zhongguo kangzhan wengi shi" (History of the Literature and Arts of Resistance in China) (Shanghai: Xiandai chubanshe, 1947).

58 Wang Yao, *Zhongguo xin wenxue shigao* (Beijing: Kaiming shudian, 1951) Zhang Yingjin's important study of modern Chinese literary historiography, "The Institutionalization of Modern Literary History in China, 1922–1980" (*Modern China* 20.3 [July 1994]: 347–77), discusses Wang Yao's *Draft History* as the dominant university textbook of modern Chinese literary history through the 1970s (358–60).

59 It is difficult to translate the Chinese term *sanwen* consistently because it has two basic meanings and is often used inconsistently in Chinese. The narrower meaning is "literary essay" and should be applied to nonfictional artistic prose writing; the broader meaning is supposed to coincide with the English word *prose* and is too broad to be of much analytical value. The latter includes reportage and historical narrative as well as expository and polemical writing, whether or not they are meant to be artistic. I use "literary essay" to render *sanwen* to reflect the more common usage. When used in conjunction or contrast with other narrow designations such as *suibi*, *xiaopin*, and *suxie*, *sanwen* should be understood in the narrow sense, although depending on the context *sanwen* may be a general term for all these forms or a specification of one among them. I have yet to see any indication, however, that *sanwen* is a specific subgenre that has features that can be contrasted with *suibi*, *zawen*, *xiaopin*, and *suxie* in formal terms.

60 Rudolf Wagner covers this history in minute detail in *Inside a Service Trade*, 245–324.

61 Hebei shida zhongwenxi xiezuo jiaoyanshi (Composition Workshop of the Hebei Normal University Chinese Department); "Baogao wenxue sanshi nian" (Thirty Years of Reportage Literature), BWYZX, vol. 2, 780.

62 "Baogao wenxue sanshinian," 781. The third and fourth volumes of *One Day in Central Hebei*, a large collective reportage project discussed in chapter 6, were published for the first time in 1963.

63 Tian Zhongji, "Texie baogao fazhan de yige lunkuo: *Texie baogao ji bianji de yidian ganshou*" (An Outline of the Development of Feature Stories and Reportage: Impressions on the Editing of *Selected Feature Articles and Reportage*), BWYZX, vol. 2, 763.

64 *Zhongguo xiandai wenxue shi cankao ziliao: Sanwen xuan* (Research Materials on Modern Chinese Literature: A Selection of Literary Essays) (Shanghai: Shanghai jiaoyu chubanshe, 1979).

65 The society was originally devoted to the study of Agnes Smedley, Anna Louise Strong, and Edgar Snow, but later it came to include research on all reportage on China written by foreigners.

66 I will often use the word *landscape* as shorthand for this notion because it serves as both a noun and a verb and also connotes human endeavors to shape and depict spatial environments.

67 The source of this idea is Henri Lefebvre, *The Production of Space* (London: Blackwell, 1991). However, Lefebvre, frustrated with what he considered to be the saturation of French philosophy with linguistic methodologies and concepts, claimed to be wholly uninterested in the literary implications of his theory.

68 Nicos Poulantzas, *Political Power and Social Classes*, 13–16, as discussed in Frederic Jameson, *The Political Unconscious: Narrative as a Socially Symbolic Act* (Ithaca: Cornell University Press, 1981), 94–95.

69 It is Lefebvre who associates social spaces with modes of production and conceives their interaction in the manner described (*The Production of Space*, 86–87).

70 Elias Canetti, *Crowds and Power* (New York: Viking, 1963), 29–63.

71 See, for example, Lydia Liu, *Translingual Practice: Literature, National Culture, and Translated Modernity—China, 1900–1937* (Stanford: Stanford University Press, 1995); Jonathan Chaves, "The Expression of Self in the Kung-an School: Nonromantic Individualism," in *Expressions of Self in Chinese Literature*, ed. Robert E. Hegel and Richard C. Hessney (New York: Columbia University Press, 1985), 123–50; and Kirk Denton, *The Problematic of Self in Modern Chinese Literature: Hu Feng and Lu Ling* (Stanford: Stanford University Press, 1998).

72 Thomas Moran, "True Stories: Contemporary Chinese Reportage and its Ideology and Aesthetic," Ph.D. diss., Cornell University, 1994; Yingjin Zhang, "Narrative, Ideology, Subjectivity"; Xiaomei Chen, "Genre, Convention and Society."

1. TRAVEL: WRITING A WAY OUT

1 Yin-hwa Chou, "Formal Features of Chinese Reportage and an Analysis of Liang Qichao's 'Memoirs of My Travels in the New World,'" *Modern Chinese Literature* I.2: 201–17.

2   Ibid., 206, quoting Ding Wenjiang (Ting Wen-chiang), *Liang Rengong xiansheng nianpu changbian chugao* (A Detailed Chronology of the Life of Mr. Liang Rengong: Preliminary Draft) (Taipei: Shijie Press, 1958), 75.

3   Richard E. Strassberg, ed., *Inscribed Landscapes: Travel Literature from Imperial China* (Berkeley: University of California Press, 1994); Wen-chiang Ting, "On Hsü Hsia-k'o (1586–1641), Explorer and Geographer," *New China Review* 3.5 (1921): 225–337.

4   Immanuel C. Y. Hsü, *The Rise of Modern China* (New York: Oxford University Press, 1970), 110. See also Liang Qichao, *Intellectual Trends of the Late Ch'ing Period*, trans. Immanuel Hsu (Cambridge: Harvard University Press, 1959), 29–32.

5   See Zhong Shuhe, ed., *Zouxiang shijie congshu* (From East to West: Chinese Travelers before 1911) (Changsha: Yuelu, 1980–86), for a rich selection of works like this, including Liang Qichao's *Xin dalu youji* (Travels in the New World) and Kang Youwei's *Ouzhou shiyi guo youji erzhong* (Two Travelogues from Eleven European Countries). I am indebted to the late Xiao Qian for bringing this astounding series to my attention.

6   The earliest instance I know of is in "Wuchan jieji wenxue yundong xin de qingshi ji women de renwu" (New Trends in the Proletarian Literary Movement and Our Tasks), (August 15, 1930), SNZWZX, 147–54.

7   For a representative collection of translations of Chinese *youji* over the centuries, see Strassberg, *Inscribed Landscapes*. For a standard Chinese collection, see Ye Youming and Bei Yuanchen, eds., *Lidai youji xuan* (Changsha: Hunan renmin chubanshe, 1980). For an overview of studies and editions, see James Hargett, "Yu-chi wen-hsüeh," *The Indiana Companion to Traditional Chinese Literature*, ed. William H. Nienhauser Jr. (Bloomington: Indiana University Press, 1986).

8   For a concise discussion of various texts and oral traditions connected with this journey, see C. T. Hsia, *The Classic Chinese Novel* (Bloomington: Indiana University Press, 1968), 115–25.

9   See James M. Hargett, *On the Road in Twelfth Century China: The Travel Diaries of Fan Chengda (1126–1193)*, Munchener ostasiatische Studien, no. 52 (Stuttgart: Steiner Verlag Weisbaden, 1989).

10 For a rare description of Xu Xiake's voluminous travelogues, see Ting, "On Hsü Hsia-k'o," 225–337. See also Hargett, "Yu-chi wen-hsüeh," 936–39; and Strassberg, *Inscribed Landscapes*, 317–34.

11 Immanuel C. Y. Hsü, *The Rise of Modern China* (New York: Oxford University Press, 1970), 110. See also Liang Qichao, *Intellectual Trends of the Late Ch'ing Period*, trans. Immanuel Hsü (Cambridge: Harvard University Press, 1959), 29–32; and Benjamin A. Elman, *From Philosophy to Philology: Intellectual and Social Aspects of Change in Late Imperial China* (Cambridge: Council on East Asian Studies, Harvard University Press, 1984), 174–75. I am indebted to Richard Lufrano for bringing

Gu Yanwu, who is rarely discussed in connection with literature, to my attention.

12 For an excerpt from one of Gu's travelogues, see Strassberg, *Inscribed Landscapes*, 353–60.

13 Guo Songtao, *Lundun yu Bali riji* (London and Paris Diary), comp. Yang Jian.

14 Liang Qichao, "Wushi nian zhongguo jinhua gailun," (An Outline of China's Evolution in the Past Fifty Years) in *Shenbao wushi zhounian jinian wenji* (Essays Commemorating the Fiftieth Anniversary of Shenbao), cited in Zhong Shuhe, introduction to *Lundun yu Bali riji*, 2–3.

15 Qu Qiubai, *Exiang jicheng* (Journey to the Land of Hunger) in ZBWC I.2, 13–87.

16 Tsi-an Hsia, *The Gate of Darkness: Studies on the Leftist Literary Movement in China* (Seattle and London: University of Washington Press, 1968), 3–54.

17 A key term on the government side of the lively debates about reportage in the 1980s is *zhenshixing*, which I translate as "actuality." See, for example, Huang Gang, "Baogao wenxue de shidai tezheng jiqi bixu yanshou zhenshi de dangxing yuanze" (*The Historical Characteristics of Reportage and the Party Principle That It Must Strictly Adhere to Actuality*), BWYZX, vol. 1, 335–82.

18 "Diplomatic investigations" would seem to be a reference to late Qing travelogues or other commentaries on foreign countries.

19 Actually, as Qu points out in the opening paragraphs of *Chidu xinshi*, his systematic reports for *Chen bao* are separate from this work, in which he is consciously focusing on his personal experiences and his subjective reactions to them. This does not seem to have been the case with *Exiang jicheng*.

20 There is no reason why this should have occurred to Hsia, who reads Qu Qiubai's narratives as documents in intellectual history rather than as works of literature. See Jonathan Spence, *The Gate of Heavenly Peace: The Chinese and Their Revolution, 1895–1980* (New York: Penguin, 1982), 169–87.

21 Qu Qiubai, *Chidu xinshi* (A Personal History in the Red Capital), ZBWC I.2, 94.

22 Paul Pickowicz, *Marxist Literary Thought in China: The Influence of Ch'ü Ch'iu-pai* (Berkeley: University of California Press, 1981), 192–221.

23 Zou Taofen, *Pingzong jiyu chuji* (Notes of a Wanderer, First Collection) (Shanghai: Shenghuo shudian, 1934); *Pingzong jiyu erji* (Notes of a Wanderer, Second Collection) (Shanghai: Shenghuo shudian, 1934); *Pingzong jiyu sanji* (Notes of a Wanderer, Third Collection) (Shanghai: Shenghuo shudian, 1935); *Pingzong yiyu* (Recollections of a Wanderer) (Shanghai: Shenghuo shudian, 1935). All four volumes are reprinted in ZBWC I.4, and all citations below refer to this edition.

24 Zhao Xiaqiu, *Zhongguo xiandai baogao wenxue shi* (A History of Modern Chinese Reportage Literature) (Beijing: Renmin University Press, 1987), 169.

25 Margo Speisman Gewurtz, *Between America and Russia: Chinese Student Radicalism and the Travel Books of Tsou T'ao-fen, 1935–37* (Toronto: University of Toronto Press, 1975), 24–25. Subsequent references will be given in the text.

26 Zhou Enlai had written similar dispatches himself when he was a student in Lyon around 1920; though not very literary in nature, these narratives of the activism of Chinese work-study students in France have been included in the *Compendium of Chinese Reportage Literature*, where they are given the distinction of being the earliest pieces of modern Chinese reportage by a known author.

27 *China's Northwest Corner* was published in Shanghai by *Dagong bao guan* in 1934 after appearing serially in the newspaper; it is reprinted in ZBWC 2:1, 11–208. For a discussion of Fan's place in the burgeoning Chinese war correspondence industry, see Chang-tai Hung, *War and Popular Culture: Resistance in Modern China, 1937–1945* (Berkeley: University of California Press, 1994), 156–57. Hung gives a more detailed treatment of the work under discussion in his "Paper Bullets: Fan Changjiang and New Journalism," *Modern China* 17.4 (1991): 427–68.

28 A Chinese *li* is said to be about one-third of a mile.

29 See, for example, the collective battlefield diary of a group of professors and urban writers in Liao Quanjing, Wen Tianxing, and Wang Daming, eds., *Zuojia zhandi fangwentuan shiliao xuanbian* (Selected Writings of the War Area Interview Group (Chengdu: Sichuan sheng shehui kexue yuan, 1984), discussed in chapter 5.

30 Examples of this narratorial attitude can be found in the section on guerrilla consciousness in chapter 5.

31 Readers interested in additional works by Fan Changjiang are referred to his second book-length report, *Saishang xing* (Border Journeys), also included in ZBWC, 2:1.

2. PUBLIC DEMONSTRATIONS: THE MISE-EN-SCÈNE OF HISTORY

1 This paradigm is applied to the 1989 Beijing prodemocracy demonstrations in Joseph W. Esherick and Jeffrey N. Wasserstrom, "Acting Out Democracy: Political Theater in Modern China," *Journal of Asian Studies* 49.4 (1990): 835–65. Esherick and Wasserstrom's article sheds a great deal of light on the demonstration phenomenon itself; I focus here rather on the special features and implications of written accounts of such events.

2 See Jacques Derrida, "The Theater of Cruelty and the Closure of Representation," in *Writing and Difference*, trans. Alan Bass (Chicago: University of Chicago Press, 1978), 232–50.

3 "Yizhou zhong Beijing gongmin de da huodong" (The Great Citizens' Movement in Beijing This Week), ZBWC, I.1, 358–62.

4 Marston Anderson, *The Limits of Realism: Chinese Fiction in the Revolutionary Period* (Berkeley: University of California Press, 1990), 44.

5 Vera Schwarcz discusses the engagement of May Fourth intellectuals in the May Thirtieth movement, stressing the primacy of blood images in their writings, in her chapter "The Crucible of Political Violence, 1925–1927," in *The Chinese En-*

lightenment: *Intellectuals and the Legacy of the May Fourth Movement of 1919* (Berkeley: University of California Press, 1986), 145–94.

6 Ibid., 148.

7 ZBWC, 1:1, 13–18, 22–24, and 27–29, respectively.

8 Ye Shengtao, "Wuyue sayi ri jiyu zhong" (In the Driving Rain on May 31), ZBWC, I.1, 22.

9 Zheng Zhenduo, "Liu yue yi ri," ZBWC, I.1, 27.

10 "Housewives Paradise" is a sarcastic reference to a department store on Nanjing Road, perhaps Wing On (Yong An) or Sincere (Xian Shi).

11 Mao Dun, "Wuyue sanshi ri de xiawu" (On the Afternoon of May 30), ZBWC, I.1, 13. Note the explicitly theatrical terms Mao Dun uses to describe the massacre. "Men of civilization" (*wenming ren*) is a sarcastic reference to Western cultures common at the time that later becomes a code word for Japan as a fascist and imperialist force.

12 Schwarcz, *The Chinese Enlightenment*, 156. Mao Dun also discusses *Gongli ribao* in his *Wo zouguo de daolu* (The Road I Have Walked) (Beijing: Renmin wenxue chubanshe, 1981), 271–76.

13 This was probably Li Dazhao; see Schwarcz, *The Chinese Enlightenment*, 156.

14 Zhu Ziqing, "Zhizhengfu da tusha ji," (The Great Massacre at the Government Administration Building), ZBWC, I:1, 50. Zhu's text is discussed at some length by Vera Schwarcz in *The Chinese Enlightenment*, 156–57.

15 Anderson, *The Limits of Realism*, 182.

16 This is despite the fact that according to Vera Schwarcz's sources, the police were all Sikhs.

17 Mao Dun, "The Afternoon of May Thirtieth," 15.

18 Ye, "In the Driving Rain on May 31," 23. Ye is describing the faces of a procession of students marching in honor of the dead.

19 Lu Dingyi, "Wusa jie de Shanghai" (Shanghai on the Anniversary of May Thirtieth), ZBWC, I:1, 36–37. The word *Chinamen* appears in English in the text.

20 The full title is "Robison Road: Extra Edition of Issue Ten of the Fourth XX Cotton Factory Wall Newspaper," and it is signed Tu Ru. Xu Naixiang and Qin Hong, eds. *Zhongguo xiandai wenxue zuozhe biming lu* (Pseudonyms of Modern Chinese Literary Authors) gives Tu Ru as a pseudonym of Xia Yan, adding that the text was published in *Wenxue daobao* vol. 1, issues 6 and 7 combined (Changsha: Hunan wenyi chubanshe, 1988). My thanks to Michel Hockx for bringing this latter citation to my attention.

21 *Guamindang* is a pun on Guomindang, the Nationalist Party.

22 See John Israel and Donald W. Klein, *Rebels and Bureaucrats: China's December 9ers* (Berkeley: University of California Press, 1976), esp. chap. 3, "Students in the Streets," 87–136. Israel and Klein use, among other things, firsthand accounts of Chinese participants and foreign observers such as Nym Wales in their dis-

cussion of the events of December 1935, but there is no mention of the Chinese text later anthologized as reportage on these events, which I discuss here.

23 "Ji shier yue ershisi ri Nanjing lu" (Nanjing Road on December 24), *Haiyan* (Petrel), January 20, 1936; "Shier yue ershisi ri xuji" (December 24 Continued), *Haiyan*, February 20, 1936.

24 The two will merge to become almost indistinguishable in the reportage of the countryside, discussed in chapters 4 and 5.

25 The Juren Tang housed the administrative offices of the He Yingqin warlord government within the same walls as the Forbidden City. It is now occupied by the Communist government.

26 "Fennu de huoshan baofa" (The Furious Volcano Erupts), ZXWD, 1927–1937, 13:360.

27 This is a large intersection (which at the time had) an imposing decorative arch just west of Xinhua Gate on the main east-west thoroughfare in Beijing, Chang'an Avenue.

28 Wang Rujuan, "Rexue huiliuzhe" (The Hot Blood Converges in Torrents), ZXWD, 1927–1937, 13:385–96.

29 In fact, John Israel and Donald Klein have shown that the movement was overwhelmingly organized by Communist Party members. This is the general thrust of the chapter mentioned above and is borne out by the entire book, which paints a picture of the "December 9ers" as an elite cohort of Communist Party members who went on to have more or less illustrious political careers in the People's Republic.

30 Lu Fen [Shi Tuo], "Qingyuan zhengpian" (Main Account of a Petition Demonstration), (January 1932), ZXWD, 1927–1937, 13:131–48; "Qingyuan waipian" (Apocryphal Account of a Petition Demonstration), reprinted in *Living Record*, 35–62. It would be easy to argue that these two works are not reportage, to begin with because they were originally published explicitly as fiction (xiaoshuo) and were referred to as such in a memoir written by the author in the early 1980s (Shi Tuo [Lu Fen], autobiographical note to *Zhongguo xiandai wenxue yanjiu congkan* (Modern Chinese Literature Research Serial) 1980:2, 281–84). On the other hand, one of them was included in one of the most authoritative anthologies of reportage literature (ZXWD, 1927–1937, vol. 13: Reportage) by the author himself, who was the editor of that volume. The reason I discuss them here is not so much to insist that they are reportage as to show how they shed light on the artistic depiction of urban struggle.

31 Lu Fen, "Qingyuan waipian" (Apocryphal Account of a Petition Demonstration), *Wenxue zhoubao* 1.1 (June 10, 1932), 151.

32 He does this by changing the tones of zhuyi.

33 The term guojia zhuyi, literally "nationalism," has fascist overtones, especially for leftists; on the other hand, minzu zhuyi, which conflates nationality with eth-

nicity, is accepted equally across the political spectrum. The implications of this interesting detail of vocabulary go far beyond the scope of this volume.

34 Ding Ling, "Duo shi zhi qiu" (An Eventful Autumn), ZXWD, 1927–1937, 13:84–116.

35 I go into more detail on "An Eventful Autumn" in my article "Narrative Subjectivity and the Production of Social Space in Chinese Reportage," in Rey Chow, ed. *Modern Chinese Literary Studies in the Age of Theory: Reimagining a Field* (Durham, Duke University Press, 2000), 25–46.

36 C. T. Hsia, *A History of Modern Chinese Fiction* (New Haven: Yale University Press, 1971), 262–72. Hsia does discuss Ding Ling's proletarian fiction but only the 1931 story "Shui" (Water) as an example of how "bad" such literature is. Based on Hsia's account, Ding appears not to have been writing from 1931 to "the early forties" (263).

37 In another fascinating piece, "You qingyuan er bu qingyuan jixiang" (A Detailed Account of a Demonstration That Never Was) by Zi Ye (ZXWD, 1927–1937, 13:370–77), students commandeer a train from Shanghai to Nanjing, driving it themselves for a stretch, but they are turned back before they reach their destination.

38 This assumption underlies Rudolf Wagner's treatment of the sketch in *Inside a Service Trade: Studies in Contemporary Chinese Prose* (Cambridge: Harvard University Press, 1992), chaps. 16–18 (311–76).

39 Yi Qun, quoted in Lan Hai (Tian Zhongji), *Zhongguo kangzhan wenyi shi* (A History of Chinese Resistance Literature and Art) (Shanghai: Xiandai chubanshe, 1947), 82.

40 These refer to the years of 1919, 1925, 1931, 1932, and 1937, respectively.

41 This process is by no means confined to a certain period and in fact continues to accumulate dates even to the present day (April 5, 1976, and June 4, 1989, are more recent examples).

42 See, for example, Huang Gang, "Zongxu" (General Introduction), in *Compendium of Chinese Reportage Literature*, ZBWC, I.2: "from this Compendium, our dear readers can come to understand certain vivid scenes from each historical period of the revolutionary struggle of the leaders of the Chinese Communist Party; today's younger readers can better strengthen their knowledge of the wretched lives of the people in the old China and from the heroic accomplishments of the people of our country as they strove for and constructed a new, socialist China can gain confidence in the widespread even more vigorous realization of the 'Four Modernizations'" (3).

43 Moreover, in the past twenty years deaths of political leaders become occasions for political demonstrations that start out as memorial ceremonies, such as the April 5 demonstration in 1976 at Tian'anmen, initially mourning Zhou Enlai, and the demonstrations in May 1989, mourning Hu Yaobang.

44 This is not meant to imply that it is a more "concrete" nationalism than territoriality; note, for example, the ambiguous status of ethnic minorities, including the largely Manchu student body of Northeastern University in the December Ninth texts, vis-à-vis the Han majority in the vague formulation "the Chinese people."

3. LABOR REPORTAGE AND THE FACTORYSCAPE

1 Rudolf G. Wagner, *Inside a Service Trade: Studies in Contemporary Chinese Prose*, Harvard-Yenching Institute Monographs, no. 34 (Cambridge: Harvard University Press, 1992), 328.

2 "Tangshan meikuang zangsong gongren da canju" (The Tragic Burial Alive of Workers at the Tangshan Coal Mine), ZBWC, I:1, 363–65. This is also one of the earliest works included in ZBWC, second only to "The Great Citizens' Movement in Beijing This Week."

3 Cang Jian, "Kuanggong shouji" (A Miner's Notebook), ZBWC I.1, 135. This, like Tu Ru's "Robison Road," is a product of the League of Left-Wing Writers' Worker Correspondents Movement. The style, footnotes, and content all suggest that this is not the narrator's own work but was based on an interview.

4 Li Qiao, "Xi shi ruhe liancheng de" (How Tin Is Smelted, 1937), ZBWC, I.1, 344–57.

5 Lou Shiyi, "Fangche de hongsheng" (The Thundering of the Looms), ZXWD, 1927–1937, 13:185–86.

6 Peng Zigang, "Zai jiqi pangbian" (Beside the Machines), ZXWD, 1927–1937, 13:463–72.

7 See SNZWZX, 215.

8 Xia Yan [Shen Duanxuan], "Baoshen gong" (Indentured Laborers), ZBWC, I.1, 265–77.

9 Yangshupu is known primarily as a factory district. The second character of the street name is elided with Xs in the text.

10 Here and elsewhere, I use the word *iterative* in contrast to *narrative* to refer to the telling of an ongoing state of affairs or the building of a tableau rather than the telling of a sequence of events. Generally speaking, literary nonfiction features the iterative mode much more than does fiction.

11 *Lugu de* literally means "revealing the bone," a grim pun.

12 See Emily Honig, *Sisters and Strangers: Women in the Shanghai Cotton Mills, 1919–1949* (Stanford: Stanford University Press, 1986).

13 Xia Yan, "'Baoshen gong' yu hua," (Reflections on Indentured Workers, 1936), ZXWD, 1927–1937, 13:74–83.

14 Yang Chao, "Baofanzuo" (The Boarders), ZXWD, 1927–1937, 13:325–29.

15 Ji Hong, "Canguan Zhabei shizhou chang" (A Visit to the Zhabei Porridge Kitchen), ZXWD, 1927–1937, 13:705–13.

16   Ji Hong, "Canguan nü qingnian hui laogong xuexiao ji" (A Visit to the Young Women's Association Labor School), ZXWD, 1927–1937, 13:714–22.

17   Ding Ling, "Bayue sheng huo" (Eight Months of My Life), ZXWD, 1927–1937, 13:116–22.

18   Huang Gang's *Tamen shi shenglizhe* (They Are the Victors) (Shanghai: Laodong chubaushe, 1951, ZBWC, II.5, 110–35) is an exception to this generalization.

19   Georg Lukács, "Reification and the Consciousness of the Proletariat," in *History and Class Consciousness: Studies in Marxist Dialectics*, ed. Georg Lukács (Cambridge: MIT Press, 1968), 90.

20   He continues: "The disciplinary pyramid constituted the small cell of power within which the separation, coordination, and supervision of tasks were imposed and made efficient; an analytical partitioning of time, gestures, and bodily forces constituted an operational schema that could easily be transferred from the groups to be subjected to the mechanisms of production; the massive projection of military methods onto industrial organization was an example of this modeling of the division of labor following the model laid down by the schemata of power" (Paul Rabinow, ed., *The Foucault Reader* [New York: Pantheon, 1984]), 210.

21   That the expression of such consciousness is unprecedented assumes that it is qualitatively different than existing literary subjectivities. See Lukács, "Reification," esp. 163–65.

4. WAR CORRESPONDENCE I: TERROR AND THE WOUND

1   Xie Bingying, "Tajinle weidade zhanchang—Taierzhuang" (Stepping onto the Great Battlefield: Taierzhuang), in Wu Dongquan, ed. *Fenghuo suiyue* (Taipei: Liming, 1987), 208–9.

2   Peter Monteath, "The Spanish Civil War and the Aesthetics of Reportage," in *Literature and War*, ed. David Bevan (Amsterdam: Rodopi, 1990), 69–85. Monteath points out that the war in Spain attracted star reporters from all the major newspapers in Europe, the United States, and the Soviet Union (69).

3   I will not go into detail on the political and military history of the period covered in this and the next chapter. For analytical studies, see John Hunter Boyle, *China and Japan at War, 1937–1945: The Politics of Collaboration* (Stanford: Stanford University Press, 1972); Hsi-sheng Ch'i, *Nationalist China at War* (Ann Arbor: University of Michigan Press, 1982); and F.F. Liu, *A Military History of Modern China, 1924–1949* (Princeton: Princeton University Press, 1956). Works that focus on the social and cultural aspects of the war include Chang-tai Hung's *War and Popular Culture* and James C. Hsiung and Steven I. Levine, eds., *China's Bitter Victory: The War with Japan, 1937–1945* (Armonk, NY: M. E. Sharpe, 1992). For an account of the War of Resistance by an American journalist, see Frank Dorn,

The Sino-Japanese War, 1937–1941: From Marco Polo Bridge to Pearl Harbor (New York: Macmillan, 1974).

4   Works published in literary journals of the time, if they were not organized into generic sections, usually included a generic reference in parentheses after the title in the table of contents. Such references, whether provided by authors or added by editors, are not definitive, as they are not based on a common understanding of the form.

5   See my discussion of the formation of this canon in the introduction.

6   See Zhao Xiaqiu, *Zhongguo xiandai baogao wenxue shi* (History of Modern Chinese Reportage Literature) (Beijing: Renmin University Press, 1987), 240–41, 246–47. This argument dovetails with the Japanese proletarian writer Kawaguchi Hiroshi's association of European reportage with the material changes brought about in the cultural sphere by the Industrial Revolution. See Kawaguchi Hiroshi [Chuankou hao], "Baogao wenxue lun" (On Reportage Literature), trans. Shen Duanxian (Xia Yan), 1932, in BWYZX, 2:1182–91.

7   Zhao Xiaqiu makes this observation (*History*, 239–40) but does not elaborate.

8   See "Wei xuanbu jieshu muji yuanzhu pinbing zuojia jijin yundong gongqi" (Public Announcement of Our Declaration to Discontinue the Fund-Raising Campaign for the Foundation for Assisting Poor and Ailing Artists), in Wen Tianxing, Wang Daming, and Liao Quanjing, eds., *Zhonghua quanguo wenyijie kangdi xiehui shiliao xuanbian* (Collected Materials on the All China Association for Resistance in Literature and the Arts) (Chengdu: Sichuan sheng shehui kexue yuan chubanshe, 1983), 306–8.

9   *Fenghuo* was initially entitled *Nahan* (Battle Cry) in Shanghai on August 25, 1937, changing its name to *Fenghuo* with its second issue on August 29. *Qiyue* was established on September 11, 1937, in Shanghai and *Wenyi zhendi* in April of 1938 in Guangzhou. *Kangzhan wenyi*, Wenxie's official literary magazine, was launched the following month in Hankou.

10 See Zhao, *History* 243–46, for a thorough list of short reportage works that appeared in these and other journals during the early months of the War of Resistance.

11 "Notice for Contributions," *Nahan*, inaugural issue, August 25, 1937.

12 Hu Feng, "Lun suxie" (On the Sketch), in *Hu Feng pinglun ji*, ed. Hu Feng (Beijing: Renmin wenxue chubanshe, 1984), 1:67–69. By "creation," Hu is referring to the major genres of fiction, poetry, and drama; he does not in so doing suggest that *zawen* and *suxie* are not creative.

13 Hu Feng, "Lun zhandou qi de yige zhandou wenyi xingshi" (On a Fighting Art Form in a Period of Fighting), in *Minzu zhanzheng yu wenyi xingge* (The National War and Artistic Style [December, 1937]) (Chongqing: Xiwang she, 1946 [Shanghai printing]), 131–44.

14 Cf. Yunzhong Shu, *Buglers on the Home Front: The Wartime Practice of the Qiyue School* (Albany: State University of New York Press, 2000), 48–49, 106–7. Shu's book examines all aspects of the *Qiyue* group's literary production, devoting two chapters to reportage. See also Rudolf Wagner's reading of Hu Feng's criticism as disapproving of reportage in general. Rudolf Wagner, *Inside a Service Trade: Studies in Contemporary Chinese Prose* (Cambridge: Harvard University Press, 1992), 351.

15 Mao Dun, *Zhongguo de yiri* (One Day in China) (Shanghai: Shenghuo chubanshe, 1936). See also the partial translation in Sherman Cochran, Andrew C. K. Hsieh, and Janis Cochran, eds., *One Day in China: May 21, 1936* (New Haven: Yale University Press, 1983).

16 I discuss this at greater length in the context of literary mobilization in general in my article "The Battlefield of Cultural Production: Chinese Literary Mobilization during the War Years," *Journal of Modern Literature in Chinese* 2.1 (1998): 83–103.

17 Zhu Zuotong and Mei Yi, eds., *Shanghai yiri* (Shanghai: Huamei chuban gongsi, 1938), iv.

18 Mao Dun, "Inaugural Statement," *Wenyi zhendi* 1.1 (April 16, 1938): 1.

19 Ah Ying (Qian Xingcun), ed., *Shanghai shibian yu baogao wenxue* (The Shanghai Incident and Its Reportage) (Shanghai: Nanqiang shuju, 1932).

20 "Baiyi nüren lizan" (Tribute to the Women in White), Ah Ying, ed., *Shanghai shibian yu baogao*, 108.

21 Another notable collection of reportage that stemmed from the Shanghai Incident is Weng Zhaoyuan, *Songhu xuezhan huiyilu* (Memoirs of the Bloody Songhu Battle) (Shanghai: Shenbao yuekan chubanshe, 1932).

22 These were spontaneous but not necessarily independent. Internal evidence suggests that most of these texts were written by three or four people who either traveled to the front together or at least were kept together by their military escorts once they got there. In "Bu pa si de tongzhimen" (Fearless Comrades), the writer compares himself, Huang Zhenxia of *Dawan bao*, and Wan Guo'an of *Shishi xinbao* (China Times) to "the Three Musketeers."

23 "Cong Shanghai shibian shuo dao baogao wenxue" (From the Shanghai Incident to a Discussion of Reportage), in Ah Ying, ed., *Shanghai shibian yu baogao*, 3–4; emphases in original). The word *reportage* appears in French where it is italicized.

24 Zou Taofen, for example, was very much aware of his moral influence on young readers.

25 Po-shek Fu, *Passivity, Resistance, Collaboration: Intellectual Choices in Occupied Shanghai, 1937–1945* (Stanford: Stanford University Press, 1993), 13–16.

26 Luo Binji, "Jiuhu che li de xue" (Blood in the Ambulance), ZBWC, II.8, 281–82.

27 Zhao Xiaqiu, *History*, 278–79.

28 Luo Binji, "Zai ye de jiaotong xian shang" (On the Night Transport Line) ZBWC, II.8, 277–80.

29 Zhao Xiaqiu, History, 276.

30 Cao Bai, "Zheli, shengming ye zai huxi . . ." (Life Breathes Here, Too . . .), ZBWC, II.8, 47–51.

31 Cao Bai, "Fang Jiangnan yiyongjun disanlu" (A Visit to the Third Route Jiangnan Volunteer Army), ZBWC, II.8, 89–96.

32 This definition of graphic is from The New Shorter Oxford English Dictionary, 1993 ed.

33 On the typology of wounds and scars, see David Der-wei Wang, "Lu Xun, Shen Congwen, and Decapitation," in Politics, Ideology, and Literary Discourse in Modern China: Theoretical Interventions and Cultural Critique, ed. Liu Kang and Xiaobing Tang (Durham: Duke University Press, 1993), 174–87; and "Reinventing National History: Communist and Anti-communist Fiction of the Mid–Twentieth Century," in Chinese Literature in the Second Half of a Modern Century (Bloomington: Indiana University Press, 2000).

34 Ling Shuhua, "Hanyang shangbing yiyuan fangwenji" (A Visit to the Hanyang Hospital for Wounded Soldiers), in Fenghuo suiyue, ed. Wu Dongquan (Taipei: Liming wenhua shiye gufen youxian gongsi, 1987), 111–16.

35 Two of Ling's stories and a short biographical note appear in Modern Chinese Short Stories and Novellas, 1919–1949, ed. Joseph S. M. Lau, C. T. Hsia, and Leo Ou-fan Lee (New York: Columbia University Press, 1981), 195–205. Her "The Night of Midautumn Festival" appears in Columbia Anthology of Modern Chinese Literature, ed. Joseph S. M. Lau and Howard Goldblatt (New York: Columbia University Press, 1995), 111–19.

36 "Hanyang shangbing yiyuan fangwen ji," 113.

37 Bai Lang, "Wo chiyi de zouxiale futi" (Hesitantly, I Descended the Stairs), Fenghuo suiyue, 123–30. Bai Lang later joined the All China Resistance Association of Writers and Artists, accompanying its Writers' War Area Interview Group and writing of her experiences in Women shisige (The Fourteen of Us). For "Hesitantly I Descended the Stairs" she used the pseudonym Bai Wei.

38 Peng Zigang, "Yizhi shou" (A Hand) in Fenghuo suiyue, 158–66.

39 See especially "Niyu zhong" (In the Mud and Rain) and subsequent articles in the fourth section, "Zhanqu yinxiang" (Battle Zone Impressions), in The Shanghai Incident, 61–95.

40 Qiu Dongping, "Diqilian: Ji diqilian lianzhang Qiu Jun tanhua" (Company Seven: A Talk with Company Commander Qiu Jun), ZBWC, II.8, 19–28.

41 Yunzhong Shu argues that the "personal" quality of Qiyue reportage is its "most important characteristic" (Buglers on the Homefront, 88). See also his reading of "Company Seven" and many other works by Qiu Dongping (111–26).

42 Qiu Dongping, "Women zai nali dale baizhan" (We Were Defeated There), ZBWC, II.8, 29–33.

43 Bi Ye, "Hutuo he yezhan" (Night Battle at the Hutuo River), ZXWD, 1937–1949, 98–104.

44 See SNZWZX, 251–90.

45 Henri Barbusse, *I Saw It Myself*, trans. Brian Rhys (New York: Dutton, 1928), 7.

46 Egon Erwin Kisch, *Der rasende Reporter* (The Roving Reporter) (Berlin: Reiss, 1925), quoted in Monteath, "The Spanish Civil War," 72.

47 A notable exception is Qiu's autobiographical "Yige lianzhang de zhandou zaoyu" (The Battle Experience of a Company Commander, 1938), discussed at some length in Shu, *Buglers on the Homefront*, 120–26.

5. WAR CORRESPONDENCE II: GUERRILLA LANDSCAPES

1 Bi Ye, *Beifang de yuanye* (The Northern Wilderness) (Shanghai: Shanghai zazhi gongsi, 1938).

2 Liu Baiyu, "Taochu Beiping" (Escaping from Beiping), ZXWD, 1937–1949, 1–3. Beijing was renamed Beiping in 1928, when Nanjing became the capital of China. For simplicity I will refer to the city consistently as Beijing.

3 Xiao Jun, "Zai 'Dalian fan' shang" (On the Dairen Maru, 1936), ZXWD, 1937–1949, 410–15.

4 Xi Min, "Beixing tuci" (Travels in the North) and "Guofangxian shang de Shijiazhuang" (Shijiazhuang on the National Line of Defense), *Shen bao* August 13, 1937, and August 8–9, 1937, respectively; Shi Ren [Zhang Xiangshan], "Jinghuxian shang" (On the Beijing-Shanghai Line), *Shen bao*, October 4, 1937. All are reprinted in Wu Dongquan, ed., *Fenghuo suiyue* (The Days of Beacon Fires) (Taipei: Liming wenhua shiye gufen youxian gongsi, 1987).

5 The report of the association is taken from "Kangzhan yilai de zhongguo wenyijie" (Literature and Art Circles in China since the Outbreak of the War of Resistance), *Resistance Literature* 2.6 (October 15, 1938), 82–83. See Tang Tao, *Zhongguo xiandai wenxue shi* (Beijing: Renmin wenxue chubanshe, 1979), 144.

6 Wenxie documents concerning all of these activities can be found in Wen Tianxing, Wang Daming, and Liao Quanjing, eds., *Zhonghua quanguo wenyijie kangdi xiehui ziliao huibian* (Collected Materials on the All China Resistance Association of Writers and Artists) (Chengdu: Sichuan sheng shehui kexue yuan chubanshe, 1983).

7 Xie Bingying, *Congjun riji* (Army Diary) (Shanghai: Guangming shuju, 1928).

8 Chang-tai Hung, *War and Popular Culture: Resistance in Modern China, 1937–1945* (Berkeley: University of California Press, 1994), 74. Hua Mulan is a legendary woman who impersonated her aging father as a general on the battlefield when he became ill.

9 Chen Yi, "Jiangnan kangzhan zhi chun" (Springtime in Jiangnan during the War of Resistance), *Jiefang jun wenyi* (1957), ZXWD, 1937–1949, 734–47. Although Chen's text was apparently not published until 1957, it is based on a 1939 diary.

10 Yin Junsheng, "Bi Ye xiaozhuan" (A Brief Biography of Bi Ye), ZBWC II.8, 271–72.

11 Bi Ye, "Beifang de yuanye" (The Northern Wilderness) ZBWC, II.8: 235–70.

12 The Taihang Mountains, like the town of Taierzhuang, become a favorite microcosm among reportage writers for China's wartime transformations.

13 The Red Spear Society is privileged in leftist literature as a band of "good bandits," a self-organized peasant militia operating throughout East-Central China, with which the Communist Party maintained amicable relations.

14 Mao Dun's enthusiastic praise for the work may indeed stem from its practical realization of the very attributes and strategies Mao described and promoted in his 1937 article "Guanyu 'baogao wenxue'" (About "Reportage Literature"), BWYZX, 51–54.

15 Huang Gang, "Wo kanjianle Balujun" (I Have Seen the Eighth Route Army), ZBWC II.5, 39–64.

16 Huang Gang, "Yu: Chen Geng bingtuan shi zengyang zuozhande zhier" (Rain: How Chen Gang's Troops Do Battle #2), ZBWC II.5, 73–82.

17 Wei Wei, "Shui shi zui ke'ai de ren" (Who Is Most Worthy of Our Love?), ZXWD, 1949–1966, 19–22.

18 David Apter and Tony Saich, *Revolutionary Discourse in Mao's Republic* (Cambridge: Harvard University Press, 1994), 69–81.

6. SOCIALIST REPORTAGE

1 Rou Shi, "Yige weidade yinxiang" (An Impression of Grandeur), ZBWC, I.3, 89–96.

2 Jintan (*rendan* in Mandarin Chinese) is a popular, Japanese pick-me-up sold in boxes of small capsules.

3 I am indebted to Richard Lufrano for drawing my attention to Wang Ruoshui and the early 1980s debate in China on socialist alienation. For a summary, see David Kelly, "The Emergence of Humanism: Wang Ruoshui and the Critique of Socialist Alienation," in *China's Intellectuals and the State: In Search of a Relationship*, ed. Merle Goldman (Cambridge: Harvard University Press, 1987). The debate has since been analyzed brilliantly in Jing Wang, "'Who Am I?' Questions of Voluntarism in the Paradigm of 'Socialist Alienation,'" *positions: east asia cultures critique* 3.2 (1995): 448–80.

4 I have generally abbreviated this whole complex alternatively as "socialism" or "the Party," but I mean all of its elements, each of which represents the whole (the evocation of Mao's name after 1949, for example, is identical in meaning to evocations of "the spirit of communism/socialism," etc.).

5 Bonnie S. McDougall, *Mao Zedong's "Talks at the Yan'an Conference on Literature and Art": A Translation of the 1943 Text with Commentary* (Ann Arbor: Center for Chinese Studies, University of Michigan, 1980), 84.

6   The reportage collections are Ding Ling, *Huowang li: Jiti baogao wenxue* (In the Line of Fire: Collective Reportage) (Shanghai: Hujiang chubanshe, 1939); and *Xixian shenghuo* (Life on the Western Front) (Shanghai: Shenghuo shudian, 1938). Some of the works from these collections were reprinted along with later works in *Yi ke wei chutang de qiangdan* (An Unfired Bullet), ed. Ding Ling (Chongqing: Shenghuo shudian, 1938).

7   Zhao Xiaqiu, *Zhongguo xiandai baogao wenxue shi* (History of Modern Chinese Reportage Literature) (Beijing: Renmin University Press, 1987), 296.

8   Huang Gang, "Yu: Chen Geng de bingtuan shi zenyang zuo zhan de zhier" (Rain: How Chen Geng's Troops Do Battle #2) *Jiefang ribao* (Liberation Daily), April 7–8, 1942; "Wo kanjianle balujun" (I Have Seen the Eighth Route Army), *Zhongguo wenhua* (Chinese Culture) 2.3–4 (November 25, December 25, 1940).

9   Huang Gang, who passed away in 1994, though not as high-ranking as some of the other members of the Yan'an cohort, remained to the end of his life one of the foremost promoters of research on international reportage, and he maintained a strong belief in the power of reportage to transform consciousness and society.

10 This was at the intersection of Shaanxi, Gansu, and Ningxia Provinces. Yan'an was located in this border area.

11 See "Xibei zhandi fuwutuan chengli xuanyan" (Declaration of the Establishment of the Northwest War Area Service Corps), *Xinhua ribao*, August 19, 1937.

12 See Liu Zengjie et al., eds., *Kangri zhanzheng shiqi Yan'an ji kangri minzhu genjudi wenxue yundong ziliao* (Materials on Literary Movements in Yan'an and other Democratic Resistance Bases during the War Against Japan) (Taiyuan: Shanxi renmin chubanshe, 1983), 447–50.

13 Zhao Xiaqiu, *History*, 296.

14 Jin-Cha-Ji stands for Shanxi-Chahar-Hebei.

15 For these references, see the editor's note in the inaugural issue of the reformed *Wenyi tuji*, May 25, 1939.

16 Lin Fei, *Zhongguo xiandai baogao wenxue de yige lunkuo* (An Outline of Modern Chinese Reportage) (Beijing: Renmin wenxue chubanshe, 1979), 215.

17 Tang Tao, *Zhongguo xiandai wenxue shi* (History of Modern Chinese Literature), 300. See also Zhao Xiaqiu, *History*: "In the dedication to the mimeographed edition of *One Day in Central Hebei*, Cheng Zihua writes: '*One Day in Central Hebei* is the first organized collective creation of the Party, government, military, and people in central Hebei and a great experience for the mass culture movement; it is a victory flag of our advance on the battle line of a new democratic culture'" (308).

18 Ibid., 302–4.

19 Lin Fei, *An Outline*, 815.

20 Zhao Xiaqiu, *History*, 311.

21 *Zhiyuanjun yiri* (One Day in the Volunteer Army) (Beijing: Renmin wenxue chubanshe, 1956).

22 See my discussion of the image of the soldier-reporter and guerrilla consciousness in chapter 4.

23 Liu Baiyu, *Yan'an Shenghuo* (Life in Yan'an) (Shanghai: Xianshi chubanshe, 1946).

24 Patricia Stranahan's study of the *Liberation Daily* shows how Mao Zedong's manipulation of the Yan'an news media helped strengthen his own political position and influence both the making and implementation of economic policy. See Patricia Stranahan, *Molding the Medium: The Chinese Communist Party and the Liberation Daily, Studies on Contemporary China* (Armonk, NY: M. E. Sharpe, 1990).

25 Liu Baiyu, *Life in Yan'an*, 9.

26 David Holm, *Art and Ideology in Revolutionary China* (Oxford: Oxford University Press, 1991).

27 Huang Gang, "Liangge chuxi" (Two New Year's Eves), ZBWC II.5, 12–16.

28 David Apter and Tony Saich, *Revolutionary Discourse in Mao's Republic* (Cambridge: Harvard University Press, 1994), 143–44, 150–53.

29 Ibid., 134–35.

30 Rudolf Wagner's treatment of Wang Meng's "Youyou cuncaoxin" (The Loyal Heart) provides an interesting perspective on the development after 1949 of the haircut as a political and moral trope in political cartoons (*Inside a Service Trade*, 481–510).

31 Huang Gang, "Jieda huanxi: Luyi xuanchuan dui" (Everybody Is Happy: The Lu Xun Academy's Propaganda Team), ZBWC, II.5, 93–97.

32 Holm, *Art and Ideology in Revolutionary China*. According to Holm, this campaign during the Spring Festival of 1943 ended a period of experimentation with the new *yangge*; the form as performed by the Luyi troupe was explicitly praised by leaders, and performances continued well beyond the festival season. See chapters 6, "New *Yangge*: The Lu Xun Academy's Pilot Project," and 7, "High Tide: The *Yangge* Movement in Yan'an," 215–86. Holm also includes photographs of Luyi troupe performances on pages 247 and 272.

33 Huang Gang, "Juelie: Nanjing Guomindang zhengfu bengkui qian de yimu" (Final Break: A Scene before the Fall of the Guomindang Government in Nanjing), ZBWC, II.5, 104–9.

34 See, for example, Rudolf Wagner's treatment of Galina Nikolayeva's *The Director of the Machine Tractor Station and the (Woman) Chief Agronomist* as a paradigm influential in China for the depiction of love in socialist fiction (*Inside a Service Trade*, 91–102).

35 Wen Junquan and Dan Fu, "Li Jinzhi: Ji wufeng gangguan chang de yige nü caozuoshou" (Li Jinzhi: A Woman Technician in the Seamless Pipe Factory), in ZXWD, 1949–1966, 134–41.

36   Mu Qing, Feng Jian and Zhou Yuan, "Xianwei shuji de bangyang: Jiao Yulu" (A Model Country Party Secretary: Jiao Yulu), ZXWD, 1949–1966, 699–710.

37   *Voluntarism* is defined as "a theory or doctrine which regards will as the fundamental principle or dominant factor in the individual or in the universe" in the *New Shorter Oxford English Dictionary*. In discussions of Mao Zedong, the sense is that the collective spirit is capable of overcoming material limitations, and thus Mao's voluntarism was the tragic flaw of the Great Leap Forward.

CONCLUSIONS

1   Liu Binyan is particularly explicit on this point. In a symposium on contemporary literature held at Columbia University in 1992, Liu began his comments with the words, "Baogao wenxue bushi wenxue" (Reportage literature is not literature). His position is also described in Leo Ou-fan Lee, introduction to *People or Monsters? And Other Stories and Reportage from China after Mao*, ed. E. Perry Link (Bloomington: Indiana University Press, 1983), xiv. One Chinese critic devotes an entire article to this topic as well: Xie Yong, "Chuanbo xue yu baogao wenxue" (Communications Studies and Reportage), *Baogao wenxue* 5 (1989): 60–63.

2   Yuan Liangjun, interview with the author, February 1993. Yuan is a researcher at the Chinese Academy of Social Sciences' Institute for Modern Chinese Literary Studies.

3   Jeffrey C. Kinkley, "Chinese Crime Fiction and Its Formulas at the Turn of the 1980s," in *After Mao: Chinese Literature and Society, 1978–1981*, ed. Jeffrey C. Kinkley (Cambridge: Harvard University Press, 1985), 89–129.

4   Yunzhong Shu, *Buglers on the Home Front: The Wartime Practice of the Qiyue School* (Albany: State University of New York Press, 2000), 49. Shu's second and third chapters, "Antidote to Wartime Heroics: Early Qiyue Reportage" (43–63) and "From Reflection to Lyricism: The Transition from Qiyue Reportage to Qiyue Fiction" (65) are concerned entirely with reportage as a reflection of Hu Feng's literary initiatives. For evidence of the compelling attraction of the idea of a "Lu Xun tradition" in Western sinology, see Leo Ou-fan Lee, ed., *Lu Xun and His Legacy* (Berkeley: University of California Press, 1985). The reappropriation of Lu Xun by both cultural authorities and dissidents has been one of the perennial motifs of modern Chinese cultural history.

5   See Liu Kang, "Subjectivity, Marxism, and Cultural Theory in China" and Liu Zaifu, "The Subjectivity of Literature Revisited," both in *Politics, Ideology, and Literary Discourse in China: Theoretical Interventions and Cultural Critique*, ed. Liu Kang and Xiaobing Tang (Durham: Duke University Press, 1993), 23–55 and 56–69, respectively.

6   Hu Feng, "Lun zhanzheng shiqi de yige zhandou de wenyi xingshi" (On a Battling Form of Literature in an Era of War), in *Minzu zhanzheng yu wenyi xingge* (National War and Artistic Character), (Shanghai: Xiwang she, 1946), 136.

7   See, for example, Fredric Jameson, "Third World Literature in the Age of Multinational Capitalism," *Social Text* 15 (fall 1986): 65–88.

8   By "concrete," I mean realized or expressed in terms of sense-experience rather than abstract concepts.

9   See, for example, Chen Xiaomei, "Genre, Convention, and Society: A Reception Study of Chinese Reportage," *Yearbook of Comparative and General Literature* 34 (1985): 85–100; Michael Ernst Geisler, "The Literary Reportage in Germany: The Possibilities and Limitations of an Operative Genre," Ph.D. diss., University of Pittsburgh, 1981; and Zhang Yingjin, "Narrative, Ideology, Subjectivity: Defining a Subversive Discourse in Chinese Reportage," in Liu and Tang, *Politics, Ideology, and Literary Discourse in Modern China*, 211–42.

10 David Apter and Tony Saich, *Revolutionary Discourse in Mao's Republic* (Cambridge: Harvard University Press, 1994), 70–71; emphasis mine.

BIBLIOGRAPHY

ORIGINAL REPORTAGE WORKS

Ai Wu 艾蕪. "Beiguo suxie" 北國速寫. *Tai bai* 太白 2.1 (March 20, 1935).

Ba Jin 巴金. "Yidian buneng wangji de jiyi" 一點不能忘記的記憶. *Zhongliu* 中流 1.5 (November 5, 1936).

———. "Women huijianle Peng Dehuai silingyuan" 我們會見了彭德懷司令員. *Zhiyuan jun bao* 志愿軍報, April 11, 1952.

Bai Lang 白朗. "Wo chiyi di zouxiale futi" 我遲疑地走下了扶梯. *Da gong bao* 大公報, October 30, 1937.

Bai Wei 白薇. "Qiangtou sanbuqu" 牆頭三部曲. *Bei dou* 北斗 2.3-4 (July 20, 1932).

———. "Huoxian shang" 火線上. *Wenyi xinwen* 文藝新聞, April 11, 1934.

"Beiping xuesheng 'yi er, jiu' shiwei" 北平學生 '一二、九' 示威. In *Yi er, jiu yu qingnian* 一二、九與青年. N.p.: N.p., 1948.

Bi Ye 碧野. *Beifang de yuanye* 北方的原野. Shanghai: Shanghai zazhi gongsi, 1938.

———. "Hutuo he yezhan" 滹沱河夜戰. *Wenyi zhendi* 文藝陣地 1.3 (1938): 81-85.

Cang Jian 蒼劍. "Kuanggong shouji" 礦工手記. *Wenyi xinwen* 文藝新聞 50, 51, 52 (April 11, 18, 25, 1932).

Cao Bai 曹白. "Zheli, shengming ye zai huxi . . ." 這裏、生命也在呼吸 . . . *Qiyue* 七月 1.1 (1937).

Chen Huangmei. "Ji shier yue ershisi ri Nanjing lu" 記十二月二十四日南京路, *Haiyan* 海燕, January 20, 1936.

———. "Shier yue ershisi ri xuji" 十二月二十四日續記, *Haiyan* 海燕, February 20, 1936.

Chen Yi 陳毅. "Jiangnan kangzhan zhi chun" 江南抗戰之春. *Jiefang jun wenyi* 解放軍文藝 6 (1957).

Dai Shuzhou 戴叔周. "Qianxian tongxin" 前線通信. *Bei dou* 北斗 2.3-4 (July 20, 1932).

Ding Ling 丁玲. "Duoshi zhi qiu" 多事之秋. *Bei dou* 北斗 2.1, 3-4 (January 20, and July 20, 1932).

———. "Bayue shenghuo" 八月生活. *Jindai wenyi* 近代文藝 1.2 (August 20, 1936).

———. "Suxie Peng Dehuai" 速寫彭德懷. *Xin Zhonghua bao xin Zhonghua fukan* 新中華報新中華副刊 1.6 (February 3, 1936).

———. *Xixian shenghuo* 西線生活. Shanghai: Shenghuo shudian, 1938.

———. *Huowang li: Jiti baogao wenxue* 火網裡：集體報告文學. Shanghai: Hujiang chubanshe, 1939.

———. "Yi ke wei chutang de qiangdan" 一顆未出膛的槍彈. In *Yi ke wei chutang de qiangdan*, ed. Ding Ling. Chongqing: Shenghuo shudian, 1938.

Fan Changjiang 范長江. *Zhongguo de xibei jiao* 中國的西北角. Shanghai: Dagong bao guan, 1934.

"Fennu de huoshan baofa" 憤怒的火山爆發. ZXWD, 1927-1937, 13:360.

Guo Songtao 郭松濤. *Lundun yu Bali riji* 倫敦與巴黎日記. *Zouxiang shijie congshu* 走向世界叢書, ed. Zhong Shuhe 鍾叔河. Changsha: Yuelu chubanshe, 1984.

Hu Yuzhi 胡愈之. *Mosike yinxiang ji* 莫斯科印象記. Shanghai: Xin shengming shuju, 1931.

Hua Shan 華山. *Yingxiong de shiyue* 英雄的十月. Beijing: Xinhua chubanshe, 1949.

Huang Gang 黃鋼. "Liangge chuxi 兩個除夕." *Dagong bao*, August 4, 1939.

———. "Kaimaila zhi qian de Wang Jingwei" 開麥拉之前的汪精衛. *Wenyi zhanxian* 1.4 (1939).

———. "Wo kanjianle balujun" 我看見了八路軍. *Zhongguo wenhua* 中國文化 2.3-4 (1940).

———. "Yu: Chen Geng de bingtuan shi zenyang zuozhan de zhi er" 雨—陳庚的兵團是怎樣作戰的之二. *Jiefang ribao* 解放日報, April 7-8, 1942.

———. "Jieda huanxi: Luyi xuanchuan dui" 皆大歡喜—魯藝宣傳隊. *Jiefang ribao* 解放日報, April 7-8, 1943.

———. "Juelie: Nanjing Guomindang zhengfu bengkui qian de yimu" 絕裂—南京國民黨政府崩潰前的一幕. *Xinhua ribao* 新華日報, June 13, 1949.

———. *Tamen shi shenglizhe* 她們是勝利者. Beijing: Gongren chubanshe, 1951.

Hui Zhu 彗珠. "Zai shangbing yiyuan zhong" 在傷兵醫院中. *Fenghuo* 烽火 1.9 (1937).

Ji Hong 寄洪. "Canguan zhabei shizhouchang" 參觀閘北施粥廠. *Funü shenghuo* 婦女生活 4.3 (1937).

———. "Canguan nü qingnian hui laogong xuexiao ji" 參觀女青年會勞學校記. *Funü shenghuo* 4.6 (April 1, 1937).

Kang Youwei 康有為. *Ouzhou shiyi guo youji erzhong* 歐洲十一國遊記二種. *Zouxiang shijie congshu* 走向世界叢書, ed. Zhong Shuhe 鍾叔河. Changsha: Yuelu chubanshe, 1980.

Li Kan 李侃. "Yalü jiang qiao" 鴨綠江橋. *Dagong bao* 大公報, November 12, 1937.

Li Liewen 黎烈文. *Shengli de shuguang* 勝利的曙光. In *Fenghuo xiao congshu* 16 烽火小叢書. Chongqing: Fenghuo she, 1940.

Li Qiao 李喬. "Xi shi ruhe lian cheng de" 錫是如何煉成的. *Zhongliu* 中流 2.1 (March 20, 1937).

Liang Qichao 梁啟超. *Xin dalu youji* 新大陸遊記. *Zouxiang shijie congshu* 走向世界叢書, ed. Zhong Shuhe 鍾叔河. Changsha: Yuelu chubanshe, 1981.

Liang, Ruiyu 梁瑞玉, ed. *Huo de jilu* 活的紀錄. Shanghai: Tianma shudian, 1936.

Lin Ailian 林愛蓮 and Xu Shaojian 徐紹建, eds., *Zhongguo xin wenxue daxi, 1937–1949.* Vol. 13: *Baogao wenxue juan* 中國新文學大係報告文學卷. 20 vols. Shanghai: Shanghai wenyi chubanshe, 1990.

Lin Keduo 林克多. *Sulian jianwenlu* 蘇聯見聞泉. Shanghai: Kaiming chubanshe, 1949.

Ling Shuhua 凌叔華. "Hanyang shangbing yiyuan fangwenji" 漢陽傷兵醫院訪問記. *Dagong bao* 大公報, October 10, 1937.

Liu Baiyu 劉白羽. "Taochu Beiping" 逃出北平. *Qiyue* 七月 1.1 (1937).

———. *Yan'an shenghuo* 延安生活. Shanghai: Xianshi chubanshe, 1946.

———. *Shidai de yinxiang* 時代的印象. Harbin: Guanghua shudian, 1948.

———. *Zaochen de taiyang* 早晨的太陽. Shanghai: Haiyan chubanshe, 1950.

———. *Wei zuguo er zhan* 為祖國而戰. Beijing: Tianxia chubanshe, 1951.

———. *Dui heping xuanshi* 對和平宣示. Shanghai: Xinwenyi chubanshe, 1953.

———. *Mosike fangwenji* 莫斯科訪問記. Beijing: Renmin wenxue chubanshe, 1955.

———. *Huoju yu taiyang* 火炬與太陽. Beijing: Zuojia chubanshe, 1956.

Lou Shiyi 樓適夷. "Xiangzhe bao feng yu qianjin" 向著暴風雨前進. *Wenxue yuebao* 文學月報 1.3 (October 15, 1932).

———. "Zhandi de yi ri" 戰地的一日. *Xiandai* 現代 1.1 (May 1, 1932).

———. "Fangche de hongsheng" 紡車的轟聲. *Liangyou* 良友 80 (September 1933).

———. "Heian de yi jiao" 黑暗的一角. In *Zhongguo de yiri* 中國的一日, ed. Mao Dun Shanghai: Shenghuo shudian, 1936.

Lu Dingyi 陸定一. "Wusa jie de Shanghai" 五卅節的上海. *Hongshui* 洪水 2.20 (1926).

Lu Fen 蘆焚. "Qingyuan waipian" 請願外篇. *Wenxue yuebao* 文學月報 (June 1932).

———. "Qingyuan zhengpian" 請願正篇. *Bei dou* 北斗 2.1 (1932).

Luo Binji 駱賓基. "'Wo you you gebo jiu xing'" 我有右胳膊就行. *Fenghuo* 烽火 1.3 (September 19, 1937).

———. "Jiuhu che li de xue" 救護車裡的血. *Fenghuo* 1.2 (September 12, 1937).

———. "Zai ye de jiaotong xian shang" 在夜的交通線上. *Fenghuo* 1.4 (September 26, 1937).

Mao Dun [Shen Yanbing] 茅盾 [沈雁冰]. "Bao feng yu" 暴風雨. *Wenxue zhoukan* 文學週刊 180 (1925).

———. "Wuyue sanshi ri de xiawu" 五月三十一日的下午. *Wenxue zhoukan* 文學週刊 172 (1925).

Mao Dun 茅盾, ed. *Zhongguo de yiri* 中國的一日. Shanghai: Shenghuo chubanshe, 1936.

Mu Qing 穆青, Feng Jian 馮健, and Zhou Yuan 周原. "Xianwei shuji de bangyang: Jiao Yulu" 縣委書記的榜樣—焦裕祿. *Renmin ribao* 人民日報, February 7, 1966.

Peng Zigang 彭子岡. "Zai jiqi pangbian" 在機器旁邊. *Funü shenghuo* 婦女生活 3.1 (1936).

———. "Yizhi shou" 一隻手. *Dagong bao* 大公報, December 28–29, 1937.

Qian Xingcun 錢杏邨 [Ah Ying 阿英]. "Ye" 夜. *Bai hua* 1.2 (November 5, 1928).

Qian Xingcun, ed. *Shanghai shibian yu baogao wenxue* 上海事變與報告文學. Shanghai: Nanqiang shuju, 1932.

Qian Xingcun. "Cheng huang miao de shushi" 城皇廟的書市. *Ye hang ji* 夜航集. Shanghai: Liangyou tushu yinshua gongsi, 1935.

Qiu Dongping 丘東平. "Di qi lian: Ji di qi lian lianzhang Qiu Jun tanhua" 第七連—記第七連連長丘俊談話. *Qiyue* 七月 1.6 (1938).

———. "Women zai nali dale baizhang" 我們在那里打了敗仗. *Qiyue* 七月 1.7 (1938).

———. *Dongping xuanji* 東平選集. Shanghai: Xin wenyi chubanshe, 1953.

Qu Qiubai 瞿秋白. *Exiang jicheng* 餓鄉記程. Shanghai: Shangwu yinshuguan, 1922.

———. *Chidu xinshi* 赤都心史. Shanghai: Shangwu yinshuguan, 1924.

Rou Shi 柔石. "Yi ge weida de yinxiang" 一個偉大的印象. *Shijie wenhua* 世界文化 1.1 (September 10, 1930).

Shi Ren 時任 (Zhang Xiangshan 張香山). "Jinghuxian shang" 京滬線上. *Shen bao* 申報 October 4, 1937.

Shu Qun 舒群. "Guilai zhi qian" 歸來之前. *Zhongliu* 中流 1.2 (September 20, 1936).

Sima Wensen 司馬文森. "Yuebei sanji" 粵北散記. *Wenyi zhendi* 文藝陣地 3.1–4.1 (1939).

Sima Wensen, ed. *Baogao wenxue xuan* 報告文學選. Hong Kong: Zhi yuan shuju, 1949.

Song Zhidi 宋之的. "Yi jiu san liu nian chun zai Taiyuan" 一九三六年春在太原. *Zhongliu* 中流 1.1 (September 5, 1936).

"Tangshan meikuang zangsong gongren da canju" 唐山煤礦葬送工人大慘劇. *Laodong yin* 勞動音 1.1 (November 7, 1920).

Tu Ru 突如 (Xia Yan 夏衍). "Laobosheng lu" 勞勃生路. *Wenxue daobao* 文學道報 1.6–7 (October 23, 1931).

Wang Jue 王玨. "Lianyun gang shang de huo" 連雲港上的火. *Dagong bao* 大公報, November 17, 1937.

Wang Rujuan 王汝娟. "Rexue huiliuzhe" 熱血匯流著. *Dazhong shenghuo* 大眾生活 1.10 (1936).

Wang Xiyan 王西彥. "Sige jidan" 四個雞蛋. *Qiyue* 七月 3.5 (1938).

Wei Wei 魏巍. "Shui shi zui ke'ai de ren" 誰是最可愛的人. In *Shui shi zui ke'ai de ren*. Beijing: Renmin wenxue chubanshe, 1952.

Wen Junquan 溫俊權 and Dan Fu 單復. "Li Jinzhi: Ji wufeng gangguan chang de yige nü caozong shou" 李金芝－記無縫鋼管廠的一個女操縱手. In *Zhongguo xinwenyi daxi, 1949-1966: Baogao wenxue ji*, ed. Mu Qing. Beijing: Zhongguo wenyi chuban gongsi, 1987.

Weng Zhaoyuan 翁照垣. *Songhu xuezhan huiyilu* 淞滬血戰回憶祿. Shanghai: Shenbao yuekan chubanshe, 1932.

Wu Dongquan 吳東權, ed. *Fenghuo suiyue* 烽火歲月. Taipei: Liming wenhua shiye gufen youxian gongsi, 1987.

Wu Xiru 吳奚如. "Zai Tanggu" 在唐沽. *Hai yan* 海燕 1.1 (January 20, 1936).

Wu Zuxiang 吳組湘. "Taishan fengguang" 泰山風光. *Wenxue* 文學 5.4 (October 1, 1935).

Xi Min 西民. "Guofangxian shang de Shijiazhuang" 國防線上的石家莊. *Shen bao* 申報, August 8-9, 1937.

———. "Beixing tuci" 北行途次. *Shen bao* 申報, August 13, 1937.

Xia Yan 夏衍 [Shen Duanxian 沈端先]. "Baoshen gong" 包身工. *Guangming* 光明 1.1 (June 10, 1936).

———. "'Baoshen gong' yu hua" '包身工' 餘話. *Funü shenghuo* 婦女生活 3.9 (November 16, 1936).

Xiao Jun 蕭軍. "Zai 'Dairen maru' shang" 在 '大連凡' 上. *Hai yan* 海燕 1.1 (January 20, 1936).

Xiao Qian 蕭乾. *Xiao shuye* 小樹葉. Shanghai: Shangwu yinshu guan, 1937.

———. "Jian wen" 見聞. In *Fenghuo xiao congshu* 烽火小叢書. Chongqing: Fenghuo she, 1939.

———. "Ping-Sui suoji" 平綏瑣記. *Rensheng caifang* 人生采訪. Shanghai: Wenhua shenghuo chubanshe, 1947.

———. *Traveller without a Map*. Trans. Jeffrey Kinkley. London: Hutchinson, 1990.

Xie Bingying 謝冰瑩. *Congjun riji* 從軍日記. Shanghai: Guangming shuju, 1928.

———. "Tajinle weida de zhanchang—Taierzhuang" 踏進了偉大的戰場－台兒莊. In *Fenghuo suiyue* 烽火歲月, ed. Wu Dongquan. Taipei: Liming wenhua shiye gufen youxian gongsi, 1987.

Yang Chao 楊潮. "Bao fan zuo 包飯作." *Tai bai* 太白 1.8 (January 1, 1935).

Yang Shuo 揚朔. "Mao Zedong texie" 毛澤東特寫. *Ziyou Zhongguo* 自由中國 1.2 (1938).

———. "Tongguan zhi ye" 童關之夜. In *Fenghuo xiao congshu* 烽火小叢書. Chongqing: Fenghuo she, 1939.

Ye Shengtao 葉聖陶. "Wuyue sayi ri jiyu zhong" 五月卅一日急雨中. *Wenxue zhoukan* 文學週刊 179 (June 28, 1925).

Ye Yiqun 葉以群. "Yige yinxiang" 一個印象. *Wenxue yuebao* 文學月報 1.3 (1932).

———. *Zhandou de suhui* 戰鬥的素繪. N.p.: Zuojia shuwu, 1943.

"Yi zhou zhong Beijing de gongmin da huodong" 一週中北京公民的大活動. *Meizhou pinglun* 每週評論, May 11, 1919.

Yin Fu 殷夫. "Jianfang de yi ye" 監房的一夜. *Mengya* 萌芽 1.3 (March 1, 1930).

Zheng Zhenduo 鄭振鐸. "Liu yue yi ri" 六月一日. *Wenxue zhoukan* 文學週刊 181 (1925).

Zhiyuanjun yiri 志願軍一日. Beijing: Renmin wenxue chubanshe, 1956.

Zhongguo zuojia nongcun duwu xiehui 中國作家農村讀物協會, ed. *Baogao wenxue xuan* 報告文學選. Beijing: Zuojia chubanshe, 1963–64.

Zhou Enlai 周恩來. "Lü Ou tongxin: Qingong jianxue sheng zai Fa zui hou zhi mingyun" 旅歐通信－勤工儉學生在法最後之命運. *Yi shi bao* 益世報 December 18, 1921–January 9, 1922.

Zhu Ziqing 朱自清. "Zhizhengfu da tusha ji" 執政府大屠殺記. *Yu si* 語絲 72 (March 29, 1926).

Zhu Zuotong 朱作同, and Mei Yi 梅益, eds. *Shanghai yiri* 上海一日. Shanghai: Huamei chuban gongsi, 1938.

Zhuo Fu 拙夫. "Yi qun 一群." *Wenyi* 文藝 1.1 (1933).

Zou Taofen 鄒韜奮. *Pingzong jiyu chuji* 萍蹤寄語初集 (Notes of a Wanderer, First Collection). Shanghai: Shenghuo shudian, 1934.

———. *Pingzong jiyu erji* 萍蹤寄語二集 (Notes of a Wanderer, Second Collection). Shanghai: Shenghuo shudian, 1934.

———. *Pingzong jiyu sanji* 萍蹤寄語三集 (Notes of a Wanderer, Third Collection). Shanghai: Shenghuo shudian, 1935.

———. *Pingzong yiyu* 萍蹤憶語 (Recollections of a Wanderer). Shanghai: Shenghuo shudian, 1937.

STUDIES

Alber, Charles J. "Ting Ling and the Front Service Corps. In *La littérature chinoise au Temps de la Guerre de résistance contre le Japon (de 1937 a 1945).* Paris: Éditions de la Fondation Singer-Polignac, 1982.

Altenbaugh, Richard J. "Proletarian Drama: An Educational Tool of the American Labor College Movement." *Theater Journal* 34.2 (1982): 197–210.

Anderson, Benedict. *Imagined Communities: Reflections on the Origin and Spread of Nationalism.* London: Verso, 1983.

Anderson, Marston. "Narrative and Critique: The Construction of Social Reality in Modern Chinese Literature." Ph.D. diss., University of California, Berkeley, 1985.

———. *The Limits of Realism: Chinese Fiction in the Revolutionary Period.* Berkeley: University of California Press, 1990.

Apter, David, and Tony Saich. *Revolutionary Discourse in Mao's Republic.* Cambridge: Harvard University Press, 1994.

Bakhtin, M. M. *The Dialogic Imagination.* Trans. Michael Holquist. Austin: University of Texas, 1981.

Balk, Theodor. "Egon Erwin Kisch and His Reportage: On the 50th Year of a Noted Revolutionary Reporter." *International Literature* 4 (1935): 67.

Barbusse, Henri. *We Others: Stories of Fate, Love, and Purity.* New York: Dutton, 1918.

———. *Under Fire.* Trans. W. Fitzgerald Wray. London: Dent, 1926.

———. *I Saw It Myself.* Trans. Brian Rhys. New York: Dutton, 1928.

———. *Stalin: A New World Seen through One Man.* Trans. Vyvyan Holland. New York: Macmillan, 1935.

Benjamin, Walter. "The Author as Producer." Trans. Edmund Jephcott. In *Reflections: Essays, Aphorisms, Autobiographical Writings,* ed. Peter Demetz. New York: Schocken, 1986.

Bevan, David, ed. *Literature and War.* Rodopi Perspectives on Modern Literature, no. 3. Amsterdam: Rodopi, 1989.

Bhabha, Homi K., ed. *Nation and Narration.* London: Routledge, 1990.

Birch, Cyril, ed. *Chinese Communist Literature.* New York: Praeger, 1963.

Blau, Herbert. *The Impossible Theater: A Manifesto.* New York: Macmillan, 1964.

———. *Blooded Thought: Occasions of Theater.* New York: Performing Arts Journal Publications, 1982.

———. *Take up the Bodies: Theater at the Vanishing Point.* Chicago: University of Illinois Press, 1982.

———. "The Thin, Thin Crust and the Colophon of Doubt: The Audience in Brecht." *New Literary History* 21.1 (1989): 175–97.

Bo, Chuan 泊船. "Baogao wenxue lun" 報告文學論. *Wenyi xinwen* 文藝新聞 no. 58, June 6, 1932.

Borland, Harriet. *Soviet Literary Theory and Practice during the First Five-Year Plan, 1928–1932.* New York: King's Crown Press, 1950.

Bourdieu, Pierre. *Field of Cultural Production: Essays on Art and Literature.* New York: Columbia University Press, 1993.

Boyle, John Hunter. *China and Jpana at War, 1937–1945: The Politics of Collaboration.* Stanford: Stanford University Press, 1972.

Britton, Roswell S. *The Chinese Periodical Press, 1800–1912.* Taipei: Ch 'eng-wen, [1933] 1966.

Buchsbaum, Jonathan. *Cinema Engagé: Film in the Popular Front.* Urbana: University of Illinois Press, 1988.

Carden, Patricia. "Reassessing Ovechkin." In *Russian and Slavic Literature,* ed. Richard Freeborn, R. R. Milner-Gulland, and Charles A. Ward. Columbus: Slavica, 1976.

Chen, Xiaomei. "Genre, Convention, and Society: A Reception Study of Chinese Reportage." *Yearbook of Comparative and General Literature* 34 (1985): 85–100.

Cheng, Yung-fa. *Making Revolution: The Communist Movement in Eastern and Central China, 1937–1945.* Berkeley: University of California Press, 1986.

Ch'i, Hsi-sheng. *Nationalist China at War*. Ann Arbor: University of Michigan Press, 1982.

Chorney, Harold. "The End of the Proletariat: Class Consciousness and the Essence of Being in George Lukács." In *George Lukács and His World: A Reassessment*, ed. Ernest Joos. New York: Peter Lang, 1987.

Chou, Yin-hwa. "Formal Features of Chinese Reportage and an Analysis of Liang Qichao's 'Memoirs of My Travels to the New World.'" *Modern Chinese Literature* 1.2 (1985): 201–17.

Chow, Rey, ed. *Modern Chinese Literary Studies in the Age of Theory: Reimagining a Field*. Durham: Duke University Press, 2000.

Clark, Katarina. *The Soviet Novel: History as Ritual*. Chicago: University of Chicago Press, 1981.

Clifford, Nicholas R. *Shanghai, 1925: Urban Nationalism and the Defense of Foreign Priviledge*. Ann Arbor: University of Michigan Press, 1979.

Cochran, Sherman, Andrew C. K. Hsieh, and Janis Cochran, eds. *One Day in China: May 21, 1936*. New Haven: Yale University Press, 1983.

Davis, Lennard, and M. Bella Mirabella, eds. *Left Politics and the Literary Profession*. New York: Columbia University Press, 1990.

Denton, Kirk. *The Problematic of Self in Modern Chinese Literature: Hu Feng and Lu Ling*. Stanford: Stanford University Press, 1998.

Denton, Kirk, ed. *Modern Chinese Literary Thought: Writings on Literature, 1893–1945*. Stanford: Stanford University Press, 1996.

Derrida, Jacques. "The Theater of Cruelty and the Closure of Representation." Trans. Alan Bass. In *Writing and Difference*. Chicago: University of Chicago Press, 1978.

Dickens, Charles. *American Notes*. London: Harper and Brothers, 1842.

Dikotter, Frank. *Discourse of Race in Modern China*. London: Hurst, 1992.

Dirlik, Arif. *Revolution and History: The Origin of the Marxist Historiography in China, 1919–1939*. Berkeley: University of California Press, 1978.

Dorn, Frank. *The Sino-Japanese War, 1937–1941: From Marco Polo Bridge to Pearl Harbor*. New York: Macmillan, 1974.

Dutrait, Noel. "La litterature de reportage chinoise." *Europe: Revue litteraire mensuelle* 53 (1985): 77–85.

Eagleton, Terry. "Ideology, Fiction, Narrative." *Social Text* 1.2 (1979): 62–80.

Eastman, Lloyd E. *The Abortive Revolution: China under Nationalist Rule, 1927–1937*. Cambridge: Harvard University Press, 1974.

Elman, Benjamin A. *From Philosophy to Philology: Intellectual and Social Aspects of Change in Late Imperial China*. Cambridge: Harvard University Press, 1984.

Erenburg, Ilia Grigorevich. *The Storm*. New York: Gaer Associates, 1949.

———. *People and Life, 1891–1921*. Trans. Anna Bostock and Yvonne Kapp. New York: Knopf, 1962.

————. *In One Newspaper: A Chronicle of Unforgettable Years*. Trans. Anatole Kagan. New York: Sphinx, 1985.

Esherick, Joseph W., and Jeffrey N. Wasserstrom. "Acting out Democracy: Political Theater in Modern China." *Journal of Asian Studies* 49.4 (1990): 835–65.

Fan Quan 范全. *Zhanzheng yu wenxue* 戰爭與文學. Shanghai: Yongxiang yinshuguan, 1946.

Fang Hanqi 方漢奇. *Zhongguo jindai baokan shi* 中國近代報刊史. 2 vols. Taiyuan: Shanxi renmin chubanshe, 1981.

Felbert, Ulrich von. *China und Japan als Impuls und Exempel: Fernostliche Ideen und Motive bei Alfred Doblin, Bertolt Brecht, und Egon Erwin Kisch*. Forschungen zur Literatur- und Kulturgeschichte, no. 9. Frankfurt am Main: Lang, 1986.

Ferrari, Arthur C. "Proletarian Literature: A Case of Convergence of Political and Literary Radicalism." In *Cultural Politics: Radical Movements in Modern History*, ed. Jerold M. Starr. New York: Praeger, 1985.

Foley, Barbara. *Telling the Truth: The Theory and Practice of Documentary Fiction*. Ithaca: Cornell University Press, 1986.

Forster, Georg. *Werke in vier Banden*. 4 vols. Frankfurt am Main: Insel Verlag, 1967.

————. *A Journey from Bengal to England through the Northern Part of India, Kashmire, Afghanistan, and Persia, and into Russia by the Caspian Sea*. London: R. Faulder, 1798.

Fu, Poshek. *Passivity, Resistance, and Collaboration: Intellectual Choices in Occupied Shanghai, 1937–1945*. Stanford: Stanford University Press, 1993.

Fudan University, Chinese Department, ed. *Zhongguo youxiu baogao wenxue xuanping* 中國優秀報告文學選評. Shanghai: Fudan University Press, 1982.

Galik, Marian. *Mao Tun and Modern Chinese Literary Criticism*. Münchener Ostasiatische Studien, no. 2. Weisbaden: Franz Steiner Verlag, 1969.

Ge, Gongzhen 戈公振. *Zhongguo baoxue shi* 中國報學史. Beijing: Sanlian shudian, 1955.

Geisler, Michael Ernst. "The Literary Reportage in Germany: The Possibilities and Limitations of an Operative Genre." Ph.D. diss., University of Pittsburgh, 1981.

Geissler, Rudolf. *Die Entwicklung der Reportage Egon Erwin Kischs in der Weimarer Republik*. Cologne: Paul-Rugenstein Verlag, 1982.

Gewurtz, Margo Speisman. *Between America and Russia: Chinese Student Radicalism and the Travel Books of Tsou T'ao-fen, 1935–37*. Toronto: University of Toronto Press, 1975.

Gillin, Donald G. *Warlord: Yen Hsi-shan in Shansi Province, 1911–1949*. Princeton: Princeton University Press, 1967.

Gloversmith, Frank, ed. *Class, Culture, and Social Change: A New View of the 1930s*. Atlantic Highlands, NJ: Humanities Press, 1980.

Goldman, Merle, ed. *Modern Chinese Literature in the May Fourth Era*. Harvard East Asian Series, no. 89. Cambridge: Harvard University Press, 1977.

Goldman, Merle, Timothy Cheek, and Carol Lee Hamrin, eds. *Chinese Intellectuals and* the State: In Search of a New Relationship. Harvard Contemporary China Series, no. 3. Cambridge: Harvard University Press, 1987.

Gorky, Maxim. "The Disintegration of Personality." In On Literature: Selected Articles. Moscow: Foreign Languages Publishing House, n.d.

Gotz, Michael. "The Pen as Sword: Wartime Stories of Qiu Dongping." In La litterature chinoise au temps de la guerre de resistance contre le Japon (de 1937 à 1945). Paris: Editions de la Fondation Singer-Polignac, 1980.

Gunn, Edward. "Comments on Sources for Literature in Japanese-Occupied Shanghai and Peking (1937-1945)." In La litterature chinoise au temps de la guerre de resistance contre la Japon (de 1937 à 1945). Paris: Editions de la Fondation Singer-Polignac, 1980.

———. "Literature and Art of the War Period." In China's Bitter Victory: The War with Japan, 1937–1945, ed. James C. Hsiung and Steven I. Levine. Armonk, NY: M. E. Sharpe, 1992.

Guo Moruo 郭沫若. "Yingxiong shu" 英雄樹. Chuangzao yuekan 創造月刊 1.8 (1928).

Hargett, James M. On the Road in Twelfth Century China: The Travel Diaries of Fan Chengda (1126–1193). Munchener ostasiatische Studien, no. 52. Stuttgart: Steiner Verlag Weisbaden, 1989.

Herzen, Aleksandr Ivanovich. The Memoirs of Alexander Herzen, Parts I and II. New York: Russell and Russell, 1967.

———. From the Other Shore and The Russian People and Socialism. Oxford: Oxford University Press, 1979.

———. Who Is to Blame? A Novel in Two Parts. Ithaca: Cornell University Press, 1984.

Heyne, Eric. "Toward a Theory of Literary Nonfiction." Modern Fiction Studies 33 (1987): 479–90.

Holm, David. Art and Ideology in Revolutionary China. Oxford: Oxford University Press, 1991.

Honig, Emily. Sisters and Strangers: Women in the Shanghai Cotton Mills, 1919–1949. Stanford: Stanford University Press, 1986.

Hsia, C. T. The Classic Chinese Novel: A Critical Introduction. New York: Columbia University Press, 1968.

———. A History of Modern Chinese Fiction. New Haven: Yale University Press, 1971.

Hsia, Tsi-an. The Gate of Darkness: Studies on the Leftist Literary Movement in China. Far Eastern and Russian Institute Publications on Asia, no. 17. Seattle: University of Washington Press, 1968.

Hsiung, James C., and Steven I. Levine, eds. China's Bitter Victory: The War with Japan, 1937–1945. Armonk, NY: M. E. Sharpe, 1992.

Hsü, Immanuel C. Y. The Rise of Modern China. New York: Oxford University Press, 1970.

Hsu, Lee-Hsia Ting. Government Control of the Press in Modern China, 1900–1949. Cambridge: Harvard University Press, 1974.

Hu Feng 胡風. "Lun zhanzheng shiqi de yige zhandou de wenyi xingshi 論戰爭時期 的一個戰鬥的文藝形式." In *Minzu zhanzheng yu wenyi xingge* 民族戰爭與文一性 格. Shanghai: Xiwang she, 1946.

———. *Hu Feng pinglun ji* 胡風評論集. 3 vols. Beijing: Renmin wenxue chubanshe, 1984.

———. "Lun suxie 論速寫." In *Hu Feng pinglun ji* 胡風評論集, ed. Hu Feng. Beijing: Renmin wenxue chubanshe, 1984.

Huang Gang 黃鋼. "Baogao wenxue de shidai tezheng jiqi bixu yanshou zhenshi de dangxing yuanze" 報告文學的時代特征及其必須嚴守真實的黨性原則. In *Baogao wenxue yanjiu ziliao xuanbian* 報告文學研究資料選編, ed. Wang Ronggang. Jinan: Shandong renmin chubanshe, 1983.

Huang Gang, Hua Shan, and Li You, eds. 黃鋼、華山、理由. *Zhongguo baogao wenxue congshu* 中國報告文學叢書. 19 vols. Wuhan: Changjiang wenyi chubanshe, 1981–83.

Huang, Joe C. *Heroes and Villains in Communist China: The Contemporary Chinese Novel as a Reflection of Life.* New York: Pica, 1973.

Huang Tianpeng 黃天鵬. *Zhongguo xinwen shiye* 中國新聞事業. Shanghai: Lianhe shudian, 1930.

Huazhong shifan xueyuan Zhongguo yuyan wenxue xi 華中師范學院中國語言文學 係, ed. *Zhongguo dangdai wenxue shigao* 中國當代文學史稿. Beijing: Kexue chubanshe, 1962.

Hung, Chang-tai. *Going to the People: Chinese Intellectuals and Folk Literature, 1918–1937.* Harvard East Asian Monographs, no. 121. Cambridge: Harvard University Press, 1985.

———. "Paper Bullets: Fan Changjiang and New Journalism." *Modern China* 17.4 (1991): 427–68.

———. *War and Popular Culture: Resistance in Modern China, 1937–1945.* Berkeley: University of California Press, 1994.

Isaacs, Harold. *The Tragedy of the Chinese Revolution.* Stanford: Stanford University Press, 1951.

Israel, John, and Donald W. Klein. *Rebels and Bureaucrats: China's December 9ers.* Berkeley: University of California Press, 1976.

Jameson, Fredric. *Marxism and Form: Twentieth Century Dialectical Theories of Literature.* Princeton: Princeton University Press, 1971.

———. *The Political Unconscious: Narrative as a Socially Symbolic Act.* Ithaca: Cornell University Press, 1981.

———. "Third World Literature in the Age of Multinational Capitalism." *Social Text* 15 (fall 1986): 65–88.

Jiang Guangci 蔣光慈. "Xiandai zhongguo wenxue yu shehui shenghuo" 現代中國 文學與社會生活. *Taiyang yuekan* 太陽月刊 1.1 (1928).

Jordan, Donald A. *The Northern Expedition: China's National Revolution of 1926–1928.* Honolulu: University of Hawaii Press, 1976.

Judge, Joan. *Print and Politics: Shibao and the Culture of Reform in Late Qing China.* Stanford: Stanford University Press, 1996.

Judd, Ellen R. "Revolutionary Drama and Song in the Jiangxi Soviet." *Modern China* 9.1 (1983): 132–35.

Karatani, Kojin. *Origins of Modern Japanese Literature.* Trans. Brett de Bary. Postcontemporary Interventions (series). Durham: Duke University Press, 1993.

Kawaguchi Hiroshi 川口浩. "Baogao wenxue lun" 報告文學論. Trans. Shen Duanxian (Xia Yan) 沈端先 (夏衍). In *Baogao wenxue yanjiu ziliao xuanbian* 報告文學研究資料選編, ed. Wang Ronggang 王榮綱. 2 vols. Jinan: Shandong renmin chubanshe, 1932.

Keith, M., and S. Pile, ed. *Place and the Politics of Identity.* London: Routledge, 1993.

Kelly, David. "The Emergence of Humanism: Wang Ruoshui and the Critique of Socialist Alienation." In *China's Intellectuals and the State: In Search of a Relationship,* ed. Merle Goldman. Cambridge: Harvard University Press, 1987.

Kisch, Egon Erwin. *Der Rasende Reporter.* Berlin: Erich Reiss, 1924.

———. *Secret China.* Trans. Michael Davidson. London: John Lane, 1935.

———. "Yige weixian de wenxue ticai" 一個危險的文學體材. *Shidai de baogao* 時代的報告 2 (1981): 193–94.

Kubiak, Anthony. *Stages of Terror: Terrorism, Ideology, and Coercion as Theater History.* Bloomington: Indiana University Press, 1991.

Lamarque, Peter, ed. *Philosophy and Fiction: Essays in Literary Aesthetics.* Aberdeen: Aberdeen University Press, 1983.

Lan Hai 藍海 [Tian Zhongji 田仲濟]. *Zhongguo kangzhan wenyi shi* 中國抗戰文藝史. Shanghai: Xiandai chubanshe, 1947.

Laughlin, Charles A. "The Battlefield of Cultural Production: Chinese Literary Mobilization during the War Years." *Journal of Modern Literature in Chinese* 2.1 (1998): 83–103.

———. "Narrative Subjectivity and the Production of Social Space in Chinese Reportage." *boundary 2* 25.3 (1998): 25–46.

Lee, Leo Ou-fan. *The Romantic Generation of Modern Chinese Writers.* Cambridge: Harvard University Press, 1973.

Lee, Leo Ou-fan, ed. *Lu Xun and His Legacy.* Berkeley: University of California Press, 1985.

Lee, Leo Ou-fan, and Andrew Nathan. "The Beginnings of Mass Culture: Journalism and Fiction in the Late Ch'ing and Beyond." In *Popular Culture in Late Imperial China,* ed. David Johnson, Andrew J. Nathan, and Evelyn S. Rawski. Studies on China, no. 4. Berkeley: University of California Press, 1985.

———. *Shanghai Modern: The Flowering of a New Urban Culture in China, 1930–1945.* Cambridge: Harvard University Press, 1999.

Lefebvre, Henri. *The Production of Space*. Trans. D. Nicholson-Smith. London: Blackwell, 1991.

Li, Chi. *The Travel Diaries of Hsü Hsia-k'o*. Hong Kong: Chinese University of Hong Kong, 1974.

Li, Yu-ning. *The Introduction of Socialism into China*. New York: Columbia University Press, 1971.

Liang, Qichao. *Intellectual Trends of the Late Ch'ing Period*. Trans. Immanuel C. Y. Hsü. Cambridge: Harvard University Press, 1959.

————. "Zhongguo weiyi zhi wenxue bao Xin xiaoshuo" 中國唯一之文學報新小說. In *Ershi shiji Zhongguo xiaoshuo lilun ziliao* 二十世紀中國小說理論資料, ed. Chen Pingyuan 陳平原 and Xia Xiaohong 夏曉虹. Beijing: Beijing University Press, 1989.

Liao Quanjing 廖全京, Wen Tianxing 文天行, and Wang Daming 王大明, eds. *Zuojia zhandi fangwentuan shiliao xuanbian* 作家戰地訪問團史料選編. Chengdu: Sichuan sheng shehui kexue yuan chubanshe, 1984.

Lin Fei 林非. "Zhongguo xiandai baogao wenxue de yige lunkuo" 中國現代報告文學的一個輪廓. *Shidai de baogao* 時代的報告 (1980): 209–79.

Lin Huanping. *Collected Essays on the Literature of the War of Resistance*. Hong Kong: Minge chubanshe, 1939.

Lin, Yu-sheng. *Crisis of Chinese Consciousness: Radical Anti-traditionalism in the May Fourth Era*. Madison: University of Wisconsin Press, 1979.

Lin, Yutang. *A History of the Press and Public Opinion in China*. New York: Greenwood, 1968.

Lindner, Rolf. *Die Entdeckung der Stadtkultur: Sociologie aus der Erfahrung der Reportage*. Frankfurt am Main: Suhrkamp, 1990.

Link, E. Perry, Jr., ed. *People or Monsters: and Other Stories and Reportage from China after Mao*. Bloomington: University of Indiana Press, 1983.

Liu Baiyu 劉白羽. "Kangri shiqi Zhongguo wenxue de fazhan daolu" 抗日時期中國文學的發展道路. In *La litterature chinoise au temps de la guerre de resistance contre le Japon*. Paris: Editions de la Fondation Singer-Polignac, 1980.

Liu, Frederick F. *A Military History of Modern China, 1924–1949*. Princeton: Princeton University Press, 1956.

Liu, Kang. "Subjectivity, Marxism, and Cultural Theory in China." In *Politics, Ideology, and Literary Discourse in China*, ed. Kang Liu and Xiaobing Tang. Durham: Duke University Press, 1993. 23–55.

Liu, Kang, and Xiaobing Tang, eds. *Politics, Ideology, and Literary Discourse in Modern China: Theoretical Interventions and Cultural Critique*. Durham: Duke University Press, 1993.

Liu, Lydia. *Translingual Practice*. Stanford: Stanford University Press, 1991.

Liu, Zaifu. "The Subjectivity of Literature Revisited." In *Politics, Ideology, and Literary*

Discourse in China, ed. Kang Liu and Xiaobing Tang. Durham: Duke University Press, 1993. 56–69.

Liu Zengjie 劉增杰, Zhao Ming 趙明, Wang Wenjin 王文金, Wang Jieping 王介平, Wang Qinshao 王欽韶, eds. Kangri zhanzheng shiqi Yan'an ji kangri minzhu genjudi wenxue yundong ziliao 抗日戰爭時期延安及抗日民主根據地文學運動資料. 2 vols. Zhongguo xiandai wenxue yundong, lunzheng, shetuan ziliao congshu 中國現代文學運動、論爭、社團資料叢書. Taiyuan: Shanxi renmin chubanshe, 1983.

Lounsberry, Barbara. The Art of Fact: Contemporary Artists of Nonfiction. New York: Greenwood, 1990.

Lukács, Georg. "Reportage oder Gestaltung? Kritische Bermerkungen anläßlich eines Romans von Ottwalt." Linkskurve 4 (1932): 4.

———. "Reification and the Consciousness of the Proletariat." In History and Class Consciousness: Studies in Marxist Dialectics, ed. Georg Lukács. Cambridge: MIT Press, 1968.

Ma Feng. 馬烽 "Jin-Sui bianqu kangri genjudi wenxue yundong gaikuang" 晉綏邊區抗日根據地文學運動概況. In La litterature chinoise au temps de la guerre de resistance contre le Japon (de 1937 à 1945). Paris: Editions de la Fondation Singer-Polignac, 1980.

Ma Liangchun and Zhang Daming, eds. 馬良春、張大明. Sanshi niandai zuoyi wenyi ziliao xuanbian 三十年代左翼文藝資料選編. Chengdu: Sichuan renmin chubanshe, 1980.

Madden, David, ed. Proletarian Writers of the Thirties. Carbondale: Southern Illinois University Press, 1968.

Mally, Lynn. Culture of the Future: The Proletkult Movement in Revolutionary Russia. Studies on the History of Society and Culture 9 Berkeley: University of California Press, 1990.

Manhua xuanchuan dui 漫畫宣傳隊, ed. Kangzhan manhua 抗戰漫畫. Hankou: Quanguo manhua xuanchuan zuojia xiehui, 1938.

Mao Dun [Shen Yanbing] 茅盾 (沈雁冰). "Gao wenxue yanjiuzhe" 搞文學研究者. Xuesheng zazhi 學生雜志. 12 (1925): 109–20.

———. "Lun wuchan jieji yishu" 論無產階級藝術. Wenxue zhoukan 文學週刊 172, 173, 175, 196 (1925): 2–4, 9–12, 27–29, 200–202.

———. "Guanyu 'baogao wenxue'" 關於'報告文學'. Zhongliu 中流 1.11 (1937).

———. "Shangwu yinshuguan bianji shenghuo zhi yi" 商務印書館編輯生活之一. Xin wenxue shiliao 新文學史料 1.1 (1978): 1–12.

McDougall, Bonnie. Mao Zedong's "Talks at the Yan'an Conference on Literature and Art": A Translation of the 1943 Text with Commentary. Ann Arbor: Center for Chinese Studies, University of Michigan, 1980.

McGowan, Moray. "Comedy and the Volksstuck." In Brecht in Perspective, ed. Graham Bartram and Anthony Waine. New York: Longman, 1982.

Merrill, John C. *The Dialectic in Journalism*. Baton Rouge: Louisiana State University Press, 1989.

Miller, G. E. *Shanghai, the Paradise of Adventurers*. New York: Orsay, 1937.

Mindich, David T. Z. *Just the Facts: How "Objectivity" Came to Define American Journalism*. New York: New York University Press, 1998.

Monteath, Peter. "The Spanish Civil War and the Aesthetics of Reportage." In *Literature and War*, ed. David Bevan. Amsterdam: Rodopi, 1990.

Moran, Thomas. "True Stories: Contemporary Chinese Reportage and Its Ideology and Aesthetic." Ph.D. diss., Cornell University, 1994.

Mu Qing 穆青, ed. *Zhongguo xin wenyi daxi, 1949–1966*. Vol. 13: *Baogao wenxue juan* 中國新文藝大係報告文學卷. Beijing: Zhongguo wenlian chuban gongsi, 1987.

Naquin, Susan, and Evelyn S. Rawski, eds. *Chinese Society in the Eighteenth Century*. New Haven: Yale University Press, 1987.

Ng, Mau-sang. *The Russian Hero in Modern Chinese Fiction*. New York: State University of New York Press, 1988.

Nienhauser, William H., Jr., ed. *The Indiana Companion to Traditional Chinese Literature*. Bloomington: Indiana University Press, 1986.

Ovechkin, Valentin. "Tan texie." *Wenyi bao* (1955): 37, 45.

Peck, David. "Joseph North and the Proletarian Reportage of the 1930s." *Zeitschrift für Anglistik und Amerikanistik* 33.3 (1985): 210–20.

Pickowicz, Paul. *Marxist Literary Thought in China: The Influence of Ch'ü Ch'iu-pai*. Berkeley: University of California Press, 1981.

Pike, David. "Marxism-Leninism and Literary History in the German Democratic Republic: From Proletarian Revolutionary Literature to Socialist Realism, 1917–1945." *Internationales Archiv für Sozialgeschichte der Deutschen Literatur* 7 (1982): 148–98.

Polewoi, Boris. "Zhunque, zhunque, zai zhunque." *Shidai de baogao* (1980): 126–29.

Price, Jane L. *Cadres, Commanders, and Commisars: The Training of the Chinese Communist Leadership, 1920–45*. Boulder: Westview, 1976.

Rabinow, Paul, ed. *The Foucault Reader*. New York: Pantheon, 1984.

Rabinowitz, Paula. "Ending Difference/Different Endings: Class, Closure, and Collectivity in Women's Proletarian Fiction." *Genders* 8 (July 1990): 62–77.

———. *They Must Be Represented: The Politics of Documentary*. New York: Verso, 1994.

Radishchev, Aleksandr Nikolaevich. *A Journey from St. Petersburg to Moscow*. Trans. Leo Wiener. Cambridge: Harvard University Press, 1958.

Robin, Regine. *Socialist Realism: An Impossible Aesthetic*. Stanford: Stanford University Press, 1992.

Ross, Kristin. *The Emergence of Social Space: Rimbaud and the Paris Commune*. Minneapolis: University of Minnesota Press, 1988.

Rühle, Jürgen. *Literature and Revolution: A Critical Study of the Writer and Communism in the Twentieth Century*. Trans. Jean Steinberg. New York: Praeger, 1969.

Saltykov, Mikhail Evgrafovich. *The History of a Town*. Oxford: Meeuws, 1980.

———. *The Golovlyov Family*. New York: Penguin, 1988.

Scarry, Elaine. *Resisting Representation*. London: Oxford University Press, 1994.

Schaff, Adam. *Marxism and the Human Individual*. Trans. Olgierd Wojtasiewicz. New York: McGraw-Hill, 1970.

———. *History and Truth*. New York: Pergamon, 1976.

———. *Alienation as a Social Phenomenon*. New York: Pergamon, 1980.

Schechner, Richard. "Invasions Friendly and Unfriendly: The Dramaturgy of Direct Theater." In *Critical Theory and Performance*, ed. Janelle G. Reinelt and Joseph R. Roach. Ann Arbor: University of Michigan Press, 1992.

Schoeps, Karl-Heinz. "From Distancing Alienation to Intuitive Naivete: Bertolt Brecht's Establishment of a New Aesthetic Category." *Monatshefte: Fur Deutschen Unterricht, Deutsche Sprache und Literatur* 81.2 (1989): 186–98.

Schramm, Wilbur. "The Soviet Communist Theory of the Press." In *Four Theories of the Press: The Authoritarian, Libertarian, Social Responsibility, and Soviet Communist Concepts of What the Press Should Be and Do*, ed. Fred S. Siebert, Theodore Peterson, and Wilbur Schramm. Urbana: University of Illinois Press, 1956.

Schudson, Michael. *Origins of the Ideal of Objectivity in the Professions: Studies in the History of American Journalism and American Law, 1830–1940*. New York: Garland, 1990.

Schutz, Erhard. *Kritik der literarischen Reportage: Reportagen und Reiseberichte aus der Weimarer Republik uber die USA und die Sowjetunion*. Munich: Fink, 1977.

Schwarcz, Vera. *The Chinese Enlightenment: Intellectuals and the Legacy of the May Fourth Movement of 1919*. Berkeley: University of California Press, 1986.

Schwartz, Benjamin. *Chinese Communism and the Rise of Mao*. New York: Harper Torchbooks, 1967.

Seume, Johann Gottfried. *A Tour through Part of Germany, Poland, Russia, Sweden, Denmark, etc., during the Summer of 1805*. London: Phillips, 1807.

———. *Mein Leben, Spaziergang nach Syrakus im Jahre 1802, Mein Sommer 1805*. Bibliothek deutscher Klassiker, no. 85. Frankfurt: Deutscher Klassiker Verlag, 1993.

Shanghai "gudao" shiqi wenxue baokan pianmu 上海孤島時期文學報刊篇目. Shanghai: Shanghai shehui kexue yuan (SASS) chubanshe, 1986.

Shanghai tushuguan guancang zhongwen baozhi fukan mulu (1898–1949) 上海圖書館館藏中文報紙副刊目錄. Shanghai: Shanghai tushuguan, 1985.

Shea, G. T. *Leftwing Literature in Japan: A Brief History of the Proletarian Literary Movement*. Tokyo: Hosei University Press, 1964.

Shen Congwen 沈從文. "Lun texie" 論特寫. *Yishi bao* 益世報, January 13, 1948.

Shu, Yunzhong. *Buglers on the Home Front: the Wartime Practice of the Qiyue School*. Albany: State University of New York Press, 2000.

Siegel, Christian Ernst. *Die Reportage*. Stuttgart: Metzler, 1978.

————. *Egon Erwin Kisch: Reportage und Politischer Journalismus*. Studien zur Publizistik, no. 18. Bremen: Schunemann, 1973.

Sims, Norman, ed. *Literary Journalism in the Twentieth Century*. New York: Oxford University Press, 1990.

Singer-Polignac, Fondation. *La litterature chinoise au temps de la guerre de resistance contre le Japon (de 1937 à 1945)*. Paris: Editions de la Fondation Singer-Polignac, 1980.

Smith, Anthony. *The Newspaper: An International History*. London: Thames and Hudson, 1979.

Smith, Iris. "Peirce on the Politics of the Epic Theater." In *Semiotics 1984*, ed. John Deely. Lanham, MD: University Press of America, 1985.

Smitten, Jeffrey. "Approaches to the Spatiality of Narrative." *Papers on Language and Literature* 14.3 (summer 1978): 296–314.

Spence, Jonathan. *The Gate of Heavenly Peace*. New York: Penguin, 1982.

Spivak, Gayatri Chakravorty. *In Other Worlds: Essays in Cultural Politics*. New York: Routledge, 1987.

Stallybrass, Peter, and Allon White. *The Politics and Poetics of Transgression*. Ithaca: Cornell University Press, 1986.

Stranahan, Patricia. *Molding the Medium: The Chinese Communist Party and the Liberation Daily*. Armonk, NY: M. E. Sharpe, 1990.

Strassberg, Richard E., ed. *Inscribed Landscapes: Travel Literature from Imperial China*. Berkeley: University of California Press, 1994.

Strout, Cushing. *The Veracious Imagination*. Middletown, CT: Wesleyan University Press, 1981.

Tang Tao 唐弢. *Zhongguo xiandai wenxue shi* 中國現代文學史. 3 vols. Beijing: Renmin wenxue chubanshe, 1979.

Tian Zhongji 田仲濟. "Zhongguo baogao wenxue jianshi" 中國報告文學簡史. *Baogao wenxue* 報告文學 1:3 (1984): 68–70.

Ting, Wen-chiang. "On Hsü Hsia-k'o (1586–1641), Explorer and Geographer." *New China Review* 3.5 (1921): 225–337.

Todorov, Tzvetan. *The Poetics of Prose*. Trans. Richard Howard. Ithaca: Cornell University Press, 1973.

Tolstoy, Leo. *The Sebastopol Sketches*. New York: Penguin, 1986.

Wagner, Rudolf. "Xiao Jun's Novel *Countryside in August* and the Tradition of 'Proletarian Literature.'" In *La litterature chinoise au temps de la guerre de resistance contre le Japon (de 1937 à 1945)*. Paris: Editions de la Fondation Singer-Polignac, 1980.

————. "Liu Binyan and the Texie." *Modern Chinese Literature* 2.1 (1986): 63–98.

————. *Inside a Service Trade: Studies in Contemporary Chinese Prose*. Harvard-Yenching Institute Monograph 5, no. 34. Cambridge: Harvard University Press, 1992.

Walker, Martin. *Powers of the Press: The World's Great Newspapers*. London: Quartet Books, 1982.

Wang, David Der-wei. *Fictional Realism in Twentieth-Century China: Mao Dun, Lao She, Shen Congwen*. New York: Columbia University Press, 1992.

———. "Lu Xun, Shen Congwen, and Decapitation." In *Politics, Ideology, and Literary Discourse in Modern China: Theoretical Interventions and Cultural Critique*, ed. Liu Kang and Xiaobing Tang. Durham: Duke University Press, 1993.

Wang, Jing. "'Who Am I?' Questions of Voluntarism in the Paradigm of 'Socialist Alienation.'" *positions: east asia cultures critique* 3.2 (1995): 448–80.

Wang Ronggang 王榮綱, ed. *Baogao wenxue yanjiu ziliao xuanbian* 報告文學研究資料選編. 2 vols. Jinan: Shandong renmin chubanshe, 1983.

Wang Yao 王瑤. *Zhongguo xin wenxue shigao* 中國新文學史稿. Revised ed. Shanghai: Shanghai wenyi chubanshe, 1982.

Weber, Ronald. *Hemingway's Art of Nonfiction*. Basingstoke: Macmillan, 1989.

Wen Tianxing 聞天行, Wang Daming 王大明, and Liao Quanjing 廖全景, eds. *Zhonghua quanguo wenyijie kangdi xiehui shiliao xuanbian* 中華全國文藝界抗敵協會史料選編. Chengdu: Sichuan sheng shehui kexue yuan chubanshe, 1983.

White, Hayden V. *Metahistory: The Historical Imagination in Nineteenth Century Europe*. Baltimore: Johns Hopkins University Press, 1973.

———. *Tropics of Discourse: Essays in Cultural Criticism*. Baltimore: Johns Hopkins University Press, 1978.

———. *The Content of the Form: Narrative Discourse and Historical Representation*. Baltimore: Johns Hopkins University Press, 1987.

Williams, Raymond. *Marxism and Literature*. Oxford: Oxford University Press, 1977.

———. *Problems in Materialism and Culture: Selected Essays*. London: New Left Books, 1980.

Wilson, Dick. *The Long March, 1935: The Epic of Chinese Communism's Survival*. New York: Weybright and Talley, 1971.

Winterowd, W. Ross. *The Rhetoric of the "Other" Literature*. Carbondale: Southern Illinois University Press, 1990.

Wong, Wang-chi. *Politics and Literature in Shanghai: The Chinese League of Left-Wing Writers, 1930–1936*. Manchester: Manchester University Press, 1991.

Wylie, Raymond F. *The Emergence of Maoism: Mao Tse-tung, Ch'en Po-ta, and the Search for Chinese Theory, 1935–1945*. Stanford: Stanford University Press, 1980.

Xie Yong 謝泳. "Chuanbo xue yu baogao wenxue" 傳播學與報告文學. *Baogao wenxue* 報告文學 1:5 (1980): 60–63.

Yang Rupeng 揚如鵬. "Baogao wenxue de chansheng he fazhan" 報告文學的產生和發展. *Baogao wenxue* 報告文學 1 (1984): 64–67.

Yin Junsheng 尹均生. "Guoji baogao wenxue fazhanzhong de yipie" 國際報告文學發展中的一瞥. *Shidai de baogao* 時代的報告 (1981): 176–81.

———. "Zhou Enlai: Zhongguo baogao wenxue de zaoqi shijianzhe 周恩來——中國報告文學的早期實踐者. *Shidai de baogao* 時代的報告 2 (1981): 8–11.

———. "Lu Xun dui waiguo baogao wenxue de jieshao" 魯迅對外國報告文學的介
紹. *Shidai de baogao* 時代的報告 3 (1982): 78–79.

———. "Baogao wenxue: Wuchanjieji geming shidai xinxing de duli de wenxue
yangshi" 報告文學無產階級革命時代新型的獨立的文學樣式. In *Baogao wenxue
yanjiu ziliao xuanbian* 報告文學研究資料選編, ed. Wang Ronggang 王榮綱.
2 vols. Jinan: Shandong renmin wenxue chubanshe, 1983.

Yin Junsheng and Yang Rupeng 楊如鵬. *Baogao wenxue zongheng tan* 報告文學縱橫談.
Chengdu: Sichuan renmin chubanshe, 1983.

Yuan Ying 袁鷹, Zhu Baozhen 朱寶蓁, and Wu Peihua 吳培華. "Baogao wenxue
zuotanhui jiyao" 報告文學座談會記要. *Baogao wenxue yanjiu ziliao xuanbian* 報告
文學研究資料選編, ed. Wang Ronggang 王榮綱. 2 vols. Jinan: Shandong
renmin chubanshe, 1983.

Zhang Deming 張德明, ed. *Taiwan baogao wenxue xuan* 台灣報告文學選. Changsha:
Hunan wenyi chubanshe, 1988.

Zhang, Yingjin. "Narrative, Ideology, Subjectivity: Defining a Subversive Discourse
in Chinese Reportage." In *Politics, Ideology, and Literary Discourse in Modern China:
Theoretical Interventions and Cultural Critique*, ed. Liu Kang and Xiaobing Tang.
Durham: Duke University Press, 1993.

———. "The Institutionalization of Modern Literary History in China,
1922–1980." *Modern China* 20.3 (1994): 347–77.

Zhao Xiaqiu 趙遐秋. *Zhongguo xiandai baogao wenxue shi* 中國現代報告文學史.
Beijing: Renmin University Press, 1987.

Zhu Zinan 珠自南. *Baogao wenxue zuojia de baogao* 報告文學作家的報告. Nanjing:
Nanjing chubanshe, 1990.

Charles A. Laughlin is Associate Professor of East
Asian Languages and Literatures at Yale University.

Library of Congress Cataloging-in-Publication Data
Laughlin, Charles A.
Chinese reportage : the aesthetics of historical experience /
Charles A. Laughlin.
p. cm. — (Asia-Pacific)
Includes bibliographical references and index.
ISBN 0-8223-2959-X (alk. paper)
ISBN 0-8223-2971-9 (pbk. : alk. paper)
1. Reportage literature, Chinese—History and criticism. I. Title.
PL2404 .L38   2002   079'.51—dc21   2002005512